The African Human Rights Judicial System

"The author has set the perennially relevant subject of human rights in the international context, while discerningly illuminating its anchorage-mechanisms in the national constitutional system and, in particular, in the adjudicatory scheme within the judicial organ. In this remarkably focused work, Dean Franceschi has placed before the readership fresh lines of legal scholarship, laying bare much information and learning that had not been accessible earlier."
—Justice J. B. Ojwang, Ph.D. (Cantab); CBS; Justice of the Supreme Court of Kenya

"Starting with the obligation of the international community to protect human rights, Luis Franceschi pulls together various strands of, and interaction between, constitutional and international law to explore the important question of the respect for, and the enforcement of, human rights. Of particular interest is his analysis of the history and jurisdiction of African commissions and courts to supplement the national protection of human rights."
—Professor Yash Pal Ghai, CBE, Fellow of the British Academy

"Dr Luis Gabriel Franceschi's study is beyond any doubt of great added value to the abundant literature on human rights in Africa. It is a comprehensive analysis of the whole African institutional framework aimed at the protection of human rights in the Continent. It embraces not only the continental mechanisms established under the African Charter on Human and Peoples' Rights, i.e. the Commission and the Court, but also the sub-continental regional judicial bodies established within the framework of the Regional Economic Communities. Dr Franceschi's study also captures the ongoing metamorphosis of the African Court on Human and Peoples' Rights, which is on the verge of being entrusted with four new kinds of jurisdiction: general legal issues, African Union constitutional issues, staff appeals, and criminal matters. This expansion of the jurisdiction of the African Court raises crucial questions to which Dr Franceschi has brought clear responses.

The author also examines the major challenges faced by the African human rights system, including, inter alia, the domestication and consideration of international law by national judges, as well as the search for appropriate and effective ways to enforce the decisions of the African Court at the municipal level, without any interference from the political organs of the States involved. These are some of the reasons why I strongly recommend the reading of this book to anyone interested in the past, the present and the future of the African Human Rights System."
—Justice Dr Fatsah Ouguergouz, Judge and former Vice-President of the African Court on Human and Peoples' Rights

The African Human Rights Judicial System: Streamlining Structures and Domestication Mechanisms Viewed from the Foreign Affairs Power Perspective

By

Luis Gabriel Franceschi

CAMBRIDGE
SCHOLARS
PUBLISHING

The African Human Rights Judicial System:
Streamlining Structures and Domestication Mechanisms
Viewed from the Foreign Affairs Power Perspective,
by Luis Gabriel Franceschi

This book first published 2014

Cambridge Scholars Publishing

12 Back Chapman Street, Newcastle upon Tyne, NE6 2XX, UK

British Library Cataloguing in Publication Data
A catalogue record for this book is available from the British Library

The research carried out was supported by the African Rule of Law Programme
of the Konrad Adenauer Stiftung

Konrad
Adenauer
Stiftung

ISBN (10): 1-4438-5509-X, ISBN (13): 978-1-4438-5509-9

To you, reader, for having the courage to share my modest knowledge on this dear subject.

TABLE OF CONTENTS

LIST OF ABBREVIATIONS

AfDB	African Development Bank
ACCNNR	African Convention on the Conservation of Nature and Natural Resources
ACERWC	African Committee of Experts on the Rights and Welfare of the Child
ACRWC	African Charter on the Rights and Welfare of the Child
ACJ	African Court of Justice
ACJHR	African Court of Justice and Human Rights
ACJHPR	African Court of Justice and Human and Peoples Rights
ACHPR	African Commission on Human and Peoples' Rights
AChHPR	African Charter on Human and Peoples Rights
ACtHPR	African Court on Human and Peoples' Rights
ADRDM	American Declaration of the Rights and Duties of Man
AGLDF	Adolescent Girls' Legal Defense Fund
AHRLR	African Human Rights Law Reports
AICT	African International Courts and Tribunals
AMU	Arab Maghreb Union
AMUIJ	Arab Maghreb Union *Instance Judicaire*
ASurICL	Annual Survey of International and Comparative Law
ASEAN	Association of Southeast Asian Nations
AU	African Union
AUC	African Union Commission
BEC	Bio-Energy Centre
BCLI	British Columbia Law Institute
CAADP	Comprehensive Africa Agriculture Development Programme
CCA	Cultural Charter for Africa
CD	Capacity Development
CDHR	Centre for Development and Human Rights
CDSF	Capacity Development Strategic Framework
CEDAW	Convention on the Elimination of All Forms of Discrimination Against Women
CEMIRIDE	Centre for Minority Rights Development
CKRC	Constitution of Kenya Review Commission
CoE	Committee of Experts on Constitutional Review (Kenya)

COMESA	Common Market for East and Sothern Africa
CSG	Continental Steering Group
CTBT	Comprehensive Nuclear Test Ban Treaty
CTBTO	Comprehensive Nuclear-Test-Ban Treaty Organization
CVK	Central Electoral Committee of Ukraine
DPD	Dewan Perwakilan Daerah of Indonesia
DPR	Dewan Perwakilan Rakyat of Indonesia
EAC	East African Community
EACJ	East African Court of Justice
ECCAS	Economic Community of Central African States
ECHR	European Court of Human Rights
ECOWAS	Economic Community of West African States
ECPHRFF	European Convention for the Protection of Human Rights and Fundamental Freedoms
EEC	European Economic Commission
eKLR	Kenya Law Reports, Electronic Edition
EN	Equality Now
ESC	European Social Charter
ESCR-Net	International Network for Economic, Social and Cultural Rights
ESCWA	Economic and Social Commission for Western Asia
EWLA	Ethiopian Women Lawyers' Association
FIS	Front Islamique du Salut (Algeria)
FJEA	Foreign Judgments (Reciprocal Enforcement) (Extension of Act) Order
FLN	Front de Libération Nationale (Algeria)
FGM	Female Genital Mutilation
GATT	General Agreement on Tariffs and Trade
GG	Grundgesetz für die Bundesrepublik Deutschland
IACtHR	Inter-American Court of Human Rights
IACHR	Inter-American Commission of Human Rights
ICC	International Criminal Court
ICCPR	International Covenant on Civil and Political Rights
ICESR	International Covenant on Economic, Social and Cultural Rights
ICJ	International Court of Justice
ICRC	International Committee of the Red Cross
IGAD	Intergovernmental Authority for Development
IGO	International Governmental Organisation
IHRDA	Institute for Human Rights and Development in Africa
IJHR	International Journal of Human Rights,

IOC	Indian Ocean Commission
IUCN	International Union for Conservation of Nature
KANU	Kenya African National Union
MDGS	Millennium Development Goals
MOU	Memorandum of Understanding
NAP	National Action Plan on Human Rights
NCICK	National Cohesion and Integration Commission of Kenya
NCGD	National Commission on Gender and Development
NEPAD	New Partnership for Africa's Development
NGO	Non-Governmental Organisation
NQHR	Netherlands Quarterly of Human Rights
OAU	Organisation of African Unity
ODIHR	Office for Democratic Institutions and Human Rights
OECD	Organisation for Economic Co-operation and Development
PCIJ	Permanent Court of International Justice
PIDA	Program of Infrastructure Development in Africa
PTA	Preferential Trading Area
REC	Regional Economic Community
RIAA	Reports of International Arbitral Awards
SADC	Southern African Development Community
SADCC	Southern African Development Coordination Conference
SSC	South/South Cooperation
TJRC	Truth, Justice and Reconciliation Commission
UEMOA	Unión Economique et Monétaire de l'Afrique de l'Ouest
UDHR	Universal Declaration of Human Rights
UN	United Nations
UNDP	United Nations Development Programme
UNEP	United Nations Environmental Programme
UNESCO	United Nations Educational, Scientific and Cultural Organization
UNGA	United Nations General Assembly
UNIDROIT	International Institute for the Unification of Private Law (Institut International pour l'Unification du Droit Prive)
UN-INSTRAW	United Nations International Research and Training Institute for the Advancement of Women
UNTS	United Nations Treaty Series
WILDAF	Women in Law and Development in Africa
WTO	World Trade Organisation

TABLE OF CASES

A,B, & C v. Ireland, ECHR, 2010

Abatielos Case, ICJ, 1952

Admissions case, ICJ 1948, 15 AD

Adams v. Cape Industries Plc, 1990

African Commission on Human and Peoples' Rights v. Great Socialist Peoples' Libyan Arab Jamahiriya, ACtHPR, Order for Provisional Measures of 25th March 2011.

African Commission on Human and People's Rights v. The Republic of Kenya, Application No. 006/2012.

Antigua and Barbuda Caribbean Court of Justice Act, 2004

Attorney-General for Canada v. Attorney-General for Ontario, 1937, A.C. 326

Armstrong v. Bidwell(US-1903)

B v. Kenya, Com. 283/03

Barberá, Messeguer & Jabardo v. Spain A.146

Burdov v. Russia ECHR (2009), App. No. 33509/04

Buron v. Denman, U.K.

Centre for Minority Rights Development (Kenya) and Minority

Rights Group Int. on behalf of Endorois Welfare Council v. Kenya, Comm276/2003

Centre for Free Speech v. Nigeria No. 206/97, 1999

Civil Liberties Organization in respect of the Nigerian Bar Association v. Nigeria Comm 101/93

Collectif des Veuves et Ayant-droit et Association Mauritanienne des Droits de l'Homme v. Mauritania, ACHPR, Act. Rep., 2000.

Colt Industries v Sarlie (No 2) 1966

Commission Nationale des Droits de l'Homme et des Libertés v. Chad, Com 74/92

Constitutional Rights Project (in respect of Zamani Lakwot and 6 Others) v. Nigeria C. No. 87/93

Curtis Doebbler v. Sudan, Com. 235/00

Dale Power Systems Plc v. Witt & Bush Ltd, 2001

Democratic Republic of Congo v. Burundi, Rwanda and Uganda, ACHPR, Com. 227/99

Ephrahim v. Pastory (Tanzania)

Free Legal Assistance Group, Lawyers' Committee for Human Rights, Union Interafricaine des Droits de l'Homme, Les Témoins de Jehovah v. DRC, C. 100/93

Foster v. Neilson, US - 1829

Great Britain v. Costa Rica - 18 October 1923, in the case of Aguilar-Amory and Royal Bank of Canada claims, RIAA I, at 369-401.

Halaoui v. Grosvernor Casinos Limited, 2002

Handyside v. The United Kingdom, (Application no. 5493/72), Strasbourg, 1976

HMB Holdings Ltd v. Cabinet of Antigua and Barbuda, 2007

Huri-Laws v. Nigeria, Com. 225/98

Katanganese Peoples' Congress v Zaire, Comm 75/92

Media Rights Agenda and Others v. Nigeria, Com. 105/93, 128/94, 130/94, 152/96

Mike Campbell (PVT) Ltd et al v The Republic of Zimbabwe, SADC (T) Case No. 2/2007

Michelot Yogogombaye v. the Republic of Senegal, Application No. 001/2008

Moscow National Bank Ltd. (London) v. GU Eye microsurgery, UK

Olajide Afolabi v. Federal Republic of Nigeria (ECOWAS, 2004)

Pan Am Pharmaceuticals Inc (USA) v. Russian Cardiology,KGA40/10556-04

State v. Petrus, Court of Appeal of Botswana, [1985]

R v. Bottrill, ex p. Kuechenmeister, U.K.

Rattigan v. Chief Immigration Officer (Zimbabwe)

Reparation for Injuries Suffered in the Service of the United Nations case, ICJ Reports, 1849

Rentpool B.V. vs. OOO 'Podjemniye Technologii', 2009

Rights International v. Nigeria No. 215/98, 1999

Ruiz-Mateos v. Spain, A 262

Salaman v. Secretary of State for India, U.K.

Sawhoyamaxa Indigenous Community v. Paraguay C No. 146

Sir Dawda K Jawara v. The Gambia, Com 147/95 & 149/96

Society of Lloyd's v Price; Society of Lloyd's v Lee, 2005

Social and Economic Rights Action Center and the Center for Social and Economic Rights v. Nigeria, Comm. No. 155/96, 2001

State v. Ncube - 1987, Zimb. L. Rep. 246 (Zimbabwe)

S.S. Wimbledon case (Government of His Britanic Majesty v. German Empire), PCIJ, Series A, 17 Aug 1923, File E-b II.

Territorial Jurisdiction of the International Commission of the River Oder case, 1929

The Djibouti v. France, Certain Questions of Mutual Assistance in Criminal Matters, ICJ, 2008

The King v. Burgess, ex parte Henry, 1936, SS C.L.R. 608

Uganda v. Matovu, High Court of Uganda, 2002

West Rand Central Gold Mining Co. v. The King(1905)

Zipporah Wambui Mathara, Bankruptcy, Kenya - 2010.

ACKNOWLEDGMENTS

First and foremost, I would like to thank all the beautiful Kenyan people who have adopted me. Here in this fantastic country I have spent the best years of my life. A special thought is given to those who have suffered human rights abuses.

I would like to thank Ángel Gómez-Montoro, President of the University of Navarra, Justice Fatsah Ouguergouz, a prolific writer, international lawyer and judge of the African Court on Human and Peoples' Rights. Justice Fatsah gave me valuable insights; he was the first person at the Court with whom I discussed my ideas and his encouragement gave the final direction this book has taken. I also acknowledge the help of Justice Gerald Ninyungeko, President of the African Court on Human and Peoples' Rights, Justice Bernard Ngoepe, Justice Elsie Thompson and Justice Sylvain Ore, whose time and guidance opened my eyes in various matters. My gratitude is also expressed to Fidelis Katonga, the Court's librarian, who was instrumental in facilitating my access to literature and materials.

I also need to mention my mentors Gustavo Linarez-Benzo, Justice J.B. Ojwang and Prof. Patricia Kameri-Mbote, who were instrumental in the beginning of my legal career and are now scholars of worldwide recognition. I should not omit Yash Pal Ghai, who has dedicated precious time to our discussions and kindly availed to me useful material.

Special thanks to Njahira Gitahi, Francis Osiemo, Santana Monda, Bonface Oduor and Christopher Ndegwa who carefully checked and formatted the draft.

I thank in a special way all my colleagues and students at Strathmore Law School. Their support has been fantastic!

I dedicate this book to my family, who has been patient, encouraging and supportive. From them I have learnt the divine and human value of work. And finally, and perhaps most importantly, to my parents, whose generosity and dedication has always been a source of inspiration for me. As I have written many times before, I am the eighth-born; had they stopped somewhere before I would not have seen this world!

FOREWORD

The special quality of Dean Franceschi's book is that it identifies and focuses upon one of those critical connecting interstitial bands to conventional pedagogic areas of public law: and as a result, this work is truly the prospector's, rather than the learner's, place of recourse.

Dean Franceschi weaves a sensitive yarn between the traditional platforms of public international law, and domestic constitutional law – building upon the special themes of human rights, and the foreign affairs power attached to the executive agency.

The author has set the perennially relevant subject of human rights in the international context, while discerningly illuminating its anchorage-mechanisms in the national constitutional system and, in particular, in the adjudicatory scheme within the judicial organ. Human rights is perspicuously portrayed as the pith and kernel of good governance universally; the domestic constitutional law, with its judicial accompaniment, is presented as the overriding norm that girds the fundamentals of human rights to the operational machinery on the national ground; and in this scenario, the vital role of the foreign affairs power is highlighted: it is the instrumentality that signifies the individual State's approach to, and mode of participation at, the forum of conception of international obligations – including obligations bearing on the fulfilment of the human-rights mandate.

In one of the patent instances of originality, Dean Franceschi urges that the foreign affairs power – itself an incident of the national Constitution – flows into the workings of international norm via its access to, and involvement at the platform of international legal obligations. As the author remarks:

> "....universal human rights impose certain checks and balances on powers that were traditionally reserved to the State over its subjects, thus arousing important questions over the nature of State sovereignty. Furthermore, universality has also come to mean the legal transference of certain jurisdictional prerogatives onto the international community, which is now bestowed with an innovative *locus standi* in certain human rights matters...."

In this remarkably focused work, Dean Franceschi has placed before the readership fresh lines of legal scholarship, laying bare much information and learning that had not been accessible earlier. Thanks to the book's origin in a thoroughly-executed doctoral-research initiative, at the University of Navarra, in Spain, its documentation is extensive, intensive, and by itself, a goldmine of reference for the avid reader: not to mention the work's bearing at a rare linguistic intersection – drawing from the mutually enriching strands in parallel traditions of scholarship.

For this special research initiative that touches on such fundamental issues of constitutional thought and practice, and at a time when Africa stands at a crossroads impelled by imperatives of good governance, Dean Franceschi's study merits high commendation. Learners of the law, as they clear prescribed modules, guided by standard texts, will be significantly enriched by this work of unlimited scholarly and intellectual effect.

JACKTON B. OJWANG, Ph.D. (*Cantab*); CBS;
Fellow of the Kenya National Academy of Sciences;
Professor of Law of the University of Nairobi
and Justice of the Supreme Court of Kenya

31 December, 2013

INTRODUCTION

The fact that the State is not an *absolute entity* prompts the existence of limitations that are actualized in the form of constitutional checks and balances. Checks and balances are regulators or valves that limit the strength, technique and manner with which the State may exercise power over its subjects and the extent of those powers. Those checks and balances fasten the State to the rule of law as may be required for the protection and enforcement of rights. Checks and balances may be found, inside, in the different layers of powers within the structures of the State, or outside, in the supranational quasi-judicial and judicial bodies.

In the *domestic field*, constitutions seem to be the most efficacious legal instruments in ensuring the highest degree for the protection of human rights.[1] This protection is conceived through properly drafted bills of rights. A well-conceived bill of rights should guarantee access to justice, including the possibility of protecting its own citizens against abuses perpetrated by the State itself. Additionally, this protection needs to be enforced through active, independent and autonomous judicial systems.[2]

In the *international field*, there has not been a consensus on the best means and ways to safeguard human rights. In some instances, such abuses may require the involvement of a neutral party. This involvement may be *de facto*, through the so-called 'responsibility to protect'[3] or *de*

---

[1] See Silva Bascuñán, A., *Tratado de Derecho Constitucional*, Editorial Jurídica de Chile, vol. XI, Santiago, 2006, at 46.

[2] See Brewer-Carías, A., *Constitutional Protection of Human Rights in Latin America: a comparative study of 'amparo' proceedings*, Cambridge University Press, New York, 2009, at 417. Brewer-Carías asserts that after two centuries of constitutional tradition of inserting very extensive human rights aspirations and declarations in the constitutions of Latin-America, it has become clear that the solution necessitates an independent and autonomous judiciary.

[3] The concept of 'responsibility to protect' was first developed by the *International Commission on Intervention and State Sovereignty* ('ICISS'), on its 30th October 2001 report entitled 'The Responsibility to Protect', which was accompanied by a comprehensive supplementary volume of valuable research material. According to Ingo Winkelmann, the ICISS identified four basic criteria for military intervention

iure, through judicial decisions emanating from international or regional human rights courts. The fact is that once a State accepts, from a legal perspective, the universality of human rights, it opens a *Pandora* box with unimaginable effects on both the international and the national legal systems.

This has challenged the traditional understanding of the concept of State, sovereignty and domestication of international law. Hersch Lauterpacht asserts that the State "is an expression of the legal order operating within a defined territory."[4] This legal order requires identity. However, this identity was jeopardized in most African States by the unilateral colonial inclusion of heterogeneous societies within defined colonial boundaries with practical disregard to ethnicity. In fact, in East Africa alone, peoples experience – even today – the turmoil of having been split by foreign powers in a race to ransack a continent before and after the World Wars. The effects are still evident and it is perhaps too late to mend them. The fact is that there are nations within each country and those nations often spill over into neighbouring countries.[5] This scenario makes national identity and a true democratic process challenging.

---

for human protection purposes: (1) the threshold of large scale loss of life or large scale, e.g. ethnic cleansing; (2) the precautionary principles of right intention, last resort, proportional means and reasonable prospects, i.e. proportionality; (3) the requirement of right authority; and (4) sound operational principles: clear mandate, unity of command, protection of a population as the prime objective, appropriate rules of engagement and maximum possible co-ordination with humanitarian organizations [See Winkelmann, I., "Responsibility to Protect", *Max Planck Encyclopedia of Public International Law*, *www.mpepil.com*, Oxford University Press, (2006), No. 5. See also "Responsibility to Protect", *Report of the International Commission on Intervention and State Sovereignty*, published by the International Development Research Center, Ottawa, Canada, December 2001, at paras 4.19 and 4.20.]

[4] Lauterpacht, H. "The Subjects of International Law", in Lauterpacht (ed), *International Law. Being the Collected papers of Hersch Lauterpacht*, vol. I – The General Works, Cambridge University Press, London, 1970, at 148.

[5] For example, the colonial boundaries partitioned the Maasai and Luo between Kenya and Tanzania, the Luhya, Luo and Teso between Uganda and Kenya, the Tutsis and Hutus in Rwanda and Burundi, the Somali people between Kenya and Somalia and so on and so forth. The division was so arbitrary that, for example, the former Vice-President of Kenya, H.E. Moody Awori, had a brother who was a minister in the Ugandan Cabinet of President Museveni, for in spite of having the same father and mother one registered as Kenyan while the other registered as Ugandan.

African constitutions have been drawn, legal structures created and international organs established, sometimes, with little connection to reality.[6] Therefore, the relation between the national and international judicial systems, which appears to be a theoretical challenge to the legal mind in the West, turns into a vivid challenge – legal as well as political – for most African systems. It is not just a matter of finding the best channels to domesticate international law or decisions. It is also a constitutional challenge that involves separation of powers, institutionalisation of checks and balances and a properly defined regulation of the foreign affairs power. Africa is home to some of the most extraordinary legal minds of the modern world.[7] Innovative jurisprudence and brilliant scholarly thought is here intermingled with a deficient political will of what seems to be an inadequately trained political class that constantly challenges the rule of law.[8]

Furthermore, there has been a mushrooming of supranational judicial organs, whose extent and nature is unclear as well as the opportunity and

---

[6] The legal tradition was determined by the colonizing power: Liberia (American Colonization Society), Libya (Italy; Britain/France), Egypt (Britain), Sudan (Britain), Tunisia (France), Morocco (France/Spain), Ghana (Britain/Germany), Guinea (France), Cameroon (Germany; France/Britain), Senegal (France), Togo (Germany; France), Mali (France), Madagascar (France), DR Congo (Belgium), Somalia (Italy), Benin (France), Niger (France), Burkina Faso (France), Côte d'Ivoire (France), Chad (France), Central African Republic (France), Congo (France), Gabon (France), Nigeria (Britain), Mauritania (France), Sierra Leone (Britain), South Africa (Britain), Tanzania (Germany; Britain), Rwanda (Germany; Belgium), Burundi (Germany; Belgium), Algeria (France), Uganda (Britain), Kenya (Britain), Malawi (Britain), Zambia (Britain), The Gambia (Britain), Botswana (Britain), Lesotho (Britain), Mauritius (Britain), Swaziland (Britain), Equatorial Guinea (Spain), Guinea-Bissau (Portugal), Mozambique (Portugal), Cape Verde (Portugal), Comoros (France), São Tomé and Príncipe (Portugal), Angola (Portugal), Seychelles (Britain), Djibouti (France), Zimbabwe (Britain), Namibia (Germany; South Africa).

[7] For example, Yash Pal Ghai, Mohamed Bedjaoui, J.B. Ojwang, Patricia Kameri-Mbote, Migai-Akech, PLO Lumumba, J. Okoth-Ogendo, Makau Mutua, Enoch Dumbutshena, F. Ouguergouz, Gérard Niyungeko, Sophia A. B. Akuffo, Bernard Makgabo Ngoepe, Desmond Orjiako, Charles Okidi, Joseph Nyamihana Mulenga, George W. Kanyeihamba, and many others.

[8] For example, the recent crisis in Ivory Coast, the Kenyan post-election violence and the inconsistent political statements that have followed the involvement of the International Criminal Court, the persistent constitutional reforms that aim at allowing additional presidential terms of office as happened in recent years in Uganda, Cameroon and Egypt.

necessity of their mediation or even 'intrusion' to safeguard, protect or restore the rule of law. These are essential and relevant questions for our time. Perhaps international law theories have not grown at the same speed at which international organizations and jurisprudence have developed. Thus, important questions immediately arise as to whether access to supranational jurisdictions should be granted to the individual; what should the power and legal foundation for the enforcement of human rights international decisions be; who should enforce them; whether international decisions imply the usurpation of sovereignty; how should these decisions be domesticated and enforced.

According to Ayala Corao, for international matters, including human rights as may be applicable, international bodies with appropriate jurisdiction may be called to intervene.[9] According to Boye, "in spite of the appreciable but very recent effort to codify the rules of international public law, the decisions rendered by international courts, including international arbitration courts, remain an essential source of international law. The problem raised is whether, and to what extent, the municipal judge takes such decisions into consideration when he is called on to adjudicate a case in which the question raised has already been subject of a decision by an international court."[10]

A greater challenge emerges when the State accesses or ratifies human rights treaties that may go beyond the consecrated constitutional rights or ratifies treaties allowing human rights extra-territorial jurisdictions to enter into play. The matter is complex; it is precisely here where constitutional law and international law are deeply related through what is known as the Foreign Affairs Power (FAP).[11]

Therefore, the protection of human rights may be challenged, on the one hand, by poorly drafted constitutional dispensations and, on the other,

---

[9] See Ayala Corao, C.M. "La Ejecución de Sentencias de la Corte Interamericana de Derechos Humanos", *Estudios Constitucionales*, vol. 5, Universidad de Talca, (2007), at 128.

[10] Boye, A., "The Application of the Rules of International Public Law in Municipal Legal Systems", in Bedjaoui, M. (ed), *International Law: Achievements and Prospects*, UNESCO & Martinus Nijhoff Publishers, Paris, 1991, at 295.

[11] See generally Ojwang, J.B., and Franceschi, L.G., "Constitutional Regulation of the Foreign Affairs Power in Kenya: A Comparative Assessment", *Journal of African Law*, vol. 46, Cambridge University, (2002), at 43-58. Ojwang and Franceschi argue that the FAP consists mainly of four identifiable elements: 1. Treaty-making; 2. Diplomacy; 3. War and Peace; and 4. Recognition of States and Governments.

by a disjointed interplay between the domestic and supranational legal orders. This goes hand in hand with a suitable regulation of the foreign affairs power, which not only opens avenues for domestication, but it also triggers the creation of international governance structures. These structures may play a vital role in monitoring, validating and enforcing human rights, even when the rule of law and the political will may be deficient at the domestic level.[12]

Certainly, the relationship between domestic and supranational systems needs to be harmonised. This process includes not only the necessity to harmonise laws, it also involves a proper understanding of the nature of international decisions as the ultimate result of the exercise of the 'foreign affairs power', and the subsequent obligation of the State to guarantee their enforcement at the domestic level.

As Gonzalo Aguilar argues, a human rights system is an integrated organic regulatory body, which is not susceptible of dissections, and which cannot be separated.[13] To dissect human rights is unnatural and discriminatory. Human beings cannot enjoy a higher degree of protection in international law than within the domestic system. In this sense, human rights standards call on the State, first, to aim at the highest possible standard, which is done primarily through the constitution's bill of rights. Second, to respect international law's peremptory norms and the treaties it has ratified or acceded. Third, to realise that if the State fails to protect human rights the political society has the right to activate available and legal means to secure such protection.

Hence, the present study deals with these two interconnected yet often forgotten realities of the constitutional order in Africa: First, the 'foreign affairs power' that gives the specific organs of the State the capacity to

---

[12] See *Daily Nation*, Special Report by Alphonce Shiundu, Wednesday 22nd December 2010, at 19. In 2007-2008 Kenya suffered widespread post-election violence. More than 1,000 were murdered and approximately 300,000 lost their property. After disagreeing on the establishment of a local tribunal to try these cases the country requested the ICC to intervene. The hidden hope of the political class was that nothing would be achieved by the ICC. However, once the ICC incriminated 6 high-level suspects there was uproar and the Kenyan Parliament passed a motion requesting the President to withdraw from the Rome Statute. The Vice President of Kenya started lobbying African countries to pressure the AU to request the deferral of the 6 cases and the AU agreed.

[13] Aguilar Cavallo, G., "La Internacionalización del Derecho Constitucional", *Estudios Constitucionales*, vol. 5, No. 001, Centro de Estudios Constitucionales, Santiago de Chile, (2007), at 231.

create and empower universal, regional and sub-regional governance and judicial structures.[14] Secondly, the 'international judicial function in Africa', with focus on the African Court on Human and Peoples' Rights and the upcoming merger with the African Court of Justice. In this regard, we have proposed what seem to be the best domestication channels for supranational human rights judicial decisions in Africa. We have also proposed amendments to the so-called 'Protocol on the Statute of the African Court of Justice and Human Rights.'

---

[14] This is usually achieved through multilateral diplomacy.

CHAPTER ONE

THE LINK BETWEEN CONSTITUTIONAL AND INTERNATIONAL HUMAN RIGHTS LAW

The 1994 genocide in Rwanda awakened the international conscience and brought to question concepts and systems for the protection of human rights. The broader international community became aware of their duty to mediate and actually get involved whenever and wherever there was a systematic and widespread abuse of Human Rights; when a State was unable or reluctant to protect its own citizens from avoidable human rights catastrophes – mass murder, rape, starvation, etc.[1]

---

[1] See UNGA, "World Summit Outcome", *Res.* 60/1 (2005), at paras 138 and 139. The paragraphs read: "138. Each individual State has the responsibility to protect its populations from genocide, war crimes, ethnic cleansing and crimes against humanity. This responsibility entails the prevention of such crimes, including their incitement, through appropriate and necessary means. We accept that responsibility and will act in accordance with it. The international community should, as appropriate, encourage and help States to exercise this responsibility and support the United Nations in establishing an early warning capability. 139. The international community, through the United Nations, also has the responsibility to use appropriate diplomatic, humanitarian and other peaceful means, in accordance with Chapters VI and VIII of the Charter, to help to protect populations from genocide, war crimes, ethnic cleansing and crimes against humanity. In this context, we are prepared to take collective action, in a timely and decisive manner, through the Security Council, in accordance with the Charter, including Chapter VII, on a case-by-case basis and in cooperation with relevant regional organizations as appropriate, should peaceful means be inadequate and national authorities are manifestly failing to protect their populations from genocide, war crimes, ethnic cleansing and crimes against humanity. We stress the need for the General Assembly to continue consideration of the responsibility to protect populations from genocide, war crimes, ethnic cleansing and crimes against humanity and its implications, bearing in mind the principles of the Charter and international law. We also intend to commit ourselves, as necessary and appropriate, to helping States build capacity to protect their populations from genocide, war crimes, ethnic cleansing and crimes against humanity and to assisting those which are under stress before crises and conflicts break out." See

As a consequence, a new concept has taken shape: "The Responsibility to Protect", also referred to as R2P. The R2P is the result of a deeper comprehension in the international community of the need to intercede on behalf of the victims of a system that is unable or unwilling to protect. Certainly, 'intervention' has always been a repugnant term in both constitutional and international law. However, the balance between the duty to protect human rights anywhere in the world and the nation's right to self-determination and autonomy has shaped an exciting debate in the legal field: The State has the duty to protect and the international community has the subsidiary duty to guarantee that protection. Thus, the classical model of State sovereignty would seem to weaken against the centeredness and universality of human rights.

Edward Luck says that "today, the UN member States are united in their support for the goals of 'Responsibility to Protect' but less so on how to achieve them."[2] He adds:

> "At the 2005 World Summit, the assembled heads of State and government agreed that R2P rests on three pillars: First, the responsibility of the State to protect its population from genocide, war crimes, ethnic cleansing, and crimes against humanity, and from their incitement. Second, the commitment of the international community to assist States in meeting

---

also UNGA, "Implementing the Responsibility to Protect", *Report of the Secretary-General*, A/63/677, 12 Jan2009, available at: *http://www.unhcr.org/refworld/docid/4989924d2.html*. See also Winkelmann, I., "Responsibility to Protect", *Max Planck Encyclopedia of Public International Law*, *www.mpepil.com*, Oxford University Press, (2006), No. 4. According to Winkelmann, 'the very notion of the responsibility to protect was first developed by the International Commission on Intervention and State Sovereignty ('ICISS'), which was established by Canadian Foreign Minister Lloyd Axworthy on 14 September 2000 and co-chaired by Gareth Evans (Australia) and Muhamed Sahnoun (Algeria). Ten more Commissioners were drawn from around the globe. A high-level advisory board provided further guidance. On 30 September 2001, the ICISS published its report entitled 'The Responsibility to Protect', which was accompanied by a comprehensive supplementary volume of valuable research material.' On this regard, see "Responsibility to Protect", Report of the International Commission on Intervention and State Sovereignty, published by the International Development Research Center, Ottawa, Canada, December 2001, at VIII. Available at: *https://docs.google.com/viewer?url=http%3A%2F%2Fwww.iciss.ca%2Fpdf%2FCommission-Report.pdf*

[2] Luck, E.C., "The United Nations and the Responsibility to Protect", *Policy Analysis Brief*, The Stanley Foundation, August 2008, at 1. Available at: *www.humansecuritygateway.com/documents/TSF_theUNandR2P.pdf&pli=1*

> these obligations. Third, the responsibility of the member States to respond in a timely and decisive manner when a State is manifestly failing to provide such protection."[3]

When former UN secretary-general Kofi Annan was called in 2008 to mediate the postelection crisis in Kenya he declared:

> "I saw the crisis in the R2P prism with a Kenyan government unable to contain the situation or protect its people. I knew that if the international community did not intervene, things would go hopelessly wrong. The problem is when we say 'intervention,' people think military, when in fact that's a last resort. Kenya is a successful example of R2P at work."[4]

The R2P is a subsidiary measure to guarantee the respect for human rights. As a subsidiary measure it is only used when all other means have failed. This means that the R2P will find application when the State in question is unable or unwilling to protect human right catastrophes, i.e. when the rule of law is rendered ineffective, inefficient or its systems have been shattered.

It is therefore essential for law-makers to be able to put into place the necessary legal foundations that may regulate the activation and extent of the so-called 'responsibility to protect'. This is essential if this R2P is to be effectively used and not abused.

Thus, the recourse to the R2P brings into play two essential components of the State: Sovereignty, which has traditionally been the protective wall that ensured self-determination, and the foreign affairs power, as the channel that allows a State to relate to the outside world, beyond that protective wall. Both sovereignty and the foreign affairs power are primarily regulated through constitutional law and/or practice.

In this chapter we look into the nature of these two areas of constitutional law that bring the State into contact with other States: the foreign affairs power, its constitutional regulation and practice, which serves as the constitutional gateway that ultimately allows the supranational judicial bodies to play a role in securing the protection of universal human rights within States, vis-à-vis the concept of sovereignty, which aims at preventing foreign intervention and defends the right to self-determination.

---

[3] *Ibid.*

[4] Annan, K. in Luck, E.C., *op. cit.* Available at: *www.humansecuritygateway.com/ documents/TSF_theUNandR2P.pdf&pli=1*

Foreign Policy, Foreign Affairs and the Constitution

Samuel Blay argues that "territorial integrity and political independence are two core elements of Statehood. Territorial integrity refers to the territorial 'oneness' or 'wholeness' of the State [while] political independence refers to the autonomy in the affairs of the State with respect to its institutions, freedom of political decisions, policy making, and in matters pertaining to its domestic and foreign affairs."[5]

Foreign affairs are directed by what is known as international policy, which refers to the course of action or decisions desired and taken by a section of the government of a State in pursuit and promotion of national interests in the international systems.[6] International policy actualizes itself through the conduct of international relations.

There are three key factors for the successful conduct of international policy in a constitutional democracy. First, is the personal or psychological factor, i.e. identification. This refers to the need and the convenience of achieving a satisfactory degree of identification with the political society,[7] i.e. between people, government and State so that they are fused into one image, and they all travel in the same direction. Second, political. International policies must be compatible with domestic policies. In addition, international policies are made by popular legitimised authorities and, although there may be no recognisable form of democratic participation, the State is meant to be one with the people who are its nation so as to achieve a satisfactory degree of identification. And third, legal international policy evolves in a context where there is an imperative need to find a balance between *separation of powers* and administrative effectiveness.

This identification is one of the most important elements for political integration. The key to foreign policy as a tool for nation building is that foreign policy can create a situation in which the people can perceive a threat to their communal identity, or an opportunity to protect and enhance it. Foreign policy can create a situation in which the whole national

---

[5] Blay, S., "Territorial Integrity and Political Independence", *Max Planck Encyclopedia of Public International Law*, *www.mpepil.com*, Oxford University Press, (2011), No. 1.

[6] Katete Orwa, "Foreign Relations and International Co-operation", *Kenya Official Handbook*, Ministry of Information and Broadcasting, (1988), at 1.

[7] See generally Maritain, J., *Man and The State*, University of Chicago Press, Chicago, 1951. Maritain calls it *body politic*.

community can be perceived as sharing the same experience in relation to a foreign actor.[8]

Thus, international policies develop and evolve into international relations, which describe the process and consequences of interactions with other States, government and peoples. International relations is not, then, the relation of super-structures, it is also a downward relation with governments and Non-State Actors; it is the relation among *political societies*.

Hence, identification between people, government and State is a substantial component of nation building and a key success for internal and international politics. The problem is how to achieve adequate levels of identification. The answer may be by establishing proper constitutional checks and balances so that the actions or decisions taken in foreign policy become as objective as possible. This does not mean that every person has the right to act in foreign policy decision-making, as this is not the way identification is necessarily achieved. Identification could be achieved instead by, for example, enhancing parliament's participation in foreign policy or by enhancing democracy in the exercise of international relations. This may be achieved by way of referendum in certain specified cases.

Thus, while identification is essential in foreign policy decision-making, it should not be ignored that foreign policy decision-making is intrinsically political. This implies that government leaders and decision-makers should routinely monitor domestic political conditions and incorporate them into their foreign policy calculations.[9] One goal for foreign policy-makers acting in their concurrent role as national decision political leaders is maintaining and, if possible, enhancing the political support base necessary for holding on to political power.[10] Thus, foreign policy-makers must balance foreign policy concerns with their need to

---

[8] See Bloom, W., *Personal Identity, National Identity and International Relations*, Cambridge University Press, Cambridge, 1990, at 81 and 82.

[9] See Hagan, J. D., *Political Opposition and Foreign Policy in Comparative Perspective*, Lynne Rienner Publisher, London, 1993, (Introductory remarks).

[10] See Reynolds P.A., *An Introduction to International Relations*, Longman, London, 1992, at 5.Although no political system commands total support from all its members all the time, it is certain that for any system to survive it must command the active support of some politically significant members of that time, and a residual coercive power to constrain the remainder or to handle a temporary crisis. We think that this support is appropriately found, in this case, by way of parliamentary intervention in international policy-making.

maximise domestic political support for their regime. When foreign policy considerations are inconsistent with the regime's political situation at home, political leaders must adjust foreign policy to make it more compatible with those domestic realities.[11]

All this evolves in a context where there is an imperative need to find a balance between separation or rather *dilution* of powers[12] and administrative effectiveness. Governmental affairs must be conducted effectively, expeditiously and inexpensively. No administrative rule-making procedure is acceptable if it does not take this into consideration because what is needed is a system of rule-making which can strike a sensible balance between the need for adequate public participation and the need for efficient government.[13] Thus, the executive must certainly be controlled, and those controls must be efficient and adapted to the country's peculiar background and circumstances because, says Ojwang:

---

[11] See Henkin, L., *Foreign Affairs and the Constitution*, W.W. Norton & Company, New York, 1972, at 4. By domestic policy we understand those concerning the government and its citizens and which therefore do not admit or recognise the rights of other governments to complain.

[12]See Wade E.C.S. and Philips G., *Constitutional Law*, 6th Edition, Longmans, London, 1960, at 22.We have designated it *dilution* of power because the word separation in the context of common law may not be desirable as it is exposed and applied in the civil law system. Wade says that separation of power may mean, or as it is understood today, in three different ways: a) *that the same person should not form part of more than one of three organs of government, e.g. that Ministers should not sit in Parliament;* b) *that one organ of government should not control or interfere with the exercise of its function by another organ, e.g. that Ministers should not be responsible to Parliament;* c) *that one organ of government should not exercise the function of another, e.g. that Ministers should not have legislative powers*. Nevertheless, Montesquieu (*Esprit des Lois, Book XI, chapter 6*), who first formulated this doctrine, based his exposition on the British Constitution. Although he followed the usual meaning of legislative and judicial power, by the executive he meant only 'the power of executing matters falling within the law of nations', i.e. making war and peace, sending and receiving ambassadors, establishing order, preventing invasion. And separation of power in this context did not mean no influence or control over the acts of each other, but only that neither should exercise the whole power of the other, which is neither desirable nor would it help to achieve the identification sought. (See also Jennings, I., *The Law and the Constitution*, 5th Ed., University of London Press, London, 1959 App. 1) In this context, dilution which means control in contra-position to concentration of power seems a more appropriate term.

[13] Bonfield, A. E., "Military and foreign affairs function rule-making under the APA", *Michigan Law Review*, vol. 71 (1972), at 222.

> "[T]he control of executive power in Africa presents certain unusual problems. The sorts of the scale of the power in question are new and have no specific well-recognised means of control. What techniques of control are employed, thus, have necessarily to be novel also. Like the modern State and its organs of power-exercise, the means of power-control available is of foreign origin. It has been transplanted, as part of an entire constitutional model, from a European country. In the very nature of things, it could take an indefinite length of time before organs of power-control thus imported could gain general acceptance and legitimacy. But the position in Africa has been complicated further by the changing nature of the social, economic and political conditions in which the organs of power-control, evolved in a relatively settled environment have been applied."[14]

Therefore, an adequate foreign policy system of checks and balances must be found taking into consideration the country's own circumstances and domestic policies and the experience that may be gathered from other States, as far as applicable. The manner foreign policy is domestically conducted affects the international community and its law. International law has traditionally been defined as a set, body or sum of rules or usage which civilised States have agreed shall be binding upon them in their dealings with one another. This set of rules is said to be formed by convention or customary means. This is by way of treaties, conventions, and other agreements based on international relations.[15] In addition, according to Hersey, international law may be defined as a set of rules observed and enforced by the States in order to preserve the peace of nations and to facilitate international commerce. The purpose of international law is to promote international co-operation and to achieve international peace and security. International law embodies certain rules relating to human relations throughout the world, which are generally observed by mankind and enforced primarily through the agency of governments of the independent communities into which humanity is divided.[16] Along the same lines, Green defines international law as the

---

[14] Ojwang, J.B., *Legislative Control of Executive Powers: A Comparative Study of the British and French-derived Constitutions of Kenya and Cote d'Ivoire*, University of Cambridge, Ph.D. dissertation, Cambridge, 1981, at 327.

[15] Tunkin, G. I., *Teoriia Mezhdunarodnogo Prava*, (Translated by Butler, W. E. as *Theory of International Law*) Harvard University Press, Cambridge, Massachusetts, 1974, at 271. Tunkin based his definition on Lord Alverstone's approach in *West Rand Central Gold Mining Co. V. The King* (1905).

[16] Hershey, A.S., *The Essentials of International Public Law and Organisation*, Revised Edition, The Macmillan Company, New York, 1927, at 1. Hersey made use of Stowell's views on international law.

body of rules of conduct enforceable by external sanctions, which confer rights and impose obligations primarily, though not exclusively upon sovereign States and which owe their validity both to the consent of the States as expressed in custom and treaties and to the fact of the existence of an international community of States and individuals.[17]

However, those who adhere to the view that international law is a set of rules among States (and, perhaps, international organisations), have found themselves in increasing opposition to those who adopt the social process theories.[18] Oppenheim says that international law refers simply to customs which have grown up among States and regulate relations between them. It is a law not above, but between sovereign States and is therefore a weaker law than municipal law which is over individuals[19] and it may also be seen as common consent where States consent to customary rules of the international community because the inter-relations of States with each other necessitates some rules of international conduct.[20]

For others, international law is defined as co-operation. Hershey defined international relations as the co-operation between the international community of States which is governed by a body of principles and customs which are generally recognised as binding upon the members;[21] and therefore international relations, Hershey continues, are aimed at satisfying collective needs of member States.[22]

Finally, international law has also been denied the category of law. One theory which enjoyed wide acceptance is that international law is not true law, but a code of conduct of moral force only.[23] John Austin, the leading proponent of this theory said that there was no visible authority with legislative power or any determinate power over the society of States. Austin concluded that international law was not true law but 'positive international morality' only analogous to the rules binding a club or society. The positive moral rules, Austin argues, "are laws improperly so

---

[17] Green, L.C., *Law and Society*, Oceana Publications Inc. Dobbs Terry, New York, 1975, at 133.

[18] See Detter De Lupis, I., *The Concept of International Law,* Norstedts Förlag, Stockholm, 1987, at 16.

[19] Oppenheim, L., *International Law*, 7th Edition, vol. I, Longmans, 1963, at 18.

[20] *Ibid*, at 14.

[21] Hershey, A.S., *The Essentials of International Public Law and Organisation*, Revised Edition, The Macmillan Company, New York, 1927, at 1.

[22] *Ibid.*

[23] Starke, J.G., *Introduction to International Law*, 9th ed., Butterworths, London, 1984, at 17.

called, may be styled laws or rules set or imposed by opinion: for they are merely opinions or sentiments held or felt by men in regard to human conduct."[24] He further described it as consisting of "opinions or sentiments current among nations generally."[25]

It is Ingrid Detter De Lupis, who as a noteworthy defender of International law, refers to it as a normative system laying down rules and obligations. This normative system may be created and continuously revised by a process triggered by customs acquired through common consent and co-operation. It is a comprehensive process of authoritative decision, transcending the boundaries of particular territorial communities, which the peoples of the world establish and maintain for the purpose of clarifying and implementing their common interests.[26]

The development of international law has been shaped by important factors that have defined our modern understanding and conduct in foreign relations. These are:

The first was based on Grotius' views that the law of nations was neither made nor supported by the power of a sovereign State, but on natural law which, he said, contains 'dictates of right reason' and which provided usage common to the laws of all nations.[27] The Greek law of nature had given inspiration to the rules of Roman *jus gentium*; and the *jus gentium* thus inspired had given force and practical application to the rule of right reason, on which international law ultimately rests. Individuals, Hobbes says, organise themselves in order to drive these relations and work in co-operation to ensure their self-preservation by giving all powers to a sovereign. According to Hobbes any division of these powers would destroy the sovereign, and therefore he prefers one singular sovereign.[28]

---

[24] Austin, J., 'The Province of Jurisprudence Determined', 1832, available at *HeinOnline* (*http://heinonline.org*). Austin also argues that Von Martens, a writer of celebrity, had named an international law department as "positive international law," or "practical international law." Austin says that had he named that department "positive international morality," the name would have hit its import with perfect precision. See Austin, J., "The Province of Jurisprudence Determined", (1832). Available at HeinOnline (*http://heinonline.org*), Sat Apr 16 11:52:25 2011.

[25] See Starke, J.G., *op. cit.*, at 19.

[26] Detter De Lupis, I., *op. cit.*, at 16 and 17.

[27] Holdsworth, Sir W. S., *A History of English Law*, Vol. V, Sweet & Maxwell, London, 1966, at 25-60.

[28] Hobbes, T., *Leviathan*, Forgottenbooks, Reprinted in 2008, at 128. Available at:

Locke, instead, attempted to provide firm assurance of the individual's rights by assigning separate co-ordinated powers to the monarchs and the parliament on the one hand and, on the other, by reserving the right of revolution against a government that had become unconstitutionally oppressive.[29] John Locke says that when individuals came together into societies the government eventually assumed a federative power to drive these relations and co-operation, and this included authority over 'war and peace, leagues and alliances, and all the transactions with all persons and communities' outside of the State.[30] This federative power granted the government the prerogative to conduct and safeguard the interests of civil society in international affairs, and any injury done to a member of the society by outsiders was regarded as an injury to the society as a whole.[31]

The second is the idea of maintaining a balance of power, which will necessarily emerge whenever there are several neighbouring and independent States. In ancient Greece and in medieval Italy, wars and alliances were used to prevent the predominance of some of these States. In the Sixteenth Century, the influence of this idea was felt throughout Western Europe. The foreign policy of Wolsey was inspired by this idea and the foreign policy of the early part of Elizabeth's reign was determined to a large extent by her knowledge that maintenance of the balance of power would practically compel Spain to take England's side against France.[32] After the French Revolution, the consciousness of the importance of keeping a balance of power reached the people. The juridical conscience of a free people created new forms of relationship between international law and constitutional law.[33]

The third is related to the increase of permanent and peaceful relations between countries, the growth of stable machinery for discussion of their

---

http://books.google.co.ke/books?id=Q4nPYeps6MC&printsec=frontcover&dq=thomas+hobbes+leviathan&hl=en&ei=6BlYTb8ryesB_PC7a4H&sa=X&oi=book_result&ct=result&resnum=1&ved=0CCsQ6AEwAA#v=onepage&q=one%20sovereign&f=false.

[29] Locke, J., *Two Treatises on Government*, 7th Ed, J. Wiston Editor, London, 1689, at 347.

[30] *Ibid.*, at 187ss. See also Prakash, S. B. and Ramsey, M. D., "The Executive Power over Foreign Affairs", *Yale Law Journal*, vol. 111, (2001), at 266-267.

[31] Locke, J., *op. cit.*, at 187ff.

[32] Maritain, J., "The Concept of Sovereignty", published in Stankiewicz, J. W. (ed), *In Defense of Sovereignty*, Oxford University Press, New York, 1969, at 51.

[33] See Mirkine-Guetzevitch, B., "Droit international et droit constitutionnel", *Recueil des Cours*, vol. 38, Académie de Droit International, The Hague, (1931), at 311-463.

differences and the consequent evolution of legal rules as to the working of this machinery and the principles applicable to settle these differences. The importance of the law which regulated peaceful relations among States was as great as the importance of the law which regulated their relations in time of war.

And the fourth is brought about by the international use of cooperation as a means of advancement, of instituting open governance models, and as a way of increasing redistribution of wealth.

Therefore, international law nowadays is not only a set of rules, nor a process, but somehow a complex and living reflection of the foreign policy of countries and the foreign policy is expressed through and by virtue of the power conferred by the constitution of each country to a specific structure or structures within the State. Thus, Pastor Ridruejo argues that the primary creators of international law are the States. This creation is actualised through two main channels: the written norm through treaty-making and the unwritten norm through customary law.[34]

This is how, it may be said, international law as a normative system is deeply influenced by the sum of constitutional regulations relating to the foreign affairs power and its exercise, because foreign relations are constructed through the exercise — at the domestic level — of what is known as the foreign affairs power.

Foreign affairs law is, at its root, constitutional law.[35] How a country conducts its diplomacy, makes international agreements and conducts itself in all foreign matters, is governed by its constitution or constitutional practice.[36] Foreign affairs, therefore, is a wide term which expresses more than mere relations. Affairs include matters and things as well as relationships and a constitutional grant of plenary legitimate power.[37] It means that foreign affairs are matters relating to foreign countries, i.e. affairs other than domestic and specifically, matters having to do with the interests of the home country in foreign countries.[38]

---

[34] See Pastor Ridruejo, J.A., *Curso de Derecho Internacional Público y Organizaciones Internacionales*, 3rd Edition, Tecnos ed, Madrid, 1989, at 31.

[35] Ramsey, M. D., *The Constitution's Text in Foreign Affairs*, Harvard University Press, Cambridge, 2007, at 1.

[36] See *Ibid.*

[37] Lane, P.H., *A Manual of Australian Constitutional Law*, 4th Ed, LawBook Co, Sydney, 1997, at 140.

[38] See Bonfield, A. E., "Military and foreign affairs function rule-making under the APA", *Michigan Law Review*, vol. 71 (1972), at 258.

In this context, foreign affairs may be identified as a function. A function is an activity specially fitted for, appropriate to or expected of something because of its peculiar nature, attributes, or qualifications. The foreign affairs function, thus, Bonfield says, may be an activity specially fitted for, appropriate to, or expected of international relations — the interests of a State in foreign States — due to the peculiar nature or attributes of such relations. In addition, power may be defined as the competence to decide and act on a specific function.[39] Hence the foreign affairs power is the competence to decide and act in matters having to do with the interests, ideals and principles of the home State in foreign States.

Having defined the power in question, the question immediately arises: How is this power exercised? In the *Reparation for Injuries* case the International Court of Justice (ICJ) remarked that powers expressly granted have been held to imply others.[40] Henkin, paraphrasing this ICJ decision says that "Foreign Affairs Power expressly granted have been held to imply others: for example, the power to make treaties implies the power to terminate or break them. And some powers taken together have been found to 'result' in others."[41] For example the power to appoint and to receive ambassadors results in the power to conduct diplomatic relations or the power to do other things involved in maintaining relations with a foreign country. Foreign affairs powers have also been spawned from general grants, for example the provision vesting the executive power in the President.[42] Nevertheless, for any implication of powers there must be a first principle or general power granted, so that others may be implied.[43] The question then arises: Where is this first principle so that

[39] See Witzch, G., "Foreign Relations and International Integration According to the Basic Law of the Federal Republic of Germany", *Indian Journal of International Law*,vol 7, (1967), at 45. See also Bonfield, A. E., "Military and foreign affairs function rule-making under the APA", *Michigan Law Review*, vol. 71 (1972), at 258.

[40] ICJ *Reports* (1948), case for *The Reparation for Injuries Suffered in the Service of the United Nations*, at 179-186.

[41] Henkin, L., *op. cit.*, at 17.

[42] This used to be the case, for example, in the former Constitution of Kenya, where there was no other mention about the conduct of international affairs.

[43] See Foley, M., *The Silence of the Constitutions*, Routledge, London, 1989, at 2-3. Foley argues that there is an *unwritten dimension in constitutions that is separate in scale and nature to the standard notion of 'unwritten' conventions. In contrast to conventions which are determinable and amenable to description, 'constitutional abeyances' represent a form of tacit and instinctive agreement to condone, and even cultivate, constitutional ambiguity as an acceptable strategy for*

other powers may be implied? The first logical answer would be: in the constitution. However, foreign affair power may also be perceived as extra-constitutional or pre-constitutional as it belongs to the nature itself of a State and the State cannot do without it. Prakash, for example, argues that in every circumstance a power cannot be inferred from nothing and that a theory to support the exercise of the foreign affairs power necessarily begins with the national Constitutional text. Prakash asserts that:

> "[I]t must be based upon a reading of actual words in the Constitution, not deduced from some broader theory of government (whether one's own or one purportedly held by the Framers). It does not, however, end with the text. Words have no meaning in a vacuum, shorn of their context. To discern that context, one must look outside the text. Indeed, even when legal texts contain definitions, the definitions themselves are composed of words that must be understood by reference to meanings 'external' to the text… Further, we think the appropriate context from which to discern the meaning of the words in a legal document is the context in which they were written."[44]

Once the power is inferred, accepted as existent and eventually exercised the checks and balances emerge as a natural and practical consequence of a democratic process. In the case of the foreign affairs power we could state that it is a limited power in that it is not a power at large as the altogether general State law-making power is.[45] It is limited by its nature in the national and international sphere. In the national sphere, partly because it is a power laid out in a particular kind of instrument—a constitution which may impose specific limitations, and partly it is determined by domestic politics and factors, otherwise the unity of country policy may be disrupted and identification lost. In the international sphere it is limited partly by the peremptory norms of international law (*jus*

---

resolving conflict. It is called constitutional *abeyance* because it implies a dormant suspension attitude of wilful neglect, protective obfuscation, and complicity in non-exposure in order to preserve the effectiveness of abeyance in deferring conflicts and containing unresolved points of issue. *Abeyances refer to those constitutional gaps which remain vacuum for positive and constructive purposes.* Constitutional abeyance may be desirable when the constitution has established the power but not all the circumstances for it to be carried out, leaving thus a range of freedom for decisions. Nevertheless, we see abeyance inconvenience when the ambiguity refers to the power itself.

44 Prakash, S. B. and Ramsey, M. D., "The Executive Power over Foreign Affairs", *Yale Law Journal*, vol. 111, (2001), at 234.

45 See Lane, P.H., *op. cit.*, at 55.

cogens), which any act of the foreign affairs power is to abide by, and partly by the specific regulations of any international negotiation the State gets involved in. For example, if the State is a party to a bilateral or multilateral treaty, the implementing law must adhere itself to the terms of the treaty.

Prakash and Ramsey argue that there are four constitutional principles or maxims that delineate and restrict the constitutional exercise of the foreign affairs powers by implication. First, the executive "enjoys a 'residual' foreign affairs power by virtue of the executive power." Second, "in line with the theory of residual powers, the President's executive power over foreign affairs is limited by specific allocations of foreign affairs power to other entities. Thus, the President has a circumscribed version of the traditional executive power over foreign affairs." Third, "Congress, in addition to its specific foreign affairs powers, has a derivative power to legislate in support of the President's executive power over foreign affairs and its own foreign affairs powers. However, contrary to the conventional view, these derivative powers do not extend to a general and independent authority over all foreign affairs matters. In particular, Congress cannot establish relations with a foreign country or establish foreign policy." And fourth, "the President's executive power over foreign affairs does not extend to matters that were not part of the traditional executive power, even where they touch upon foreign affairs. In particular, the President cannot claim power over appropriations and law-making, even in the foreign affairs arena, by virtue of the executive power. That is to say, the President is not a law-maker, even in foreign affairs."[46]

Indeed, there is a clear reciprocal interplay and influence between international and constitutional law, where the international legal order seems to have developed a particular primacy over the internal order. This is so, due to the paramount influence each constitutional system plays within the co-relation between foreign policy, international law and diplomacy. This correlation, according to Tunkin, has three aspects: "The influence of foreign policy upon the development of international law; the converse influence of international law upon the foreign policy of a State; and the use of international law by States as a support for foreign policy."[47]

---

[46] See Prakash, S. B. and Ramsey, M. D., "The Executive Power over Foreign Affairs", *Yale Law Journal*, vol. 111, (2001), at 234-235.
[47] Tunkin, G. I., *Teoriia Mezhdunarodnogo Prava*, (Translated by Butler, W. E. as *Theory of International Law*) Harvard University Press, Cambridge, Massachusetts, 1974, at 271.

As each of these aspects evolves and States find the need to implement their foreign policy through foreign relations, the elements of the foreign affairs power become visible and identifiable. Those elements of the Foreign Affairs Power are usually intermingled but for academic purposes we group them into four, as follows: Treaty-making; diplomacy; war and Peace and, finally, the recognition of States and Governments.

Two of these four elements, i.e. treaty-making and diplomacy, are directly and constantly involved in the design and making of international human rights structures, bodies and decisions.[48] In one way or another, these two elements partly determine the vigour of the external activity in modern States. This impact extends from States to international organisations, which as the initial result of treaty-making and diplomacy, may themselves create further structures and bodies. Such relations and structures affect the essence of the political and social life of a country and its relations with other members of the international community. Therefore, this requires external checks and balances which should be established by the constitution for they affect the very core of separation of powers. It may be said that the exercise of the foreign affairs power is in itself a section of the constitutional powers vested by the constitution in a specific organ and we focus our attention on this matter in the following section.

The Regulation of the Foreign Affairs Power in Constitutional Law

According to Prakash and Ramsey, the constant recourse of scholars and judges to the constitution in search for the allocation of foreign affairs powers, have revealed one trait: "They have given up on the exclusive reference to the constitutional text."[49] Constitutions usually contain

---

[48] Certainly *war and peace* and *recognition of States and governments* are also related to human rights. For example, the presence of *de facto* State of war immediately calls for the application of humanitarian laws, and the recognition of a State or government may be beneficial or detrimental to the rule of law of its subjects. Nevertheless, they are not *per se* the immediate cause of international human rights structures, which is our focus on this study. International structures of governance are created through diplomatic negotiations and treaty-making, even though the remote cause may be explicit or implicit recognitions of States and governments, or sometimes a post-war situation as happened with the United Nations.

[49] See Prakash and Ramsey, *op. cit.*, at 231.

enormous abeyances or gaps that must be filled by reference to sources beyond the text: practice, convenience, necessity, national security, international relations law and theory, inherent rights of sovereignty, and so forth.[50] However, as we said before, a power cannot be inferred from nothing and a theory of foreign affairs necessarily begins with the Constitution's text and then develops through jurisprudence and explicitly or implicitly accepted practices. This means that the foreign affairs power should have a constitutionally expressed dimension, and this is usually clarified and guided throughout time by judicial review.

Certainly, all modern States have constitutions but possession and publication of a constitution does not necessarily make a government constitutional. In modern times a democratic constitutional government should defend, uphold and foster procedural stability, accountability, representation, division of power with proper checks and balances, openness and disclosure.

The concurrent presence of these characteristics guarantees the existence of a democratic constitutional government. And these characteristics turn into requirements when referred to the specific functions of government, one of them being the exercise of the foreign affairs power. Therefore, the following questions seem to necessitate an accurate answer: Should the law address the regulation of the foreign affairs power? And if so, Should it be designed, regulated and framed within the constitution or should it be left open as an abeyance?[51]Third, should it be conceived as an executive function or be placed on other State organs? And fourth, should the judiciary intervene in the regulation or development of the foreign affairs power? We think the answer should be positive on the following grounds:

First, the conduct of the foreign affairs power affects the very essence of the political and social life of a country—its relation with other members of the international community. This has become particularly important in the last decades as the evolution of external life somewhat determines the quality of life at the domestic level and, consequently, affects its subjects directly. Moreover, there is an increase in interdependence as trade, technology transfer, investment, travel, migration and other transactions are continuously multiplying.[52] Its legal regulation is essential

---

[50] See *Ibid.*

[51] On the concept of abeyance refer to Foley, M., *The Silence of the Constitutions*, Routledge, London, 1989, at 2-3.

[52] See more on interdependence in Sullivan, M.P., "Transnationalism, Power Politics, and the Realities of the Present System", in Williams, M. (ed),

for "it provides the mechanisms, forms, and procedures by which nations maintain their relations, carry on trade and other forms of intercourse, resolve differences and disputes"[53] and it gives some predictability and uniformity to the action of subjects in international relations.[54]

The second reason is related to the appropriate place for that regulation. We argue that the exercise of the foreign affairs power requires external checks and balances which should be established by the constitution for they affect the political balance suspended on the fence of separation of powers. Constitutional government has come to suggest limited government and constitutions have become a blueprint for a system of government. They share out authority among a set of different branches in which limitations are implied, or should be implied. Constitutions should lay the foundation for external checks and the separation of powers, as "this separation of powers is designed, at least in part, to safeguard the people's liberties,"[55] which is an essential feature of any democratic system. But in a democratic system any given individual or group of individuals, if unrestrained by external checks, will tyrannize others because the elimination of external checks produces tyranny.[56] Therefore, it can be affirmed that the exercise of the foreign affairs power is in itself a section of the constitutional powers vested by the constitution in a specific organ. Consequently, as a power, it would have to be subject to external checks because the absolute accumulation of powers in the same hands implies tyranny. In order to establish those external checks on the exercise of the foreign affairs power it would seem correct to affirm that the constitution, as the source, pillar and foundation of the power itself, must provide for external checks to be applied.

International Law in the Twentieth Century: A Reader, Macmillan Education, London, 1989, at 255.

[53] Henkin, L., "The Role of Law and its Limitations", in Williams, M. (ed), *International Law in the Twentieth Century: A Reader*, Macmillan Education, London, 1989, at 189.

[54] *Ibid.*, at 197.

[55] Henkin, L., *Foreign Affairs and the Constitution*, W.W. Norton & Company, New York, (1972) at 3.

[56] See Dahl, R.A., *A Preface to Democratic Theory*, Charles R. Walgreen Foundation Lecturers, University of Chicago Press, Chicago, 1956, at 6. According to Dahl, *'external check'* consists of the application of rewards and penalties, or the expectation that they will be applied, by some source other than the given individual himself and *'tyranny'* is every severe deprivation of a natural right. This is an approach close to Madison's.

Third, the foreign affairs power is an 'executive function', which refers to what pertains to the executive power, something that belongs to the office of the executive, that is, he who 'carries out' as in the US Constitution, where the President is given the duty to 'take care that the laws be faithfully executed.' However, Mansfield argues that this would make the President an 'errand boy.' Taking care to execute the law faithfully is only one of the duties imposed on the presidency for the performance of which he is given several enumerated powers. Moreover, he is vested with the executive power which, according to Hamilton's famous argument,[57] has a nature of its own that is not exhausted by the enumerated powers, and he, in most countries, takes an oath not to faithfully execute the law but to faithfully execute his office.[58]

In Machiavelli's thought, the Prince should be the executive, because execution is sudden, decisive, energetic, extra-ordinary and extra-legal. In his *Prince* Machiavelli vests the primacy of war and foreign affairs in the executive. However, it was John Locke who first conceived the executive in its modern form. Locke offered the doctrine of the separation of powers, in which the executive appears as a power subject to the supremacy of the legislative.[59] The legislative power is conceived by Locke as a supreme

---

[57] Hamilton, A., "Pacifus", no. 1, in Syrett, H. C. (ed.), 26 Volumes, Columbia University Press, New York, XV, *Federalist,* vol. 70,(1973) at 33-43.

[58] Mansfield, H. C., "The Modern Doctrine of Executive Power", *Presidential Studies Quarterly*, Spring (1987), at 237.

[59] See Locke, J., *op. cit.*, nos. 145-148. Actually, John Locke speaks of the executive and the federative powers, which are distinct in themselves but usually united in practice. Locke states that: "There is another power in every commonwealth which one may call natural, because it is that which answers to the power every man naturally had before he entered into society. For though in a commonwealth the members of it are distinct persons, still, in reference to one another, and, as such, are governed by the laws of the society, yet, in reference to the rest of mankind, they make one body, which is, as every member of it before was, still in the state of Nature with the rest of mankind, so that the controversies that happen between any man of the society with those that are out of it are managed by the public, and an injury done to a member of their body engages the whole in the reparation of it. So that under this consideration the whole community is one body in the state of Nature in respect of all other states or persons out of its community. § 146. This, therefore, contains the power of war and peace, leagues and alliances, and all the transactions with all persons and communities without the commonwealth, and may be called federative if any one pleases. So the thing be understood, I am indifferent as to the name. § 147. These two powers, executive and federative, though they be really distinct in themselves, yet one comprehending the execution of the municipal laws of the society within itself

collective body which is placed in the hands of 'diverse persons' who assemble and then separate so that they themselves become subject to the laws.[60]

These developments evolved in the modern concept of the executive who — according to Ojwang — "is the organ, person or group of persons recognised as having the competence to perform the execution of laws, maintenance of public order, management of State property, foreign policy, military operation, the provision of such services as education, public health, transport as well as State assistance and insurance or other public functions."[61] Therefore, to affirm that foreign affairs is an executive function is logical. Yet, to say that foreign affairs is 'exclusively' an executive function is not justified. Certainly, there is an obvious need to conduct governmental affairs effectively, expeditiously and inexpensively and, it must be said, no administrative rule-making procedure is acceptable unless it takes account of this consideration fairly. Consequently, procedural requirements that unduly fetter agency action, or frustrate its purposes, are obviously misdirected.[62] But it seems a mistake to exalt presidential over parliamentary expertise in the conduct of foreign affairs for the mere interest of making it expeditious and effective.[63] Effectiveness and promptitude do not mean, however, that executive functions as such should be unlimited within the set of rules regulating the function because "the exercise of the executive power in any State ought to be conducted within a framework of appropriate checks"[64] and this is usually done through the constitution.

Fourth, although the foreign affairs power is essentially, although not exclusively, an executive function, it is bound to be guided and steered through judicial intervention so as to guarantee the fulfilment of procedures and the resolution of conflicting legislations. Therefore, the

---

upon all that are parts of it, the other the management of the security and interest of the public without with all those that it may receive benefit or damage from, yet they are always almost united."

[60] See *Ibid.*, at 237 and ff.

[61] Ojwang, J.B., *Constitutional Development in Kenya*, Act Press, Nairobi, 1990, at 76.

[62] Bonfield, A. E., "Military and foreign affairs function rule-making under the APA", *Michigan Law Review*, vol. 71 (1972), at 222.

[63] Berger, R., "The Presidential Monopoly of Foreign Treaties", *Michigan Law Review*, vol. 71, (1972-73), at 56.

[64] Ojwang, J. B., *Application of Treaties, Legislative Control of Executive Powers*, Downing College, Cambridge, August 1981, at 220.

judiciary in this regards plays a role in modern democracies that should not be disregarded or ignored. Judicial decisions have practically shaped human rights systems in the last two decades, and the way international judicial decisions are incorporated into the municipal arena means a lot to the modern conduct of foreign affairs. Nevertheless, the dilemma between effectiveness and promptitude on the one side, and checks and balances, on the other, must not be resolved by getting rid of either. Instead, proper and effective checks and balances must be found for each function within each constitutional system.

The constitutional regulation of the foreign affairs power is relevant for the enforcement of international judicial decisions on two main accounts: it expresses the attitude and legal posture of a State towards international law in general, and it establishes the legal system for international law domestication, including international judicial decisions. In this regard, domestication systems may find legal or political obstacles that are usually based on the application of the theory of sovereignty. It seems therefore important to clarify certain aspects of the development of sovereignty and its interplay between international law and human rights.

The foreign affairs power is, then, the constitutional avenue whereby a State may allow international involvement in its domestic matters. Thus, States have traditionally built their sense of identification around the constitutional order, which jealously safeguard its sphere of influence through the application of the concept of sovereignty. Sovereignty is often used as a stopgap measure or as a self-defence mechanism to prevent foreign intervention or regulate the extent of its possible impact on national or domestic matters. Even the act of negotiating a treaty that would seem to curtail sovereignty would traditionally be seen as an act of sovereignty itself.

Nevertheless, the foundation of the first human rights instruments and structures has drastically changed the relationship between international and domestic organs. States have got together and constituted bodies with judicial powers and jurisdiction over matters, persons or situation that used to be considered purely domestic. International human rights systems have challenged traditional international law concepts, such as sovereignty. The concept of sovereignty seems to have evolved a great deal and the world is witnessing a rapid metamorphosis in the approach towards the sovereign State with human rights systems. This will be analysed in the next section.

The Foreign Affairs Power and Sovereignty

On 19th March 2009 Justice Lord Hoffmann, of Britain, stated, that human rights are "universal in abstraction but national in application."[65] Justice Hoffmann goes on to explain that:

> "The fact that the 10 original Member States of the Council of Europe subscribed to a statement of human rights in the same terms did not mean that they had agreed to uniformity of the application of those abstract rights in each of their countries, still less in the 47 States which now belong. The Strasbourg court … has no mandate to unify the laws of Europe on the many subjects which may arguably touch upon human rights. … The application of many human rights in a concrete case, the trade-offs which must be made between individual rights and effective government, or between the rights of one individual and another, will frequently vary from country to country, depending upon the local circumstances and legal tradition. … The problem is the Court; and the right of individual petition, which enables the Court to intervene in the details and nuances of the domestic laws of Member States. Not only that: the right of individual petition, which was optional until 1998 but is now compulsory, has produced a flood of such petitions which is overwhelming the Court."[66]

Justice Hoffmann's postulate on human rights being "universal in abstract but national in application" expresses his frustration and that of many a judge to what they perceive as interference and abuse of jurisdiction, in this specific case, by the European Court of Human Rights. Nevertheless his argument could perhaps also justify historical abuses such as the apartheid system in South Africa, or the killing of Tutsis by the Hutu majority in 1994 in Rwanda, or Hitler's Holocaust, or perhaps other non-extreme State perpetrated abuses that could be justified through the ambiguous 'margin of appreciation.' The dilemma Justice Hoffmann puts forward goes beyond the mere conception and application of human rights. It is a dilemma that has come about due to the interplay between traditional concepts, such as State sovereignty, and the protection of universal human rights, that has brought into play the post-World War II mushrooming of international bodies with powers and functions that seem

---

[65] Hoffmann, J., "The Universality of Human Rights", *Judicial Studies Board Annual Lecture* given on 19th March 2009.
[66] *Ibid.*

to conflict or oppose what used to be the exclusive sphere of State operation.[67]

The mandate to make treaties was traditionally reserved to the king by virtue of his *imperium* or *suma potestas*. This fact led to what Anne Peters describes as a close association of treaty making power and sovereignty,[68] which was also reaffirmed by the PCIJ in the S.S. "Wimbledon" case. In this case, Germany argued that the terms of a treaty should be restrictively interpreted because limited Germany's sovereignty. The PCIJ rejected Germany's plea by stating that "the right of entering into international engagements is an attribute of State sovereignty."[69]

---

[67] See Maritain, J., *Man and The State*, University of Chicago Press, Chicago, 1951, at 8 ff. Maritain, distinguishes two terms, *State* and *Body Politic*, which have been commonly but mistakenly used as synonymous. Although they point at the same reality, they differ as the part differs from the whole. The *Body Politic* or *Political Society* is the whole and the State is the topmost part of this whole. The *Political Society* comes together in rational ways for the pursuit of the common good. It is composed of parts and units, such as the family, whose essential rights and freedoms are anterior to itself. It also comprises of particular societies born from the free initiative of citizens whose autonomy should be respected. The State is the part of the Political Society that specializes in the interests of the whole through the rule of law, the promotion of common welfare and public order and the administration of public affairs. Maritain then concludes that "the State is not the supreme incarnation of the Idea, as Hegel believed; the State is not a kind of collective superman; the State is but an agency entitled to use power and coercion, and made up of experts or specialists in public order and welfare, an instrument in the service of man. Putting man at the service of that instrument is political perversion. The human person as an individual is for the body politic and the body politic is for the human person as a person. But man is by no means for the State. The State is for man." Maritain's view, defined as *instrumentalist* places the state at the service of the person, in opposition to the *absolutist* or *substantialist* view that make the State subject of rights, a moral person, enjoying supreme authority for its own sake. In the certain models (e.g. American model) the State gains legal personality *de iure* by the promulgation of a 'constitution' as the act that gives birth to the State; and *de facto* by the recognition of other states or governments as an existing reality. In other cases (e.g. European context) State pre-existed the constitution through the political pact. However, it is the constitution the one that organizes that State and gives it the necessary legal structure.

[68] Peters, A., "Treaty Making Power", *Max Planck Encyclopedia of Public International Law*, *www.mpepil.com*, Oxford University Press, (2011), No. 15-16.

[69] PCIJ, *S.S. Wimbledon case* (Government of His Britanic Majesty v. German Empire), Series A, 17 Aug 1923, File E-b II, at 25. In this case, however, there was a dissenting opinion by Justice Schucking stating that: "According to the teaching of writers on international law, all treaties concerning servitudes must be

According to the Wimbledon principle, the very act of ratifying a treaty that imposes restrictions on the exercise of sovereignty is, in itself, an act of sovereignty. In fact, sovereignty was the foundation of the treaty making power[70] and this capacity was not subject to any limit imposed by the subject matter, but internal rules of the State.[71] However, more recent developments have added new perspective to this principle. As Peters asserts "less than sovereign States enjoy only a limited treaty making power, whose extent depends on the special case. States in point, which are de facto not fully sovereign because their governmental powers are exercised or supervised by international institutions, are for example Bosnia-Herzegovina after 1995, or Kosovo after 2008."[72]

In fact, there are also sub-units with certain treaty-making powers within States as is the case of *Länders* in Austria and Germany, the *cantons* in Switzerland, Hong Kong after 1997, and the regions and communities in Belgium, which after the 1993 constitutional revision, became the only European Federal State where the constituent entities enjoy an exclusive competence in international relations.[73] Nevertheless, treaties concluded by such units are ultimately considered federation treaties which are entered into by delegated powers, and the 'parent' State will have the final responsibility over the subject.[74]

However, treaties that transfer judicial powers and functions from the State to universal and regional bodies seem to be placed at a different level and the categorization of units or delegated powers do not apply. The transference of judicial powers is more likely to be due to the natural development of constitutional checks and balances in democratic societies that believed in the universality of human rights.[75] Therefore, this power

---

interpreted restrictively in the sense that the servitude, being an exceptional right resting upon the territory of a foreign State, should limit as little as possible the sovereignty of that State." PCIJ, *Ibid.*, Dissenting Opinion of Judge Schucking, at 43.

[70] Vienna Convention on the Law of Treaties, Article 6 states: 'Every State possesses capacity to conclude treaties'.

[71] Peters, A., *op. cit.*, at 17.

[72] *Ibid.*, at 18

[73] See Polakiewicz, J., *Treaty-making in the Council of Europe*, Council of Europe Publishing, Strasbourg,1999, at 50.

[74] Peters, A., *op. cit.*, at 32.

[75] The foundation of the PCIJ and its successor the ICJ fostered the creation of multiple international bodies vested with judicial powers and trans-boundary jurisdictions. For example, the International Criminal Court, the European Court of Justice, The European Court of human Rights, the Inter-American Court of justice,

transference brought into place a new scenario, distinct from what the PCIJ had envisaged at Wimbledon. In this new scenario, States were not entering into treaties that would limit their sovereignty by performing or refraining from performing a particular act. In this case, States are actually abdicating their duty to perform the judicial function within certain conditions and circumstances, even from an internal perspective, in order to secure the protection and safeguard of universal human rights. This shift within international human rights law has deeply changed the outlook of human rights protection vis-à-vis traditional views on sovereignty, and what had until then been called 'sovereignty' should now be subjected to revision. Consequently, a State may be said to be 'sovereign' in respect to other States, in the sense that they are equal; but 'autonomous' towards the inside, towards its subjects, and this autonomy is subjected to checks and balances that guarantee the ultimate end of human rights protection: the actual enjoyment of those rights.

As Lauterpacht conceived it, "statehood cannot be a permanent veil between the international legal order and individual human beings,"[76] for States are simply groups of human beings. For Lauterpacht, sovereignty had no real essence of its own and it should be conceived as a "bundle of rights and powers accorded to the State by the legal order" which was subject to division and limitation.[77]

Sovereignty is not, according to Antonio Perez, a word about things – that is, the things owned by the sovereign State. Neither is it about words – that is, the discourse through which States participate in international governance. "Rather, sovereignty must be about how persons, who in the past have been objects of State ownership, become subjects who come to speak for themselves."[78]

Thus, the veil between the international legal order and the individual human being is lifted when domestic legislation divides and limits the rights and powers accorded to the State. Domestic legislation achieves this target through a twofold task: on the one hand, by creating systems to

---

the Inter-American Court of Human Rights, The African Court on Human and People's Rights, the Caribbean Court of Human Rights (still under study), the SADC Tribunal, the ECOWAS Court, the East African Court of Justice, etc.

[76] Koskenniemi, M., "Lauterpacht: "The Victorian Tradition in International Law", *European Journal of International Law*, vol. 8, (1997) at 224 ff.

[77] *Ibid.*

[78] Perez, A. F., "Who Killed Sovereignty - or: Changing Norms Concerning Sovereignty in International Law", *Wisconsin International Law Journal*, vol. 14, (1995-1996), at 490.

determine the circumstances and conditions for accession or ratification of treaties and, on the other, by instituting mechanisms for the domestication and enforcement of decisions issued by the supranational judicial bodies it has accessed or ratified. Both tasks are accomplished through the constitutional regulation of what is known as the Foreign Affairs Power, which represents in practical terms the meeting point of two essential disciplines of law: constitutional and international law.

Conclusion

The acceptance of universal human rights has created new a scenario, where a large number of situations seem to fall outside the traditional realm of international law. For example, universal human rights impose certain checks and balances on powers that were traditionally reserved to the State over its subjects, thus arousing important questions over the nature of State sovereignty. Furthermore, universality has also come to mean the legal transference of certain jurisdictional prerogatives onto the international community, which is now bestowed with an innovative *locus standi* in certain human rights matters or situations.

Thus, the international community has gained where State powers have been curtailed or diminished by supranational checks and balances.

Hence, the foreign affairs power, a constitutionally limited power, may be used to negotiate, create, ratify or access supranational structures for the better fulfilment of the State's mission. In doing so, two elements of the foreign affairs power come into play: treaty making and diplomacy. These two elements will be studied in depth in the following chapter.

CHAPTER TWO

CONSTITUTIONALITY'S IMPACT ON FOREIGN AFFAIRS

Treaty-making, Diplomacy and Constitutional Practice

In the first chapter we have seen that the foreign affairs power has four elements and that two of them, treaty-making and diplomacy, are essential triggers of international relations among States and of structures of judicial nature and their relations. These structures of judicial nature, also known as international, regional or sub-regional courts and tribunals, and their jurisprudence are important sources of law in modern international law.

Treaty making, diplomacy and their practical applications and impact on constitutional practice are studied in this chapter in greater depth. These two subjects have an important two-fold impact on the matter under study: on the one hand, treaty-making and diplomacy will affect the way judicial structures are conceived, the nature international judicial decisions will be reached and the general mechanisms for implementation. On the other hand, once an international decision is issued, treaty making and diplomacy will play an essential role in its domestication process and its eventual enforcement.

The Treaty-Making Process

Treaties or international agreements are one of the most important means by which States relate to one another and give birth to international rights and duties, structures and different organs in the sphere of international law. Hence, they are key elements constituting foreign affairs powers. This has contributed to and furnished the creation of a comprehensive set of rules known as the law of treaties.[1] It is not our

---

[1] In this regard, the *Vienna Convention on the Law of Treaties*, signed at Vienna 23 May 1969 and which entered into force on 27 January 1980, constitutes a landmark on this subject. It stipulates in its Preamble: '*Believing that the codification and*

intention to give a detailed picture of the law of treaties, but to explain basic concepts so as to affirm the importance of a clear understanding of treaty law in the international community and the importance of developing a consistent set of rules in the municipal legal system.

1. The Nature of Treaties

The nature of a treaty and its validity is defined by the subject of the treaty,[2] the consent expressed, and the object or aim of the treaty.

The *1969 Vienna Convention on the Law of Treaties*, defines treaty in its Article 2, 1(a) as "an international agreement concluded between States in written form and governed by international law, whether embodied in a single instrument or in two or more related instruments and whatever its particular designation."[3] This definition, which omitted agreements between States and international organisations or between international organisations only, was later complemented by the *1986 Vienna Convention on the Law of Treaties between States and International Organisations or between International Organisations*. This convention defines treaties in its Article 2, 1(a) as: "an international agreement governed by international law and concluded in written form: (i) between one or more States and one or more international organizations; or (ii) between international organizations, whether that agreement is embodied

progressive development of the law of treaties achieved in the present Convention will promote the purposes of the United Nations set forth in the Charter, namely, the maintenance of international peace and security, the development of friendly relations and the achievement of co-operation among nations...' The scope of this convention was later expanded by the *Vienna Convention on the Law of Treaties between States and International Organisations or Between International Organisations* signed on 21 March 1986.

[2] By '*subject*' we do not refer to the theme or substance of the treaty but rather to the act of being a party. Each party, in this sense, is a subject to the treaty.

[3] The *Vienna Convention* compiles the customary international law and practice on this subject. It may be understood as a set of rules of international law governing the conclusion, validity, effects, interpretation, modification, suspension, and termination of treaties. It was adopted in 1969 at a conference convened by a resolution of the UN General Assembly. Representatives from 110 nations participated, UN member States as well as several non-members including Switzerland. The International Law Commission prepared the draft. The convention went into force in January 1980 after ratification by 35 nations.

in a single instrument or in two or more related instruments and whatever its particular designation."[4]

Indeed, in most States, the constitution determines the faculties and powers relating to foreign relations, granted to different organs within the government structure. Almost invariably, Mwagiru says, the "Head of State, irrespective of whether he is the holder of actual political power or not, is granted the capacity to represent the country on the international scene. In particular, he ratifies international treaties."[5] Where the function of head of government exists separately from the head of State, the head of government or the government as a collective body may be granted the capacity of giving final approval to certain treaties which do not need ratification power.[6]

The burden to ensure that all municipal law requirements are met for the conclusion of an agreement rests, in most cases, with the Head of State.[7] Besides, in the international arena the Head of State must notify other negotiating States of any restriction of his representative, as stipulated by Article 47 of the 1969 Vienna Convention on the Law of Treaties.[8]

Finally, "in order to create a binding agreement, consensus between parties is necessary."[9] States reach consensus by agreeing on the terms of a treaty; thereafter they express consent to be bound by the treaty. Consent is to be understood as the manifestation of the will to be bound by the treaty provisions. It is an essential element in any agreement.[10]

---

[4] *UNTS,* vol., 1155, No. 331.

[5] Mwagiru, M., *Diplomacy: From Theory to Practice*, paper presented at the *Seminar on Diplomacy, Culture and Media of the Institute of Diplomacy and International Studies*, University of Nairobi, 1-3 August, 1991, at 4.

[6] *Ibid.*

[7] This, however, depends on the municipal constitutional law.

[8] Article 47 of the 1969 *Vienna Convention* on the Law of Treaties says: *If the authority of a representative to express the consent of a State to be bound by a particular treaty has been made subject to a specific restriction, his omission to observe that restriction may not be invoked as invalidating the consent expressed by him unless the restriction was notified to the other negotiating States prior to his expressing such consent.*

[9] Blix, H., "The Requirement of Ratification", *British Year Book of International Law,* vol. 30, (1953), at 353.

[10] Consensus comes from Latin and etymologically it means *agreement.*

In this respect, States are free to choose the procedure for the entry into force of an agreement. In "most modern treaties it is either expressly stated or clearly implied by what procedure they are to come into force."[11]

2. Consent as an essential element for the validity of treaties

In treaty law there are different ways of 'expressing consent', which is the essence of a treaty. According to Jutta Brunnée, "Treaty law most readily reflects the idea of consensual international law. Individual States' explicit consent remains central, in both the initial adoption and subsequent development of treaties. In the latter context, attenuated forms of consent, such as consent that is presumed subject to opt-out, are increasingly common. Nonetheless, States usually retain full control over the binding commitments that they take on."[12]

This consent may be understood, Budislav Vukas says, "as accepting the obligation or the right provided for them in the treaty." Vukas adds that "as far as the obligations are concerned, they arise for a third State or a third organization from a provision of a treaty if two conditions are satisfied: (a) the parties to the treaty must have intended the provision to be the means of establishing the obligation for a third State or a third organization; and (b) the third State or the third organization must have expressly accepted that obligation in writing."[13]

The 1969 Vienna Convention on the Law of Treaties provides in Article 11 that "the consent of a State to be bound by a treaty may be expressed by signature, exchange of instruments constituting a treaty, ratification, acceptance, approval or accession, or by any other means if so agreed."[14] By 'signature' it is understood the endorsement by the person or envoy duly authorised according to international law requirements and in fulfilment of the municipal law demands of the negotiating party. Signature does not necessarily express a legal commitment to bind the

---

[11] Blix, H., *op. cit.,* at 352.

[12] Brunnée, J., "Consent", *Max Planck Encyclopedia of Public International Law, www.mpepil.com*, Oxford University Press, (2010), No. 20.

[13] Vukas, B., "Treaties, Third-Party Effect", *Max Planck Encyclopedia of Public International Law, www.mpepil.com*, Oxford University Press, (2007), No. 10 & 11.

[14] The *1986 Vienna Convention on the Law of Treaties between States and International Organisations or between International Organisations* accordingly extends this provision to international organisations.

represented party to the agreement signed.[15] Article 12 of the 1969 Vienna Convention on the Law of Treaties declares,

> "1. The consent of a State to be bound by a treaty is expressed by the signature of its representative when:(a) the treaty provides that signature shall have that effect; (b) it is otherwise established that the negotiating States were agreed that signature should have that effect; or (c) the intention of the State to give that effect to the signature appears from the full powers of its representative or was expressed during the negotiation. 2. For the purposes of paragraph 1: (a) the initialling of a text constitutes a signature of the treaty when it is established that the negotiating States so agreed;(b) the signature ad referendum of a treaty by a representative, if confirmed by his State, constitutes a full signature of the treaty."[16]

If there is a defect of consent the treaty is invalid; for example, when the defect affects the treaty-making power of a party or its involvement in a treaty. In this regard, we find the defect of Coercion of a State. A treaty is void if its conclusion has been procured by the threat or use of force in violation of the principles of international law embodied in the Charter of the United Nations.[17] A treaty may also be invalid if there has been coercion of a representative of a State; for example, when the expression of a State's consent to be bound by a treaty has been procured by the coercion of its representative through acts or threats directed against him shall be without any legal effect.[18] Corruption of a representative of a State

---

[15] See Starke, J.G., *Introduction to International Law*, 9th ed., Butterworths, London, 1984, at 475. When the final draft of the treaty has been agreed upon, the instrument is ready for signature *The text may be made public for a certain period before signature*. The act of signature is a most formal matter, even in the case of bilateral treaties. In multilateral conventions, signing is done at the closing session (*séance de clôture*). The delegates step up to the table and sign on behalf of the Head of State or government by whom he is appointed unless parties agree to do away with the requirement of signature. It is essential for a treaty because it serves to authenticate the text according to Article 10 to the Vienna Convention which sets this rule that the text may be authenticated by such procedure as is laid down in the treaty itself, or as agreed to by the negotiating States, or in the absence of such agreed procedure, by signature, signature *ad referendum*, initialling by the representative of those States, or by incorporation in the Final Act of the conference. Authentication may also be done by resolution of an international organisation. Signing of a treaty must be done by each delegate in the presence of each other and in the same place and at the same time. The date of the treaty is taken to be the date on which it was signed.

[16] See *Vienna Convention on the Law of Treaties*, Article 12.

[17] 1969 *Vienna Convention*, Article 52.

[18] 1969 *Vienna Convention*, Article 51.

is also an invalidating cause of a treaty. If the expression of a State's consent to be bound by a treaty has been procured through the corruption of its representative directly or indirectly by another negotiating State, the State may invoke such corruption as invalidating its consent to be bound by the treaty.[19]

A defect of consent may be invoked if consent was given on grounds of some erroneous matter, for example, if the party had actually known the matter it would not have accepted to be bound by the treaty. First, error may be invoked by a State "if the error relates to a fact or situation which was assumed by that State to exist at the time when the treaty was concluded and formed an essential basis of its consent to be bound by the treaty. Nevertheless, this does not apply if the State in question contributed by its own conduct to the error or if the circumstances were such as to put that State on notice of a possible error. An error relating only to the wording of the text of a treaty does not affect its validity. In this case, article 79 of the 1969 Vienna Convention applies."[20]Secondly, Fraud, "if a

---

[19] 1969 *Vienna Convention*, Article 50.

[20] 1969 *Vienna Convention*, Article 48. In the same Convention, Article 79 reads: 1. *Where, after the authentication of the text of a treaty, the signatory States and the contracting States are agreed that it contains an error, the error shall, unless they decide upon some other means of correction, be corrected: (a) by having the appropriate correction made in the text and causing the correction to be initialled by duly authorized representatives; (b) by executing or exchanging an instrument or instruments setting out the correction which it has been agreed to make; or (c) by executing a corrected text of the whole treaty by the same procedure as in the case of the original text.* 2. *Where the treaty is one for which there is a depositary, the latter shall notify the signatory States and the contracting States of the error and of the proposal to correct it and shall specify an appropriate time-limit within which objection to the proposed correction may be raised. If, on the expiry of the time-limit: (a) no objection has been raised, the depositary shall make and initial the correction in the text and shall execute a procès-verbal of the rectification of the text and communicate a copy of it to the parties and to the States entitled to become parties to the treaty; (b) an objection has been raised, the depositary shall communicate the objection to the signatory States and to the contracting States.* 3. *The rules in paragraphs 1 and 2 apply also where the text has been authenticated in two or more languages and it appears that there is a lack of concordance which the signatory States and the contracting States agree should be corrected.* 4. *The corrected text replaces the defective text ab initio, unless the signatory States and the contracting States otherwise decide.* 5. *The correction of the text of a treaty that has been registered shall be notified to the Secretariat of the United Nations.* 6. *Where an error is discovered in a certified copy of a treaty, the depositary shall*

State has been induced to conclude a treaty by the fraudulent conduct of another negotiating State, the State may invoke the fraud as invalidating its consent to be bound by the treaty."[21] And third, a change of circumstances. Certainly, not any change could justify defect of consent. It must be a fundamental change of circumstances which has occurred with regard to those existing at the time of the conclusion of a treaty, and which was not foreseen by the parties.[22] However, a fundamental change of circumstances may not be invoked as grounds for terminating or withdrawing from a treaty,[23] and if a party invokes a fundamental change of circumstances as a ground for terminating or withdrawing from a treaty it may also invoke the change as a ground for suspending the operation of the treaty.[24]

Once the signature is appended to a treaty, there may be a process of 'approval', which is an act in the municipal law carried out by each State according to its own constitutional procedures, for example, the approval the legislature may grant to the Head of State to conclude a treaty.[25] This process of approval is at times mistakenly called 'ratification'. This confusion has developed a wrong conception that has degenerated into having two different meanings for ratification. On the one hand, ratification is seen as the act in the municipal law, which is believed to be the approval given by the legislative body of a State authorising the Head of State to conclude a treaty. On the other hand, ratification in the international sense means the final and formal expression of consent to be bound by the treaty, carried out after approval by the legislature. This confusion is obvious, for instance, Article 52(1) of the 1958 French

---

execute a procès-verbal specifying the rectification and communicate a copy of it to the signatory States and to the contracting States.

[21] 1969 *Vienna Convention*, Article 49.

[22] It may not be invoked as a ground for terminating or withdrawing from the treaty unless: *(a) the existence of those circumstances constituted an essential basis of the consent of the parties to be bound by the treaty; and (b) the effect of the change is radically to transform the extent of obligations still to be performed under the treaty.*

[23] In the following cases: (a) if the treaty establishes a boundary; or (b) if the fundamental change is the result of a breach by the party invoking it either of an obligation under the treaty or of any other international obligation owed to any other party to the treaty.

[24] 1969 *Vienna Convention*, Article 62.

[25] In the case of international organisations, for example, the approval is given according to the requirements, if any, provided for by their constitutive instruments.

Constitution reads: "The President of the Republic shall negotiate and ratify treaties." But in Article 53 approval by Parliament is placed at par with ratification, as if Parliament were the one ratifying a treaty, which does not seem the case or else it would contradict Article 52(1). Article 53 reads, (1) "Peace treaties, commercial treaties and treaties, or agreements relating to international organisation, or implying a financial commitment on the part of the State, or modifying provisions of a legislative nature, or relating to the status of persons, or entailing a cession, exchange or addition of territory, may be ratified or approved only by act of Parliament."

In the United Kingdom, McNair asserts, the expression often used of 'Parliamentary ratification' is incorrect. "It is the Crown who ratifies, not Parliament, though Parliament may be invited to approve and where necessary to legislate."[26]

Moreover, under the U.S. Constitution the treaty-making power is vested in the President, with the advice and consent of the Senate. An important treaty usually is negotiated by the State Department and then submitted to the Senate for 'approval' by a two-thirds vote of the members present. The Senate may make its approval dependent on the inclusion of amendments, reservations, or other declarations that require acceptance by the other parties involved. After final approval, the treaty goes to the President for ratification.

However, 'ratification',[27] in the international and proper sense, means "the procedure whereby the executive power of a State —traditionally the Head of State — signifies its final consent to an agreement."[28] Ratification also means "the international procedure whereby a treaty enters into force, namely the formal exchange or deposit of the instruments of ratification,[29]

---

[26] McNair, A. D., *The Law of Treaties*, Clarendon Press, Oxford, 1961, at 130.

[27] Acceptance has also been used to mean 'ratification' apparently to avoid the constitutional difficulties brought up by the word ratification in some States. In the U.K.'s customary practice, for example, the instrument of *Acceptance* is identical to that of ratification. The only change is the substitution of words.

[28] Blix, H., *op. cit.,* at 352.

[29] See *Armstrong v. Bidwell* (1903), 124 Fed. 690, 692: *The exchange of the ratifications was like the delivery of a deed, and until that was done, the transaction was not complete. ... Until the ratifications were exchanged, it was competent for either Power, or both, to recede or rescind its action.* This passage indicates well that an instrument of ratification, until exchanged for the corresponding instrument, is what English lawyers call an escrow.

or the actual document,[30] sealed or otherwise authenticated, whereby a State expresses its willingness to be bound by the treaty."[31] Nonetheless, ratification in the municipal or constitutional sense is not more than 'the approval of ratification' given by the competent organ in the municipal law (for example legislature) to the organ meant to ratify a treaty (the executive.) In the past ratification was "little more than a formality"[32] because the full powers granted to plenipotentiaries contained the promise of the 'sovereign' to ratify as far as the plenipotentiary acted within the limits of his powers.

Therefore, as McNair asserts, ratification is not a

> "mere formality like the use of a seal, or parchment, or tape. Ratification has a value which should not be minimised. The interval between signature and the ratification of a treaty gives the appropriate departments of the Governments that have negotiated the treaty an opportunity of studying the advantages and disadvantages involved in the proposed treaty as a whole, and of doing so in a manner more ... comprehensive than ... while negotiating the treaty. However careful may have been the preparation of the instructions, it rarely happens that the representatives of both parties succeed in producing a draft which embodies the whole of their respective instructions; concession[s] ... and ... element[s] of compromise are present in practically every negotiation. It is therefore useful that in the case of important treaties, Governments should have the opportunity of reflection afforded by the requirement of ratification."[33]

Likewise, Anzilotti, stresses that ratification is not "un acte confirmatif, mais la véritable déclaration de volonté de stipuler; il ne valide pas un acte déjà existant, mais il donne existence à un acte nouveau."[34] Today, the Full Powers granted to plenipotentiaries contain no promise of ratification and, if the treaty so requires, ratification "is an indispensable condition for bringing [a treaty] into operation. It is not, therefore, a mere formal act, but an act of vital importance."[35]

---

[30] Often referred to as instruments of ratification.

[31] McNair, *op. cit.,* at 130.

[32] *Ibid.*

[33] *Ibid*, at 133.

[34] Ratification is not *an act of confirmation, rather it is the true declaration of the will to stipulate; it does not validate an existing act but it engenders the reality of a new act.*' [See *Cours de Droit International*, 1929, at 370].

[35] ICJ *Report* 1952, *Abatielos case*, at 43. Earlier, in 1929, the Permanent Court of International Justice (PCIJ) had ascertained this rule in *the Territorial Jurisdiction of the International Commission of the River Oder* case [PCIJ, 1929, River Oder] as follows: *with respect to this, it must be pointed out that Article 338* [of the

Hence, the general rule has settled for ratification. A treaty is not binding upon a contracting party unless it has been ratified.[36] However, in the absence of express provisions to the contrary (no ratification), ratification is in any case necessary with regard to treaties which require parliamentary approval or authorisation of ratification in accordance with the constitutional law or practice of the countries concerned.[37] Thus, ratification is an essential requirement, unless the treaty itself dispenses with it[38] or it can be implied from the negotiation that the parties had the

---

Treaty of Versailles] *expressly refers to a 'Convention'; unless the contrary be clearly shown by the terms of that article, it must be considered that reference was made to a Convention made effective in accordance with the ordinary rules of international law amongst which is that rule that conventions, save in certain exceptional cases, are binding only by virtue of their ratification.*

[36] After the *1986 Vienna Convention on the Law of Treaties between States and International Organisations or between International Organisations,* ratifications done by international organisations have acquired the name of *act of formal confirmation*. Article 2(b-bis) provides: *act of formal confirmation means an international act corresponding to that of ratification by a State, whereby an international organization establishes on the international plane its consent to be bound by a treaty.*

[37] Oliver, C.T., "Historical Development of International Law: Contemporary Problems of Treaty Law", *Recueil Des Cours*, vol. 88 II, Académie de Droit International, The Hague, (1955), at 437.

[38] There are examples of ratification by one party only, such as Agreement of 29th June 1948 between Denmark and the U.S.A concerning economic co-operation. Article 12 reads: *This agreement shall be subject to ratification by Denmark. It shall come into force on the day on which notice of such ratification is given to the government of the U.S.A.* (UNTS, vol. 22., 1948, at 217); Agreement of 17 April 1947 between The Netherlands and Greece concerning Air Transport UNTS 32 (1949) at 115; Financial Agreement of 9 April 1946 between Canada and France 43 UNTS 1949. The consensus can also be given by proclamations (UNTS 43. 1949 at 156 – Agreement of 4 July 1946 the U.S.A. and The Philippines) by publication, by exchange of telegrams, or of notes. By Publication: Agreement of 25 Feb 1949 between Belgium and Luxembourg concerning the reciprocal communication free of charge of copies of civil status certificates and nationality records, Article 5: *'This arrangement is not subject to ratification. It shall come into force when each of the two parties has approved and published it in accordance with its domestic law.'*(UNTS, 47 (1950) at 7), [See Blix, *op. cit.*, at 355.] An example is also given by McNair: the 1902 Anglo-Japanese Alliance, which provided in Article 6 that the agreement *shall come into effect immediately after signature.*

intention of dispensing with or ruling out the requirement of ratification.[39] It is a definitive expression of consent which should be made once the required municipal approvals have been duly obtained.[40] Blix asserts that it is generally accepted that "if agreement requires ratification it is binding only when the exchange of the instruments of ratification takes place. There is no duty to ratify a signed treaty even if full powers have been issued which seems to create such an obligation or a treaty expressly provides that it shall be ratified."[41] And this is so, according to Charles

---

[39] See McNair, *op. cit.,* at 137. In the U.K. ratification is unnecessary in the following cases: (a) Inter-governmental Agreements, whether or not they expressly provide that it shall be unnecessary. It may happen that the constitutional law or practice of the other contracting party renders the ratification or an inter-Governmental agreement necessary or desirable, and in that event the Government of the United Kingdom is prepared to exchange ratifications; (b) Treaties containing a term expressly dispensing with ratification; (c) Where a Final Protocol or other agreement made subsequent to a principal treaty which is awaiting ratification stipulates that the Final Protocol or other subsequent agreement shall take effect upon ratification of the principal treaty and 'without any other special ratification', for instance, the Final Protocol supplementing the Anglo-Portuguese Commercial Treaty of 12 August 1914; (d) Protocols or Declarations or Additional Articles or other instruments, by whatever name they may be called, which merely modify or add to or extend a former instrument, do not usually require ratification unless the principal instrument to which they are supplemental was ratified; (e) Many Exchanges of Notes, agreements establishing *modi vivendi* or other provisional arrangements, and agreements prolonging the duration of commercial treaties take effect without ratification.

[40] McNair, *op. cit.,* at 135.McNair states that *to withhold ratification lightly and without adequate reason, or in the hope of obtaining some new concession in the same or another subject of negotiation, is a breach of courtesy and 'bad business'; but Governments usually realize from their own experience that the Government of the other contracting party may meet with insurmountable political difficulties which preclude ratification.*

[41] Blix, H., "The Requirement of Ratification", *British Year Book of International Law,* vol. 30, (1953), at 352. Blix also presents some interesting statistics: Some 1300 instruments reproduced in the UNTS I, 1946 – Vol. 79 (1951) provides good material: 300 expressly or by clear implication provide for ratification. 425 expressly or by clear implication provide entry into force by signature; five of them expressly dispense with ratification. 250 are exchanges of notes which, expressly or by clear implication, state the manner in which they are to come into force, normally by the very exchange of signed notes. Only a few require ratification. 90 expressly provide for entry into force upon evidence which may be given, for example, by exchange of notes. 60 contain express provisions of other nature for entry into force. They cannot be classified in any of the above.

Rousseau, inasmuch as a State should not be exposed to possible errors of its plenipotentiaries.[42]

Finally, 'accession', according to Rousseau means,[43] "l'acte juridique par lequel un État qui n'est pas partie à un traité international se place sous l'empire des dispositions de ce traité."[44]

Article 12 of the Harvard Draft Convention on the Law of Treaties expresses itself in similar terms: "As the term is used in this Convention, an accession to a treaty is an act by which the provisions of a treaty are formally accepted by a State on behalf of which the treaty has not been signed or ratified."[45]

However, both the 1969 Vienna Convention on the Law of Treaties and the 1986 Vienna Convention on the Law of Treaties between States and International Organisations or between International Organisations, do not define accession properly inasmuch as they consider accession as being equal to ratification.[46] Both conventions consider accession to be the manifestation of consent of a State to be bound by a treaty. Accession of non-negotiating States has become a common practice and, nowadays, most multilateral treaties negotiated by international organisations are publicly opened for accession by any interested party. This matching of concepts emerged due to the fact that the effects of accession are similar to

---

[42] Rousseau, C., *Principes Généraux du Droit International Public*, vol. I., Pedone, Paris, 1944, at 190.

[43] Rousseau, C., *op. cit.,* at 152. Rousseau used the term '*adhésion*' which is also understood as accession, adherence or adhesion.

[44] Accession is the juridical act whereby a State which is not a party in an international treaty, places itself under the power of the dispositions of the treaty.

[45] Harvard Draft Convention on the Law of Treaties, A/CN.4/23. Report on the Law of Treaties by J.L. Brierly, Special Rapporteur. Extract from the *Yearbook of the International Law Commission* 1950, vol. II.

[46] 1969 *Vienna Convention*, Article 2 reads: (b) *'ratification', 'acceptance', 'approval' and 'accession' mean in each case the international act so named whereby a State establishes on the international plane its consent to be bound by a treaty.'* Article 2 of the 1986 Convention provides: '(b) *'ratification' means the international act so named whereby a State establishes on the international plane its consent to be bound by a treaty; (b bis) 'act of formal confirmation' means an international act corresponding to that of ratification by a State, whereby an international organization establishes on the international plane its consent to be bound by a treaty; (b ter) 'acceptance', 'approval' and 'accession' mean in each case the international act so named whereby a State or an international organization establishes on the international plane its consent to be bound by a treaty.*

those of ratification. The acceding party, in principle, becomes a party with equal rights and duties as the original parties.

There are two kinds of accession. The first one is accession from the traditional and historical point of view, which means an act whereby a State becomes party to a treaty already signed by other States, although it may not necessarily be in force yet; and the second one is accession in a modern sense, which refers to the act whereby a State binds itself to an instrument intended to become a treaty drafted by an international organisation and publicly opened for accession.[47] This has become a common practice in international organisations. Article 83 of the 1969 Vienna Convention on the Law of Treaties provides that the "Convention shall remain open for accession by any State belonging to any of the categories mentioned in article 81. The instruments of accession shall be deposited with the Secretary-General of the United Nations."[48]

2.1 Obligations Born from Treaties

From the international law perspective, an obligation born from a treaty is, first and foremost, legal.[49] This is especially relevant in the area

[47] For example Article XIII of the *International Convention on Civil Liability for Oil Pollution Damage* says: *The present Convention shall remain open for signature until 31st December 1970 and shall thereafter remain open for accession.* And Article 14 of the Vienna Convention for the Protection of the Ozone Layer says, *This Convention and any Protocol shall be opened for accession by States and by regional economic organizations from the date on which the Convention or the protocol concerned is closed for signature*...The Preamble of the 1946 Convention on the Privileges and Immunities of the United Nations reads, *Consequently the General Assembly by a Resolution adopted on the 13 February, 1946, approved the following Convention and proposed it for accession by each Member of the United Nations.* In its final article it provides, '*Section 31. This convention is submitted to every Member of the United Nations for accession.' 'Section 32. Accession shall be effected by deposit of an instrument with the Secretary-General of the United Nations and the convention shall come into force as regards each Member on the date of deposit of each instrument of accession.*'

[48] 1969 *Vienna Convention*, Article 81 affirms that the *Convention shall be open for signature by all States Members of the United Nations or of any of the specialized agencies or of the International Atomic Energy Agency or parties to the Statute of the International Court of Justice, and by any other State invited by the General Assembly of the United Nations to become a party to the Convention...*

[49] Certainly, a treaty may impose moral obligations upon the subject, but in this study we are strictly concerned with the legal subject.

of human rights, for when a State ratifies a human rights treaty it is assuming or reaffirming[50] an obligation to protect and safeguard those specific rights of its subjects or aspects thereof. Human rights are not created through treaty-making, they are not born from the treaty itself nor from the State's will to be bound; they are born from the person's and the people's dignity. Therefore, human rights treaties do not give birth to the right itself; instead, human rights treaties give birth to the legal obligation of the State to protect that right, thus, shifting the treaty beneficiary from the State to the person, and in Africa also the peoples.[51]

International agreements or treaties may bring about external effects and internal effects. The external ones bind a State to fulfil an international obligation. All international agreements produce external effects for the mere fact of being 'international', but not all will necessarily produce internal effects. For example, an agreement for mutual cooperation in case of aggression by a third party or a declaration recognizing as compulsory the jurisdiction of the International Court of Justice, in conformity with Article 36, paragraph 2, of the Statute of the International Court of Justice, signed by Kenya at Nairobi, on 12 April 1965 may not necessarily make an impact on the internal affairs of Kenya. However, internal effects refer to those agreements which are intended to produce some change in the domestic legal system. These agreements will fall within either of the two following categories: The first one encompasses those agreements which officials intend to have applied within their territorial boundaries,[52] and the second one, those agreements which, in order to accomplish an international obligation, require that some change be made in the internal law of the country.[53]

External and internal effects depend primarily on the fulfilment of the legal formalities established by law. For example, a treaty will have international effects if it fulfils the international law requirements, i.e. that signature, ratification, or other formalities have been performed according

---

[50] It may be said 'assuming' if such rights were not contemplated by the domestic laws; while 'reaffirming' refers to those human rights already safeguarded by domestic constitutional or statutory provisions.

[51] We will analyse later the concept of 'peoples' as subjects of human rights as conceived by the African Charter.

[52] For instance, the 1989 *United Nations Convention on the Rights of the Child* which Kenya signed on 26 January 1990, and ratified on 30 July 1990.

[53] For instance, the *East African Community Mediation Agreement*, which required the enactment of the *East African Community Mediation Agreement Act* (Cap. 4) of 1984.

to law. If these formalities are fulfilled it is said to be a valid treaty; it has validity. Similarly, a treaty will have internal effects if it fulfils the municipal law requirements for treaty making.[54] If these requirements are not fulfilled the treaty may be valid, but there is inability to perform. Hence inability to perform is caused by a breach in the domestic law requirements, and it induces what is known as imperfect ratification.[55]

Therefore, invalidity and inability to perform are two different concepts from a legal point of view. A treaty which a Government may be unable to implement without the co-operation of the legislature can be, nevertheless, internationally valid.[56] In this regard, Anzilotti postulates that in an imperfect ratification, it would be wrong for a State to declare a treaty to be null and void since the treaty is binding.[57]

If attention is now focused on those agreements requiring internal application and on the manner in which they are incorporated into the legal municipal arena, the need arises of giving an answer to the following questions: First, how is a treaty incorporated into the domestic or municipal arena? Second, what hierarchical position does a treaty possess in the domestic legal system once incorporated? And third, what happens if a treaty is not consistent with the domestic law?

2.2 Treaty Domestication Mechanisms: Incorporation of treaties into the domestic realm

The rules governing the conclusion of treaties are laid down partly by national constitutions — varying from one country to another — and partly by international customary law, supplemented by the 1969 Vienna Convention on the Law of Treaties and the 1986 Vienna Convention on the Law of Treaties between States and International Organisations or between International Organisations.[58] National constitutions present two

---

[54] Constitutional law plays a key role in this regard. The formalities established by the constitution for the conclusion of treaties will determine whether a party has the necessary executive or legislative power to give effect to the treaty.
[55] See Reuter, P., *Introduction to the Law of Treaties*, Printers Publishers, London, 1989, at 40. Imperfect ratification occurs when 'two States conclude a treaty and, after their representatives have declared it to be binding, one of them claims not to be bound because some of its own constitutional requirements have not been complied with.'
[56] McNair, *op. cit.,* at 59.
[57] Anzilotti, D., "Volonta e responsabilita nella stipulazione dei trattati intemazionali", *Rivista di Diritto Internazionale*, (1910), at 3ff.
[58] See Reuter, P. *op. cit.,* at 35.

approaches to the conferment of legal character to those treaties requiring internal application.[59] On the one hand, there is what is known as 'parallelism' or 'dualism', which is the legal acknowledgement of the co-existence of the two independent juridical orders, i.e. international and constitutional. Consequently, agreements need special legislation before they become part of the law of the land. On the other hand, 'Internationalism' or 'monism' — initiated by the Austrian school —and which refers to the acknowledgement of the interplay between the internal and the international order without contradiction, and therefore agreements made under certain conditions automatically become law of the land.[60]

The dualist theory perfectly agreed with the international reality before the First World War and British Common Law was spread across its former colonies. However, the radical transformation of international life after the War, the creation of new forms of international law, new legal bodies not foreseen before the War, gave pre-eminence and marked the success of the Austrian school, the monist school, which propounded the primacy of international law.[61] It is worth mentioning that the work of Triepel[62] enhanced progress in this regard. He asserts that it is necessary to admit the fact that international law and internal law form a logical unity. This leads us to substitute the dualist theory with the monist, which in essence identifies the international legal system with the internal. Another monist advocate, Verdross,[63] suggests that the choice of primacy rests on juridical logic.[64]

---

[59] Some authors like Boris Mirkine-Guetzevitch speak of a third group called *Nationalisme constitutionnel* that is the acknowledgement of the primacy of internal law although this would imply a complete negation of the existence of international law which does not correspond to today's reality. See *infra* note no. 60.

[60] See Mirkine-Guetzevitch, B., "Droit international et droit constitutionnel", *Recueil des Cours*, vol. 38, Académie de Droit International, The Hague, (1931), at 312.

[61] *Ibid*, at 313.

[62] Triepel, M., "Les Rapports entre le Droit Interne et le Droit International", *Recueil des Cours*, vol. 1, The Hague, (1923), at 85-87. His legal thought is based on earlier works of Hans Kelsen.

[63] See Verdross, A., "Le Fondement Du Droit International", *Recueil des Cours*, Académie de Droit International, vol. I, The Hague, (1927), at 268-270. Verdross' attempts to depict the main social conditions characteristically begun with a philosophical point of view. Relying on this perspective he wrote: *'on n'arrive pas à comprendre les faits sociaux si l'on ne pénètre pas les pensées qui sont à leur base.'*

[64] See generally Kelsen, H., *Principles of International Law*, The Lawbook Exchange Ltd, New Jersey, 2003. See also Verdross, A., *op. cit.,* at 270.The

For Kelsen,[65] the two systems cannot co-exist in the same political entity. A State, under the same circumstances, is either monist or dualist. Nevertheless, the co-existence of both systems in the international order is a historical reality. The fact is that for some States, concluded treaties are considered part of the law of the land (monism),[66] and for others they are not (dualism).[67]

In monist systems, treaties become law of the land automatically. However, they are not always self-executing or immediately operative.[68] Monism represents a step forward in the development of binding rules of international law and their enforcement. It is, however, still developing and has found, at times, barriers for its acceptance. For some States monism is believed to fit only cases

> "where legal integration is matched by a complete social integration, i.e. where international society is strong enough for more restricted social structures and relationships to converge and harmonise within it. But

---

essentials of the monist theory can be seen in Hans Kelsen's postulates. He affirms that monism is indispensable and that *two parallel juridical orders cannot co-exist*. Similarly, this was stated by the International Court of Justice when it said: *Èu égard du droit international ... les lois nationales sont des simples faits ... au même titré que les décisions judiciaires ou les mesures administratives*. (In regard to international laws ... the national law are simple facts ... with the same value as judicial decisions or administrative measures.)

[65] Verdross, A., *op. cit.*, at 270.

[66] For example, US Constitution, Article 6(2) says: *...all treaties made, or which shall be made, under the authority of the United States, shall be supreme law of the land*. However, although they become *the supreme Law of the Land*, some treaties require legislative action before they can receive effect in American courts. In this regard see the case of *Foster* v. *Neilson*, 1829. See also McNair (*op. cit.* at 81), where he explains that in the United Kingdom, instead, with a very limited class of exceptions, no treaty is self-executing; no treaty requiring municipal action to give effect to it can receive that effect without the co-operation of Parliament, either in the form of a statute or in some other way. In the case *Attorney-General for Canada v. Attorney-General for Ontario and Others* (1937) the Privy Council held that a treaty comprises any agreement between two or more sovereign States and that 'within the British Empire, there is a well-established rule that the making of a treaty is an executive act, while the performance of its obligations, if they entail alteration of the existing domestic law, requires legislative action.' [Wilson, G., *Cases and Materials in Constitutional and Administrative Law*, Cambridge University Press, Cambridge, 1966, at 452-453]

[67] Examples of dualist constitutions are studied later in chapter II where there is a more elaborate analysis on selected world constitutions.

[68] See *supra* note 66, *Foster v. Neilson* (1829).

> where international society is practically non-existent and States jealously close themselves to the outside world and keep their foreign relations under strict control, then hardly any international rules will penetrate the municipal shell.[69] These prejudices, Reuter continues, are a fair reflection of the ideal of a State rejecting legal integration essentially because there is no social integration and no intention of bringing it about."[70]

The fact is that there is a growing monist approach in most modern constitutions as well as in traditionally dualists systems.[71]

Dualism, on the other hand, is not directly related to the approval the legislature usually grants before ratification, which may also be there in a monist system. Rather, it rests on the requirement of having statutory law being passed by Parliament before giving any legal internal effect to an already ratified treaty. This may obstruct the fulfilment of international obligations because there is no possibility of giving internal effect to treaties unless they are consistent with existing legislation, or a statute is passed by Parliament.[72]

There is no doubt, however, that either system, monist or dualist, can bring about certain difficulties such as those relating to the supremacy and temporal validity of treaties, in reference to domestic law on the one hand, and discrepancies between the national constitution and the treaty, on the other. The resolution of such discrepancies is the subject matter of our study below.

3. The Incorporation of Treaties into the Domestic Legal System and the Question of Hierarchy

In principle, the burden to ensure that all municipal law requirements are met for the conclusion of an agreement rests, in most cases, with the authority in charge of ratification, who must notify other negotiating States of any restriction, even those relating to its own authority to ratify. This is stipulated by Article 47 of the 1969 Vienna Convention on the Law of Treaties, which states: "If the authority of a representative to express the

---

[69] Reuter, P., *op. cit.,* at 38.
[70] *Ibid.*
[71] See generally Waters, M.A., "Creeping Monism: The Judicial Trend Toward Interpretive Incorporation of Human Rights Treaties", *Columbia Law Review*, vol. 107, (2007), at 628-705.
[72] It is important to understand that there can be as many designs of systems as countries in the world. We have tried to present in this chart the most common features of systems in operation in the world.

consent of a State to be bound by a particular treaty has been made subject to a specific restriction, his omission to observe that restriction may not be invoked as invalidating the consent expressed by him unless the restriction was notified to the other negotiating States prior to his expressing such consent."[73]

In monist systems, supremacy may determine that the treaty is above the constitutional norm, at par with the constitution or below the constitution but above other legislative provisions.[74] For instance, in the US, the Supreme Court has developed the constitutional theory where "a treaty made 'under the authority of the US' can create rights and impose obligations in situations where the Federal Government could not act in the absence of a treaty, and all courts, including State courts, must give effect to the treaty as the supreme law of the land."[75] In principle, a treaty in the United States, is placed at par with federal laws and it is meant to be considered and applied as such by all courts. An interesting case is the *R. Asakura Case*, where the Supreme Court upheld the contention of Asakura, deciding that the "treaty required a broad construction, even if the result was to override the local law."[76] In France, in the event of a conflict between a law and a treaty, the treaty prevails.[77] The position is stated in Article 55 of the French Constitution which provides: "Duly ratified or approved treaties or agreements shall, upon their publication,

---

[73] 1969 *Vienna Convention on the Law of Treaties*, Article 47 says: *If the authority of a representative to express the consent of a State to be bound by a particular treaty has been made subject to a specific restriction, his omission to observe that restriction may not be invoked as invalidating the consent expressed by him unless the restriction was notified to the other negotiating States prior to his expressing such consent.*

[74] This matter is studied further and more in depth in Chapter II, 3 *infra*.

[75] Oliver, C.T., *op. cit.*, at 440.

[76] See Oliver, C.T., *op. cit.,* at 464.Asakura was a Japanese citizen who resided in Seattle, Washington State since 1904. In 1915 he became a pawn-broker. In 1921 the city of Seattle enacted an ordinance requiring the Licensing of pawn-brokers. The ordinance prohibited any alien to be licensed as a pawn-broker. Asakura refused to abide by the ordinance's prohibition. He argued that this contradicted the Japanese-American Treaty of 1911, which reciprocally provided for nationals of each country to have the right *to carry on trade* in the other. The Supreme Court of Washington State rejected his contention, saying that 'trade' in the treaty did not include the money-lending activity but only *those callings in which an individual has an inherent right to engage*. The U.S. Supreme Court disagreed with this conclusion and upheld the contention of Asakura, deciding that the treaty required a broad construction, even if the result was to override the local law.

[77] The price for this supremacy is that the ratification must be authorised by law.

override laws, subject, for each agreement or treaty, to its application by the other party."In the Netherlands most but not all treaties must be approved by the *Staten-Generaal*, and only after they have been so approved will they override inconsistent law.

In dualist systems, it is implied that the legislature must be involved and pass statutory law for making a treaty internally operative. In view of this, the problem of hierarchy is somehow solved by the legislature itself. Once a treaty is made into a statute it automatically becomes a norm of the rank Parliament has given to it, thus following the maxim: 'special law prevails over general law.' Nevertheless, this practice has created interesting problems in some Commonwealth countries with a federal structure. For instance, in 1937 the Judicial Committee of the Privy Council held that the Parliament of Canada had no power to enact legislation to carry out certain undertakings in the International Labour Conventions regarding matters under the Canadian Constitution left to the Provinces.[78]Section 91 of the British North America Act,[79] "gives the

---

[78] Case *Attorney-General for Canada v. Attorney-General for Ontario and Others* [1937] A.C. 326, 347-8. *Supra* note 66.

[79] The British North America Act (1867), also known as the Constitution Act, 1867, together with the Constitution Act, 1982, constitutes Canada's fundamental law. It determines the structure of government, the allocation of powers between federal and provincial authorities, and the interpretation of other statutes. Its operation is modified by custom and precedent derived from Canada's British legacy and legal decisions. The British North America Act was passed by the British Parliament in 1867. It created the Dominion of Canada out of the United Province of Canada (which became Québec and Ontario), New Brunswick, and Nova Scotia and provided for entry of other colonies or British possessions into the new federation. The act had originated in negotiations among colonial politicians in 1864. It established a system of government modelled on British parliamentary practice with Britain's monarch as Canada's sovereign. Over the years, court decisions, compromises, and amendments have served to modify the provisions of the act. In 1931, Canada secured full control of its foreign affairs as a result of the Statute of Westminster. The Supreme Court became the country's final court of appeal in 1949. Although the 1867 Constitution did establish a workable system of government, it did not prevent disputes over the division of powers in overlapping areas of authority such as taxation and in new areas such as broadcasting, social policy, and language rights. The conviction gradually grew that the Constitution required major revision, but efforts to secure provincial agreement on how to amend it repeatedly failed. In the 1970s, Prime Minister Pierre Trudeau took up the cause anew and eventually all the provinces except Québec endorsed a new agreement, which became the Constitution Act of 1982. Prime Minister Brian Mulroney attempted to secure Québec's approval of the new Constitution in 1987

Canadian Parliament exclusive power to legislate in certain fields, while Section 92 gives the Provinces exclusive authority to legislate in certain other fields, including property, civil rights, and the administration of justice. The Central Government cannot make a treaty internally effective on those matters not in its exclusive competence."[80]

3.1 Primacy and Temporal Validity of Treaties

Regarding temporal validity of treaties, different jurisdictions apply diverse rules. For example, in French law, a treaty properly ratified will have an immutable effect on national law, prior or subsequent, so long as it has not been denounced.[81] In the United States, where there is a conflict between a treaty approved by Senate, and other legislation, the later in time prevails internally;[82] the treaty, in either case, would still express an international obligation. In the case of a conflict between earlier legislation and later executive agreement (non-Senate-consented international agreements), legislation seems to prevail because if a treaty has been approved by Senate, it is placed at par with legislation made by Congress. On the contrary, executive agreements are not at par with legislation for they are made without Senatorial approval.[83] In dualist systems the issue is solved as in internal laws: "the latter prevails over the former and special law over general law."

3.2 The Question of Unconstitutional Treaties

There may be circumstances whereby a treaty is defective from a constitutional point of view. As has been stated,[84] article 27 of the 1969

with the Meech Lake Accord, which required the unanimous assent of all provinces within a three-year period. As a result of a new language dispute and English-Canadian concerns over identification of Québec as a 'distinct society,' however, the Accord was never ratified by the Provinces. (See Rutherford P. F. W., Encarta Encyclopaedia)

[80] Appeal Cases 326, 347-8. This also happens in Australia: *The King* v. *Burgess, ex parte Henry* (1936) SS C.L.R. 608. See Oliver, C.T., *op. cit.,* at 445.

[81] See Oliver, C.T., *op. cit.,* at 446.

[82] This situation could cause confusion if the treaty demands the fulfilment of a condition, permanent in character, in the municipal law. When a treaty is overridden by internal law, its implementation becomes impossible in international law. The ideal situation would be that, once the treaty is overridden by an internal law, such a State requests the termination of the treaty.

[83] See Oliver, C.T., *op. cit.,* at 441.

[84] See *supra* note 42, on how this matter was resolved by the Vienna Convention on the Law of Treaties.

Vienna Convention on the Law of Treaties asserts that "a party may not invoke the provisions of its internal law as justification for its failure to perform a treaty"[85] unless the national rule violated is of fundamental importance or the violation is manifest, i.e. "the violation was objectively evident to any State conducting itself in the matter in accordance with normal practice and in good faith."[86]

Additionally, for the last sixty years both the Permanent Court of International Justice (PCIJ) and its successor the International Court of Justice (ICJ)[87] have adopted interpretations that tend to promote the application of appropriately concluded treaty provisions, regardless of barriers in the domestic order. Indeed, the PCIJ said in its Advisory Opinion on the *Greco-Bulgarian Communities* that: "In the first place, it is

---

[85] 1969 *Vienna Convention on the Law of Treaties*, Article 27. The same article, however, provides that this rule is without prejudice to article 46. Article 46 reads: *A State may not invoke the fact that its consent to be bound by a treaty has been expressed in violation of a provision of its internal law regarding competence to conclude treaties as invalidating its consent unless that violation was manifest and concerned a rule of its internal law of fundamental importance. 2. A violation is manifest if it would be objectively evident to any State conducting itself in the matter in accordance with normal practice and in good faith.*

[86] 1969 *Vienna Convention*, article 46.

[87] The Permanent Court of International Justice (PCIJ) was established under the Covenant of the League of Nations. During its existence, the PCIJ heard a total of 66 cases. It also rendered a total of 27 advisory opinions and 32 judgments. The PCIJ underwent its first major revision in 1926. This was followed by a significant overhaul of its rules followed in 1936. World War II marked the end of the PCIJ. It held its last wartime session in The Hague in February 1940. Delegates at the Dumbarton Oaks Conference in Washington, DC discussed the development of a new International Court of Justice, which would work in association with the United Nations. Another delegate's conference held in San Francisco approved the new International Court of Justice (June 1945) as one of the principal organs of the United Nations (Article VII) and as the UN's chief judicial organization (Article XCII). In October 1945, the members of the PCIJ held their last session. The judges of the PCIJ all resigned on 31 January 1946, and the election of the first Members of the International Court of Justice took place on 6 February 1946, at the First Session of the United Nations General Assembly and Security Council. In April 1946, the PCIJ was formally dissolved, and the International Court of Justice, meeting for the first time, elected as its President Judge José Gustavo Guerrero (El Salvador), the last President of the PCIJ. The Court appointed the members of its Registry (largely from among former officials of the PCIJ) and held an inaugural public sitting, on the 18th of that month. The first case was submitted in May 1947. It concerned incidents in the *Corfu Channel* and was brought by the United Kingdom against Albania.

a generally accepted principle of international law that in the relations between Powers who are contracting Parties to a treaty, the provisions of municipal law cannot prevail over those of the treaty."[88] Two years later, in 1932, the PCIJ reiterated its stand in an Advisory Opinion in the case of the *Treatment of Polish Nationals and Other Persons of Polish Origin or Speech in the Danzig Territory*[89] when the Court asserted that "a State cannot adduce as against another State its own Constitution with the view of evading obligations incumbent upon it under international law or treaties in force."[90]

Indeed, States have adopted diverse methods to deal with such cases. In the United States, the Supreme Court held in 1957 in *Reid v. Covert*, that "no agreement with a foreign nation can confer power on the Congress, or on any other branch of Government, which is free from the restraints of the Constitution."[91] Spiro adds that "there is perhaps no element of the foreign relations law canon more universally held than the

---

[88] P.C.I.J. Advisory Opinion, No. 17, 1930, case of the *Greco-Bulgarian Communities*, File F. c. XIX. Docket XVIII. Available at:
http://www.icj-cij.org/pcij/serie_B/B_17/01_Communautes_greco-bulgares_Avis_consultatif.pdf

[89] Danzig was a Polish port on the Baltic Sea north of Warsaw, and is now known as Gdańsk. Section VIII, Article 87 of the Treaty of Versailles (1919) brought about important territorial changes for Poland, which lost some 71,000 km², including the port of Danzig, which was ceded to the principal allied and associated powers. Danzig was recognised as a free city administered under the League of Nations but subject to Polish jurisdiction in regard to customs and foreign relations. See the Treaty of Versailles (1919) available at *http://net.lib.byu.edu/~rdh7/wwi/versa/versa2.html*

[90] P.C.I.J. Series A/B, No. 44, 4th February 1932, case of *Treatment of Polish Nationals and Other Persons of Polish Origin or Speech in the Danzig Territory*. Available at
http://www.icj-cij.org/pcij/serie_AB/AB_44/01_Traitement_nationaux_ polonais_ Avis_consultatif. pdf.

The Court denied the Polish Government the right to submit to organs of the League of Nations questions concerning the application to Polish nationals of certain provisions of the Constitution of the Free City of Danzig, on the ground that according to generally accepted principles, a State cannot rely, as against another State, on the provisions of the latter's Constitution, but only on international law and international obligations duly accepted. For a further analysis of this decision, see Kelsen, H., *Principles of International Law*, The Lawbook Exchange Ltd, New Jersey, 2003, at 195.

[91] See Supreme Court of the United States, *Reid, Superintendent, District of Columbia Jail, v. Covert*, No. 701, October Term, 1955, 354 U.S. 1; 77 S. Ct. 1222; 1 L. Ed. 2d 1148; 1957 U.S. Lexis, 729

proposition that constitutional rights prevail as against inconsistent international agreements. (…) Even as other elements of modern foreign relations law have come under vigorous assault, this constraint on the treaty power has gone unchallenged. Indeed, across the political spectrum, the rule is counted among those whose deep entrenchment eliminates the need for justification."[92]

However, in France a treaty in conflict with the constitution cannot be given the approval by Parliament for ratification until the constitution is revised.[93] In Germany, a treaty in conflict with the *Grundgesetz für die Bundesrepublik Deutschland* cannot take effect for being unconstitutional.[94] However, those treaties which refer to norms of *jus cogens* can be automatically integrated by virtue of Article 25 of the German Basic Law: "The general rules of public international law constitute an integral part of federal law. They take precedence over statutes and directly create rights and duties for the inhabitants of the federal territory."[95] In Kenya, legislative approval of a treaty is not required at any instance by the 2010 Constitution, except as provided for by article 71.[96] And in Uganda, the Constitution declares among the National Objectives and Directives

---

[92] Spiro, P.J., "Treaties, International Law, and Constitutional Rights", *Stanford Law Review*, vol 55, 1999. Available at:
http://www.lexisnexis.com/hottopics /lnacademic/?sfi=AC00NBGenSrch&csi=7353&shr=t

[93] Constitution of France (1958), Article 54.

[94] See Article 59 of the 1949 German Basic Law (last amended on 29th July 2009): (1) *The President represents the Federation in its international relations. He concludes treaties with foreign countries on behalf of the Federation. He accredits and receives envoys.* (2) *Treaties which regulate the political relations of the Federation or relate to matters of federal legislation require the consent or participation, in the form of a federal statute, of the bodies competent in any specific case for such federal legislation. As regards administrative agreements, the provisions concerning the federal administration are applicable.*

[95] Consequently there is a dilemma in the German case. By signing an agreement, the German State commits itself and in virtue of the general principle *pacta sunt servanda*, the State must fulfil its duty; otherwise the State would be contravening a general rule of public international law which would also be unconstitutional.

[96] Regarding agreements dealing with natural resources, the 2010 Constitution of Kenya, article 71 states that *A transaction is subject to ratification by Parliament if it — (a) involves the grant of a right or concession by or on behalf of any person, including the national government, to another person for the exploitation of any natural resource of Kenya.* It also states that Parliament shall enact legislation providing for these types of transaction that require Parliamentary ratification. All other transactions do not require any Parliamentary approval.

Principles of State Policy, Principle XXVIII, that "the foreign policy of Uganda shall be based on the principles of ... (b) respect for international law and treaty obligations." This directive principle would provide general support for any international commitment that Uganda may enter, and by not complying with such a commitment the State would be violating the principle. However, in case of a conflict between this principle and Section 2(2), the Ugandan constitution may prevail.[97]

The United Kingdom, by entering into treaties, undertakes the obligation of enacting the necessary laws, if there were none, to allow the internal application of a treaty.[98] Although the conduct of foreign affairs is the Crown's prerogative, the experience has developed a custom whereby the Crown seeks legislation prior ratification of certain kinds of treaties. This avoids embarrassment to the Executive, for example that the Crown ratifies a treaty and Parliament rejects to pass a statute, and also guarantees the internal execution of treaties as may be necessary.[99] McNair summarises these treaties in respect of which legislation is needed as: treaties creating a direct or a contingent financial obligation; treaties that involve changes in or additions to the law; and treaties that affect the acquisition or cession of territory.[100]The rationale behind these limitations

[97] Uganda Constitution, Article 2(2) establishes: (2) *If any other law or any custom is inconsistent with any of the provisions of this Constitution, the Constitution shall prevail, and that other law or custom shall, to the extent of the inconsistency, be void.*

[98] For example, the 1929 *Warsaw Convention* settling uniform rules as to the international carriage of goods by air was adopted into the British law by the *Carriage by Air Act 1932*. This Convention was revised at The Hague in 1955 and the revised version was enacted by the *Carriage by Air Act 1961*. The 1961 Vienna Convention on diplomatic immunities was enacted by the *Diplomatic Privileges Act 1964* and the *Consular Relations Act 1968* gave municipal effect to the 1963 Vienna Convention on Consular Relations. More examples are given by Walker, D., *The Scottish Legal System*, 6th Ed., W. Green/Sweet & Maxwell, Edinburgh, 1992, at 563.

[99] It is understood that if there is legislation already in force, there is no need for a new one.

[100] See McNair, *op. cit.*, at 83ff: Treaties for which parliamentary sanction in form of statute is required for municipal execution: (i) *Treaties in the United Kingdom requiring a change in or an addition to the Law administrated in the Courts.* (ii) *Treaties granting new powers to the Crown.* (iii) *Treaties creating a Direct or a Contingent Financial Obligation upon Great Britain.* There are other cases when the Crown, out of prudence (*ex abundantia cautela*), consults Parliament upon treaties, either (i) before signature or (ii) after signature and before ratification. This practice is becoming more common under the *Ponsoby Rule* of submitting

is founded on necessary check and balances that have imposed constitutional and democratic limitations on royal prerogatives.

Diplomatic Relations

Diplomacy is always considered from the point of view of international law. However, its national regulation as an element of the foreign affairs power is paramount for the adequate advancement of diplomatic relations. This regulation in the municipal legal order, as we explained before, belongs to the constitutional order. It is therefore relevant to study the definition and nature of diplomacy as well as the instruments diplomacy makes use of as relational means whereby a sovereign country deals with its counterparts.

Diplomacy has also been said to be an art because a diplomat would be considered more or less successful depending on his astuteness to handle a difficult situation.[101] Finally, diplomacy was considered an exclusively State function because only States would send and receive ambassadors.

However, modern diplomacy is witnessing the rapid growth of multilateralism. As Amitav Acharya says,

> "Post-war multilateralism helped to define, extend, embed and legitimize a set of sovereignty norms, including territorial integrity, equality of States and non-intervention. Today, multilateral institutions are under increasing pressure to move beyond some of these very same principles, especially non-intervention, as part of a transformative process in world politics. Without multilateralism, it is highly doubtful that the post-war international order would have been so tightly and universally built upon the norms of sovereignty. And without multilateralism, transition from this normative order now would be difficult and chaotic."[102]

---

treaties to Parliament in order to ensure publicity for treaties and to afford opportunity for their discussion in Parliament if desired. [See Wilson, G., *Cases and Materials in Constitutional and Administrative Law*, Cambridge University Press, Cambridge, 1966, at 453.]

[101] See Heatley, P. D., *op. cit.* at 41. Bismarck, for instance, would advise ambassadors to write diplomatically and to be polite but without irony. Even in a declaration of war, Bismarck advised, one observes the rules of politeness.

[102] Acharya, A., in Newman, E. and others (Editors), *Multilateralism Under Challenge*, United Nations University Press, Tokyo, 2006, at 95.

Diplomacy today encompasses three distinct but interrelated meanings:[103] First, it means the 'conduct' of international relations. Second, it also means the 'study' and analysis of foreign policy.[104] And finally, it has a 'procedural and normative' character. The procedural aspect is concerned to examine the actual process of the peaceful conduct of relations between States.[105] The normative aspect is concerned with statement and analysis of the rules of diplomacy. This is what may be called the international law of diplomacy.

In an effort to arrive at a unified and comprehensive definition, Mwagiru asserts that diplomacy "is the study of the relations between actors in international relations and the mechanism, process and rules by which those relations are rendered functional."[106] This definition includes also other actors in the international scene apart from States. Thus, 'diplomatic relations', within this context, may be said to make specific reference to those "mechanisms and processes whereby any of the actors in the international relations put into practice its foreign policy."[107]

Certainly, the goal of diplomacy is to further the State's interests, which are dictated by geography, history, and economics. In this context priority is given to safeguarding its independence, security, and integrity—territorial, political, and economic. This aims at reserving wide freedom of action to the State. Besides, diplomacy seeks maximum national advantage without using force and preferably without causing resentment.[108] Diplomacy is an alternative to war to achieve a nation's goals. Its weapon is words, and it often, but not always, seeks to preserve peace. Diplomacy may employ coercive threats; its range, flexibility, and effectiveness are

---

103 Mwagiru, M., Paper presented at the *Seminar on Diplomacy, Culture and Media of the Institute of Diplomacy and International Studies*, University of Nairobi, 1-3 August, (1991), at 2.

104 See Watson, A., *Diplomacy: The Dialogue Between States*, Routledge, London, 1991, at 20.

105 Satow, Sir E. M., *Satow's Guide to Diplomatic Practice*, 5th Edition, Longman, London, 1979, at 3.

106 Mwagiru, M., Paper presented at the *Seminar on Diplomacy, Culture and Media of the Institute of Diplomacy and International Studies*, University of Nairobi, 1-3 August, (1991), at 4.

107 Heatley, P. D., *Diplomacy and the Study of International Relations,* Clarendon Press, Oxford, 1919, at 4. Policy is defined by Heatley as *the application of mind and means to conditions for an object, immediate or distant, or both.* On Foreign Policy, see Chapter I *supra.*

108 See Von Glann, *Law Among Nations*, 2nd Ed., The Macmillan Co., London, 1970, at 393.

linked in part to the relative power of the State or States using it and at the same time it seeks to create goodwill toward the State it represents.

These goals are to be reached through the exercise of diplomatic relations, and diplomatic relations are carried out through diplomatic missions. The functions of diplomatic missions are clearly spelt out by the 1961 Vienna Convention on Diplomatic Relations. Article 3 of the Convention says that the functions of a diplomatic mission consist *inter alia* in:

> "(i) Representing the sending State in the receiving State;
>
> (ii) Protecting in the receiving State the interests of the sending State and of its nationals, within the limits permitted by international law;
>
> (iii) Negotiating with the Government of the receiving State;
>
> (iv) Ascertaining by all lawful means conditions and developments in the receiving State, and reporting thereon to the Government of the sending State;
>
> (v) Promoting friendly relations between the sending State and the receiving State, and developing their economic, cultural and scientific relations."

As a general rule, the Diplomatic Service is conducted by the office of foreign affairs or its equivalent. Notes and other communications concerning relations with other countries are usually signed by the Minister of Foreign Affairs, or on his behalf.[109] However, at present, this office normally deals with other matters which were not traditionally considered to fall within the ambit of diplomacy, such as the ever-increasing complexity and diversity of relationships with international organisations, particularly with the advent of multilateral diplomacy.

Multilateral diplomacy "deals with regional or global issues and is used with a plurality of States through an international organization or at international conferences; they do not exclude but naturally complement each other."[110]

---

[109] See Satow, Sir E. M., *Satow's Guide to Diplomatic Practice*, 5th Edition, Longman, London, 1979, at 12.

[110] Roncati, E., "Diplomacy", *Max Planck Encyclopedia of Public International Law*, *www.mpepil.com*, Oxford University Press, (2008) para. 12.

The drama generated by the World Wars brought forth a tide of pragmatism in international law in which States, traditionally the main actors in international law, were joined by other 'secondary subjects' that progressively emerged, e.g. inter-governmental organizations or international governmental organizations (IGOs). This new phenomenon was more concerned with making these new 'subjects' work than with the intellectual coherence and consistency of legal thought and practice.[111]

Already in 1948, only three years after the UN foundation, the ICJ stated in the *Reparation for Injuries Case*:

> "the Court's opinion is that fifty States, representing the vast majority of the members of the international community, had the power, in conformity with international law, to bring into being an entity possessing objective international personality, and not merely personality recognized by them alone, together with capacity to bring international claims."[112]

An International Governmental Organization has broadly been defined as a body based on a formal instrument or agreement between three or more States possessing a permanent secretariat performing on-going assignments.[113] International Governmental Organizations, a term coined to "describe an organization set up by agreement between two or more States,"[114] were usually formed by agreements between States, which were the main actors in their constitution. Their recognition as subjects of international law has been progressively established[115] and it is usually

[111] Carty, A., "International Legal Personality and the End of the Subject: Natural Law and Phenomenological Responses to New Approaches to International Law", *Melbourne Journal of International Law*, vol. 6, (2005) at 535.

[112] ICJ *Reports* (1948), case of *The Reparation for Injuries Suffered in the Service of the United Nations*, at 185.

[113] See generally Delbruck, J., "Structural Changes in the International System and its. Legal Order: International Law in the Era of Globalization", *Swiss Review of International and European Law*, vol. 1, (2001), at 36. However, the term also covers mixed organizations. A mixed organization is a non-governmental organization (NGO) entrusted with functions typical of a State, for example, the International Committee of the Red Cross (ICRC) and the International Union for Conservation of Nature (IUCN). Further, in the modern international system states there has been a shift towards institutionalized cooperation.

[114] Malanczuk, P., *Akehurst's Modern Introduction to International Law*, Seventh Edition, Routledge ed., London, 1997, at 92.

[115] Oppenheim, L., *Oppenheim's International Law*, Edited by Jennings, R and Watts, A., 9th Edition, Longmans, New Jersey, 1996, at 16-22.

pegged to their objectives, depending on their reason for being.[116] Sometimes such organisations were created with a broad mandate, encompassing all fields of political, economic, social, and cultural life of the international community.[117]

International or inter-State organisations have existed since, at least, 1815.[118] Nevertheless, it was after the First World War that they acquired such relevance in international law. Since then, their relevance and number have increased vertiginously. As Starke says, "under modern practice the number of exceptional instances of individuals or non-State entities enjoying rights or becoming subjects to duties directly under international law, has grown. (…) The doctrinaire rigidity … has been tempered."[119]

---

[116] A modern European example is found in the formation of the European Union (EU). The European Community Treaty (ECT), which is the founding treaty, confers powers onto a new legal person in order to carry out certain functions. Their powers are, however, not necessarily limited to the constituent treaty. They can be extended to do what is necessary to perform those functions granted effectively. See Reparation for Injuries Suffered in the Service of the United Nations' case, ICJ, 1949, Confirmed by the 'Certain Expenses' case, ICJ, 1962. In the case of the EU, the ECT gives the EU authority to legislate, to execute administrative functions, and to adjudicate legal disputes through the European Court of Justice (ECJ). The EU also has the power to directly reach the citizens of member governments, whether natural persons or juridical corporate entities. European Community Treaty, Arts. 220-249. Another example is the World Trade Organization (WTO). At the end of World War II, several new global organizations were formed with the mandate of economic and political stability. The US wanted a trade organization that would regulate world trade [See Elaine Hartwick and Richard Peet (2003), at 190] Four preliminary conferences on trade were convened under United Nations auspices. The most important of these meetings was the Geneva Conference of 1947. This conference produced an interim measure known as the General Agreement on Tariffs and Trade (GATT). GATT became the main international basis for managing trade in the post- war period. [See Jackson, J. H., "Editorial Comment: International Law Status of WTO DS Reports: Obligation to Comply or Option to 'Buy-Out'?", *American Journal of International Law*, vol. 98, (2004), at 109].

[117] McWhinney E., *Supreme Law and Judicial Law-Making: Constitutional Tribunals and Constitutional Review*, Martinus Nijhoff Publishers, Dordrecht, 1966, at 112.

[118] *Ibid.*

[119] Starke, J.G., *Introduction to International Law*, Tenth Edition, Butterworths, London, 1989, at 70.

International Governmental Organizations may be born from a resolution[120] or by a declaration.[121] However, the acceptance of International Organizations as subjects of international law is not automatic or immediate. It is rooted on the organisation's constitutive act and it will depend on its mission and functions. The Vienna Convention on the Law of Treaties between States and International Organizations or between International Organizations, establishes in Article 2, that "for the purposes of the present Convention 'treaty' means an international agreement governed by international law and concluded in written form: (i) between one or more States and one or more international organizations; or (ii) between international organizations."[122] The same Convention's article 6 stipulates that "the capacity of an international organization to conclude treaties is governed by the rules of that organization."[123]

In most recent times International Governmental Organizations have come together and have institutionalized forms of cooperation that reveals their own personality separate from the States that constituted them. By their nature, these bodies may be conceived in specific ways and with a specific mission. Some may have legislative powers that can pass resolutions and directives[124] or binding judgments[125] or quasi-judicial decisions,[126] etc. Certainly, most States nowadays are members of a dense

---

[120] This is the case with the formation of Comprehensive Nuclear-Test-Ban Treaty Organization (CTBTO) [See *www.ctbto.org*].

[121] The Association of Southeast Asian Nation (ASEAN) is an example of such [*www.aseansec.org*]. The ASEAN was formed on 8th August, 1967 by the Bangkok Declaration. The main reason for its formation was the promotion of economic cooperation of Southeast Asian States. The organization was also formed to fill the vacuum of authority that was vacant after the exit of colonial masters. A second example is the Asian Pacific Economic Cooperation (APEC) [*www.apec.org*]. The idea of APEC was firstly publicly broached by former Prime Minister of Australia, Mr. Bob Hawke, during a speech in Seoul, Korea in January 1989. Later that year, 12 Asia-Pacific economies met in Canberra, Australia and signed a declaration for the establishment of APEC. The purpose of forming APEC was to promote free trade and economic cooperation throughout the Asian-Pacific region.

[122] See Vienna Convention on the Law of Treaties between States and International Organizations or between International Organizations, A/CONF.129/15, 21 March 1986.

[123] *Ibid,* Article 6.

[124] For example, the United Nations General Assembly.

[125] The International Court of Justice, the International Criminal Court, the International Regional Courts, etc.

[126] The African Commission on Human and People's Rights.

and often complex network of International Governmental Organizations.[127] The great majority of International Governmental Organizations are still conceived in a traditional State-centred fashion as intergovernmental *fora* for cooperation. These types of Organizations usually tend to have limited agendas.[128] Yet, there are International Governmental Organizations that deal with universal matters such as international security, the economy, environmental protection, etc. Such bodies tend to be more globally focused and may have autonomous regulatory, administrative, and judicial areas of authority.[129]

The act of investing an International Governmental Organizations with regulatory and judicial competence implies the transference of some State power. This was the case, for example, in the formation of the Permanent Court of International Justice, which was the first attempt at creating a global forum of justice. Unfortunately, the Permanent Court's parent body, the League, was unsuccessful and unable to prevent World War II.[130] These failures led to the need of a stronger International Governmental Organization that would secure world peace and prevent the horror of another world war.

Hence, the idea of the United Nations came into being. Its structure was decided by the United States, the United Kingdom, the Soviet Union and China at the Dumbarton Oaks meeting of 1944 and the subsequent 1945 Yalta Summit.[131] The UN was meant to be a peace and security organization and it became the primary venue for the diffusion of international tensions in the post-World War II period.

The foundation of the United Nations brought with it a drastic change in the world order. Until then, States would constantly reclaim their right to war. With the appearance of the UN, the founding States transferred their right to the use of force onto a Security Council, which was entrusted

---

[127] Delbrück, J., "Prospects for a Word (Internal) Law?: Legal Developments in a Changing International System", *Indiana Journal of Global Legal Studies*, vol. 9, (2001-2002), at 408.

[128] For example, The Universal Postal Union (UPU), the World Meteorological Organization (WMO), or the World Tourism Organization, etc.

[129] Delbrück, J., "Transnational Federalism: Problems and Prospects of Allocating Public Authority Beyond the State", *Indiana Journal of Global Legal Studies*, vol. 11, (2004), at 36.

[130] Thompson, A. and Snidal, D., *International Organizations*, University of Chicago, Chicago, 1999, at 695-696. Available at: *http://encyclo.findlaw.com/9800book.pdf*

[131] *Ibid.*

with the primary responsibility of authorizing and overseeing military action[132] and maintaining international peace and security. This Council was also bestowed with the power to issue decisions binding on its member States.[133]

The idea of a United Nations' powerful Security Council had already been in gestation for a number of years, perhaps ever since nations realized that the League's structure was too weak to succeed in such a turbulent Twentieth century. The Covenant of the League of Nations envisaged the foundation of the Permanent Court of International Justice (PCIJ). Although its life and work was cut short by the Second World War,[134] the PCIJ marked the beginning of a process that would lead to the foundation of the International Court of Justice and later on to the mushrooming of international courts and tribunals. Ever since, States have transferred judicial powers and functions onto regional and universal bodies.[135]

Acts originating from International Governmental Organizations may require in dualist States implementation by statute, unless there is already an existing law on the subject.[136] In such a situation, the State would have

---

[132] Koskenniemi, M., "Place of Law in Collective Security", *Michigan Journal of International Law*, vol. 17, Issue 2 (1996), at 456 ff.

[133] UN *Charter*, articles: 24 and 25. For example, the Security Council has directed binding decisions to individual States directing them to stop acts of aggression or refrain from the threat of use of force [See Delbrück, *op. cit.*, at 442-464]. Resolution 1373 also contains legislative provisions taken from the Convention for the Suppression of the Financing of Terrorism adopted by the General Assembly [UNGA, Res. 54/109, 54th Sess., 76th plen. mtg., U.N. Doc.]

[134] See further information on the PCIJ and the ICJ in *supra* note no. 87.

[135] The foundation of the international court fostered the creation of multiple international bodies vested with judicial powers and trans-boundary jurisdictions. For example, the International Criminal Court, the European Court of Justice, the European Court of Human Rights, the Inter-American Court of justice, the Inter-American Court of Human Rights, the African Court on Human and People's Rights, the Caribbean Court of Human Rights, the SADC Tribunal, the ECOWAS Court, the East African Court of Justice, etc.

[136] Walker, R. J. and Ward, R., *English Legal System*, Seventh Ed. Butterworths, London, 1994, at 21. Walker and Ward say that it would be a mistake to regard English and European Law as two separate systems of law because the European one, by virtue of the Treaty of Rome, has become a significant source of English law as stated in *HP Bulmer Ltd v J Bollinger SA*. Although this is the current trend, it is still a fact that the English legal system is dualist, and therefore, it requires statutory law to incorporate foreign decisions or agreements into its municipal law.

the obligation to legislate in order to enforce decisions from the emanating organ.[137]

The fact is that once an International Organization is constituted it is bestowed with a type of legal personality which allows it to enter into relationships by setting into motion the elements of the foreign affairs power for the attainment of its objectives. This personality may be sui-generis and restricted according to the organization's nature and function. It is not above the State's personality but at par with it. As the ICJ stated in 1980 in the case of the Interpretation of the Agreement of 25 March 1951 between the WHO and Egypt:

> "Article 44 of the WHO Constitution empowers the World Health Assembly to define geographical areas in which it is desirable to establish a regional organization and, with the consent of a majority of the members of the Organization situated within the area, to establish the regional organization. It also provides that there is not to be more than one regional organization in each area… But States for their part possess a sovereign power of decision with respect to their acceptance of the headquarters or a regional office of an organization within their territories; and an organization's power of decision is no more absolute in this respect than is that of a State. As was pointed out by the Court in one of its early Advisory Opinions, there is nothing in the character of international organizations to justify their being considered as some form of 'super-State' (Reparations for Injuries Suffered in the Service of the United Nations, Advisory Opinion, I.C.J. Reports 1949, p. 179)."[138]

The International Organization is therefore the legal expression of a larger reality. This legal expression is of different nature than those who gave birth to it and from those in charge of directing it. This being, the International Organization, is granted by law the most appropriate status to describe the reality before our eyes. This protection or status granted by the law is what is known as juristic personality. This personality is neither below nor above the State, but at par. It is not built on sovereignty or territoriality, but functionality and therefore it extends as far as the mission entrusted to the organization by the constitutive instrument.[139]

---

[137] See Walker, R. J. and Ward, R., *English Legal System*, 7thEdition, Butterworths, London, 1994, at 21.
[138] ICJ Reports, case of *Interpretation of the Agreement of 25 March 1951 between the WHO and Egypt*, 1980, at 73 (No. 12 and 37)
[139] See Peters, A., *op. cit.*, para. 45. Examples of provisions of founding documents containing treaty making authorizations are given by Anne Peters as follows: Arts 43, 57, 63, 105 (3) United Nations Charter; Arts 2, 3 (2), 54 (3), 87 (5) Statute of

The Foreign Affairs Power in Constitutional Practice

Having looked into the theoretical frame of the foreign affairs power and two of its elements – treaty-making and diplomacy – it now seems appropriate to examine the impact caused by the constitutional regulation of the foreign affairs power on those two elements which are essential tools for the construction of any supranational human rights system, and specifically, the African Human Rights system. Furthermore, it is also important to take into consideration that the enforcement of decisions emanating from supranational human rights organs will find their actual fulfilment if the constitutional systems of domestication and enforcement are in place at the domestic level.[140]

The Constitution of a State is the most important part and dimension of its basic law. Constitutions have been classified as: Written – formal and codified document embodying the rules and relationships of Government,

---

the International Criminal Court (ICC); Art. 41 (2) Convention Establishing European Free Trade Association ((concluded 4 January 1960) 370 UNTS 3) (European Free Trade Association (EFTA)); Arts 5 (c) and 12 (b) Convention on the Organisation for Economic Cooperation and Development ((done 14 December 1960, entered into force 30 September 1961) 888 UNTS 181; Organization for Economic Co-operation and Development (OECD)); Art. 41 Agreement Establishing the Common Fund for Commodities ((adopted 27 June 1980, entered into force 19 June 1989) (1980) 19 ILM 896; Common Fund for Commodities (CFC)); Art. XIII (2) Constitution of the Food and Agricultural Organization ((adopted 16 October 1945, entered into force 16 October 1945) 145 BSP 910; Food and Agriculture Organization of the United Nations (FAO)); Art. 40 (b) Statute of the Council of Europe ((signed 5 May 1949, entered into force 3 August 1949) CETS No 1; Council of Europe (COE)); Art. IV (4) Articles of Agreement of the International Bank for Reconstruction and Development ((done and entered into force 27 December 1945) 2 UNTS 134; loan and guarantee contracts with States which are arguably international law instruments; International Bank for Reconstruction and Development (IBRD)).

140 The study of the constitutional regulation of the foreign affairs power will highlight the importance of clear constitutional directions on the conduct of this power and the interplay of its checks and balances. To achieve this we have looked at how different constitutions in Europe and Africa deal with the subject. We will not attempt an exhaustive comparative study, but a quick review of several constitutions in Europe that have played an essential role in Africa's colonization and the subsequent conception of African legal systems, and we will also review several African constitutions from different geographical or cultural regions that may represent those existing diverse legal traditions in Africa. The study, though not exhaustive, may reveal the essential importance constitutional law plays as an enforcement mechanism of decisions emanating from International Organizations.

and unwritten –informal collection of rules, customs and traditions that pertain to the accepted organisations of authority but which do not possess any collective force that affords them a superior status to either the governing institutions or their decisions. However, there has been a long argument on whether an unwritten constitution is a constitution at all. Alexis de Tocqueville's conclusion was that England, for example, had 'no constitution.'[141]Evidently, "if a constitution means a written document then," Ivor Jennings says, "obviously Great Britain has no constitution."[142]

The classification, Foley says, is shown to break down on 3 counts:

(1) Should the British Constitution be accepted as an unwritten constitution, it would become (with the possible addition of Israel) the only one of its kind in the world. By virtue of this fact alone, the typology's usefulness is undermined. (2) The confusion is said to derive from the absence of a central and singular document of codified constitutional rules. The modernist reply is to draw attention to the fact that most of what is regarded as comprising the British Constitution is ascertainable historical process and may consist of an accumulation of principles and practices. Nevertheless, its identity and meaning are discoverable by reference to statutes, judicial decisions, conventions and constitutional commentaries and these taken together are said to be more explicit than the written constitutions of other countries. Consequently the British Constitution's mark of destruction is not that it is unwritten, but that it is unassembled or uncodified. It exists in written fragments that may or may not have collective identity but which in theory do admit of being collected together in written form. C. K. Wheare offers a corrective formula: 'The truth about Britain can be stated not by saying that she has an unwritten constitution but by saying that she has no written constitution. (3) Drawing attention to the unwritten elements of the written constitutions. From being devoid of the sort of unwritten components known to characterise the British Constitution, other constitutions are recognised as being similarly dependent upon conventions for their adaptability. Therefore, 'no constitution will be completely 'written' or completely 'unwritten', completely 'codified' or completely 'uncodified'.[143]

---

[141] See generally Tocqueville, A., *Democracy in America*, Regnery Publishing, Washington DC, 2002.
[142] See Jennings, I., *The Law and the Constitution*, 5th Ed., University of London Press, London, 1959.
[143] See Foley, M., *op. cit.,* at 4.

This being so, a constitution like that of Britain is, to Carl Friedrich, "just as much written as the American or French constitutions, that is to say embodied in written documents of all kinds even though not codified or assembled in a single document."[144]

In addition, there is the unwritten dimension which comprises other legal instruments, customs and history that shape the conduct of State affairs. Indeed, in order to study the basic law (*droit constitutionnel*) of a State it is not enough to analyse only the articles of the constitution (*loi constitutionnelle*). It is necessary to know the circumstances and the so-called spiritual background (*Geistlicher Hintergrund*) that led to the drafting of the document and the development of judicial thought and decisions.

It is not possible to fully understand the constitution of any State by reading the text alone. On how the text came into existence, the conditions that prevailed at the time have to be taken into account, so as to gain a more complete understanding of such a constitution and be able to grasp the fundamental ideas and the basic reasoning underlying the constitution.[145]

The constitutional regulation of the foreign affairs power brings to light the process for treaty domestication, appointment of ambassadors and heads of diplomatic missions, the regulation of war and recognition of States and Governments. It is also necessary to understand how the judiciary has interpreted and managed these constitutional provisions throughout time and space. In this regard, the process of enforcement of foreign judgments becomes — along with treaty domestication — an important tool where domestic legislation is influenced by international law. The enforcement of foreign judgments is the reciprocal recognition and enforcement of judgments between States. This is frequently regulated by bilateral treaty or multilateral international conventions. Enforcing foreign judgments involves the application of the local court's powers to

144 Friedrich, C., "Constitutions of Modern States, Constitutions and Constitutionalism", in Sils, P. L. (ed) *The International Encyclopaedia of the Social Sciences*, Vol. 3, New York, 1968, at 318.

145 At the beginning of each constitution we have tried to give a general short political context of the State. Most constitutions have been consulted in original texts, while some are translations made by the *International Constitutional Law* site of Berne University (SZ). The translation of the Argentinian Constitution was done by this author.

give effect to the foreign court's decision without the plaintiff having to re-litigate the merits of the dispute.[146]

Regarding diplomatic relations, the constitutional regulation of diplomacy is relevant as far as it determines the power to appoint heads of diplomatic missions and the extent of the powers granted to those agents to bind the State.

In relation to the power appoint, the majority of constitutions tend towards considering two main possibilities: exclusive or shared power. It is 'exclusive' when that power is vested in a sole entity of the State, in this case the executive. However, it may be totally exclusive, when the power is vested in the President alone, or partially exclusive, when other substructures of State within the same power are expressly called upon to intervene, together with the President, in the appointment. Such substructures may be the cabinet or the foreign affairs minister or the prime minister. On the contrary, 'shared' power arises when the executive must count on the advice or consent of another branch or structure to make the appointment; in this case the legislature.

Totally exclusive power is the case, for example, of Cameroon and Madagascar, among others, where the President alone intervenes in the appointment. Partially exclusive is the case of Iran where the President makes the appointment upon recommendation by the Minister of Foreign Affairs.[147] It is also the case in France, where the appointment is made by the Council of Ministers,[148] and thereafter the President accredits the ambassador. Similar is the case of Japan, where the emperor makes the

---

[146] British Columbia Law Institute ('BCLI'), *Report on the Enforcement of Non-Money Judgments from Outside the Province*, Report No 8, (1999) at 6.

[147] See the 1979 Constitution of the Islamic Republic of Iran, Article 128: "The ambassadors shall be appointed upon the recommendation of the foreign Minister and approval of the President. The President signs the credentials of ambassadors and receives the credentials presented by the ambassadors of the foreign countries."

[148] See the French Constitution, Article 13 (1) "The President of the Republic shall sign the ordinances and orders decided upon in the Council of Ministers. (...) (3) Councillors of State, the Grand Chancellor of the Legion of Honour, Ambassadors and envoys extraordinary, Chief Councillors of the Cour des Comptes, Prefects, Government representatives in the Overseas Territories, General Officers, Heads of Academic Institutions and Directors of central administrations shall be appointed by the Council of Ministers. Article 14 The President of the Republic shall accredit Ambassadors and envoys extraordinary to foreign powers; foreign Ambassadors and envoys extraordinary shall be accredited to him."

appointment with the approval of the cabinet.[149] In addition, the system followed by Antigua and Barbuda may also be included here as the appointment is vested in both the Governor-General and the Prime Minister.[150]

Shared power of appointment is observed in countries where the President, with the approval of the legislature, makes the appointment. This is the case, for example, of the Russian Federation,[151] and Uganda.[152] In all of them Parliament or Congress approves the appointment. In China[153] the Standing Committee of the National People's Congress decides on the appointment and the President effects it.

Constitutions tend to make indiscriminate mention of envoys, envoys extraordinary, ambassadors, plenipotentiary representatives, diplomatic representatives, diplomatic agents,[154] minister plenipotentiary, heads of mission, and heads of permanent diplomatic missions, heads of diplomatic missions, high commissioners and papal representatives. There has been no consistent or uniform practice. Article 14 of the 1961 Vienna Convention on Diplomatic Relations aimed at unifying the criteria and terminology used for diplomatic agents. In this regard, it seems convenient

---

[149] See the 1946 Constitution of Japan (promulgated on November 3, 1946): Article 7: "The Emperor, with the advice and approval of the Cabinet, shall perform the following acts in matters of State on behalf of the people: (...) (5) Attestation of the appointment and dismissal of Ministers of State and other officials as provided for by law, and of full powers and credentials of Ambassadors and Ministers. (...) (9) Receiving foreign ambassadors and ministers."

[150] The Constitution of Antigua and Barbuda [1981] Article 101 "[In] relation to any office of Ambassador, High Commissioner or other principal representative of Antigua and Barbuda in any other country or accredited to any international organisation the Governor-General shall act in accordance with the advice of the Prime Minister…"

[151] The *Constitution of the Russian Federation* (1993), article 83(L) - Only for diplomats representing the Federation. The Constitution also provides for the possibility of diplomats representing the president in which case the appointment is made by the president alone - The Constitutions of the Russian Federation (cf. art. 83(j)).

[152] The Constitution of Uganda (1995), Section 122: "(1) The President may, with the approval of Parliament, appoint Ambassadors and Head of Diplomatic missions."

[153] The *Constitution of the People's Republic of China* (1982), Adopted at the 5th Session of the 5th National People's Congress and Promulgated for Implementation by the Proclamation of the National People's Congress on December 4, 1982. Printed by Foreign Languages Press, Beijing, 1987, article 67(13) and 81.

[154] As happens in Mexico.

that constitutions designed after the 1961 Vienna Convention should take into consideration the conceptual framework of the Convention.

In Europe, the post-war development of governance structures, have made an impact worldwide. It has begotten a culture where the rule of law has great prominence. One of the most relevant developments has been the judicial independence and the submission of rulers to an autonomous justice system. In most European legal systems, the national judiciary is largely free and law is upheld as an essential developmental component applicable to all.[155]

Some European constitutions have made a decisive impact on the formation of Africa's constitutional law as we know it today.[156] European

---

[155] See Baluarte, D. C. and De Vos, C. M., *Judgement to Justice: Implementing International and Regional Human Rights Decisions*, Open Society Justice Initiative, Open Society Foundations, New York, 2010, at 16.Nonetheless, certain regional organs, such as the European Human Rights Judicial System, have been facing serious challenges in the past few years. The European Court of Human Rights individual petitions procedure has expanded to a backlog of almost 120,000 cases. This has adversely affected the implementation of the Court's decisions. In January 2007, the year that execution of the court's judgments began to be monitored and made public, over 5,000 judgments were still listed as pending before the Committee of Ministers, the political branch of the Council of Europe responsible for supervising the Court's judgments. By the end of 2009, the figure rose to 7,887. In the past two years alone, the number of pending cases has risen at an annual rate of 18%, far outpacing the number of cases that have been closed. By the start of 2010, there were nearly 120,000 applications pending before a decision body of the Court. The Court's caseload has 'multiplied by a factor of ten' in the past decade, such that more than 90% of the Court's judgments have been delivered between 1998 and 2008. Furthermore, of the pending cases, 5 States—Russia, Turkey, Romania, Ukraine, and Italy—account for over 60% (69,100 applications) of the Court's workload. Certain States—Russia, Italy, Turkey, Bulgaria, Ukraine, in particular—pose problems for the European system. This is because they lack the capacity or political will to enforce judgments.

[156] For example, France: As one of the nations that inspired constitutionalism in the modern world and brought forward the idea of a monist system subjected to checks and balances for a controlled exercise of the foreign affairs power. Germany: An ambitious colonizer and as the country which ignited two World Wars in the first half of the century. Italy: As a coloniser with a diverse political history. Russia: As a powerful communist superpower which after the collapse of communism found itself in the midst of weak institutions, and is yet to settle. And the United Kingdom, powerful colonizer and peculiar on its own for having what has been called an unwritten constitution. Britain's organizational expertise helped create systems of governance that helped many colonies to develop a great deal.

government styles and systems have deeply influenced the modern world at large, and specifically Africa's colonization and post-independence history.

The French Constitution was adopted on 4 October 1958. It has been amended eighteen times;[157] the most recent one received the Great Seal of France on 1 October 2008. Articles 52-55 are dedicated to the foreign affairs powers in matters of treaties. Throughout the years, checks and balances have shaped the presidential powers. These controls may be grouped into 'internal checks', those found within the executive power. These are, mainly, the requirement of the Prime Minister's and, where applicable, a relevant Minister's countersignature provided for by Article 19 of the Constitution and the requirement of consent expressed by the Council of Ministers in its decisions. And there are also 'external checks', which refer to those found outside the executive power, such as authorisations required for the executive to act upon a specific matter. They may be expressed in the form of referenda[158] or Acts of Parliament.[159]

The French system is monist. Once a treaty is published it prevails over statutory provisions, whether previous or posterior to the treaty. This was affirmed by the Constitutional Council in the *Nicolo* decision of 1989.[160] Nevertheless, as stated by article 55, treaties shall override French legislation subject to its application by the other party.[161] It is also important to take into consideration that the French system also provides a basic distinction of treaties according to their nature: executive treaties, being those signed and ratified by the Executive; and treaties which must be ratified or approved only by virtue of an Act of Parliament. These are "those which involve the State in financial obligations, modify the

However, their inexperience on written constitutions threw most African colonies in a State of post-independent confusion which led to executive abuse of powers and manipulation of laws.

[157] See Prakke, L. and Kortmann, C. (ed), *Constitutional Law of 15 EU Member States*, Kluwer Legal Publishers, Deventer, 2004, at 245. (Certainly Prakke and Kortmann do not include the 18th Amendment that took place in 2008).

[158] For example, article 53(3) of the Constitution of France.

[159] For example, article 53(1) of the Constitution of France.

[160] See Prakke, L., and Kortmann, C. (ed), *op. cit.,* at 295.

[161] See article 55 of the Constitution of France.

provisions of the law, concern personal status or involve the cession, exchange or addition of territory."[162]

In Germany, a treaty in conflict with the *Grundgesetz für die Bundesrepublik Deutschland* cannot take effect for being unconstitutional.[163] However, those treaties which refer to norms of *jus cogens* can be automatically integrated by virtue of Article 25 of the German Basic Law.[164] Since its amendment of 1993, Germany's Basic Law also allows for the transfer of sovereign powers to intergovernmental institutions[165] and, furthermore, it integrates general rules of public international law into the federal law,[166] creating direct rights and taking precedence over statutory law.[167]

In Spain, according to Fernando Garrido-Falla, a treaty validly concluded is not yet a direct source of domestic law but only indirect. In

---

[162] See Article 53(1) of the Constitution of France. The original text reads: *Les traités de paix, les traités de commerce, les traités ou accords relatifs à l'organisation internationale, ceux qui engagent les finances de l'Etat, ceux qui modifient les dispositions de nature législative, ceux qui sont relatifs à l'état des personnes, ceux qui comportent cession, échange ou adjonction de territoire, ne peuvent être ratifiés ou approuvés qu'en vertu d'une loi.*

[163] See Article 59 of the 1949 German Basic Law (last amended on 29th July 2009): (1) *The President represents the Federation in its international relations. He concludes treaties with foreign countries on behalf of the Federation. He accredits and receives envoys.* (2) *Treaties which regulate the political relations of the Federation or relate to matters of federal legislation require the consent or participation, in the form of a federal statute, of the bodies competent in any specific case for such federal legislation. As regards administrative agreements, the provisions concerning the federal administration are applicable.*

[164] Consequently there is a dilemma in the German case. By signing an agreement, the German state commits itself and in virtue of the general principle *pacta sunt servanda*, the state must fulfil its duty; otherwise the state would be contravening a general rule of public international law which would also be unconstitutional.

[165] See GG, Article 24.

[166] See GG, Article 25.

[167] However, Stone and Keller say, the Federal Constitutional Court has begun to treat certain conventions such as the European Convention on Human Rights as *lex specialis* and, in 2004, the Federal Constitutional Court favoured the European Court of Human Rights (ECHR). It now requires the judiciary to enforce Convention rights even against statutes passed later in time. Nevertheless, this has not always been the case. See Keller, H. and Stone Sweet, A., "Assessing the Impact of the ECHR on National Legal Systems", *Faculty Scholarship Series*, Paper 88, 2008. Available at:
http://digitalcommons.law.yale.edu/fss_papers/88

order to become a direct source, i.e. part of internal law, it must fulfil the requirement of publication. It seems this requirement does not affect the fact that treaties are automatically considered part of internal law, but it is either a formal constitutive requirement or it may also be considered a condition which places the treaty in suspension until publication is effected.[168]

Like Germany's, Italy's Constitution conforms to the generally recognised principles of international law,[169] Italy's Constitution is dualist. Ratification does not automatically make the treaty in question enforceable. Treaties become part of internal order by reception (recezione) which gives full execution within the internal order to the agreement.[170] In Italy the incorporation has proceeded through rulings of the constitutional courts. In relation to the European Convention on Human Rights, for example, the courts' attitude has been marked by longstanding reluctance to recognize its primacy over statutes. However, a 2007 ruling of the Italian Constitutional Court declaring the unconstitutionality of a statute found to contravene Article 1 of Protocol No. 1, which may well be a landmark change.[171]

Russia, on the other hand, is dualist. The implementation of international treaties in the Russian Federation requires incorporation into federal law. This incorporation is done through the treaty's official publication. In certain cases, implementation may require the adoption of new domestic statutes or the amendment of existing ones.[172] In what appertains to the execution of foreign judgments the Russian system demands that foreign judgments and awards must be enforced within three years from their

---

[168] See Fernando Garrido Falla, *Comentarios a la Constitución*, 3ra edición, Civitas, Madrid, 2001, at 1505.

[169] 1947 Constitution of Italy, Article 10(1) reads: *Italy's legal system conforms to the generally recognised principles of international law.*

[170] See Ballin E. H., in Prakke, L. and Kortmann C. (ed), *op. cit.*, at 493.

[171] See Keller, H. and Stone Sweet, A., "Assessing the Impact of the ECHR on National Legal Systems", *Faculty Scholarship Series*, Paper 88, (2008). Available at *http://digitalcommons.law.yale.edu/fss_papers/88*

[172] See UNIDROIT "Committee Of Governmental Experts for the Preparation of a Draft Convention on Harmonised Substantive Rules Regarding Intermediated Securities", *Report of the Ad hoc Working Group on Legislative Techniques for the Implementation of the Preliminary Draft Convention on Harmonised Substantive Rules Regarding Intermediated Securities*, UNIDROIT (2006), Study LXXVIII – Doc. 26, Rome, 6/14 March 2006.

entry into legal force[173] and will be recognised if they are part of a treaty that Russia has with a particular country or it's sanctioned by Federal Law.[174] A foreign judgement cannot be reviewed as to its substance.[175] Russian courts can also recognise foreign judgments[176] based on the principle of reciprocity.[177] The court has the power to determine whether there is any reason for non-recognition or enforcement.[178]

In Algeria, the Constitution empowers the President to appoint Ambassadors and Envoys upon the proposal of the Minister of Foreign Affairs. The President is also empowered to sign and, after consultation with the National Assembly, ratify and implement treaties, conventions and international agreements;[179] Algeria's Constitution is essentially monist for it automatically incorporates treaties within its domestic legislation and grants properly ratified treaties a superior status to statutory provisions.[180] However, their rank is lower than that of constitutional norms.[181]

The Cameroonian Constitution is one of the few world constitutions bold enough to incorporate three key human rights instruments. It firmly states in its preamble: "We, the people of Cameroon… affirm our attachment

---

[173] See Maxim Kulkov, *The Moscow Times*, 13th Mar. 2007 in Lamm, C.B. and Others, "Enforcement of Foreign Arbitral Awards in Russia", *American College of Trial Lawyers*. Available at:
http://www.actl.com/AM/Template.cfm?Section=
Home&Template=/CM/ContentDisplay.cfm&ContentID=5001

[174] *Arbitrazh Procedural Code* (APC), Article 241.

[175] *Ibid.,* Article 243(4).

[176] Examples of human rights judgments for the ECHR include the case of *Burdov v. Russia* (No. 2). The case concerns Russia's failure to honour judgment debts to applicants who had suffered from radioactive emissions in the wake of the Chernobyl disaster. See ECHR (2009), App. No. 33509/04, *Burdov v. Russia,* No. 2.

[177] This was held in the case of *Rentpool B.V. v. OOO 'Podjemniye Technologii'* 7th December, 2009, supported by the *Supreme Arbitrazh Court RF* (No VAS-13688/09). In this case, a judgement issued by a Dutch district court was recognized and enforced on the basis of reciprocity and comity. The court decided to uphold these generally recognized principles of international law despite the fact that Russia has no treaty on reciprocal recognition of judgments with the Netherlands.

[178] *Arbitrazh Procedural Code*, Article 244.

[179] *Constitution of Algeria,* Article 77.

[180] *Ibid,* Article 132.

[181] *Ibid,* Article 165 and 168.

to the fundamental freedoms enshrined in the Universal Declaration of Human Rights, the Charter of the United Nations and The African Charter on Human and Peoples' Rights, and all duly ratified international conventions relating thereto…" In fact these three Conventions expressly mentioned are usually published together with the national constitution. The Constitution of Cameroon also contains a chapter on treaties and international agreements, which establishes the presidential limits to ratification of certain treaties,[182] the need to amend the constitution before ratifying an unconstitutional treaty[183] and the superior rank ratified treaties shall have over national legislation.[184] It is a modern and well-conceived monist constitution. However, as happens in many African states, reality does not follow the word and most of these great aspirations remain, for the time being, on paper.

The Constitution of Equatorial Guinea[185] grants the President the exercise of the foreign affairs power as established by article 39.[186] The President signs and ratifies treaties except peace and trade treaties and those affecting national sovereignty and territorial integrity, the ratification of which is reserved to the National Assembly.[187] The Constitution also creates a Constitutional Council which, among other functions, shall look

---

[182] *Ibid.*

[183] *Constitution of Cameroon,* Article 44.

[184] *Ibid,* Article 45.

[185] See *www.cia.gov/library/publications/the-world-factbook.* On October 12, 1968, the territory became the independent republic of Equatorial Guinea, with Francisco Macías Nguema as president. In 1972 Macías Nguema appointed himself president for life. In 1979 Macías Nguema was overthrown in a military coup, tried for treason, and executed. Lieutenant Colonel Teodoro Obiang Nguema Mbasogo, Macias nephew and the coup leader, became president. In 1982 a new constitution was enacted under which Equatorial Guinea was a single-party State, and in 1991 a new multiparty constitution was approved by public referendum. Under the 1991 constitution, the voters elect a president to a seven-year term with no term limits. On 29th November 2009, Teodoro Obiang Nguema was re-elected president by 95.8% of the voters. His closest contender, Placido Mico, obtained 3.6%. Elections have always been marred by widespread fraud. It is sad to note that Teodoro Obiang Nguema Mbasogo, a man with an extremely controversial record in human rights violations, is the current Chairman of the African Union, having been elected to that position in January 2011. Equatorial Guinea has a GDP of USD 37,500. It is number 28 in the world (between Ireland and Sweden). The next African country on the list is Gabon which ranks no. 81.

[186] *Constitution of Equatorial Guinea*, Article 39.

[187] *Ibid*, Article 64.

into the non-conformity of international treaties as provided by the Constitution.[188]

In Madagascar, the Constitution establishes the competencies in matters of diplomacy and treaties in simple and clear terms. The foreign affairs power is vested in the President. He negotiates and ratifies treaties and should be informed of any process of treaty negotiation not leading to ratification.[189] In Madagascar treaties rank below the Constitution but above statutory law. However, certain treaties must be submitted by the President to the Constitutional Court before ratification. Should a treaty require constitutional amendments, such changes need to be effected before ratification.[190]

South Africa's system is peculiar and unique in many ways. While it encourages interpretation according to international law it also places restrictions and regulations on treaty-making and states clearly that the constitution is the supreme law of the land and nothing may contradict it. The South African system is founded on a foreign affairs power bestowed upon the executive with the supervision of a National Assembly and the National Council of Provinces, which must approve binding treaties, except of a technical, administrative or executive nature, or an agreement which does not require either ratification or accession. It also stipulates that international agreements will become domestic law when they are enacted by national legislation, although self-executing provisions of an agreement that has been approved by Parliament is automatically law in the Republic unless it is inconsistent with the Constitution or an Act of Parliament. Regarding customary international law, it is considered law in the Republic unless it is inconsistent with the Constitution or an Act of Parliament.[191] Therefore, the system seems hybrid, which allows for dualism when treaties must be passed in statutory form for domestication, and it is monist for self-executing provisions which do not require statute.[192] It is also monist when it comes to the application of international law principles by national courts.[193] Furthermore, it

[188] *Ibid*, Article 94.
[189] *Constitution of Madagascar*, Article 56.
[190] *Constitution of Madagascar*, the Constitution's article 82 imposes limitations *rationae materiae*.
[191] See *Constitution of South Africa*, Article 231.
[192] *Ibid*.
[193] *Ibid*, Article 232.

encourages courts to favour international law dictates when interpreting law.[194]

The Ugandan Constitution regulates international relations in Sections 122, 123 and 124. Although the constitution does not directly limit the President's powers in treaty-making, it vests in Parliament the task of making laws to govern the ratification of treaties and international agreements. In this manner treaty-making regulations become flexible and changeable according to the needs of the country. In fact, there has been innovative jurisprudence in matters relating to automatic domestication of international agreements through the 'spirit of the law' as was the case in *Uganda v. Matovu* (2002).[195]

The 2010 Constitution of Kenya is openly monist but failed to contain instructions on signature and ratification of treaties.[196] It actually neglects to define the power to ratify, which we must say, is a rather grave omission for a monist constitution. And once this abeyance is in place, the gap must be filled through the principle of executive residual functions. Unless the omission is redressed through the enactment of a ratification statute presidential ratification will imply the legislating of norms of higher domestic rank with no checks and balances. Those norms actually have the power to abrogate any internal legislation that contradicts them as was proven by the case of *Zipporah W. Mathara*.[197] An appropriate

---

[194] *Ibid*, Article 233.

[195] In the case of *Uganda v. Matovu*, High Court of Uganda at Kampala, Oct. 21, 2002, the defendant Peter Matovu was indicted on charges of defilement. The common law in Uganda states that when considering a sexual offenses trial, the victim must be proven as truthful before the court will base a conviction on her testimony alone. In *Uganda v. Matovu*, Judge E. S. Lugayizi cited a case from 1997 which espoused the traditional reason behind this rule: '*...for all sorts of reasons and sometimes for no reason at all, women and girls tell a false story which is very easy to fabricate but extremely difficult to refute...*' However, Judge Lugayizi recognized that this traditional rule was in conflict with Uganda's legal obligations under CEDAW and held that the discriminatory rule was unconstitutional and therefore null and void. [See *Legal Tools for the Establishment of Gender Equality through International Law, www.globaljusticecenter.net*]

[196] In Kenya, legislative approval of a treaty is not required at any instance, except as provided for by article 71 of the 2010 Constitution of Kenya regarding agreements dealing with natural resources.

[197] *Zipporah Wambui Mathara, Bankruptcy Cause* (19 of 2010), in the matter of Bankruptcy Act Chapter 53 of the Laws of Kenya (2010) eKLR (24th September 2010) where Justice Koome asserted that *'by virtue of the provisions of Section*

process of ratification with relevant checks and balances must be put in place. The omission is grave indeed and it makes Kenya's Constitution the first one to become monist, giving treaties supremacy over domestic legislation with no instructions on ratification.

The United Kingdom, by entering into treaties, undertakes the obligation of enacting the necessary laws, if there were none, to allow the internal application of a treaty.[198] Although the conduct of foreign affairs is the Crown's prerogative, the experience has developed a custom whereby the Crown seeks legislation prior ratification of certain kinds of treaties. This avoids embarrassment to the Executive, for example that the Crown ratifies a treaty and Parliament rejects to pass a statute, and also guarantees the internal execution of treaties as may be necessary.[199] McNair summarises these treaties in respect of which legislation is needed as: Treaties creating a direct or a contingent financial obligation; treaties that involve changes in or additions to the law; and treaties that affect the acquisition or cession of territory.[200] The rationale behind these limitations is founded on necessary checks and balances that have imposed constitutional and democratic limitations on royal prerogatives.[201]In British constitutional practice acts of State meant unchallengeable acts, i.e. "essentially an act of sovereign power, and hence cannot be challenged, controlled, or interfered with by municipal courts" (*Salaman v. Secretary of State for India*). Moreover, acts of State seem to have been used by the Crown as a shield in actions brought by private individuals, such as cases of aliens outside British territory (*Buron v. Denman*); in cases of enemy aliens within British territory (*R v. Bottrill, ex p. Kuechenmeister*); and in

---

2(6) of the Constitution of Kenya 2010, International Treaties, and Conventions that Kenya has ratified, are imported as part of the sources of the Kenyan Law. Thus the provision of Article 11 of the International Covenant on Civil and Political Rights which Kenya ratified on 1st May 1972 is part of Kenyan law…'

[198] A good number of examples are given by Walker, D., *The Scottish Legal System*, 6th Ed., W. Green/Sweet & Maxwell, Edinburgh, 1992, at 563.

[199] If there is legislation already in force, there is no need for a new one.

[200] See McNair, *op. cit.,* at 83ff. For example the *Geneva Convention* of 1906, in respect of Articles 23, 27 and 28 to which Great Britain had to make a reservation because legislation was needed (and eventually passed, the Geneva Convention Act, 1911), to prevent the improper use of the name or emblem of the 'Geneva Cross' or 'Red Cross'.

[201] On the concept of royal prerogatives see generally Blackstone, Sir W., *Commentaries on the Laws of England*, Clarendon Press, Oxford, 1765. Reprinted by Dawsons of Pall Mall, London, 1966, III.

cases of acts done by the Crown in British protectorates with reference to the local inhabitants.[202]

Conclusion

Two of the four elements of the foreign affairs power, i.e. treaty-making and diplomacy, are essential triggers of international relations among States and of structures of judicial nature, which are also known as international, regional or sub-regional courts and tribunals.

We have said that multilateral diplomacy deals with regional or global issues and is used with a plurality of States through an international organization or conferences. These international organizations are vested with relative treaty-making powers that extend as far as the organisation's constitutive instrument may allow.

As it is widely accepted in international law theory and jurisprudence, treaty-making capacity is built upon an assumption of legal or juristic personality that allows the international organisation in question to present itself at par with States. Thus, the juristic or legal personality of an International Organization, therefore, is not a fiction nor is it created by any external power. It exists where a collectivity has a social value by virtue of pursuing an interest worthy of legal protection.

Whereas the legal personality of a State is absolute, in the sense that it brings all the attributes and prerogatives proper to State treaty-making, the legal personality of international organisations is relative, in the sense that it exists for specific purposes and within specific functions, as it may be stipulated by its constitutive instrument.[203]The International Organization is treated in the eyes of the law as a legal person because it is the legal expression of a larger reality that is the State and, ultimately, the people, by whom it is created, for whom it exists and without which it cannot subsist.

---

[202] Charles II (1661), *Act declaring the sole Right of the Militia to be in King and for the present ordering & disposing the same*. Another example is found in the exclusive power of the Crown to mobilise armed forces: *The sole supreme government, command and disposition of the Militia and all forces by sea and land and by all forts and places of strength is and by the laws of England ever was the undoubted right of his Majesty and his royal predecessors.*

[203] See Boczek, B.A., *International law: A dictionary*, Scarecrow Press, Lanham, 2005, at 73.

Furthermore, when the aim of the organisation is to dispense justice, it follows that its judicial decisions should have the strength of municipal decisions, and they must be executed in a similar fashion. From this perspective, the power granted to an international organisation must be perceived as an internationally devolved power whereby a specific political society directly or indirectly[204] allows the State to commit itself to constitute or access an international body whose decisions, directions and/or recommendations will be binding on the State and/or other subjects of international law to whom it may be directed and as may be necessary to achieve the common good.[205]

---

[204] Indirectly by exercising the electoral power of choosing representatives; directly by referendum on prior to ratification of specific treaties as was the case, for example, in Costa Rica, (2007) the first referendum held in Costa Rica was for the approval of the free trade agreement with Central America and the Dominican Republic. It was approved by a minimum number of votes (49.030 votes). Results were 51.62% voted in favour and 48.38% against it. It is currently the only FTA in the world that has been approved on a referendum. Other examples are: Denmark, where referendums are held for the approval of new European Union treaties; Ireland, where the constitution so requires; France, where article 88-5(1) establishes that: "Any government bill authorizing the ratification of a treaty pertaining to the accession of a State to the European Union is submitted to referendum by the President of the Republic." United Kingdom, where the only referendum to be put to the entire UK electorate was the United Kingdom European Communities Membership referendum in 1975. It was held two years after British accession to the European Economic Community to gauge support for continued membership. Ukraine (2006), when the Central Electoral Committee of Ukraine (CVK) recognized as valid more than 3 million voters' signatures which were collected in the call for the Referendum on Ukraine joining NATO and for the Referendum on joining Common Economic Space.

[205] After World War II, there was an increased interest in IGOs. This is despite the proponents of realism pointing out the failures of the League to achieve its purposes. David Mitrany's functionalist theory also contributed to the formation of IGOs. He argued that States could either choose to isolate themselves under the guise of sovereignty or surrender some of their 'sovereignty' for purposes of development. Advancements in technology and the desire to promote the general welfare were only achievable through interstate cooperation that required IGOs. His theory was further supported by the Neofunctionalism theory. The Neofunctionalism theory was to the effect that successful collaboration in one area increases the benefits of cooperation in related areas. Such collaboration generates joint pressure from domestic interest groups and international officials to extend the realm of cooperation. [See Haas, 1964; Lindberg and Scheingold 1971; Nye, 1971; Groom and Taylor, 1975]. There are further contemporary theories on the concept of IGOs in relation to their sovereignty. An example of such a theory is the

The mushrooming of international institutions in general, and specifically of supranational courts, represents another stage in the process of maturation of international law, where traditional concepts need to be reworked and adapted to the new circumstances of a more globalized and flexible scenario.[206]

The powers granted to an international organisation are more extensive and complex than simple delegated powers may suggest. It seems to fall into the realm of *devolved powers*[207] whereby a State entrusts the exercise and care of certain functions to a distinct 'legal person', which has been

---

rationalist regime theory. This theory is by Robert Keohane's, in his 1984 book, *After Hegemony*. He argues that world politics is characterized by institutional deficiencies inhibiting mutually advantageous cooperation [Keohane, R. (1984), at 85] Therefore, IGOs will serve to fill in these gaps to facilitate cooperation among States on a decentralized basis. Moreover, clustering common issues into an institution would lead to interaction among States. This continued interaction reduced the need to cheat and enhanced the value of reputation. This would finally lead to the creation of decentralized enforcement founded on the principle of reciprocity [Keohane, R. (1984), at 145]. Hence, it is in the interest of States to form IGOs. This is despite concerns over the issue of sovereignty. States would find it more efficient to operate within IGOs as compared to other modes of international cooperation e.g. countless bilateral agreements [Aggarwal, 1985]. In conclusion, IGOs are essential in today's world, where the process of globalization has pushed cultures towards the outside and where the traditional concept of State no longer satisfies the widening needs of the *political society*.

206 Iles, A., "Recent Developments", *Harvard International Law Journal*, vol. 36, (1995) at 219. Alistair Iles explains this process of maturation in terms of new environmental trends applied to desertification.

207 Devolution of power is a political phenomenon defined as "the practice in which the authority to make decisions in some sphere of public policy is delegated by law to sub-national territorial assemblies (e.g., a local authority). Devolution entails transferring governmental or political authority – with the powers of the constituent units determined by legislation rather than by the Constitution." [CKRC, Constitution of Kenya Review Commission (2005) Final Report, Final Draft, Approved for Issue at 95th Plenary Meeting of the Constitution of Kenya Commission Held on 10th February 2005 pp. 223, 224.] Devolution has therefore been linked with democratization, to the extent that it may be used to create a situation where government is 'of the people, by the people and for the people'. Warioba observes that international courts do not have power of enforcement because there is no world executive similar to national governments." [Warioba, J.S., Frowein, J.A., Wolfrum, R.(eds.) "Monitoring Compliance with and Enforcement of Binding Decisions of International Courts" in the *Max Planck Yearbook of United Nations Law*, vol. 5, Kluwer International, The Netherlands, 2001, at 49.]

created and endowed of certain characteristics and functions that make it susceptible of possessing a certain degree of autonomy as its nature may require. In this regard, we identify with Malanczuk, *mutatis mutandis*, the following characteristics of International Organizations that are subjects of international law: the organ has the authority of adopting binding acts; the organization's secretariat is composed of persons who are not representatives of a State; the organ's decisions have effects on individuals and corporations; the Constituent treaty forms a new legal order; and, finally, the validity of the organ's decisions and the parties compliance are subject to judicial review by independent judicial bodies.[208]

Therefore, certain international organisations enjoy certain attributes and powers that are bound to make an impact on the domestic legal scenario and may possibly have a direct effect on the citizenry. The strength of that impact is determined primarily by the constitutional processes established for ratification, accession or acceptance of a treaty and its domestication process. Thus, the impact and strength of an international organization is measured by the nature of its mission and objectives, which are conceptualized, designed and executed in concordance with constitutional law of the State parties.

As it has been pointed out, ratification or accession to a treaty is usually regulated by Constitutional law, which distributes the powers and functions within the State and puts in place the necessary checks and balances to guarantee identification between, among others, peoples and policies. Thus, from a domestic point of view, the creation of international organizations and the authority bestowed on them are primarily the result of the exercise of certain powers and functions constitutionally given to specific State offices.

The fulfilment or the aim of a treaty that has been negotiated, signed and ratified or accessed may have certain effects at the national level. These treaties need to be incorporated into the domestic forum. This incorporation process may be through a monist or dualist system and it is governed by Constitutional law and practice. Indeed, an inappropriate or poorly designed constitutional system for domestication and enforcement of international law can frustrate and has actually frustrated the enforcement of many a treaty.

---

[208] See Malanczuk, P., *Akehurst's Modern Introduction to International Law*, 7th Edition, Routledge ed., London, 1997, at 96.

In the next chapter, we will analyse in depth the African System of Human Rights, its genesis and history, its virtues and weaknesses. We will focus on the African Court on Human and Peoples' Rights and see the necessary steps Africa should take to enhance the enforcement of this Court's decisions.

CHAPTER THREE

THE CREATION OF INTERNATIONAL GOVERNMENTAL INSTITUTIONS: THE AFRICAN HUMAN RIGHTS SYSTEM

The power that allows the State to create an international organization may be used for constituting organs of judicial nature. Judicial decisions from such bodies will not, in principle, follow the same domestication process as foreign judgments, for they do not come from a foreign court but from a supranational court. In this regard, international decisions will follow the process as may be specified in the constitutive instruments creating them. This process is legally guided by the regulation of the foreign affairs power at the national level, which has a two-fold impact on the formation of international governmental institutions. On the one hand, it gives the structures of the State clear instructions and delineation of functions that allow them to participate in the creation of international bodies and systems and bestow them with specific powers. On the other, decisions and recommendations from those international bodies find their application at the municipal level through domestication processes which are usually designed at the constitutional level.

Having analysed the foreign affairs power and its relevant elements from a national constitutional perspective we now need to look into the African Human Rights System: history, structures, mechanisms and organs.

Considerations on Human Rights in Africa

Society tends to generalise peoples' habits, customs and ways of being. This trend in Africa has somewhat often placed all black people under one heading (the Black Continent), one type of societal structure (Tribe), one form of conflict resolution (Violence) and one common legal judgment (Impunity). While all these exist in one way or another and they may be widespread, the African reality is drastically varied. Scientific studies point at greater racial diversity within Africa than between Africa and other Continents.[1] The forms of societal organization are also extremely diverse, and so are cultural practices, initiation rituals, language, religion, etc. For example, among the Turkana, the Elders are the decision makers, judges and religious leaders of the community. They decide when and where to graze the cattle, to emigrate to newer pastures, to attack and raid neighbouring communities; they are the contact between local government and the people. Women are not involved in decision making at community level. Women are practically slaves and a man may marry many women to increase wealth and prestige. Due to constant raids a Turkana man becomes a hero when he kills an enemy. Revenge is the order of the day. To the north of Turkana land, we find the Daasanach, or Merile. The Daasanach youth must kill an enemy (Turkana) as part of their initiation rituals and cut off the deceased's genitals as the ritual demands. He then cuts a scar on his body and the more scars he has the more prestige he acquires and his status is raised. In this way they prove their manhood and are accepted as warriors, who will defend their tribe from their enemies.

Less than one hundred kilometres from the Turkana border the Kalenjins, Luhyas, Luos, Kisiis and Tesos have opposing practices, education system and levels of development. For some of them, the Turkana or Daasanach practices sound absolutely foreign or at least superseded in time. Further south, in Nairobi, an ordinary boy will be travelling by car to school, watching South American soap operas on his favourite television channel and shopping for the latest video game at a

---

[1] See Jorde, L.B. and Wooding, S.P., "Genetic Variation, Classification and Race", in *Nature Genetics*, Vol. 36, (2004) (Published online), pp. 28-33. In this publication Jorde and Wooding consider an apportionment of Old World populations into three continents (Africa, Asia and Europe), a grouping that corresponds to a common view of three of the 'major races'. They conclude that approximately 85–90% of genetic variation is found within these continental groups, and only an additional 10–15% of variation is found between them. In other words, 90% of total genetic variation would be found in a collection of individuals from a single continent, and only 10% more variation would be found if the collection consisted of Europeans, Asians and Africans. Considering that Africa was the cradle of humanity, modern genetic studies, published by Cavalli-Sforza, Menozzi and Piazza, "The History and Geography of Human Genes", Princeton University Press, Princeton, 1994, divides humanity into four major ethnic regions, African (Khoisan), Caucasoids (Basque), Mongoloids (American Indian) and Australians (Aborigine). Throughout the study the authors argue that fossil evidence confirms the African origin of humanity. Africans have the greatest genetic distance from the rest of humanity, showing that on the human family tree, the split from the Africans occurred before the other branches.

luxurious mall. He will have undergone initiation in a modern hospital. Thus, when we speak of Africa we are facing different cultures and realities which may have only a few characteristics as common denominator. Perhaps they may be grouped together under a colonization process which in some instances deprived them of their freedom, land and resources for decades; or under a type of slavery that displaced thousands of Africans into the unknown.

Certainly, it would be dishonest to disregard European presence in 20th century Africa as the ignition point of African development. Nonetheless, the way the African State was constituted, in practical disregard for the reality on the ground, and giving more importance to the economic or political gains of the colonizing power, has caused a disjointed growth in the African system, where social rivalry between ethnic groups is largely present within the same State.

Consequently, the foundation of an African Union and the elaboration of a common African Human Rights System has been a rare and magnanimous but also risky feat. This could explain why African Human Rights instruments often tend to be general, ambiguous, full of claw-back clauses, and to a certain point uncommitted. There are some clear desires and common goals: the rejection of colonization, foreign exploitation, discrimination against the African. There are also aspirations such as the right to be like the rest of the world, particularly like the European colonizers (developed, rich and powerful). On the other hand, there is little internal commitment between government and governed, between the State and the person. This is mostly due to a disjointed and fictional 'body politic' or political society, from which the African State was abnormally born. The African State seems to have been superimposed on different African realities and peoples, legalising oppressing structures and systems of institutionalised human rights abuses and discrimination. Thus, the so-called African State seems to have been founded on foreign categories and this weakness has played a role in the poor protection of and respect for human rights which, at the same time, are also viewed by some African leaders as part and parcel of that foreign category.

The universality of human rights is construed upon the person's humanity, which makes him or her the owner of a dignity and carrier of a unique self-value. This dignity is not granted by the State; it is not a legal or mental category. It is a reality according to nature, regardless of race, sex, religion, origin, level of education or cultural practices.

Some modern scholars refute the universality of human rights and tend to view the concept as a Western imposition.[2] They debate on the existence of human rights in pre-colonial Africa. According to Howard, African proponents of human rights confuse human duties with human rights. Howard says, "the African concept of human rights is actually a concept of human duties, of what defines 'the inner' (moral) nature and worth of the human person and his or her proper (political) relations within society."[3] Others favour universality based on the general acceptance of instruments for the promotion and protection of human rights, such as the Universal Declaration of Human Rights[4] and its similarly conceived regional versions.

Nonetheless, both groups of scholars seem to have mistakenly confused Human Rights legislation and enforcement with the anthropological reality of the person. Anthropology places the person in the realm of freedom, and it is precisely the power of choice, whether potential or actual, that elevates the person above all other beings, thus making him or her subject

---

[2] See generally Donnely, J. and Howard, R., in Vincent Orlu, *The African Human Rights System*, Martinus Nijhoff, The Hague, 2001, at 9-13. Howard is also based on the mistaken view of Hegel, who placed Africa outside history and civilization.

[3] See Howard, R., "Evaluating Human Rights in Africa: Some Problems of Implicit Comparisons", *Human Rights Quarterly*, vol. 6, (1984) at 176. See also Nmehielle, V. O, *The African Human Rights System: Its Law, Practice and Institutions*, Martinus Nijhoff Publishers, The Hague, 2001, at 9. Some authors such as Richard Amoako Baah, *Human Rights in Africa: The Conflict of Implementation*, University Press of America, 2000. And in many ways Paul J. Magnarella, "Assessing the Concept of Human Rights in Africa" available at *http://www.du.edu/korbel/hrhw/volumes/2001/1-2/baah-magnarella.pdf* also agrees with Baah. Baah argues that human rights, as presented by the Universal Declaration of Human Rights focusing on the individual, are a Western concept. However, it is our view that this is a misunderstanding. When examined deeply and carefully the expert will observe that in African thought the group rights or peoples' rights were aimed at precisely protecting the person who would not survive on his or her own. This natural desire of self-preservation led the community to assert certain community customs and rights so as to guarantee survival. For example, the custom of widow inheritance and the right to inherit a next-of-kin wife aimed at securing protection and livelihood for the widow. With the advent of urban forms of life many of these institutions and survival customs were either corrupted or superseded.

[4] See *http://www.unac.org/rights/question.html*.The Declaration was ratified through a proclamation by the General Assembly on 10th December, 1948 with a count of 48 votes to none with only 8 abstentions. This was considered a triumph as the vote unified very diverse, even conflicting political regimes.

of rights and their corresponding duties. Consequently, legislation must be put in place in order to safeguard those inherent and inalienable rights that we call human, for they are proper and exclusive to the person.[5]

Therefore, to think of societies where human rights did not exist amounts to thinking of societies without humans. Yet, it is possible to accurately refer to a society without human rights legislation, protection or respect.[6]

Human Rights legislation, instruments, treaties and bodies are the result of a historical process deeply attached to democracy; to the awareness of the equality between the authority and the subject and between communities themselves. In fact, Human Rights legislation is, somehow, the outcome of accountability, and seems to defeat the Rousseaunian idea on the existence of an absolute sovereignty.[7] It is a process that is intrinsically related to the historical development of diplomacy.

Historical Appraisal of the African Human Rights System

By the 18th century diplomacy had generated a sizeable literature, written by its practitioners. One of the earliest, the Dutch diplomat Abraham de Wicquefort, in 1679 termed an envoy as "an honourable spy" and "a messenger of peace," who should be charming, silent, and indirect, though deceit was counterproductive.[8] The French diplomat François de Callières agreed in 1716, adding that a diplomat should conduct the business of his master and discover the business of others; affability and

---

[5] See Sellés Dauder, J. F., *Antropología para Inconformes*, Ediciones Rialp, Madrid, 2006, at 13. Juan Fernando Sellés argues that anthropology must be focused on the person as a transcendental being, a person who transcends culture, body, society.

[6] And this may be the case in certain existing societies even today as we have mentioned above when referring to certain Daasanach practices.

[7] See Rousseau, J.J., *The Social Contract*, Book III, chapter IV, at 160. In fact, Rousseau wrote that "If there were a nation of gods, it would be governed democratically. So perfect a government is unsuited to men." cited by Maritain, J., "The Concept of Sovereignty", *In Defense of Sovereignty*, J.W. Stankiewicz (ed), Oxford University Press, New York, 1969, at 57.

[8] Wicquefort, *L'Ambassadeur et ses Fonctions*, Daniel Steucker Edition, Cologne, 1690, at 6. Available at:
http://books.google.co.ke/books?id=Vls_AAAAcAAJ&printsec=frontcover&dq=Wicquefort+L'Ambassadeur+et+ses+Fonctions&hl=en&ei=y0FYTfKfKMTXrQfQy7WMBw&sa=X&oi=book_result&ct=result&resnum=1&ved=0CCgQ6AEwAA#v=onepage&q=h

good looks helped. He stressed that diplomacy was a profession which needed trained personnel.[9] In 1737 another French diplomat, Antoine Pecquet, was more idealistic, terming the profession a sacred calling requiring discretion, patience, accurate reporting, and absolute honesty.[10]

In the late 18th century and the 19th century the world order changed. In Europe power shifted from royal courts to cabinets. Kings disappeared or became largely ceremonial, even at international meetings, to be replaced by ministers. Foreign policy too became a matter of increasingly democratised politics. The face of Africa also changed forever. The process of industrialization the world lived through the second half of the 19th century had a deep impact on the formation of new African States.

European powers mobilized themselves in search of raw materials and areas of influence to increase their productivity. This resulted in the so-called 'scramble' for Africa.[11] European powers occupied and shared the continent. Boundaries were arbitrarily drawn following patterns mostly set by European explorers.[12] In most cases these borders disregarded the human geography and the interests of the local populations.

Thus, the modern African State was born as a fiction imposed from above. It was mostly founded on economic interests and its aim was to increase the colonizer's wealth and the exploitation of the natural riches of the colonized. This fiction-State forced the common life of radically diverse communities that had historically rivalled each other. It created a unique political structure that did not fit within the 'body politic' or political society and the desires of its peoples.

---

[9] Heatley, *op. cit.,* at 217.
[10] *Ibid.*
[11] See generally Pakenham, T., *The Scramble for Africa: White Man's Conquest of the Dark Continent from 1876 to 1912*, Random House Publishing Group, New York, 1991, 784 pp.
[12] See Jeal, T., *Stanley: The Impossible Life of Africa's Greatest Explorer*, Yale University Press, New Haven, 2007, at 246 ff. For example the borders between the Democratic Republic of Congo and Congo-Brazzaville were settled between France and Belgium following the competing expeditions and subsequent occupations of Henry M. Stanley (working for King Leopold II of Belgium) and Count Pierre Savorgnan de Brazza, a French naval officer who explored the upper Congo river. The arrival of these two men at both sides of the Congo River and their setting of camps determined the future border between the two African nations.

Unquestionably, the process also brought a wealth of education, faith and development that was until then foreign to the African context and life, and for which most Africans are tremendously grateful. This awakened in the African mind self-consciousness, self-knowledge, faith in themselves and their capacity, and desires for a free, fair and just society beyond tribal lines.

In the meantime, the horror of the World Wars had shaken Europe to the core. The Great Wars brought powers together to the negotiating table. Politics, law and economics took a dramatic shift. The face of colonial Africa was also re-shaped based on European winners and losers.

The great wars' devastation and the awareness of possessing the actual capacity to destroy each other in future, along with the expectations of market growth, drew European potencies into greater and wider deals. It renewed the belief that international multilateral bodies could serve as vehicles for negotiation and exchange. It also impacted on them the firm belief that it was necessary to make joint declarations of rights belonging to every human being, and it was a duty imposed upon every State to respect them. In a way, we could argue that the horrors humanity went through in the 20th century made the international community realise that the State should not be sovereign after all; it should be subjected to certain check and balances.

This awareness, coupled with the fact that most victims were the result of States' abuse of power, led the United Nations Charter to assert as one of its purposes the "respect for human rights and for fundamental freedoms for all without distinction as to race, sex, language, or religion."[13] Thus, the UN Charter actually stresses the principle of individual human rights, taking a significant step toward what has developed into a personalized modern Human Rights international system. This step, taken in order to guarantee peace, international security and justice, seems to have caused a gradual and sustained change in understanding the role played by sovereignty in respect to human rights' international legislation.[14]

[13] See the *United Nations Charter*, Article 1.3.

[14] This step actually opened certain checkpoints that have led to measures such as what is nowadays called humanitarian intervention as was seen in Panama and Grenada. However, this concept needs revision for it has been abused and politicized.

1. The Growth of Human Rights Awareness in Africa

We can divide Africa's modern human rights history into five more or less defined stages.[15] The first covers from 1860s to 1885 when the great explorations and incursions into Africa were driven by missionary activity and a certain geographic and commercial curiosity.[16]

The second covers from 1885,[17] when most colonies were established after the Berlin Conference until roughly the 1960s when African independence's awakening gathers momentum. Desmond T. Orjiako[18] asserts that according to the Organisation of African Unity (OAU) archives, the oldest remarkable attempt at Pan-African gathering of intellectuals was in Manchester, United Kingdom in 1900. It was presided over by Menelik II, uncle of Ethiopia's Emperor Haile Selassie I. It was in an effort to create freedom, equality and justice for African colonial subjects. Some years later, on 1st August 1904, the Pan-Africanist Leader Marcus Garvey was said to have convened another remarkable event that brought together scattered African Communities worldwide. The African Union records also point at the contributions of other prominent black nationalists, such as Sylvester Williams and George Padmore both from Trinidad, and the role of William Bourghart Dubois and Langston Hughes from the United States. By 1920, every square mile of the African

---

[15] Certainly, the stages may vary depending on regional patterns.

[16] See generally Jeal, T., *Stanley: The Impossible Life of Africa's Greatest Explorer*, Yale University Press, New Haven, 2007.

[17] See de Blij, H.J. and Muller, P.O., *Geography: Realms, Regions, and Concepts*. John Wiley & Sons, Inc., 1997, at 340.Available at *http://geography.about.com/cs/politicalgeog/ a/berlinconferenc.htm*. After the 1884-1885 Berlin Conference, Great Britain desired a Cape-to-Cairo collection of colonies and almost succeeded through their control of Egypt, Sudan (Anglo-Egyptian Sudan), Uganda, Kenya (British East Africa), South Africa, and Zambia, Zimbabwe (Rhodesia), and Botswana. The British also controlled Nigeria and Ghana (Gold Coast). France took much of western Africa, from Mauritania to Chad (French West Africa) and Gabon and the Republic of Congo (French Equatorial Africa). Belgium and King Leopold II controlled the Democratic Republic of Congo (Belgian Congo). Portugal took Mozambique in the east and Angola in the west. Italy's holdings were Somalia (Italian Somaliland) and a portion of Ethiopia. Germany took Namibia (German Southwest Africa), Tanzania (German East Africa), Rwanda, Burundi and Cameroon. Spain claimed the smallest territories- Equatorial Guinea (Rio Muni), Spanish Sahara and part of Morocco.

[18] Orjiako, D. T., "The African Union – Our Common Home". *A Keynote Address delivered at North-eastern University, Boston*, Massachusetts, 24thMarch, 2005.

Continent had been occupied or was under a protectorate of the European colonial powers, with the exception of Ethiopia, and the then Union of South Africa.

In 1948 the United Nations General Assembly adopted the Universal Declaration of Human Rights, the first comprehensive instrument among nations regarding specific personal rights and freedoms of all human beings, from all places, at all times. This document would be later followed by an array of regional declarations and treaties that gave birth to commissions and courts charged with the duty to promote, foster, protect and enforce human rights throughout the world.[19] The need for the creation of regional instruments in Africa took time to settle. Indeed, in the 40s and 50s Africa was not in a position to play human rights rhetoric.

The third period embraces 1960 and extends until 1975. This period is identified with the great independence expectations.

The fourth period includes from 1975 to 1995, which some authors have called the great disillusionment.[20] This period is characterized by the permanence in power of independence leaders and the subsequent degeneration of government structures along with corruption, repression and, in some instances, human rights abominations.[21]

---

[19] For example, the mushrooming of international inter-governmental organizations than in some way or another touch on human rights issue, include (non-exhaustive enumeration): ECOWAS (1975), Organization for the Prohibiting of Chemical Weapons (1997), Association of Southeast Asian Nations (ASEAN), Union of South American Nations-2008, Association of Caribbean States (ACS)-1994, Central American Parliament-1991, Southern African Development Community (SADC)-1980, Intergovernmental Authority on Development (IGAD)-1986, Arab Maghreb Union-1989, Indian Ocean Commission (IOC)-1984, Asia-Pacific Economic Cooperation (APEC)-1989, Pacific Islands Forum-2000, UN centre for human settlements (Habitat)-1978, UN development program (UNDP)-1965, UN environment program (UNEP)-1972, UN international research and training institute for the advancement of women (INSTRAW)-1979, Economic and Social Commission for Western Asia (ESCWA)-1973, etc.

[20] For example, Ahmed and Appiagyei-Atua, "Human Rights in Africa – A New Perspective on Linking the Past to the Present", *McGill Law Journal*, vol 41, (1995-1996), at 822.

[21] See *infra* note no. 31. Idi Amin in Uganda, Jean-Bédel Bokassa in the then Central African Empire, and Francisco Macias Nguema in Equatorial Guinea, conducted the most catastrophic systems of human rights abuse in Africa during those first years after the creation of the OAU.

The fifth and last period covers from 1995 up until our days and it could be identified with the democratic experiment. For some countries it worked out successfully; for others the future is still quite uncertain.[22] During this period Africa has also moved towards an institutional strengthening and several countries are making an effort to end political impunity.

No international instrument for the protection of human rights could be expected from the Africa in the early 20th century, for most countries were nothing but an extension of the European colonizing powers. Once the independent expectations actualized and some countries detached themselves from their colonizing power, then African legal experts began to participate in the First Congress of African Lawyers in Africa. It was held in Lagos, Nigeria, from 3rd to 7th January 1961. It was organized by the International Commission for Jurists. Paragraph 4 of its resolution, known as the 'Law of Lagos' invited African governments to "study the possibility of adopting an African Convention on Human Rights."[23]

Two years later came the historic meeting of independent African States on 25th May 1963 in Addis Ababa, Ethiopia gave birth to the Organization of African Unity (OAU). Illustrious leaders of 30 African States were gathered at the invitation of Haile Selassie I, the Emperor of Ethiopia, Former Prince Ras Tafari, who on being enthroned received the name of the 'King of Kings, the Lord of Lords and the Conqueror Lion of the Tribe of Judah.' This pompous title referred to Selassie's ancestry, the 125th descendant of the oldest dynasty in the World, a descendant of the Queen of Sheba and King Solomon.[24] Thus, the OAU was born as the official regional body of African States. Its headquarters were based in Addis Ababa, Ethiopia, a location reflecting perhaps the respected leadership and diplomatic skills of the Ethiopian emperor. Due to Africa's colonial historical background, the OAU was founded on the principles of State sovereignty and non-interference. It also postulated the fight for decolonization of Africa as it believed that Africa would not be free until

---

[22] For example, in the last 5 years, fraudulent election results have been strongly alleged in Uganda, Kenya, Ivory Coast, Nigeria, Tanzania, Zimbabwe, Mozambique, Rwanda, Central African Republic, Guinea, among others.

[23] Ouguergouz, F., *The African Charter on Human and Peoples' Rights: A Comprehensive Agenda for Human Dignity and Sustainable Democracy in Africa*, Martinus Nijhoff Publishers, The Hague, 2003, at 20.

[24] Orjiako, D. T., "The African Union – Our Common Home." A Keynote Address delivered at *The North-eastern University*, Boston, Massachusetts, and March 24, 2005.

each colony had gained independence and won the fight against segregation and apartheid in some specific States.[25]

Since its foundation, the OAU has helped to strengthen ties between African nations and in settling disputes.[26] The preamble to the Charter of the OAU recognized that the Charter of the United Nations and the Universal Declaration of Human Rights (UDHR) provided a solid foundation for peaceful and positive co-operation among States. One of the purposes of the OAU was therefore to promote international co-operation, having due regard to the Charter of the United Nations and the UDHR.

In 1967, a conference of jurists from Francophone Africa was convened in Dakar. The Dakar Declaration requested the International Commission of Jurists for assistance to study the feasibility of creating a regional system for the protection of human rights in Africa"[27]

Meanwhile, at the Tehran Conference, in 1968, celebrating the 20th anniversary of the Universal Declaration of Human Rights, the Organization for African Unity had been the only regional body that did not present a report on its activities in this field.[28] A seminar was organized in Cairo in 1969 and its participants put forward the creation of an African Commission on Human Rights. Its mandate would be mostly educational and advisory.[29]

In 1977, the United Nations General Assembly formally appealed to all States in areas where regional arrangements in the field of human rights did not exist to consider agreements with a view to establish within their respective regions suitable regional machinery for the promotion and protection of human rights.[30]Negotiations regarding how to address human

---

[25] For example in South Africa and Zimbabwe, where governments were in the hands of racial minorities and segregation was an *accepted* social system.
[26] For example, see ACHPR, Comm. 227/99: *Democratic Republic of Congo v. Burundi, Rwanda and Uganda*, where the Commission found the application admissible and finally found the Respondent States in violation of Articles 2, 4, 5, 12(1) and (2), 14, 16, 17, 18(1) and (3), 19, 20, 21, 22, and 23 of the African Charter on Human and Peoples' Rights. Available at:
http://www.achpr.org/english/_info/ index_Decision_Uganda.html
[27] Ouguergouz, F., *op. cit.*, at 22.
[28] See *Ibid*, at 28.
[29] See *Ibid*, at 29.
[30] UNGA, *Resolution* 32/127 (1977).

rights abuses which had taken place throughout the 1960s and 1970s were already on-going at the OAU.[31]

According to Ouguergouz, the year 1978 may be regarded as the pivotal moment in the conceptualization of human rights in Africa.[32] From 3rd to 7th July 1978 jurists met in Butare, Rwanda, and a few months later, in September, held the Dakar Colloquium on Human Rights and Economic Development. These meetings helped to dispel the idea that human rights abuses in Africa were a necessary flaw or a justifiable means to attain economic development. The participants again called for a human rights Convention to be concluded at a Pan-African level. They also spoke of one or more sub-regional human rights commissions to be created composed of magistrates or judges responsible for hearing complaints relating to human rights abuses.[33]

In September, another seminar was convened in Monrovia (Liberia) and the *Monrovia Proposal* was finally adopted.[34] As Ouguergouz says, the text of its fifteen articles laid down the foundations for an African Commission on Human Rights.[35]

By then, discussions about human rights in Africa had acquired special resonance.[36] First the atrocities reported in Uganda,[37] Equatorial Guinea[38]

---

[31] The OAU had failed to react to various gross violations of human rights committed by dictators like Idi Amin in Uganda, Jean-Bédel Bokassa in the then Central African Empire, and Francisco Macias Nguema in Equatorial Guinea, due to the principle of non-interference in the internal affairs of member States. As time went on there was a growing recognition of the importance of human rights, which led to the development of the African Charter.

[32] Ouguergouz, F., *op. cit.*, at 23.

[33] *Ibid*, at 25.

[34] *Ibid*, at 34.

[35] *Ibid*.

[36] See Makau, M., "The African Human Rights System, a Critical Evaluation." (2000).Available at:
http://hdr.undp.org/en/reports/global/hdr2000/papers/mutua.pdf.
Makau Mutua brings up similar points although in a different order as do several other authors.

[37] See *http://africanhistory.about.com/od/biography/a/bio_amin.htm*
President Idi Amin (b. 1925, near Koboko, West Nile province, Uganda) known as the *Butcher of Uganda* for his brutal, despotic rule, was possibly the most notorious of all Africa's post-independence dictators. Amin seized power in a military coup in 1971 and ruled over Uganda for 8 years. Estimates for the number of his opponents who were killed, tortured, or imprisoned vary from 100,000 to half a million. He was ousted in 1979 by Ugandan nationalists, after which he fled

and the Central African Empire[39] as well as the Tanzanian military invasion of Ugandan territory.[40] Second, post-colonial African States had been born out of the anti-colonial struggle for human rights. Third, black-ruled African States had used human rights principles to isolate and apply pressure on the colonial minority white-ruled States of Angola, Mozambique, Namibia, Zimbabwe and South Africa.

---

into exile. He died on 16th August 2003, in Jeddah, Saudi Arabia. During his presidency he conferred upon himself the following titles: *His Excellency President for Life, Field Marshal Al Hadji Doctor Idi Amin, VC, DSO, MC, Lord of All the Beasts of the Earth and Fishes of the Sea, and Conqueror of the British Empire in Africa in General and Uganda in Particular.*

[38] See *US Department of State*, available at: *http://www.state.gov/r/pa/ei/bgn/7221.htm*
Francisco Macias Nguema was elected first president of Equatorial Guinea in 1968. In July 1970, he created a single-party State and by May 1971, key portions of the constitution were abrogated. In 1972 Macias took complete control of the government and assumed the title of President-for-Life. The Macias regime was characterized by abandonment of all government functions except internal security, which was accomplished by terror; this led to the death or exile of up to one-third of the country's population. Due to pilferage, ignorance, and neglect, the country's infrastructure--electrical, water, road, transportation, and health--fell into ruin. Religion was repressed, and education ceased. The private and public sectors of the economy were devastated. Nigerian contract labourers in Bioko, estimated to have been 60,000, left en masse in early 1976. The economy collapsed, and skilled citizens and foreigners left.

[39] See generally Lamb, D., *The Africans*, Vintage Books, New York, 1987.The Central African Empire was the name of the short-lived, self-declared autocratic monarchy that replaced the Central African Republic on 4th December 1976. The Empire was formed when Jean-Bédel Bokassa, President of the republic, declared himself Emperor Bokassa I. The monarchy was abolished on 21st September 1979 and the name "Central African Republic" was restored. Bokassa was ousted with French support. During Bokassa's tenure thousands of people were tortured and assassinated. There are claims that more than 100 elementary school children were killed during a demonstration. Bokassa himself seems to have taken part in the mass-killing. The matter was widely aired by the international press.

[40] See Graham, M., in Murison, K. (Ed), *Africa South of the Sahara*, 34th edition, Europa Publications Limited, Volume 33, London, 2004, at 1119.Tanzanian relations with neighbouring Uganda deteriorated in the early 1970s. In September 1972 supporters of the former Ugandan president, Milton Obote, attempted an invasion of Uganda from Tanzanian territory. This prompted Uganda's Gen. Idi Amin, to accuse Tanzania of plotting against his regime. In November 1978, Uganda announced the annexation of Tanzania's bordering Kagera region, which led to a full-scale invasion by Tanzanian troops into Uganda. Amin capitulated and an interim government was proclaimed.

In 1979, a meeting of experts was convened in Dakar, from 28th November to 8th December. In his opening address, Senegalese President Léopold S. Senghor, urged the experts "to use their imagination and to draw inspiration from African traditions, bearing in mind the values of African civilisation and the real needs of Africa."[41] According to Baricako, President Senghor also "pleaded for a special place to be accorded to the right to development that, according to him, embraces economic, social and cultural rights as well as civil and political rights. He also insisted on the need to make provision for 'duties of the individual' which are in harmony with the rights granted by the society to which he/she belongs."[42] He encouraged them to assimilate without being assimilated and of borrowing from modernity only what was compatible with the deep nature of African civilization. Senghor, moreover, stressed that in the area of human rights, irresponsibility and immorality should be carefully avoided.[43] Ouguergouz asserts that the experts met the expectations and managed to produce a draft with remarkable care and speed.[44]

A few months later, the first Ministerial Conference was convened at Banjul, The Gambia, under the auspices of the Gambian Government to consider the Charter presented by the experts.[45] However, it was not entirely successful and agreement was reached only about the Preamble and 11 articles.[46]

A second Ministerial Session was held again in Banjul, in January 1981. The meeting successfully agreed on a document that was in

---

[41] Senghor, L.S., OAU Doc. CAB/LEG/67/5. See also Germain Baricako, who analyses the speech by His Excellency Léopold Sedar Senghor, President of the Republic of Senegal, in Baricako, G., "Introductory Preface: The African Charter and the African Commission on Human and People's Rights", published in Malcolm, E. and Murray, R. (Eds), *The African Charter on Human and Peoples' Rights: the system in practice 1986-2006*, 2nd Edition, Cambridge University Press, Cambridge, 2008, at 6.

[42] Baricako, G. "Introductory Preface: The African Charter and the African Commission on Human and People's Rights", published in Malcolm, E. and Murray, R. (Eds), *op. cit.*, at 6.

[43] President Senghor was, perhaps, here pre-empting the Western influence of anti-values and the possible structural ideologization of the fight for human rights in Africa.

[44] See Ouguergouz, F., *op. cit.*, at 43.

[45] This Conference took place on 9th-15th June 1980, at Banjul, The Gambia.

[46] See Ouguergouz, F., *op. cit.*, at 44.

substance what the committee of experts had drafted.[47] And in Nairobi, at the Kenyatta International Conference Centre, on 27th June 1981, close to midnight and in a hurry to get finished, the 18th Assembly of Heads of State and Government adopted the Charter without debate. Thus, Africa had at last a Human Rights Charter.

2. Initial Development of the African Human Rights System

The African Charter on Human and Peoples' Rights[48] established a quasi-judicial organ: The Commission on Human and People's Rights. Once the Charter came into force on 21st October 1986, the stage was set for the Commissioners' appointment. The first Commission members were elected by the OAU's 23rd Assembly of Heads of State and Government in June 1987 and the African Commission on Human and Peoples' Rights was formally inaugurated on 2nd November of that year.[49]

It took another decade of negotiations for the OAU to create and adopt a draft protocol establishing the basis for an African Court: The Protocol to the African Charter on Human and Peoples' Rights on the Establishment of an African Court on Human and Peoples' Rights.[50] A group of experts, mainly lawyers, met in Cape Town in 1995 and adopted the Cape Town Draft Protocol to the African Charter on Human and Peoples' Rights on the Establishment of an African Court on Human and Peoples' Rights. This was followed by the Nouakchott Draft of April 1997, and the Addis

---

[47] See Ouguergouz, F., *op. cit*, at 45-46.Mikuin-Leliel Belinda argues that apparently the approval came from the realization of the immediate importance of human rights protection against abuses already perpetrated against certain representatives of Upper Volta who had themselves taken part in previous ministerial sessions. Certainly, Doe's assassination of Dr William Tolbert (12th April, 1980) President of Liberia and head of the OAU, must have also made an impact on the delegates desires for concrete results.

[48] We will from time to time refer to it as the *Banjul Charter* or simply the *African Charter*.

[49] ACHPR, *First Annual Activity Report of the African Commission on Human and Peoples' Rights*, 2nd Nov 1987, ACHPR/RPT/1st, para. 4.

[50] *The viability of the African Commission, and by inference, the African human rights system, was seen to be severely impaired as a result of the absence of a court on human rights. This point of view had become so pronounced in Africa that during the summit of Heads of State and Government of the OAU, held in Tunis, Tunisia in June 1994, a decision was made to give more "teeth" to the African human rights system in the form of a human rights court, which would complement and reinforce the Commission*. See IHRDA, Institute for Human Rights and Development in Africa, available at *http://www.ihrda.org*

Ababa Draft of December 1997.[51] These efforts matured in the 1998 Protocol adopted by the Assembly of Heads of State and Government of the OAU on 10th June 1998 in Ouagadougou, Burkina Faso. After ratification by the required 15 States,[52] the ACtHPR Protocol[53] entered into force on 25 January 2004.[54] By January 2011, 25 Member States of the AU had ratified it.[55] The first judges of the Court were elected by the Executive Council of the AU and appointed by the Assembly of Heads of State and Government on 22nd January 2006 at its 8th Ordinary Session held in Khartoum, Sudan.[56] They were later sworn in before the Assembly on 2nd July 2006 in Banjul, The Gambia. The African Court met in Addis

---

[51] See Viljoen, F., "African Court on Human and Peoples' Rights (ACtHPR)", *Max Planck Institute for Comparative Public Law and International Law*, Heidelberg and Oxford University Press, (2010), No. 3.

[52] The *Protocol* entered into force on 25th January 2004, thirty (30) days after the deposit of the fifteenth instrument of ratification in accordance with Article 34(3).

[53] Also referred to as the *Original Protocol.*

[54] See Institute for Human Rights and Development in Africa (IHRDA), available at: *http://www.ihrda.org*. It is clear that the *success of the ACtHPR will, to a large extent, depend on the operational efficiency of the ACmHPR, as the overarching aim of the court is to supplement (complement) the ACmHPR's complaints procedure*.

[55] See EX.CL/539 (XVI) Rev.1. As of 1 January 2011, the following twenty-five (25) Member States have ratified the Protocol: Algeria, Burkina Faso, Burundi, Comoros, Côte d'Ivoire, The Gambia, Gabon, Ghana, Kenya, Libya, Lesotho, Mali, Malawi, Mauritania, Mauritius, Mozambique, Niger, Nigeria, Rwanda, Senegal, South Africa, Tanzania, Togo, Tunisia and Uganda. The following twenty-four (24) Member States have signed but not ratified the Protocol: Angola, Benin, Botswana, Cameroon, C.A.R., Chad, Congo, Djibouti, D.R.C., Egypt, Eq. Guinea, Ethiopia, Guinea, Guinea-Bissau, Liberia, Madagascar, Namibia, Seychelles, Sierra Leone, Somalia, Sudan, Swaziland, Zambia and Zimbabwe.

[56] These Judges were: Dr Gerard Niyungeko (Burundi, professor of law, incumbent of the UNESCO Chair in Education for Peace and Conflict Resolution at the University Burundi). Niyungeko is the current serving president of the Court; Mr Modibo Tounty Guindo (Magistrate in the Ministry of Justice, Mali), who served as the first Vice-President; Dr Fatsah Ouguergouz (Secretary of the International Court of Justice, Algeria); Mr Jean Emile Somda (member of the Constitutional Court, Burkina Faso); Ms Sophia Akuffo (Supreme Court judge, Ghana); Mrs Kelello Justina Masafo-Guni (High Court judge, Lesotho); Mr Hamdi Faraj Fanoush (Supreme Court judge, Libya); Mr Jean Mutsinzi (Supreme Court judge, Rwanda); Mr El Hadji Guisse (advocate, member of the UN Sub-Commission on the Promotion and Protection of Human Rights, serving as its Special Rapporteur on the right to drinking water supply and sanitation, Senegal); Mr Bernard Ngoepe (High Court President, South Africa); and Mr George Kanyeihamba (Supreme Court judge, Uganda).

Ababa, Ethiopia in November 2006 but then moved to its permanent seat in Arusha, Tanzania in August 2007. It was decided that the Court would be based in Arusha, utilizing facilities developed for the International Criminal Tribunal for Rwanda.[57]

In the meantime, the OAU had been replaced by the African Union (AU) in 2001.[58] The establishment of the AU was seen as a great opportunity to put human rights firmly on the African agenda. The AU Constitutive Act contains several amendments to the OAU Charter which have been instrumental to the functioning of the African human rights system. For example it includes the right of the Union to intervene in a Member State pursuant to a decision of the Assembly in respect of grave circumstances, namely, war crimes, genocide and crimes against humanity; the right of Member States to request intervention from the Union in order to restore peace and security; promotion of gender equality; respect for democratic principles, human rights, the rule of law and good governance; promotion of social justice to ensure balanced economic development; respect for the sanctity of human life, condemnation and rejection of impunity and political assassination, acts of terrorism and subversive activities; and condemnation and rejection of unconstitutional changes of government.[59]

The Constitutive Act of the African Union foresaw the creation of the Court of Justice of the African Union, called the African Court of Justice

[57] See the Host Agreement between Tanzania and the African Union, available at: *https://docs.google.com/viewer?url=http://www.africancourt.org/fileadmin/documents/Court/Host_agreement/agreement-Tanzania%2520and%2520AU.pdf.* However, as the Tribunal for Rwanda is still operational, the Court is currently operating from a provisional facility next to the Arusha National Park.

[58] As we said before 53 of the 54 African States are members of the AU. In 1984 Morocco withdrew once the OAU recognized the State of Western Sahara, known as the Sahrawi Arab Democratic Republic. Sahrawi is not yet fully recognised by the UN but has been recognised by more than 80 States, most of them Africans and enjoys full membership at the AU.

[59] See *http://news.bbc.co.uk/2/hi/africa/1430504.stm.* The key idea of the transformation was to empower the AU in a manner that would not have been possible at the formation of the OAU, where governments compromised on a body with more abstract powers. Under the new order, the African Union would eventually have a common parliament, central bank and court of justice. In theory, these would give ordinary Africans a greater say in their continental leadership, create and run an Africa-wide economy and make abusers of human rights accountable for their actions. Nonetheless, this is not the case yet and a decade has gone by.

(ACJ).[60] This Court of Justice's specificities were captured in its Protocol.[61] However, the African Court of Justice has never been constituted and does not seem likely to ever come into existence because in July 2004 the African Union decided that the African Court of Justice and the African Court on Human and People's Rights should be merged.[62]One year later, in July 2005, the AU Assembly decided that a draft instrument establishing the merged court should be presented for consideration. In May 2006 negotiations began on a new protocol that would integrate the two into a single court. The so-called *Merger Protocol* was finally approved in July 2008, although it is not yet in force. This merger Protocol foresees the fusion of the African Court on Human and Peoples' Rights (ACtHPR) with the African Court of Justice (ACJ) to become the African Court of Justice and Human and Peoples Rights (ACJHPR).

The process is currently stalled and somewhat confused. The process is quite political and many governments do not understand yet the nature of the Court and the importance of an expanded jurisdiction and modified procedural rules that would facilitate access to justice. Perhaps the judges themselves have not managed to convey the importance or urgency of having a working African court to their own governments.[63]

In addition to the African Charter, the OAU adopted two other important human rights instruments addressing specifically the rights of women and children. The African Charter on the Rights and Welfare of the Child was adopted by the OAU in 1990 and it entered into force in 1999. It is a comprehensive instrument that sets out rights and defines universal principles and norms for the status of children. It spells out the rights that African States must ensure for children living in their jurisdiction. Another protocol known as the Protocol to the African Charter on Human and Peoples' Rights on the Rights of Women in Africa, commonly referred to as the Maputo Protocol, was adopted by the AU on 11th July 2003 at its second summit in Maputo, Mozambique. It entered

---

[60] *Constitutive Act of the African Union*, Art. 5.

[61] This Protocol entered into force on 11thFebruary 2009, however it is not operational.

[62] See AU, Decision on the Seats of the Organs of the African Union, Assembly/AU/Dec.45 (lll) Rev.1.

[63] While all this merging process is going on an additional fact has confused the situation further: there have been 16 ratifications of the *African Court of Justice Protocol*, which has in fact already entered into force. Therefore, currently there is a merger protocol not yet in force and an *ACJ Protocol* that entered into force while the merger process was being negotiated.

into force in 2005, having been ratified by 15 member States of the AU as required. Its origin can be traced back to the meeting organized by *Women in Law and Development in Africa* (WILDAF) in March, 1995, in Lomé, Togo, which called for the development of a specific protocol to the African Charter to address the rights of women.[64] In June 1995, the OAU Assembly had mandated the Commission to develop the protocol and the OAU Secretariat received the completed draft in 1999. The process, however, stalled and the protocol was not presented at the inaugural summit of the AU in 2002. In 2003, *Equality Now*[65] hosted a conference of women's groups to pressure the AU to adopt the protocol. The lobbying was successful and the AU resumed the process, officially adopting the Protocol to The African Charter on Human and Peoples' Rights on the Rights of Women in Africa.[66]

The African Court on Human and People's Rights,[67] is a specialized judicial organ created to be an impartial arbiter between individuals and States that violate the provisions of the African Charter. This Court complements and reinforces the Commission's protective mandate. The Court's judgments on cases are final and binding upon the State parties concerned.[68] However, since its inception the Court has issued only one substantive judgement.[69]

---

[64] WILDAF is a New York-based NGO with Observer Status before the AU.

[65] EQUALITY NOW is an NGO founded in 1992. Issues of urgent concern to Equality Now include rape, domestic violence, reproductive rights, trafficking of women, female genital mutilation, and the denial of equal access to economic opportunity and political participation. It is considered a strong donor-funded lobby group promoting the feminist agenda.

[66] According to Article XXIX (1), this Protocol entered into force on 25th November, 2005, 30 days after the deposit of the 15 instrument of ratification. 27 Member States have so far ratified or acceded to the Protocol: Angola, Benin, Burkina Faso, Cape Verde, Comoros, D.R.C, Djibouti, Gambia, Ghana, Guinea-Bissau, Lesotho, Liberia, Libya, Mali, Malawi, Mauritania, Mozambique, Namibia, Nigeria, Rwanda, Senegal, Seychelles, South Africa, Tanzania, Togo, Zambia and Zimbabwe.

[67] We will often refer to it as ACtHPR.

[68] The States who have so far ratified the Court's Protocol are (as of 1st January 2011): Algeria, Burkina Faso, Burundi, Côte d'Ivoire, Comoros, Gabon, Gambia, Ghana, Kenya, Libya, Lesotho, Mali, Malawi, Mozambique, Mauritania, Mauritius, Nigeria, Niger, Rwanda, South Africa, Senegal, Tanzania, Togo, Tunisia and Uganda.

[69] Out of sixteen cases brought before the court, only one has been substantively discussed; African Commission on Human and People's Rights v. The Republic of Kenya, No. 006/2012. In all other cases, the court has found that it lacks

The African Charter on Human and People's Rights

The African Charter on Human and peoples' Rights, also known as the Banjul Charter, is the main African human rights instrument that sets out the rights and duties relating to human and peoples' rights.[70]Certainly, the African Charter is an original and innovative instrument in the field of human rights which took into consideration the specificities of African countries.[71]

The committee of experts in charge of drafting the Charter decided that it "should reflect the African conception of human rights [and] take as a pattern the African philosophy of law and meet the needs of Africa."[72]

This concern, Ouguergouz asserts, was reflected in the preamble which takes into "consideration the virtues of their historical tradition and the

---

jurisdiction to try the case before it. Even so, with the Kenyan case, the court has appeared as a toothless bulldog owing to the fact that to date the Respondent has not responded to the request for provisional measures.

[70] See EX.CL/539 (XVI) Rev.1. We have already explained that *the African Charter on Human and Peoples' Rights, which deals with the promotion and protection of human and peoples' rights, was adopted by the 18th Ordinary Session of the Assembly of Heads of State and Government, in June 1981 in Nairobi, Kenya. It entered into force on 21 October 1986 in application of Article 63(3), which requires ratification/adherence of a simple majority of Member States to come into force. All Member States have ratified the Charter. Some States registered their reservations as follows: Zambia: Article 13(3)- should be amended such that every individual has the right of access to any place, services or public property intended for use by the general public; Article 37- the Secretary-General of the Organization, rather than the Chairman of the Assembly, should draw lots to determine the terms of office of members of the Commission; and non-State Parties to the Charter should also submit reports to the Commission. Egypt entered reservations as follows: Article 8 and Article 18(3)-Application of Article 8 and Article 18 (3) of the Charter should be in the light of Islamic Shariah Law and not to its demerit; Article 9(1)- Egypt shall interpret this paragraph as being applicable only to information, the obtaining of which is authorized by Egyptian laws and regulations.*

[71] See Ouguergouz, F., "African Charter on Human and Peoples' Rights", *Max Planck Encyclopaedia of Public International Law,* Max Planck Institute for Comparative Public Law and International Law, Heidelberg and Oxford University Press, (2010). Available at: *www.mpepil.com*

[72] Draft African Charter prepared for the Meeting of Experts in Dakar, Senegal, from 28 November to 8 December 1979' CAB/LEG/67/3/Rev.1, reprinted in Heyns, C., *Human Rights Law in Africa*, Kluwer, The Hague, 2002, at 81.Cited also by Ouguergouz, *Ibid.*

values of African civilization which should inspire and characterize their reflection on the concept of human and peoples' rights."[73] The Charter goes on to stress the importance of morals and traditional values on two occasions[74] and the protection of African cultural values.[75] Ouguergouz asserts that "the Banjul Charter should consequently be viewed as a legal instrument which takes into account the specificities of the African continent. It is clearly an original legal instrument when compared to the instruments of the same kind adopted at the universal or regional levels."[76] The Charter is undeniably bewildering for any person not conversant with its history and background. It deals, for instance, with the right of peoples to "the equal enjoyment of the common heritage of mankind"[77] together with the duty of the individual "to contribute to the best of his abilities, at all times and at all levels, to the promotion and achievement of African Unity."[78] It is, thus, a regional instrument designed to reflect the history, values, traditions, and development of Africa.

Its main purpose includes: First, the establishment of bodies to promote and protect human and peoples' rights such as the Commission and, through subsequent protocols, the Court. Second, the eradication of all forms of colonialism from Africa, coordinating and intensifying cooperation and efforts to achieve a better life for the peoples of Africa and to promote international cooperation having due regard to the Charter of the United Nations and the Universal Declaration of Human Rights. And third, to achieve the total liberation of Africa, the peoples of which are still struggling for their dignity and genuine independence, and undertaking to eliminate colonialism, neo-colonialism, apartheid, Zionism and to dismantle aggressive foreign military bases and all forms of discrimination, particularly those based on race, ethnic group, colour, sex, language, religion or political opinions.

---

[73] *African (Banjul) Charter on Human and Peoples' Rights.* Adopted 27th June 1981, OAU Doc. CAB/LEG/67/3 rev. 5, 21 I.L.M. 58 (1982), entered into force 21st October 1986.
[74] *Banjul Charter*, Article 17 and 18.
[75] *Ibid*, Article 29.
[76] Ouguergouz, F., "African Charter on Human and Peoples' Rights", *op. cit.* Available at: *www.mpepil.com*
[77] *Banjul Charter*, Article 22(1).
[78] *Banjul Charter*, Article 29(8). On this point see Ouguergouz, F., "African Charter on Human and Peoples' Rights", *op. cit.* Available at: *www.mpepil.com*

1. Structure and Motivation

The African Charter sets itself into motion with a beautifully assembled 'Preamble'. It contains the philosophical foundations and common aspirations that brought together such diverse African cultures into one human rights deed. Once the drafters had laid the foundations, they launched themselves to the task of designing the upper structure as an all-round and interconnected African hut to house human rights in the Continent. It is as if the whole African family took part in the construction.

In part I and II, they had rights to shelter. The corresponding duty was to build and maintain the home. The skeleton of branches used to wall the hut corresponds to the rights enumerated from articles 1 to 29. These rights are accompanied by their related duties that act like the plaster that binds the branches together and give them the consistency they need to stay strong.

Once the walling was over, the drafters roofed the hut by putting in place the necessary mechanisms to prevent those rights from being damaged and to redress them. This was the grass-thatched roof. This roof safeguards and keeps the rights intact, protecting them against the weather's inclemency. Articles 30 to 63 provide for that roof; for those safety measures. The first chapter of this section determines the materials to be used, and it provides for the establishment and organization of the African Commission on Human and Peoples' Rights. The second and third chapters speak to us about the design, and how those materials must be arranged to achieve the expected protection. These chapters deal with the mandate and the procedure of the Commission. At the end of this part, the drafters left a beautiful footprint of the Charter's Africanness. In articles 60 to 63 they halt the construction for a moment and give some words of advice about the entrance to the hut, the door for the rights, how to admit them; how the interpretation of rights should be dealt with and how these rights should be understood and discerned by the Commission's workings. It sounds like the elders' advice to the future generations so as to maintain the proper Africanness of the rights and their understanding.

Finally, in part III, on general provisions, from articles 64 to 68, the drafters give directions on how to occupy the hut, on how to access it and how to go about possible necessary changes that the threats of time and weather may require.

2. Charter Innovations in the African Context

The African Charter on Human and Peoples' Rights does not distinguish between classes of rights. In this, the African Charter is essentially different from other human rights instruments.[79] For the African Charter all rights are interdependent despite the different measures required to implement them. For instance, the right to education and the right to health are mingled with the right to freedom of speech and association. Further, its preamble categorically states that: "Civil and political rights cannot be disassociated from economic, social and cultural rights in their conception as well as universality and … the satisfaction of economic, social and cultural rights is a guarantee for the enjoyment of civil and political rights."[80]

This approach differs from previous systems such as the European and Inter-American human rights systems which do not include these diverse classes of rights in a single document. For example, the European Convention is not focused on economic, social and cultural rights. These rights are framed mostly in the European Social Charter (ESC)[81] and further contemplated within the Organisation for Security and Cooperation in Europe (OSCE).[82] On the other hand, the American system has the American Declaration of Rights and Duties of Man.[83] This Declaration contains provisions on economic, social and cultural rights, which were not captured in the American Convention on Human Rights.[84]

---

[79] For example, in The European Charter of Fundamental Rights of the European Union (2000/C 364/01) rights fall under the classification of political-economic and social rights. This is also clearly the case in the International Covenant on Civil and Political Rights and in the International Covenant on Economic, Social, and Cultural Rights.

[80] See *Banjul Charter*, Preamble.

[81] *European Social Charter*, 18th October 1961, 529 UNTS 89.

[82] Blored, A. "The Human Rights Dimension of the OSCE: Past, Present and Prospects", *Office for Democratic Institutions and Human Rights*, Bulletins No. 3, (1995), at 16.

[83] The *American Declaration of the Rights and Duties of Man* was adopted by the 9th International Conference of American States of the Organization of American States in Bogota, Colombia, on 2nd May 1948. It was the first human rights instrument, thus predating the UDHR.

[84] The *American Convention on Human Rights* was adopted at the Inter-American Specialized Conference on Human Rights, San José, Costa Rica on 22nd November 1969.

Nevertheless, as it has been pointed out before, the document acknowledges the existence of rights together while at the same time it lacks the commitment or readiness to respect or protect them.[85] The Charter also contains no derogation provisions notwithstanding the fact that in customary international law a State has a right to derogate.[86] Nonetheless, the Commission has interpreted this to mean that derogation from the rights and duties under the African Charter by member States is not permitted.[87]

2.1 The Right to Solidarity

The development of human rights has often been classified into 'first-generation' rights, namely the civil and political rights and 'second-generation' rights namely, the economic, social and cultural rights. In more recent decades, debate has arisen over the concept of a 'third classification', referred to as the 'third-generation' rights or rights of solidarity.

The authorship of this concept is attributed[88] to Karel Vasak, who used this expression to denote the new human rights which "express a certain

---

[85] See Communications 105/93, 128/94, 130/94, 152/96, *Media Rights Agenda and Others v. Nigeria*, Twelfth Activity Report, 200 AHRLR, and (ACHPR 1998). For instance, the freedom of association has to be exercised in accordance with the law. Could this mean that this right is subject to the domestic laws of member States? The commission has clarified the matter by holding that it does not mean domestic law. The term 'law' has been interpreted by the Commission to mean that rights have to be exercised in accordance with international law standards. Further provisions with claw-back clauses are: the right to life [The African Charter on Human and Peoples' Rights, Art. 4], the right to liberty and security of the person, [The African Charter on Human and Peoples' Rights, Art. 6], the freedoms of conscience, profession and religion [The African Charter on Human and Peoples' Rights, Art. 8], the right to movement and residence, [The African Charter on Human and Peoples' Rights, Art. 12], the right to participate in government [The African Charter on Human and Peoples' Rights, Art. 13].

[86] Higgins, R., "Derogation Under Human Rights Treaties", *British Yearbook of International Law*, vol. 48, (1976-77), at 281.

[87] Communication 74/92, *Commission Nationale des Droits de l'Homme et des Libertés v. Chad*, 9th Activity Report, (2000) AHRLR 66 (ACHPR 1995); Communications 54/91, 61/91, 98/93, 164-169/97,210/98, *Malawi African Association, Amnesty International, Ms Sarr Diop/UIDH/RADDHO, Collectif des Veuves et Ayanst-droit* and *Association Mauritanienne des Droits de l'Homme v. Mauritania*, 13th Activity Report; (2000) AHRLR 149 (ACHPR 2000).

[88] According to Ouguergouz, F., *op. cit.*, at 290.

conception of communal life, and can only be realized through the efforts of all who participate in life in society: individuals, States, other public or private entities."[89] These rights include the right to development, the right to peace, the right to the environment, the right of ownership of the common heritage of mankind and the right to communicate. Except for the right to communicate, the other rights have been incorporated into the African Charter, which we shall discuss below.[90] Before turning to their discussion, we should highlight the criticisms that have been labelled against these classifications of human rights.

The first pertains to the subject of these rights. While the subject of the first and second generation rights is easily traceable to the individual, it is argued that with respect to the third generation rights, it is not certain whether their subject is the individual or a group of individuals being the State, the international community, the whole of mankind or all the above. Further, it may be said the subject of the rights is variable according to the right that is concerned e.g. the right to the common heritage of mankind may involve the whole of mankind, while the right to development may take on sub-national (e.g. marginalized groups within a State), national, regional and even international dimensions.

Secondly, the novelty of the third generation rights has been challenged since they may be traced to other international human rights instruments as for example the *International Bill of Human Rights*[91] which recognizes that the fulfilment of individual human rights is dependent on human solidarity and participation in communal life. Furthermore, their contribution to human rights theory has also been questioned since the concept, it is argued, does more to obscure than clarify human rights theory.[92]

---

[89] See Vasak, K., "Pour une troisième génération des droits de l'homme", in Swinarski, C. (ed.), *Studies and Essays on International Humanitarian Law and Red Cross Principles in honour of Jean Pictet*, Martinus Nijhoff Publishers, Geneva, The Hague, ICRC, 1984, at 839.

[90] For a detailed analysis of the preliminary draft Third United Nations Covenant on Human Rights, see Ouguergouz, F., *op. cit.*, at 291-292.

[91] The *International Bill of Human Rights* consists of the *Universal Declaration of Human Rights* (1948), the *International Covenant on Civil and Political Rights* (1966) and its two Optional Protocols, and the *International Covenant on Economic, Social and Cultural Rights* (1966).

[92] Alston, P., "A Third Generation of Solidarity Rights: Progressive Development or Obfuscation of International Human Rights Law?", *Netherlands International Law Review*, vol. 29, No. 3, (1982), at 308.

Thirdly, the third generation rights have been criticized for their non-justiciable nature, though Karel Vasak responded to this criticism by stating that the justiciability of a norm is not a condition for its existence but only its enforcement.[93] The positivist school of thought does not regard rights that are not legally enforceable as human rights. For this school of thought, a right, to be taken seriously, must be sanctioned by a legal authority and must be based upon appropriate enforceable legislation. Therefore, these 'rights' should be considered, from a legal perspective, social aspirations, goals, statements of objectives.

According to the Centre for Development and Human Rights (CDHR) human rights, which precede law and are derived not from law but from the concept of human dignity, should not be confused with legal rights. CDHR further states that there is nothing in principle to prevent a right from being internationally recognised as a human right even if it is not individually justiciable. It is inappropriate to assert that human rights cannot be invoked if they cannot be legally enforced.[94]

The fact is that both views are not necessarily opposed. Certainly there are so-called human rights that are not immediately enforceable and from a strict legal perspective they are human or social aspirations. However, any action directly opposed against them could trigger a legal action. In this sense they are actually rights.[95] The fact that everyone has a right to development does not grant *locus standi* to demand its application in a court of law, but in our opinion the presence of an aggressor or unjust or unfair obstacle placed by an identifiable aggressor could trigger a legal action grounded on such guaranteed social aspiration.

We shall now analyse the rights of solidarity as they are captured in the African Charter.

---

[93] See Vasak, K., *op. cit.*, at 839. The matter is extensively discussed by Ouguergouz, F., *op. cit.*, at 289 ff.

[94] Centre for Development and Human Rights, *The Right to Development: A Primer*, Sage Publications, New Delhi, 2004, at 60.

[95] See Bedjaoui, M., "The Right to Development", in Bedjaoui, M. (ed), *International Law: Achievements and Prospects*, UNESCO & Martinus Nijhoff Publishers, Paris, 1991, at 1194. Bedjaoui speaks of the possibility of an *actio popularis*.

2.1.1 The Right to Development

The 'right to development' was coined by Senegalese Judge Keba M'Baye, former Vice-President of the International Court of Justice.[96] According to M'Baye, all fundamental rights and freedoms are linked with the right to existence to a higher standard of living and therefore to development.[97] Moreover, the right to development, according to M'Baye, had already been implied in several United Nations documents such as the United Nations Charter and the Universal Declaration of Human Rights. Both recognised the limits to State sovereignty and the duty to cooperation.[98] The right to development was later formally recognised by the 1977 Resolution 4 (XXXIII) of the United Nations Commission on Human Rights.[99]

Shivji argues that,

> "M'Baye, while not defining development in any precise manner, distinguishes it from growth and argues that development is a metamorphosis of structures involving 'a range of changes in mental and intellectual patterns that favour the rise of growth and its prolongation in historical time.' In short, M'Baye views development as a comprehensive integrated process including, but not confined to, economic development. He further argues that the right to development is a collective right and belongs to a group. Although he does not seem to stick decisively to this view when he says development concerns 'all men', 'every man' and 'all of man' and therefore it is superfluous 'to indulge in rhetorical speculation on whether the right to development is really a collective or an individual right."[100]

Nonetheless, the subject of this right was also been vested on the individual by the 1986 UN General Assembly Resolution on the Right to

[96] See Welch, C.E., *Human Rights in Africa: Roles and Strategies of Non-governmental Organizations*, University of Pennsylvania Press, Philadelphia, 1995, at 165.M'Baye chaired the group of experts who drafted the first draft. His vision of human rights in Africa won him the title of father of African human rights.

[97] See Baehr, P.R., *The Role of Human Rights in Foreign Policy*, Second Edition, Macmillan, Hampshire, 1996, at 136.

[98] See Shivji, I.G., *The Concept of Human Rights in Africa*, Codesria, London, 1989, at 31.

[99] Baehr, P.R., *op. cit.*, at 136.

[100] Shivji, I.G., *op. cit.*, at 31.

Development.[101] However, as an individual human right it seems not to add a real meaningful content to the concept of human rights.

Article 22 of the African Charter states:

> 1. "All peoples shall have the right to their economic, social and cultural development with due regard to their freedom and identity and in the equal enjoyment of the common heritage of mankind.
> 2. States shall have the duty, individually and collectively, to ensure the exercise of the right to development."

The Charter decisively adopts the approach of situating the subject of the 'right to development' in the people. The 'right to development' stems from and is closely linked to the 'right to self-determination', which connection is evident from the reference to the peoples' freedom and identity. Moreover, the approach adopted by the Charter is to regard development as holistic, embracing the economic, social and cultural spheres of society, which is a departure from the stance initially adopted by international institutions such as the United Nations and international financial institutions that framed development with reference to a more or less exclusive economic growth.

Moreover, advocates in favour of the right to development have argued that it is meaningful only when developed countries play an active role and cooperate with developing countries towards the establishment of a new international economic order, which is marked by justice and equity in global economic relations. This position has also been reiterated by African States in various forums such as the Assembly of Heads of State and Government.[102]

In terms of the implementation of the right to development, African States have also sought to rely on themselves by establishing regional initiatives such as the "New Partnership for Africa's Development" (NEPAD) which is "a pledge by African leaders that they have a pressing duty to eradicate poverty and to place their countries, both individually

---

[101] See UNGA, A/RES/41/128, of 4 December 1986, at the 97th Plenary Meeting, Article 1: *The right to development is an inalienable human right by virtue of which every human person and all peoples are entitled to participate in, contribute to, and enjoy economic, social, cultural and political development, in which all human rights and fundamental freedoms can be fully realized.*

[102] Conference on Security, Stability, Development and Cooperation in Africa Solemn Declaration, AHG/Decl. 4 (XXXVI): The promotion of North-South and South-South Cooperation is an important strategy in Africa's development effort.

and collectively, on a path of sustainable growth and development and, at the same time, to participate actively in the world economy and body politic."[103]

NEPAD's Article 22 places the obligation to realize the right to development on State parties both individually and collectively. Nevertheless, the provision is silent on how this is to be realized. The collective initiatives that African States have embarked upon such as NEPAD offer enough evidence of the performance of this obligation.[104] Moreover, by referring to the individual obligation of State parties, it may be argued that the State holds the primary duty towards the people's right to development. It may further be argued that the State is to be held responsible for creating the conditions for there to be equality of opportunities for peoples, for it is at the level of communities that the right acquires its real meaning.[105]

---

[103] See generally OAU, *Assembly of Heads of State and Government*, 37th Session held in Lusaka, Zambia, July 2002.

[104] See Ibrahim As sane Maya (Chief Executive Officer, NEPAD Secretariat), *Promoting the African Development Agenda Through Nepad Initiatives 'Re-Positioning Nepad for Better Delivery'* Presentation at the Special Briefing Session for African Ambassadors accredited to France and delegates to the OECD Global Forum VIII on International Investment, Paris, 8th December 2009.Some NEPAD initiatives include: Agriculture and Food Security Increased ECOWAS support for CAADP and signing of Compacts by Ghana, Togo, Benin, B. Faso; Global approach to Food Security and L'Aquila G8; Partnership Platform, Abuja; Finalization of the AU/NEPAD African Action Plan; Gender: €50 million MOU signed for next 5 years of NEPAD/Spanish Fund for African Women Empowerment (June 2009); Science and Technology US$10.4 million Grant Agreement signing with Bill and Melinda Gates Foundation; Roll-Out of NEPAD Capacity Development Strategic Framework (CDSF); CDSF as first-ever Africa-wide CD strategy and tool for effective implementing capacities; 2010 Launch of CD Continental Steering Group South/South Cooperation and Aid Effectiveness; NEPAD coordination role in Africa for the Task Team on SSC and Capacity Development in context of Aid Effectiveness for 2010 Bogota and 2011 Seoul Climate Change; Completion of Demonstration Phase of NEPAD eSchools in 10 out of 16 countries; NEPAD working with Oracle Corporation towards the development of the NEPAD e-Schools Portal; Bio-Energy Centre established in Burkina Faso; NEPAD Secretariat assisted in the recent take-off of the Bio-Energy Centre in Ouagadougou in promoting the implementation of CPA *infra*structure; Support for Program of Infrastructure Development in Africa (PIDA) on regional infrastructure in collaboration with AUC, AfDB and RECs; NEPAD Transport Summit, Johannesburg, Nov 2009; Private Sector Development, etc.

[105] Benedek, W., "Human Rights in a Multi-Cultural Perspective: The African Charter and the Human Right to Development", in Ginther K. and Benedek, W.

2.1.2 The Right to the Common Heritage of Mankind

At first this concept may appear abstract and theoretical. Mohammed Bedjaoui, however, extends its understanding to world food stocks. Bedjaoui says that

> "This concept in fact affords the opportunity for a new and spectacular departure for mankind in the quest for its 'right to development'. Far from being illusory, this concept offers an outstanding chance to break free of a number of long-established factors of confrontation, domination and appropriation."[106]

When referring to the 'common heritage of mankind' Ouguergouz also focuses on the idea that

> "natural resources, which were once thought to be unlimited, are at risk of depletion through uncontrolled exploitation and that the legal regime of the spaces in which they are found needs to be redefined so that they benefit both countries currently lacking the material means to gain access to them and future generations too."[107]

In international law, the concept of the common heritage of mankind has been often invoked, although not exclusively, in relation to the law of the sea whereby the sea-bed outside the exclusive jurisdiction of States has been considered the common heritage of mankind.[108] The United Nations Convention on the Law of the Sea also recognizes the concept of the common heritage of mankind, applying it to the 'area' referred to in the abovementioned resolution. The resources in the area are not subject to appropriation; the activities conducted therein must be for peaceful purposes and be conducted in an orderly, safe and rational manner in the interests of all mankind; its benefits are to be equitably shared.[109]

(Ed), *New Perspectives and Conceptions of International Law. An Afro-European Dialogue*, Supplement 6, Vienna, at 157.

[106] Bedjaoui, M., "The Right to Development", in Bedjaoui, M. (ed), *International Law: Achievements and Prospects*, UNESCO & Martinus Nijhoff Publishers, Paris, 1991, at 1198.

[107] Ouguergouz, F. *op. cit.*, at321.

[108] For instance, the UNGA, *Res.* 2749 (XXV) of 17th December 1970, states: *The sea-bed and ocean floor, and the subsoil thereof beyond the limits of national jurisdiction, (hereinafter referred to as the 'area') as well as the resources of the area, are the common heritage of mankind.*

[109] See Ouguergouz, F. *op. cit.*, at327.

The need to respect the 'common heritage of mankind' has also brought into light resolutions such as 1803 (XVII) of 14 December 1962, on the permanent sovereignty over natural resources, which seeks to limit the exploitation of resources by other States or parties without the express consent of the 'owner' State. This aims at preventing abuses such as illegal diamond trade witnessed in Liberia and Sierra Leone or Congo's gold scandals. This will also encourage States to regulate quantity and extraction methods so as to prevent depletion.

The African Charter stipulates that all peoples have the right to the equal enjoyment of the common heritage of mankind.[110] Although it still remains an abstractly defined right, it has been reasoned that the Charter is narrowing down the right by identifying peoples as its beneficiaries.[111] Furthermore, it has been stated that the beneficiary may be interpreted to mean peoples within a State and not only the people forming a State.[112]

2.1.3 The Right to Peace and Security

In pre-colonial Africa, before resorting to war, the parties had to try and settle any dispute peacefully. In Togo the conduct of such peace initiatives was entrusted to nobles of the conflicting parties; in Burkina Faso to the imperial guards; in Burundi and Rwanda to notables; and in Uganda and Kenya to elders. Parties would not resort to war unless these efforts had been unsuccessful.[113] There were also rules governing the start of hostilities such as the beating of drums or blowing of horns, and war activities were subject to certain rules and principles affecting, for example, the behaviour of warriors, the conduct of war, the treatment of non-combatants, etc.[114]

In China, one of the classics of literature on military strategy, the Art of War by *Siun Tseu*, written about 500 BC contained important humane requirements during combat such as "a commander must show intelligence, sincerity, humanity, courage and dignity; he must respect prisoners of war ... and should avoid using needless violence; a commander should not seek

---

[110] *African Charter*, Article 22 (1).
[111] Ouguergouz, F. *op. cit.*, at331-332.
[112] This clearly brings forward the reality of the diversity and strong ethnic differences within the African State. Further, see below for a discussion of the designation of 'people' as a legal subject in the Charter.
[113] Ndam Njoya, A., "The African Concept of Humanitarian Law", in *International Dimensions of Humanitarian Law*, Edited by Henry Dunant Institute and UNESCO, Martinus Nijhoff, Dordrecht, 1988, at 6.
[114] *Ibid.*, at 7.

the total annihilation of the enemy."[115] The Code of *Mañava-dharma-sãstra* (200 BC – 200 AD), compendium of laws, morals and customs of the people of India also contained norms pertaining to the protection of victims of war. According to this Code a soldier would be allowed neither to kill an enemy by using a hidden weapon nor to attack one who had surrendered or was severely wounded or fleeing.[116]

In the Islamic world there is no distinction, as such, between the various types of war or armed conflicts. A war could aim at propagating the Islamic faith or against schismatics or rebels, but the rules governing the conduct of war would be the same inasmuch as they were laid down by the same divine authority and would cover all conflicts regardless of their nature.[117] Islamic rules of war were based on mercy, clemency and compassion, and a fighter should not transgress the limits of the basic principles of the Islamic legal system: justice and equity.[118]

The concept of *Bellum Justum* (just war) developed further in the Christian world. This came about as a consequence of the Christianisation of the Roman Empire.[119] Force could be used provided it complied with requirements of justice and it was employed as the ultimate sanction for the maintenance of an ordered society. War was to be embarked upon to punish wrongs and restore the peaceful *status quo,* but no further. Augustine enunciated a fundamental principle of self-defence by which just wars were justified on the basis that the wrong suffered at the hands of the adversary would be worse than the war itself.[120]

The Christian concept of just war was developed further by Thomas of Aquinas in the 13th Century, who inferred that for a war to be just it had to fulfil three conditions: First, *auctoritas principis* (principle of authority)

---

[115] Adachi, S., "The Asian Concept", *in International Dimensions of Humanitarian Law,* Edited by Henry Dunant Institute and UNESCO, Martinus Nijhoff, Dordrecht, 1988, at 13.

[116] *Ibid.*, at 13.

[117] Hamed, S., "The Islamic Concept of Humanitarian Law", in *International Dimensions of Humanitarian Law*, Edited by Henry Dunant Institute and UNESCO, Martinus Nijhoff, Dordrecht, 1988, at 32.

[118] In the 2nd Sura of the Koran, among the instructions of Mohammed to his troops, formal prohibition of mutilation, torture and any other degrading treatment of enemies in war, are found.

[119] Shaw, M.N., *International Law*, 3rd ed., Grotius Publications Limited, Cambridge, 1991, at 16-21.

[120] See Augustine of Hippo, *De Civitate Dei*, Penguin Books, Edition of 2004, Book XIX § VII.

under which a war must be conducted by the authority of a prince, not privately. A privately undertaken war would be called nowadays a "mercenary activity". Second, *causa justa* (a just cause): there should be a just cause to engage in war. And third, *intentio recta* (right intention): not only the just cause but the right intention to promote good, and avoid evil on the part of the belligerents.[121]

For centuries scholars searched for just causes so as to justify war but it was Grotius who, without neglecting the importance of just causes as such, emphasised the duty of the belligerents to observe certain rules of warfare. It would take time for this doctrine to be accepted as a firm principle of international law.[122]

Since time immemorial, Cassese says, war would involve suffering for both combatants and civilians, although during the 17th and 18th century war tended to become a *game of professionals*, where civilians would not suffer direct involvement in war actions.[123] Nevertheless the invention of *gunpowder* was one of the chief instruments in freeing the world from the dominion of physical force.[124] Thus, war became an extended instrument with no differentiation of combatant and civilian. It turned into a mass instrument of annihilation for which special skills and physical strength

---

[121] See Aquinas, T., *Summa Theologica*, Secunda Secundae, Questio 40, Article 1 on Whether it is Always Sinful to Wage War, Christian Classics, Westminster, Maryland, 1920.

[122] Grotius, *De Iure Belli Ac Pacis*, Libri tres, Vol. 2. Cited by Draper, G.I.A.D., "The Development of International Humanitarian Law", in *International Dimensions of Humanitarian Law*, Edited by Henry Dunant Institute and UNESCO, Martinus Nijhoff, Dordrecht, 1988, at 68.Grotius was horrified at the excesses in the Thirty Years War. He wrote: "*Throughout the Christian world I observed a lack of restraint in relation to war such as even barbarous races would be ashamed of. I observed that men rush to arms for slight causes, or no cause at all, and that when arms have once been taken up, there is no longer any respect for law, divine or human; it is as if, in accordance with a general decree, frenzy had openly let loose for the committing of all crimes.*" The Thirty Years War concluded at the "*Peace of Westphalia*" in 1648. The Spanish-Dutch treaty, terminating the Eighty Years' War between Spain and the Dutch and the German phase, was signed on Jan. 30, 1648. The treaty of Oct. 24, 1648, comprehended the Holy Roman emperor Ferdinand III, the other German princes, France, and Sweden. England, Poland, Muscovy, and Turkey were the only European powers that were not represented at the two. (See E.B., M. Edition).

[123] Cassese, A., *International Law in a Divided World*, Clarendon Press, Oxford, 1994, at 255.

[124] See Cassese, *op. cit.*, at 256.

would no longer be as essential as before. Within this frame of ideas, the French Revolution yielded the concept and the crude reality of 'total wars'[125]which made armed conflicts become even crueller and bloodier.

In the 19th century, humanitarian ideals on warfare began to develop. His precursor is Henry Dunant with his work '*Un Souvenir de Sólferino'* written in 1862 after the battle of Solferino for which he was an eye witness.[126]

In 1863 Francis Lieber[127] prepared the Instructions for the Government of the Armies of the United States in the Field. This document was published as General Orders No. 100 by President Lincoln on 24thApril 1863. The Lieber Instructions, as they were later known, were the first attempt to codify the laws of war.

Eleven years later, in 1874, a conference was convened at Brussels by Tsar Alexander II, at which the Lieber Instructions were a preparatory text. This conference did not succeed but its proposals were presented at the First Hague Peace Conference of 1899 convened by Tsar Nicholas II.[128] Four Conventions were established at this Conference and, at the

---

[125] *Ibid.*, at 255.

[126] See *The Thirty Year's War,* in E.B. (2000).Dunant, J.H. (1828-1910), Swiss philanthropist and founder of the Red Cross, born in Geneva. He was brought up as a Seventh Day Adventist. His mother was deeply religious. While still young he was one of the founders of the YMCA. Dunant was appalled by the condition of the wounded he saw near the battlefield of Solferino, Italy, in 1859, during the Franco-Austrian War. In his book (translated in 1911) he suggested that neutral organizations should be established to aid wounded soldiers in time of war. In 1863 an international conference was held in Geneva and committee was established to study the issue. This committee was known as the 'committee of five' composed by General D.H. Dufour as president, Gustave Moynier, Henry Dunant, Théodore Maunoir and Louis Appia, and, at the Geneva Convention of 1864 the results of this committee became the *International Committee of the Red Cross*. In 1901 Dunant shared the first Nobel Peace Prize with the French statesman Frédéric Passy. Among Dunant's writings are *Fraternité et charité internationales en temps de guerre* (International Brotherhood and Charity in Time of War, 1864).

[127] Francis Lieber (1800-1872) was a professor of Columbia College in New York.

[128] The first conference was called for the purpose of bringing together the principal nations of the world to discuss and resolve the problems of maintaining universal peace, reducing armaments, and ameliorating the conditions of warfare. Twenty-six countries accepted the invitation to the conference issued by the minister of foreign affairs of the Netherlands and, on May 18, 1899, 101 delegates, including jurists, diplomats, and high army and naval officers, held their first

Second Conference, in 1907,[129] other thirteen Conventions were adopted including those which had failed at Brussels in 1874.[130] This extensive codification at the beginning of the 20th century was, according to Draper, the outcome of the central question of how to harmonise military needs to the dictates of humanity in times of war.[131]

---

meeting at a 17th-century villa in The Hague, the *Huis ten Bosch* (The House in the Wood). The last meeting took place on July 29, 1899. The delegates to the conference entered into three formal conventions, or treaties. The first and most important one set up permanent machinery for the optional arbitration of controversial issues between nations. This machinery took the form of the Permanent Court of Arbitration, popularly known as The Hague Court or Hague Tribunal. The second and third conventions revised some of the customs and laws of warfare to eliminate unnecessary suffering during a war on the part of all concerned, whether combatants, non-combatants, or neutrals. These two conventions were supplemented by three declarations, to stay in force five years, forbidding the use of poison gas, expanding (or dumdum) bullets, and bombardment from the air by the use of balloons or by other means. Despite the failure of the conference to limit armaments, or to provide for compulsory arbitration of international disputes—the great nations refused to adopt compulsory arbitration because it infringed on their national sovereignty—the conference was one of the most significant international conferences of modern times, because it was the first multilateral international conference on general issues since the Congress of Vienna in 1815 and pointed forward to the later League of Nations, forerunner of the United Nations. *See The Hague Conferences,* E.B. 2000.

[129] The idea of holding the Second International Peace Conference was first proposed by U.S. Secretary of State John Milton Hay in 1904, and it was called three years later on the direct initiative of the Russian government. The conference took place at The Hague from June 15 to October 18, 1907, and was attended by representatives from 44 countries. The second conference resulted in 13 conventions, which were concerned principally with clarifying and amplifying the understandings arrived at in the first conference. In particular, new principles were established in regard to various aspects of warfare, including the rights and duties of neutrals, naval bombardment, the laying of automatic submarine contact mines, and the conditions under which merchant ships might be converted into warships. The second conference recommended that a third conference be held within eight years. The government of the Netherlands actually began preparations for such a conference, to be held in 1915 or 1916; the outbreak of World War I, however, put an end to the preparations. After 1919, and until the formation of the UN in 1945, the functions of the Hague conferences were largely carried on by the League of Nations. *See The Hague Conferences in Encyclopaedia Encarta 97.*

[130] See Draper, G.I.A.D., in *International Dimensions of Humanitarian Law*, Edited by Henry Dunant Institute and UNESCO, Martinus Nijhoff, Dordrecht, 1988, at 71.

[131] Draper, G.I.A.D., *op. cit.*, at 73.

The experiences of warfare between 1914 and 1918 revealed important loopholes in the Hague Conventions. The 1917 and 1918 Berne Agreements, the 1929 Geneva Conventions, the 1925 Geneva Gas Protocol and the Protocol to the 1936 London Naval Agreement were attempts to fill those gaps. But it was after the World War II, in 1949, that the comprehensive four Geneva Conventions for the Protection of War Victims were adopted. These Conventions were a landmark in the struggle to minimise violations of the *jus in bello*. Years later, the 1949 Geneva Conventions were strengthened, and their scope widened, by the 1977 First and Second Protocols.

In the 20th century Africa has borne the brunt of the majority of the world's conflicts presently.[132] Peace and security have a deep relationship to economic and social development. It is not surprising that States that are unstable and insecure have also experienced retarded development, a reality which has plagued the African continent for decades. As Kofi Annan expressed in his 2005 report, "not only are development, security and human rights all imperative; they also reinforce each other."[133] He further stated:

> "Human rights are as fundamental to the poor as to the rich, and their protection is as important to the security and prosperity of the developed world as it is to that of the developing world. It would be a mistake to treat human rights as though there were a trade-off to be made between human rights and such goals as security or development. We only weaken our hand in fighting the horrors of extreme poverty or terrorism if, in our efforts to do so, we deny the very human rights that these scourges take away from citizens. Strategies based on the protection of human rights are vital for both our moral standing and the practical effectiveness of our actions."[134]

The importance of this relationship 'peace-security-development' has been emphasized in multilateral legally binding and non-binding instruments as well as proclaimed by scholars and diplomatic officials.[135]Article 23(1)

---

[132] As Kofi Annan stated: *Out of two dozen or more conflicts raging around the world, roughly half are in Africa*. See Kofi, A., former UN Secretary General, 4087th meeting of the *Security Council* relating to the situation in Africa and the impact of AIDS on peace and security in Africa.

[133] UNGA, "In larger freedom: towards development, security and human rights for all", *Report of the Secretary-General*, A/59, (2005), No. 16.

[134] *Ibid*, No. 140.

[135] For instance the *Universal Declaration of Human Rights* holds that recognition of the inherent dignity and of the equal and inalienable rights of all members of the

of the African Charter states that: "all peoples shall have the right to national and international peace and security." The approach adopted by African States was to anticipate and prevent situations of potential conflict, e.g. the establishment by the OAU Heads of State and Government of the Mechanism of Conflict Prevention, Management and Resolution. Africa's concern with security and peace is evident from its denuclearization treaties commenced since the establishment of the OAU and culminating in the African Nuclear Weapon Free Zone Treaty of 1996. The Charter does not mention previous disarmament legal instruments, choosing to couch this right in terms of the principle of solidarity and friendly relations. An expression of the former is in the mutual defence treaties signed by some African States. However, by referring to the principles of solidarity and friendly relations, Article 23 (2) aims particularly at the prohibition of subversive activities, which severely limits its scope in view of the reality of conflict in Africa that goes beyond this limited range of activities.

Subversive activities in Africa have been a concern of the OAU since 1963; hence Article III (5) of the OAU Charter made political assassination and subversive terrorist activities on the part of neighbouring States or any other State a principle of unreserved condemnation. This concern evolved due to the refugee problem which States endeavoured to prevent from being a source of friction between them.[136]

From Article 23(2), it may be concluded that the only subject and beneficiary of the right to peace is the people forming a State. However, the reference in Article 23(1) to national and international peace and security permits both people of a State taken as a whole and its different ethnic components taken individually.

---

human family is the foundation of peace in the world and that everyone is entitled to a social and international order in which the rights and freedoms set forth in the Declaration can be fully realized. This was also recognized by the OAU in 1998 when its then chairman acknowledged that security goes hand in hand with economic development, with social development, with democratization, with human rights… [20th *Conference of Heads of State of France and Africa*].

136 OAU (1965), *The Problem of Refugees in Africa*, AHG/Res. 26 (II), (paragraphs 2 and 3) adopted at the 2nd Ordinary Session of the Assembly of Heads of State and Government, Accra (Ghana) from 21st to 25th October 1965.

2.1.4 The Right to a Satisfactory Environment

The question of the environment has attracted significant attention in international and national law. At the universal level, one of the most notable United Nations conferences was the United Nations Conference on the Human Environment, at Stockholm, in 1972. This conference adopted the "Stockholm Declaration"[137] which may be considered the starting point for the recognition of a right to a satisfactory environment.[138] Twenty years later, this was followed by another environmental landmark, the Rio Declaration on Environment and Development.[139] Though non-binding, these instruments have provided the impetus for the development of numerous legally binding instruments. At the regional level, Article 11 of the Additional Protocol to the American Convention on Human Rights[140] states that "everyone shall have the right to live in a healthy environment and to have access to basic public services. States parties shall promote the protection, preservation and improvement of the environment."[141] In the European context, the right to a satisfactory environment has not formally acquired the form of an additional protocol to the European Convention on Human Rights nor has it been adopted as a separate instrument. However, the European Court of Human Rights has recognized a right to a clean environment on the basis of respect for private life and the home.[142]

The African Charter states that "all peoples shall have the right to a general satisfactory environment favourable to their development."[143] This formulation implies a wider connotation of environment and development which is not merely ecological. Certainly, the provision of article 24 places no precise obligation on States parties. Ouguergouz[144] points out that it might be thought that the implementation of the right of peoples to a

---

[137] Declaration of the United Nations Conference on the Human Environment, *Report on the United Nations Conference on the Human Environment-Stockholm*, 5-16 June 1972, New York, United Nations, 1973, Doc. A/CONF.48/14/Rev. 1, at 148-149.

[138] Kromarek, P., "Environment and Human Rights", *Human Rights Teaching*, vol. 3, UNESCO, (1982), at 26.

[139] Adopted by the *United Nations Conference on Environment and Development* in 1992.

[140] Adopted in San Salvador on 17th November 1988.

[141] *Protocol of San Salvador*, Article 11(1 and 2).

[142] E.g. in *Lopez Ostra v. Spain*,16798/90 [1994] ECHR 46, 9thDecember 1994.

[143] See *African Charter,* article 24 of the Charter.

[144] Ouguergouz, F. *op. cit.*, at365.

satisfactory environment would consist in States compliance with obligations in other international legal instruments both universal and regional.[145] Furthermore, the constitutions of several African States give recognition to the protection of the environment.[146] As with the other solidarity rights, the Charter seems to have created an ambiguity by stating the subject of this right to be 'all peoples' which could mean the people forming a State but also a people within a State such as the ethnic group, or all African peoples. This seems to make its protection and eventual enforcement cumbersome.

Jess Estanislao points at a wider conception of environment and development that is already taking root in scholarly circles. Estanislao asserts:

> "There are many views on development that have been put forward over decades. Inevitably, they stress economic growth, which needs to be sustained over a long period such that it leads to structural change in the economy. Many of these views reflect the search for the magic bullet that can propel peoples and nations from a State of backwardness to one of prosperity within a few generations, preferably only one or two. They tend to focus on a few – if not on only one of key factors, e.g. education, population control, opening to the rest of the world through free trade, development of credit and capital markets, the destruction of the old culture through violent revolution to give way to a new classless society, State planning, environmental protection, moral values and civic education, democracy, etc. (…) However, development, to be genuine, must be of people, by people, and for people. It must lead to the improvement of the people themselves; in other words; they have to become better. And they become so mainly by being involved in the process of development itself: they need to participate in it, necessitating the need to be better equipped for work, at which they become increasingly more productive and efficient, such that development is truly by them. And as a result, the benefits of development should redound upon them: they should be the ones to enjoy many more fruits of development and the opportunities that it opens up. Indeed, development has to be for people, for all the people, who end up having more in life---including the material,

---

[145] For a regional instrument, see *African Convention on the Conservation of Nature and Natural Resources*, adopted in Algiers on 15th September 1968.

[146] For example, the Kenyan Constitution in Articles 42, 69 and 70 provides for the right to a clean and healthy environment as well as the State's obligations and means of enforcement of this right. Other African constitutions contain numerous articles related to environmental protection, for example: (Number of times environmental protection is mentioned) Eritrea 2, Congo 7, Ethiopia 7, Madagascar 7, Mali 6, South Africa 6, Malawi 5.

> but not exclusively the material aspects---as well as wider prospects for an even better future."[147]

The African Charter encourages compliance and the building of a culture of human rights through State reporting and complaints. It establishes organs for the protection and promotion of these rights: the Commission and the Court. These organs are now playing a greater and more active role which must be praised. Nevertheless, Governments usually delay the presentation of reports and often default representation at the meetings. It is remarkable that the 2002 Activity Report of the Commission praised the record number of State parties represented at the meeting (only 36 out of 53 countries participated and this was hailed as a record participation).[148]

Report defaulting is not, however, an African problem. Kofi Anna already expressed this worldwide concern when he stated that:

> "The [human rights] treaty body system remains little known; is compromised by the failure of many States to report on time if at all, as well as the duplication of reporting requirements; and is weakened further by poor implementation of recommendations. Harmonized guidelines on reporting to all treaty bodies should be finalized and implemented so that these bodies can function as a unified system."[149]

Although a lot has been accomplished in the past two decades, there are still many aspirations and dreams enshrined in the Charter yet to be achieved and respected.

2.1.5 The duties of the individual

In the Universal Declaration of Human Rights, articles 29 and 30 specifically deal with the concept of the duties of the individual, though falling short of laying down the content of these duties. Article 29(1) provides that everyone has duties to the community in which alone the free and full development of his personality is possible. Article 30

---

[147] Estanislao, J., "A View on Development as a Calling to Continuing Improvement", Paper presented at the *7th Annual Conference*, Strathmore University, Nairobi, 28th and 29th October 2010. (Currently in Press).

[148] Fifteenth Annual Activity Report of the African Commission on Human and Peoples' Rights, (2001-2002). Available at: *https://docs.google.com/viewer?url=http%3A%2F%2Fwww.achpr.org%2Fenglish%2Factivity_reports%2Factivity15_en.pdf*

[149] UNGA, "In larger freedom: towards development, security and human rights for all", *Report of the Secretary-General*, A/59, (2005), No. 16.

provides that nothing in the declaration may be interpreted as implying for any State, group or person any right to engage in any activity or to perform any act aimed at the destruction of any of the rights and freedoms set forth therein. In this formulation, Article 30 recognises general human duties which are a corollary of the rights enshrined therein.

At the American regional level, the American Declaration of the Rights and Duties of Man[150] devotes eleven articles to the duties of the individual which include *inter alia* duties of parents towards their children, the duty to acquire education, the duty to work etc. Subsequently, the American Convention on Human Rights[151] would contain only one article on the duties of the individual, namely article 32.[152]

In the European context, the European Convention for the Protection of Human Rights and Fundamental Freedoms[153] implicitly provides for the duty of the individual in article 13 among other provisions.[154] However, Marc-Andre Eissen observes that these duties are conceived as a corollary to the rights contained in the instrument and that in this respect, the Convention would be resolutely individualistic.[155]

The African Charter devotes three articles, namely 27, 28 and 29 to the duties of the individual. It has been argued that the inclusion of the duties of the individual in the Charter is tied to the African conception of human rights and African traditional social organization along the African societal specificities put forward by Leopold Senghor[156] when he stated that:

> "Room should be made for [the] African tradition in our Charter on Human and Peoples' Rights, while bathing in our philosophy, which consists in not alienating the subordination of the individual to the community, in co-existence, in giving everyone a certain number of rights

---

[150]Adopted at the 9th *International American Conference* in March 1948, at Bogota, Colombia.
[151] Adopted on 22nd November 1969 at San José, Costa Rica.
[152] IACHR, Article 32 states: *1. Every person has responsibilities to his family, his community and mankind. 2. The rights of each person are limited by the rights of others, by security of all, and by the just demands of the general welfare in a democratic society.*
[153] Adopted on 4th November 1950.
[154] Ouguergouz, F., *op. cit.*, at398.
[155] Eissen, M.A., "La Convention et les devoirs de l'individu", in *La protection international des droits de l'homme dans le cadre europeen*, Proceedings of the Workshop organized by the Faculty of Law of Strasbourg on 14 and 15 November 1960, Dalloz, Paris, (1961), at 181.
[156] See *supra* note no. 43.

and duties. In Europe, human rights are considered as a body of principles and rules placed in the hands of the individual, as a weapon, thus enabling him to defend himself against the group or entity representing it. In Africa, the individual and his rights are wrapped in the protection of the family and other communities ... Rights in Africa ... cannot be separated from the obligations due to the family and other communities."[157]

Therefore, it is in light of this central role of the person that the Charter should be considered.[158] The idea of the person's duties to others and to society is the natural outcome of his/her exercise of rights[159]and not as Okoth-Ogendo puts it: "little more than the formulation, entrenchment, and legitimation of State rights and privileges against individuals and peoples."[160] Makau Mutua says that:

> "In my view, these criticisms, while understandable, are mistaken. African States have not notoriously violated human rights because of their adherence to the concept of duty. The disastrous human rights performance of many African States has been triggered by insecure regimes whose narrow political classes have no sense of national interest and will stop at nothing, including murder, to retain power. In any case, it is not a plausible argument that individuals should not owe any duties to the State. In fact, they do, in tax, criminal, and other laws. A valid criticism of the language of duties should rather focus on the precise meaning, content, conditions of compliance, and application of those duties. More work should be done to clarify the status of the duties in the Charter, and define their moral and legal dimensions and implications for enforcement."[161]

The challenge may be the moral and legal degree of enforcement of the duties as expressed in the Charter.

Article 27 of the Charter states that: "1. Every individual shall have duties toward his family and society, the State and other legally recognized communities and the international community. 2. The rights

---

[157] *Ibid.*

[158] Ouguergouz, F. *op. cit.*, at376. This idea is formulated in the sixth paragraph of the Preamble: *Considering that the enjoyment of rights and freedoms also implies the performance of duties on the part of everyone.*

[159] For a brief comparison, see Ouguergouz, F. *op. cit.*, at381-382.

[160] Okoth-Ogendo, H.W.O., "Human and Peoples' Rights: What Point is Africa Trying to Make?" in Cohen, Hydén and Nagan (eds.), *Human Rights and Governance in Africa*, University Press of Florida, Gainesville, 1993, at 74.

[161] Mutua, M., "The African Human Rights System, a Critical Evaluation" (2000), at 12.Available at:
http://hdr.undp.org/en/reports/global/hdr2000/papers/mutua.pdf

and freedoms of each individual shall be exercised with due regard to the rights of others, collective security, morality and common interest."[162]

It is argued that it is preferable to regard this article as an introductory provision laying down a general statement on the duties of the individual and articles 28 and 29 as specifying the content of these duties.[163] The first paragraph identifies five entities that the individual has duties toward, namely the family, society, the State, other legally recognized communities and the international community. The second paragraph may however be regarded as a claw-back clause which seems dangerous. This clause places restrictions on the rights and freedoms of the individual without making them subject to the requirement of legality.[164]

Article 28 states that: "Every individual shall have the duty to respect and consider his fellow beings without discrimination and to maintain relations aimed at promoting, safeguarding and reinforcing mutual respect and tolerance."

Here, the principle of non-discrimination is used in the context of relations between individuals. Ouguergouz argues that the reason for this lies in the heterogeneousness of African States.[165] Article 28 also lays down the duty to maintain relations aimed at promoting, safeguarding and reinforcing mutual respect and tolerance which is a general duty.

Article 29 is the most detailed of the three articles on the duties of the individual and lays down several duties totalling eight sub-articles. Article 29(1) provides that the individual shall have the duty: "To preserve the harmonious development of the family and to work for the cohesion and respect of the family; to respect his parents at all times, to maintain them in case of need."

This lays down what seems to be a general duty to the family. However, in the African context, the family extends beyond the nuclear, thus reaching out to the extended family.[166] Traditionally, the duty to preserve and work for the cohesion and respect of the family is a traditional obligation in the African context and it may be easily fulfilled.

---

[162] *African Charter*, Article 27.

[163] Ouguergouz, F. *op. cit.*, at401.

[164] Ouguergouz, F. *op. cit.*, at402

[165] *Ibid.*

[166] In many African languages (for example in *Dholuo* – around Lake Victoria or in *Shona* spoken by 80% of Zimbabweans) there is no word for cousin for they are all brothers/sisters. Even first or second cousin are meaningless terms.

It has been argued that 'family' here should also mean 'extended family.'[167] The second part lays down the duty to respect one's parents and maintain them in case of need. In the case of parents, Ouguergouz asserts, that the term parents should be understood *stricto sensu* as biological father and mother, even though in most African legal systems the duty to maintain applies, in principle, to a much wider category of persons.[168]

Certainly, there is no doubt whatsoever, that in the African Charter, family is always and exclusively understood and founded on the biological reality of man-woman, children and relatives. Even liberal authors such as Michael Gose says that, "the emphasis the Charter lays on the notion of family is, however, an expression of a specific African understanding and must be interpreted from an African point of view. Such an interpretation leads to the assumption that the term "family" cannot be understood in the traditional, narrow, Western concept…"[169]

Moreover, Corine Packer acknowledges that the family clauses

> "… were never intended to maintain the cultural subjugation of women but simply to convey the idealism with which the drafters forged the Charter. Indeed, given the historical framework which inspired the drafting of the African Charter this conclusion is very probable. Much as the duty to preserve and protect the family is placed within the hands of the State and the individual, the obligation to protect the morals and values of African society is similarly dispersed among the State (preamble and Article 18(1)), the family (Article 18(2)), and the individual (Article 29(7)). This is very much in keeping with African culture since African women are seen, and sometimes consider themselves, as the custodians and defenders of culture and cultural values. For instance, at the first African Indigenous Women's Conference held in Morocco in April 1998, one of the central issues women addressed was 'their role as treasurers of the cultural heritage of their people.' Even African music continues to project the idealistic image of the woman as the symbol of family stability and the moral fibre of the whole nation… [Women] are recognised in the Charter as the messenger and not the creator of socio-cultural values."[170]

---

[167] Ouguergouz, F. *op. cit.*, at 404.

[168] *Ibid*, at 405.

[169] Gose, M., *The African Charter on the Rights and Welfare of the Child*, Published by the Community Law Centre, University of Western Cape, Bellville, 2002, at 97.

[170] Packer, A.A.C., *Using human rights to change tradition: traditional practices harmful to Women's Reproductive Health in Sub-Saharan Africa*, Intersentia, Utrecht, 2002, at 121.

Thus, it would be insincere to attempt to justify homosexual unions as family under this instrument. The Charter clearly states in article 18 the following: "(1) The family shall be the natural unit and basis of society. It shall be protected by the State which shall take care of its physical health and morals. 2. The State shall have the duty to assist the family which is the custodian or morals and traditional values recognized by the community." Article 27 further states the specific duty as follows: "(1) Every individual shall have duties towards his family and society, the State and other legally recognized communities and the international community."[171]

In its last report to the Commission, Uganda has stated that the Ugandan Constitution recognizes the important maternal functions of women and the right to start a family. The report adds that,

> "Affirmative action provisions in the Constitutions have been adhered to in this regard, leading to at least 30% representation of women councillors, and 30% composition of women in Parliament. Affirmative action in the education system at Primary and university level has significantly resulted in increased enrolment of girls in the education system. Girl child education increased from 44.2% in 1990 to 49.9% in 2008, although their retention rates are still challenged by cultural, social and perception factors. Progress also includes the passing of laws to support the family and community values. These include the Domestic Violence Act 2010, a law that seeks to protect victims of domestic violence and to punish perpetrators. It is not only limited to physical harm, but also economic, emotional, verbal and psychological abuse which has previously gone unnoticed, and the Prevention of Female Genital Mutilation (FGM) Act. The Act criminalizes the practice of FGM, prosecution of offenders and protection of victims. There are however other critical laws that are still pending which would enable the majority of people in Uganda to attain family justice… These include: the Sexual Offences (Amendment) Bill, the Penal Code (Amendment) Act - to take into consideration the issue of criminal adultery, the Succession (Amendment) Act – to take into consideration aspects of equal inheritance between men and women… The Ministry of Gender, Labour and Social Development has also created a Family Affairs department and is in process of recruiting staff."[172]

---

[171] It seems clear that the context and intension of the drafters state family as biological parents and relatives.

[172] Periodic report by the Government of Uganda to the African Commission on Human and Peoples' Rights presented at the 49th Ordinary Session Banjul, the Gambia, 21st April 2011.

The Charter also contemplates duties to society in general. These are set out in Article 29 (4), (6) and (7). Article 29(4) provides that the individual has the duty "to preserve and strengthen social and national solidarity, particularly when the latter is threatened." The duty to strengthen national solidarity has been argued to be "only didactic, its purpose being to stimulate the individual's spirit of solidarity. Of itself, it cannot constitute an adequate legal basis for the imposition of certain duties on the individual."[173] Article 29(6) on the other hand provides for the duty "to work to the best of his abilities and competence and to pay taxes imposed by law in the interest of the society." The duty to work must be situated in the context of African States' under-development. Article 29(7) provides for the duty "to preserve and strengthen positive African cultural values in his relations with other members of the society, in the spirit of tolerance, dialogue and consultation and in general to contribute to the promotion of the moral well-being [sic] of society." It has been argued[174] that this can be seen as part of the implementation of the 1976 Cultural Charter for Africa, one of whose objectives is to develop all dynamic values in the African cultural heritage and to reject any element which is an impediment to progress.

The Charter also dedicates articles 29(2, 3 and 5) to 'Duties to the State and Others." These are provided for through various references to national community, State and country. Article 29(2) states that the individual has the duty "to serve his national community by placing his physical and intellectual abilities at its service." Article 29(3) states that the individual has the duty "not to compromise the security of the State whose national or resident he is." This duty is imposed not only on the nationals of a State but also those residing in it. This has been viewed as aimed at political refugees who have a duty not to engage in subversive activities against the State in which they reside.[175] Finally, Article 29(5) provides for the individual's duty "to preserve and strengthen the national independence and the territorial integrity of his country and to contribute to its defence in accordance with the law," which duty is naturally part of every person's civic obligations.

Finally, the Charter establishes 'duties to the international community'. Article 27(1) identifies the international community as one of the entities to which the individual owes a duty. Article 29(8) states that the individual

---

[173] Ouguergouz, F., *op. cit.*, at406-7.
[174] *Ibid*, at 407.
[175] *Ibid.*, at410

has the duty "to contribute to the best of his abilities at all times and at all levels to the promotion and achievement of African unity." This duty is similar to one of the purposes assigned to African states parties to the Constituent Charter of the Organization of African Unity, which leads Ouguergouz to observe the individual difficulty of performing this abstract duty other than by fulfilling the obligation, for instance, not to engage in subversive activities, refrain from propaganda for war or hatred, etc.[176] Furthermore, the expression 'to the best of his abilities' implies that this is an abstract duty of which specific results cannot be demanded.

Therefore, we can identify 'general' and 'special' duties in the African Charter.[177] The general duties are contained in Articles 27, 28 and 29(7). Article 27(2) lays down the limitations on the exercise of individual rights and freedoms which are the rights of others, collective security, morality and common interest. It has been argued that this provision, by setting out the criteria for a State's intervention in limiting the rights and freedoms of individuals, actually protects human rights.[178] This view was adopted by the African Commission in its decision of 31st October 1998 relating to four communications lodged against Nigeria:

> "The only legitimate reasons for limitations to the rights and freedoms of the African Charter are found in Article 27(2), that is, the rights of the Charter 'shall be exercised with due regard to the rights of others, collective security, morality and common interest'."[179]

The duty laid down in Article 28[180] has been viewed as no more than a moral one due to its generality and therefore it is placed beyond judicial control. Article 29(7) on the other hand, places an obligation to promote the moral well-being of society, which is similar to the traditional obligation to respect morality and public order. However, its reference to preserving and strengthening positive African cultural values has been marked as dangerous and compared to the elastic and ambiguous notions

---

176 *Ibid.*, at 411.

177 We follow the categorization by Ouguergouz.

178 Ouguergouz, F., *op. cit.*, at414.

179 ACHPR, Communications 105/93, 128/94, 130/94, 152/96, *Media Rights Agenda, Constitutional Rights Project, Media Rights Agenda and Constitutional Rights Project v. Nigeria, Twelfth Annual Report of the Commission-1998/1999.*

180 Article 28 says: "Every individual shall have the duty to respect and consider his fellow beings without discrimination, and to maintain relations aimed at promoting, safeguarding and reinforcing mutual respect and tolerance."

of 'public order' and 'normal standards of behavior.' However, this ought to be read in light of the limitations in Article 27(2).[181]

As regards the special duties, the duties to one's family contained in Article 29(1) are widely considered to be imposed on the individual already by domestic laws, apart from which the duties are no more than moral. With respect to the individual's duties to the State, most of them are also imposed at the national level, e.g. not to compromise the security of the State (Article 29(3)), to preserve national solidarity (Article 29(4)), to defend his country (Article 29(5)) and to pay taxes imposed by law (Article 29(6)). The duty to serve one's national community by placing one's physical and intellectual abilities at its service and the duty to work to the best of one's abilities and competence contained in Article 29(2) and (6) respectively complete the consideration of the special duties contained in the African Charter.[182]

2.1.6 The designation of 'people' as a legal subject

Generally, in international law, the concept of 'people' has arisen within the context of the right of 'peoples' to self-determination. Therefore, within this framework, 'people' have often been referred to as those who were or are under colonial or foreign subjugation.[183]

The African Charter does not define what constitutes the people. In fact, the authors made a "deliberate choice not to define certain concepts, such as that of 'peoples', in order to avoid becoming bogged down in a

[181] See Ouguergouz, F., *op. cit.*, at415.
[182] For a discussion of Articles 29 (2 and 6), see generally Ouguergouz, *op. cit.*
[183] See, for example, the *United Nations General Assembly Resolutions* 1514(XV) of 14th December 1960, and 2625 (XXV) of 24th October 1970. However, in its advisory opinion No. 2010/25, of 22 July 2010, in *Accordance with International Law of the Unilateral Declaration of Independence in Respect of Kosovo* the ICJ contextualized the right to self-determination by stating that "the international law of self-determination developed in such a way as to create a right to independence for the peoples of non-self-governing territories and peoples subject to alien subjugation, domination and exploitation' and that a 'great many new States have come into existence as a result of the exercise of this right'. The Court observes that there were, however, also instances of declarations of independence outside this context and that '[t]he practice of States in these latter cases does not point to the emergence in international law of a new rule prohibiting the making of a declaration of independence in such cases'."

complicated discussion."[184] The body of the Charter lends meaning to the concept of the people depending on the context within which the concept is used, leading one author to ponder whether the concept is 'chameleon-like.'[185]

In this light, the African Charter ascribes various meanings to the people without committing itself to a specific concept. People may mean 'State'. This view of the people is evident throughout the African Charter for example Article 23(2) states that "for the purpose of strengthening peace, solidarity and friendly relations, States parties to the present Charter shall ensure that: [...] (b) their territories shall not be used as bases for subversive or terrorist activities against the people of any other State party to the present Charter."

The people considered as the nationals of a State were not traditionally considered in international law as a subject of law; rather, it was the State representing them which was considered as the subject. However, modern human rights instruments and practice tend toward the consideration of the person and – by extension – of people as subject of human rights. This implies a paradigm shift that obliges States and international organizations to bypass considerations of sovereignty in certain cases.[186]

People may also be referred to as 'population', which is closely tied to the formulation of people as the nationals of a State. The population of a State goes beyond those who are its nationals but also includes those who are of residential status. This interpretation can be gleaned from the French version of the African Charter with respect to Article 21,[187] in which the French word "population" is used in the same breath as the word peoples. Though the word population does exist in English, this is not used in the English version of the Charter. The same is applicable to Article 16 of the Charter.[188]

---

[184] ACHPR, Decision relating to *Communications* 105/93, 128/94, 130/94, 152/96. *Media Rights Agenda, Constitutional Rights Project, Media Rights Agenda and Constitutional,* in the case of *Rights Project v. Nigeria,* text in 12th Annual Report of the Commission - 1998/1999.

[185] Ouguergouz, F., *op. cit.*, at204.

[186] We discuss this matter extensively in Chapter I, 3 *supra*.

[187] "*1. Les peuples ont la libre disposition de leurs richesses et de leurs ressources naturelles. Ce droit s'exerce dans l'intérêt des exclusif des populations...*"

[188] See The American Heritage Dictionary of the English Language, Fourth Edition by Houghton Mifflin Company, updated in 2009, available at

People may also mean 'entities under colonial or racial domination'. This conceptualization may be obtained from the reference to the liberation of the African people from colonialism, a goal which is emphatically stated from the preamble of the Charter as well as its substantive provisions. For example, paragraph 4 of the Preamble contextualises the people as those under colonial subjugation.[189] However, it has been argued[190] that this restrictive interpretation of people is an exception and is invalidated by both the Preamble itself and by the operative part of the Charter which use 'people' in a more general context. Proof of this exception is said to be found in Article 20(2) which relates to such situations: "colonized or oppressed peoples shall have the right to free themselves from the bonds of domination by resorting to any means recognized by the international community."

People may also be identified with an 'ethnic group'. Due to the ethnic plurality of the African people, it has been suggested[191] that the ethnic group may also be inferred from the concept of 'people' in the African Charter. In support of this proposition, reference is made to the prohibition of all discrimination based on the ethnic group[192] and the fact that if one refers to the traditional objective and subjective elements suggested for the definition of the people, the concept of the ethnic group fits in with it. Further, it is argued that this formulation is not foreign to international law

---

http://www.thefreedictionary.com/people. Population is understood as all the people living in a particular country, area or place. See also the Cambridge Advanced Learner's Dictionary, available at:
http://dictionary.cambridge.org/dictionary/british/population.
It may also be understood as *(sometimes functioning as plural) all the persons inhabiting a country, city, or other specified place; or the number of such inhabitants.* See Collins English Dictionary – Complete and Unabridged HarperCollins Publishers 2003, available at:
http://www.thefreedictionary.com/population.
People may be defined as *a body of persons living in the same country under one national government; a nationality; or body of persons sharing a common religion, culture, language, or inherited condition of life.* It may also be defined as *the citizens of a political unit, such as a nation or State; the electorate.* Used with '*the*'.

[189] *African Charter*, Reaffirming pledge they solemnly made in Article 2 of the said Charter to *eradicate all forms of colonialism from Africa, to coordinate and intensify their cooperation and efforts to achieve a better life for the peoples of Africa…*

[190] Ouguergouz, F., *op. cit.*, at208.

[191] See Ouguergouz, F., *op. cit.*, at 208-210, for an explanation on this.

[192] *African Charter*, Preamble, paragraph 8 and Article 2.

since the United Nations General Assembly made ethnicity one of the criteria for identifying the peoples in the non-self-governing territories.[193] It is therefore noteworthy that the African Commission has set up a working group of experts on the rights of indigenous peoples or communities in Africa.[194]

For Ruiloba, 'people' refers to the same reality as 'nation'.[195] However, Pastor Ridruejo explains that 'nation' evokes the National State born toward the end of the Modern age. In this regard, Pastor Ridruejo asserts that there are two different understandings of 'nation'. The objective view (German) and the subjective view (French). The first refers to objective elements such as language and ethnicity in a given human society. The second one – subjective – focuses on the will of a given society to consider itself a 'people', without due regard to language or ethnicity. As a matter of fact, it seems that contemporary international law has adopted an eclectic view whereby a 'people' may have objective elements such as language and ethnicity in common, together with the actual will to consider themselves a 'people'.[196]

Peoples' rights, according to the African Charter, include rights to equality, self-determination and control over natural resources, development and the entitlement to a safe environment. The African Commission has in certain instances been requested to consider the rights of peoples. One example is *Katangese Peoples' Congress v Zaire*[197] whereby the Katangese people sought to claim independence from Zaire based on Article 20(1) of

---

[193] Principle IV of GA Res. 1541(XV): '*prima facie* there is an obligation to transmit information in respect of a territory which is geographically separate and is distinct *ethnically* and/or *culturally* from the country administering it.' (*emphasis added*)

[194] See 70 ACHPR/Res.65 (XXXIV) 03.The African Commission on Human and People's Rights appointed this Group of Experts on 20th November 2003, at its 34th Ordinary Session, in Banjul, The Gambia. The group was composed of: Commissioner Andrew Ranganayi Chigovera (Chair), Commissioner Kamel Rezag Bara, Marianne Jensen (Independent Expert), Naomi Kipuri, Mohammed Khattali, Zephyrin Kalimbawas.

[195] Ruiloba Santana, E., "Una Nueva Categoría en el Panorama de la Subjetividad International; El Concepto de Pueblo", in *Estudios de Derecho Internacional. Homenaje al Profesor Miaja de la Muela*, Tecnos Ed, Madrid, 1979, vol. 1, at 303 ff.

[196] See Pastor Ridruejo, J.A., *Curso de Derecho Internacional Público y Organizaciones Internacionales*, 3rd Edition, Tecnos ed, Madrid, 1989, at 252.

[197] ACHPR, *Communication* 75/92.

the Charter. The Katangese people are only a portion of the population in Zaire.[198]

The claim for self-determination, however, did not result in the cessation of the Katangese from Zaire, as the Commission concluded that the case did not provide any evidence of violation of any rights under the African Charter. It stated that,

> "in the absence of concrete evidence of violations of human rights to the point that the territorial integrity of Zaire should be called to question and in the absence of evidence that the people of Katanga are denied the right to participate in Government as guaranteed by Article 13(1) of the African Charter, the Commission holds the view that Katanga is obliged to exercise a variant of self-determination that is compatible with the sovereignty and territorial integrity of Zaire."[199]

It is relevant to notice that the African Commission recognized the Katangese as a 'people' in the light of the Charter. This agrees with the eclectic consideration of the term 'people' as suggested above by Pastor Ridruejo.

Conclusion

Among the international structures created through multilateral diplomacy we find the African Human Rights System, whose legal frame was embodied by the African Charter on Human and Peoples' Rights. The African Charter was a great step forward in the right direction. It is imbued with innovative terms and a legal approach that makes it unique and somewhat 'African' in many ways. It portrays the joy of life, the African sense of solidarity, the positive existence of diverse ethnic groups, the suffering of slavery and a twisted colonizing history, the great aspirations of a Continent. In an unprecedented effort to make this work, the drafters considered the inclusion of specific bodies. They captured the existence of a quasi-judicial organ: The African Commission on Human

[198] Nevertheless, in its decision the Commission did not hesitate to refer to them as a people, without considering it important to determine whether Katangese consist of one or more ethnic group.

[199] See ACHPR, *Communication* 75/92.

and Peoples' Rights as a supervisory mechanism for the protection and promotion of human rights.[200]

The Commission was the only original body conceived for the exclusive promotion and protection of Human Rights in Africa. However, on 10th June 1998 a new body of judicial nature was conceived at Ouagadougou, Burkina Faso: the African Court on Human and People's Rights. The African Court on Human and Peoples' Rights has been operational since July 2006. It is the principal human rights judicial organ of the AU.

As has already been said,[201] the Constitutive Act of the African Union foresaw the creation of the Court of Justice of the African Union.[202] This Court of Justice's specificities were captured in its Protocol, which entered into force on 11th February 2009. However, the African Court of Justice has not been constituted and does not seem likely to ever come into existence because in July 2004 the African Union decided that the African Court of Justice and the African Court on Human and People's Rights should be merged.[203] To this effect they approved a merger Protocol, which is not yet operational.

Therefore, under the current African system, there are two key bodies entrusted with the promotion and care of human rights at the African level: The African Commission on Human and Peoples' Rights (ACHPR)[204] and the African Court on Human and Peoples' Rights (ACtHPR),[205] which will possibly become the African Court of Justice and Human and Peoples Rights (ACJHPR). These organs are the subject of our study in the next chapter, when we will take a closer view of the African Court and the current merger process between the African Court on Human and People's Rights and the still unborn African Court of Justice. This will allow us to identify the greatest

---

200 See Pityana, N. B., "Reflections on the African Court on Human and Peoples' Rights", *African Human Rights Law Journal*, vol. 4, (2004) at 121. See also The African Charter on Human and Peoples' Rights, Art. 30.

201 This matter is studied further and more in depth in Chapter II, 3 *supra*.

202 *Constitutive Act of the African Union*, Art. 5.

203 Decision on the Seats of the Organs of the African Union, Assembly/AU/Dec.45 (lll) Rev.1.

204 Hereinafter we may simply refer to it as the *Commission*.

205 Hereinafter we may refer to it as the *Court*.

obstacles for the proper dispensation of justice within the African human rights system.[206]

[206] There is a third body within the African system of human rights with a restricted mandate. It is the African Committee of Experts on the Rights and Welfare of the Child (ACERWC). This Committee draws its mandate from articles 32-46 of the African Charter on the Rights and Welfare of the Child, which was adopted by the Heads of State and Government of the OAU on 11 July 1990 and came into force on 29 November 1999. The Charter provides for the Establishment of an African Committee of Experts on the Rights and Welfare of the Child consisting of 11 members. The Committee was established in 2001 and it meets twice a year, usually in May and November in Addis Ababa, Ethiopia. A universal ratification and compliance campaign was launched by the ACERWC in January 2014.

CHAPTER FOUR

THE CREATION OF JUDICIAL STRUCTURES IN THE AFRICAN HUMAN RIGHTS SYSTEM AND THEIR DECISION-MAKING POWER

As has already been pointed out, the African Human Rights Charter captured the existence of a quasi-judicial organ: The African Commission on Human and Peoples' Rights as a supervisory mechanism for the protection and promotion of human rights.[1]The Commission was the only original body conceived for the promotion and protection of Human Rights in Africa. Its first members were elected by the OAU's 23rd Assembly of Heads of State and Government in June 1987, and the Commission was formally inaugurated on 2nd November of that year.[2]

The African Human Rights Charter implicitly paved the way for a judicial organ, a court, with jurisdiction over human rights matters in Africa. The constitution of this court took almost two decades to materialise, until June 1998, when the Protocol to the African Charter on Human and Peoples' Rights on the Establishment of an African Court on Human and Peoples' Rights was conceived at Ouagadougou, Burkina Faso. It entered into force on 25th January 2004. The African Court on Human and Peoples' Rights has been operational since July 2006 when it held its first session. It is the principal human rights judicial organ of the AU.

The African Court of Justice has not been constituted. Article 5 of the Constitutive Act of the African Union had foreseen the creation of the Court of Justice of the African Union. This Court of Justice's specificities were captured in its Protocol, which entered into force on 11th February 2009. However, is not operational and does not seem likely to ever come into operation because in July 2004 the African Union decided that the

[1] See Pityana, N. B., *op. cit.*, at 121.

[2] ACHPR, 2 Nov, 1987, *First Annual Activity Report of the African Commission on Human and Peoples' Rights*, 1987-8, ACHPR/RPT/1st, para. 4.

African Court of Justice and the African Court on Human and People's Rights should be merged.[3] To this effect they approved a merger Protocol, which is still under scrutiny.

This Chapter examines the structure of the African Commission on Human and Peoples' Right sand the African Court on Human and Peoples' Rights, the nature and efficacy of their decisions and the role played by sub-regional courts and bodies in the protection of human rights within the African system.

The African Commission on Human and People's Rights

Between May 1963 and mid-80s the promotion and protection of human rights within OAU Member States was not a major priority. Despite the OAU's endorsement of the principles of the Universal Declaration on Human Rights of 1948 the focus in Africa was decolonization and apartheid's eradication.[4]The OAU focused all its energies on "political and economic independence, non-discrimination and the liberation of Africa eradication of colonialism on the continent and apartheid in Southern Africa, at the expense of individual liberty."[5]

In fact, different groups, which included the Media, the Church, inter-governmental and non-government organisations (NGOs), mounted pressure on the OAU and "accused the Organisation of abandoning its primary goal of restoring dignity to the humiliated African peoples. It was accused of double standards for condemning apartheid in South Africa while failing to condemn the massive human rights violations committed by some of its own members."[6]

On 21 October 1986, the Charter came into force. Article 30 of the African Charter asserted that "an African Commission on Human and Peoples' Rights … shall be established within the Organisation of African Unity to promote human and peoples' rights and ensure their protection in Africa". This milestone meant the "acceptance of a limitation on sovereign national authority (at least on human rights related matters), albeit minimal, was hailed as a significant step by African States. The move was

---

[3] Decision on the Seats of the Organs of the African Union, Assembly/AU/Dec.45 (lll) Rev.1.

[4] See The African Commission on Human and Peoples' Rights – OAU, Information Sheet No. 1.

[5] *Ibid.*

[6] *Ibid.*

generally viewed as ushering in a new era of recognition of individuals rights as enshrined in the Universal Declaration of Human Rights."[7]

The African Commission on Human and Peoples' Rights was primarily created to "promote human and peoples' rights and ensure their protection in Africa."[8]The Commission did not have a permanent Secretariat after its inauguration. It was in November 1989 when finally the Commission's Secretariat settled in Banjul, The Gambia. The new headquarters were officially inaugurated by His Excellency, Sir Dawda Kairaba Jawara, former Head of State of the Gambia, on Monday 12th June 1989.[9]

The Commission consists of eleven members,[10] who should be chosen from among African personalities of the highest reputation, known for their high morality, integrity, impartiality and competence in matters of human and peoples' rights.[11] The Commissioners are elected by secret ballot by the Assembly of Heads of State and Government from a list of persons nominated by the State Parties to the Charter. It is of paramount importance that the Commissioners act in their personal capacity and not as representatives of their governments. No Member State may have more than one of its nationals on the Commission at any given time. The Commission elects by secret ballot its chairman and vice-chairman for a two-year renewable period. The chairman carries on the duties assigned to him by the Charter, the Rules of Procedure and the decisions of the Commission.[12] In the absence of the chairman, the vice-chairman shall represent him during that session. In the absence of both the chairman and vice-chairman, the members shall elect an acting chairman. The Commission usually meets twice a year, in March-April and October-November. However, there are provisions enabling it to meet extraordinarily if necessary. The sessions may last for ten days or more if necessary.

The Commission lays down its own rules of procedure. It is served by a full-time Secretary based in The Gambia. The Secretary General of the AU appoints the secretary of the Commission and staff necessary for the effective discharge of the Commission's duties. The AU bears the costs of the staff and services.

---

[7] *Ibid.*
[8] *African Charter*, Article 30.
[9] *Ibid.*
[10] *African Charter*, Article 31(2).
[11] *Ibid*, Article 31(1).
[12] ACHPR, *Rules of Procedure*, No. 18.

The Commission has been perhaps the most prolific body of the AU. It has produced hundreds of decisions or recommendations. Certainly, enforcement of the Commission's decisions is still a challenge. Since the African Commission has no follow-up policy to monitor the steps taken by State parties to implement its recommendations, the secretariat of the Commission has never compiled data on State compliance.[13]Since the Commission's establishment, there have been dramatically low levels of implementation of its recommendations.[14] This is partly due to the Commission's lack of an institutionalized follow-up mechanism and the non-binding legal character of its recommendations.[15] The implementation rate is currently around 12 percent.[16]

However, in 2010, the Commission adopted new rules of procedure that provided both a comprehensive follow-up process for the recommendations it makes and a process to refer cases to the African Court on Human and Peoples' Rights (ACtHPR). Under Rule 115 of the new rules of the Commission, there are specific timelines for States to respond on matters of implementation, which are followed up by specific Commissioners. Certainly, enforcement in Africa seems to be a political issue rather than a legal challenge.

---

[13] See Viljoen, F. and Louw, L., "State Compliance with the Recommendations of the African Commission on Human and Peoples' Rights,1993–2004", *American Journal of International Law*, vol 101, No. 1, (2007), pp. 1-34.

[14] Baluarte, D. C. and De Vos, C. M., *Judgement to Justice, from Judgment to Justice: Implementing International and Regional Human Rights Decisions*, Open Society Justice Initiative, Open Society Foundations, New York, 2010, at 23. Some decisions have been successfully implemented: *Pagnoulle v Cameroon*; *Constitutional Rights Project v Nigeria*; *Centre for Free Speech v Nigeria*; *Forum of Conscience v Sierra Leone*; *Modise v Botswana*, *Amnesty International v Zambia*; and *Constitutional Rights Project (in respect of Zamani Lakwot and 6 Others) v Nigeria.*

[15] Viljoen, F. and Louw, L., "State Compliance with the Recommendations of the African Commission on Human and Peoples' Rights,1993–2004", *American Journal of International Law*, vol 101, No. 1, (2007), at 1; and Okafor, O. C., "The African system on Human and Peoples' Rights, quasi-constructivism, and the possibility of peace-building within African States", *The International Journal of Human Rights*, Volume 8, Issue 4, (2004), at 413–450.

[16] See Baluarte, D. C. and De Vos, C. M., *op. cit.*, at 16.Out of 60 decisions issued by the Commission only 12% have been successfully implemented. Of these cases, 50 % involved civil and political rights; 25 % involved economic, social, and cultural rights; and only 5 % involved group rights.

1. General Mandate of the Commission: Promotion and interpretation

The mandate of the Commission, as provided for by Article 45, is "(1) to promote human and peoples' rights, (2) to ensure the protection of human and peoples' rights under the conditions laid down by the Charter, (3) to interpret the provisions of the Charter when so requested, and (4) to perform any other tasks which may be entrusted to it by the Assembly of Heads of State and Governments." In summary, the three main functions of the Commission are promotion, ensuring protection and interpretation.

The Charter gives pre-eminence to the promotion of human rights and vests a wide range of responsibilities on the Commission.[17] This task is significant, bearing in mind Africa's largely uneducated population, ignorant of its rights and poor access to enforcement means. The Commission's task of promotion includes collecting documents, undertaking studies and researches in African problems in the field of human and peoples' rights, organizing seminars, symposia and conferences, disseminating information, encouraging national and local institutions concerned with human and peoples' rights, and also making recommendations to Governments. It has held seminars on various issues.[18]

Commissioners themselves also have a duty to promote the Charter. They may go on promotional country visits during which they meet government officials, NGOs and members of the public to raise awareness about the Charter and the work of the Commission and to urge the State to take steps to implement human rights. The Commission's promotional mandate involves cooperating with other African and international institutions concerned with the promotion and protection of human and peoples' rights.

The Commission also formulates principles and rules upon which African Governments may base their legislation. For example, the Commission has been instrumental in the formulation of 'The Guidelines and Measures for the Prohibition and Prevention of Torture, Cruel,

---

[17] Umozurike, U.O., *The African Commission on Human and Peoples' Rights*, Martinus Nijhoff Publishers, The Hague, 1997, at 67ff.

[18] For example: *Workshop on Impunity in Africa*, Ouagadougou, Burkina Faso, 22-23 March 1996; *Prison Conditions in Africa*, Kampala, Uganda, 19-21 September 1996; *Mechanisms for Early Warning in Emergency Situations under Article 58 of the African Charter*, Nairobi, Kenya, 23-25 July 1996.

Inhuman or Degrading Treatment or Punishment in Africa' (2002),[19] the 'Declaration of Principles on Freedom of Expression in Africa' (2002), and 'The Principles and Guidelines on the Right to a Fair Trial and Legal Assistance in Africa' (2003). Unfortunately, Rachel Murray says, "what is apparent from the research that has been done on this issue is that the impact of the Commission's findings on the affected State is limited. Although there have been some examples of States implementing the Commission's recommendations (e.g., the Constitutional Rights Project [*in respect of Zamani Lakwot and six others] v. Nigeria*) in many instances the Commission's findings have not been taken on board."[20] Moreover, the recommendations are not binding and do not provide the State in question specific mechanisms for implementation.

According to Kithure Kindiki,

> "Another contributor to States' non-compliance by States to the Commission's recommendations is that unlike some other regional and global human rights bodies, the Commission does not have an institutionalized follow-up system to ensure the implementation of its recommendations and decisions, even though some *ad hoc* follow-up and inconsistent measures had been initiated on few occasions. The Commission has in a variety of forums attempted to follow up on the implementation of its recommendations through promotional and protective missions to state parties or by incorporating follow-up measures as part of its findings on individual communications. It has also enquired about the status of implementation of its past recommendations during the presentation of State reports, and during the consideration of other communications affecting the same States. These efforts have yielded few concrete results, if any."[21]

Furthermore, Kindiki also states that,

> "Neither the African Charter nor the Rules of Procedure of the African Commission define the status of the Commission's recommendations. Nevertheless, it is trite that by signing and ratifying the African Charter, States signify their intention to be bound by and adhere to the obligations

---

[19] Formally referred to as the *Robben Island Guidelines* (2002).

[20] Murray, R., "African Commission on Human and Peoples' Rights", *Max Planck Encyclopedia of Public International Law*, www.mpepil.com, Oxford University Press, (2007), para. 20-21.

[21] Kindiki, K., "A Review of the Efficacy of Select African Union Monitoring and Reporting Mechanisms", *State of the Union Continental Report*, published by the State of the Union Coalition, (2010) at 3. Available at *www.stateoftheunionafrica.net*.

arising there-from, even if they do not enact domestic legislation to effect domestic incorporation. This principle is expressed in article 14 of the Vienna Convention on the Law of Treaties of 1969. Therefore, while it is true that African States were not keen to surrender their sovereignty to a regional quasi-judicial body like the African Commission, by ratifying the Charter it is obvious that they were aware that they were required to abide by its provisions. Article 27 of the Vienna Convention further provides that a state 'cannot [consequently] plead provisions of its own law or deficiencies in that law' in answer to a claim it is in breach of a treaty obligation. The African Commission has adopted this position by stating that the effective implementation of the African Charter is based on the principle of *pacta sunt servanda*, which is to the effect that agreements are binding on parties, and are to be implemented in good faith."[22]

The Commission's promotion role has been stressed on numerous occasions. In her 46th Ordinary Session opening speech, Therese Sarr-Toupan, representing Honourable Attorney General and Minister of Justice of the Republic of The Gambia welcomed the participants and stressed that the promotion of human rights in Africa is the primary responsibility of States because it is only when human rights are guaranteed, promoted and protected, that human security can become a reality. She lamented the fact that "in 2009, Africa witnessed the resumption of coup d'états, social unrests, summary executions and sexual crimes, which have become the tools and weapons in the hands of junta regimes. In this regard, she urged the ACHPR to continue working with member States to implement its mandate to monitor, protect and promote human rights."[23]

In fact, Commissioners have taken the Commission's promotional role actively. In the 27th Report we also read that on 21stOctober 2009, Commissioner Atoki delivered a Statement to commemorate Africa Human Rights Day in Cotonou, Benin, during her Promotional Mission in the country. The statement, which was broadcasted on the National Television, emphasized the need for States Parties to the African Charter, NGOs, international community and other stakeholders to continue to commit to the realization of the rights enshrined in the African Charter. From 13thto 27thMay 2009, Commissioner Atoki also undertook a Promotion Mission to the Republic of Sudan, together with Commissioners Reine Alapini-Gansou, Pansy Tlakula, and Soyata Maiga.

---

[22] *Ibid.*, at 5.

[23] See ACHPR, 27th Activity Report of the African Commission on Human and Peoples' Rights. Submitted in accordance with article 54 of the African Charter on Human and Peoples' Rights, (2009).

The aim of the Promotion Mission was to inter alia promote the African Charter; exchange views and share experiences with the Government of the Republic of Sudan and major human rights stakeholders in the country on how to enhance the enjoyment of human rights in the country; discuss ways to promote human rights in the Sudan; to exchange views with relevant Sudanese authorities on Sudan's preparation for the country's general elections in 2010; and to exchange closer collaboration between the African Commission and the Republic of Sudan on one hand, and between the African Commission and civil society organization in the country.[24]

Commissioner Bitaye also undertook a Promotional Mission to the Federal Republic of Nigeria. From 14 to 18 September 2009, he was accompanied by Dr. Feyi Ogunade, Senior Legal Officer at the Secretariat. The above Mission was aimed at amongst others: promoting the African Charter; exchanging views with all human rights stakeholders, including the Government of the Federal Republic of Nigeria on the ways and means of enhancing the enjoyment of human rights in the country; and raising awareness and visibility of the African Commission and its functions, especially among the relevant government departments/institutions, and civil society organisations.[25]

Commissioners Maiga, Kayitesi, Gansou along with several other commissioners also carried out promotional visits to more than half of State members to promote human rights and facilitate the work of the Commission. Additionally, the Commission also appointed committees and taskforce teams on Prevention of Torture in Africa, on Economic, Social and Cultural Rights, on the Death Penalty and on Extractive Industries and Human Rights Violations in Africa.[26]

Rachel Murray explains that "some of the most important work of the Commission has consisted in the appointment of Special Rapporteurs and the creation of Working Groups on specific themes. Prompted mostly by NGOs eager for the Commission to focus on particular issues, the Commission has appointed a number of Special Rapporteurs, all of whom have been its own members, to look in detail at a number of issues including: extrajudicial summary and arbitrary executions; prisons and

---

[24] See *Ibid.*

[25] *Ibid.*

[26] ACHPR, 27th Activity Report of the African Commission on Human and Peoples' Rights. Submitted in accordance with article 54 of the African Charter on Human and Peoples' Rights, (2009).

other conditions of detention; women's rights; freedom of expression; refugees and internally displaced persons; and human rights defenders. The combination of NGO commitment in terms of funding and logistical support and the commitment of individual Commissioners has meant that some of them have had an impact on the areas for which they are responsible. For example, previous holders of the post of Special Rapporteur on Prisons and Conditions of Detention undertook a number of visits to places of detention in various States and on a few occasions were able to return to verify—sometimes positively—whether recommendations had been implemented. Where this support and commitment has not been available, however, the results have been far from satisfactory. The Special Rapporteur on Summary, Arbitrary and Extra-Judicial Executions being one such example, failing to produce little more than a few generalized reports in the several years of its mandate. As a result, since 2000, this important post has fallen into disuse."[27]

Regrettably, while this initially gave a push to the Commission's activities and ensured some degree of independence, the outcome was that for many years the Commission's work was imperceptible to the political players of the OAU upon whom the Commission depended on financial and political support to implement and enforce its findings and recommendations.[28]

The protecting function of the Commission, pursuant to Articles 46 to 59 of the African Charter, to ensure the protection of human and peoples' rights on the continent, is perhaps the most efficacious function from a legal perspective. The Commission has power to consider complaints, otherwise known as communications, alleging human rights violations. The communications can be submitted by individuals, NGOs or State parties to the Charter alleging that a State has violated specific rights as stipulated under the Charter. Frans Viljoen clarifies that the Charter's drafters would be surprised to see how the individual complaints procedure developed. When the drafters started their work they faced two possibilities: The former UN Human Rights Commission procedure 1503, on the one hand, and the First optional Protocol to the ICCPR (OPI) on the other. The African Charter drafters went for a careful balancing act, using somewhat abstract language. The individual communications were later

---

[27] Murray, R., "African Commission on Human and Peoples' Rights", *Max Planck Encyclopaedia of Public International Law*, *www.mpepil.com*, Oxford University Press, (2007), para. 21.

[28] *Ibid.*, para. 2.

added to the Commissions' workings through the adoption of its first Rules and Procedures in 1988.[29]

The Commission's protecting function has been commendable. During the 46thOrdinary Session, a total of seventy-nine (79) Communications were tabled before the ACHPR: eight (8) on Seizure; seven (7) on Admissibility; one (1) on Merits; and one (1) for review. The Communications seized by the Commission were directed against Tunisia, Kenya (two communications), South Africa, Libya, Sudan, Cameroon and Senegal. The Commission considered and adopted decisions on Admissibility on communications against Kenya, Gabon, Zimbabwe, Equatorial Guinea, Algeria and Malawi. The Commission also considered and declared inadmissible a Communication against Sudan. Consideration of other sixty-two (62) Communications was deferred to the 47thOrdinarySession, for various reasons, including time constraints and lack of response from one or both parties.

The Commission also adopted decisions on the merits of the followings Communications: Communication 235/00 – Curtis Doebbler v. Sudan and Communication 276 – Centre for Minority Rights Development (Kenya) and Minority Rights Group International on behalf of Endorois Welfare Council v. Kenya.[30] However, there are no enforcement mechanisms in place to adjudicate the rights as established by the Commission's decisions. As Okoth asserts, more than a year since the ruling in favour of the Endorois, the Government of Kenya has not taken any steps to implement the Commission's decision, leaving the Community frustrated. In fact, "Recent discussions before Parliament on the extent to which the Government is pursuing implementation of the Endorois decision goes to demonstrate the lack of coordinated action on the part of the State ...While the Ministry of Lands reported it was yet to receive a sealed copy of the verdict to allow it take action, ministries of Foreign Affairs and that of Justice failed to confirm before Parliament they had received formal communication on the Endorois decision... The State Law Office has also not advised relevant arms of Government or the Cabinet to facilitate enforcement of the decision [and] the Government [of Kenya] ... also continues to operate as if the Endorois decision does not exist. For example, Kenya Wildlife Service has recently sought the

---

[29] See Viljoen, F., *International Human Rights Law in Africa,* Oxford University Press, Oxford, 2007, at 319 and 320

[30] See *infra* note no.162.

declaration of Lake Bogoria as a UNESCO world heritage site without consulting the Endorois."[31]

As a quasi-judicial organ, the Commission also has a broad interpretative function. The requirement in Article 60 and 61 that it takes into account other African and international laws and customs is said to provide the Charter with an unusual touch in that it may include non-binding concepts and the jurisprudence of other bodies.[32]Practically every decision by the Commission requires an interpretation of the facts, complaint, procedure, admissibility and merits so as to reach a comprehensive and fair decision. The Commission has further adopted various recommendations and resolutions where it has interpreted various articles of the Charter. The Commission has also exercised its interpretive role in the consideration of communications. On its 18th Ordinary Session at Praia, Commissioners exchanged views in the interpretation of article 58 of the African Charter.[33] The Commission has also interpreted its rules and procedures as it happened with article 12 in 1995 at the 17th Ordinary Session in Lomé.[34]

However, the creation of the African Court on Human and Peoples' Rights has progressively taken away the exclusive interpretative function from the Commission. The more recent 2003 Protocol to the African Charter on Human and Peoples' Rights on the Rights of Women in Africa, expressively grants the interpretation powers to the Court. Article 27 states: "The African Court on Human and Peoples' Rights shall be seized with matters of interpretation arising from the application or implementation of this Protocol." The Commission, nevertheless, was granted the interpretation function in a subsidiary manner by the transitional provision foreseen in Article 32, which reads: "Pending the establishment of the African Court on Human and Peoples' Rights, the African Commission on

---

[31] See Okoth, D., "Cheers Turn to Tears for Endorois Waiting for Land", Special report, *Standard Newspaper*, Nairobi, 18th June 2011, at 10. Okoth mistakenly reports the decision as coming from the ACtHPR, while it is really a decision emanating from the ACHPR. Further information on this case is provided for in *infra* note no.162.

[32] Bello, E., "The African Charter on Human and Peoples' Rights", *Recueil des Cours*, vol. 194, (1985), The Hague, at 82. See also Umozurike, U.O., *The African Charter on Human and Peoples' Rights*, Nijhoff, The Hague, 1997, at 81ff.

[33] See ACHPR Report 18th Ordinary Session in Praia, Cape Verde from 2nd - 11th Oct 1995.

[34] See ACHPR Report 17th Ordinary Session in Lomé, Togo from 13th – 22nd March 1995.

Human and Peoples' Rights shall be seized with matters of interpretation arising from the application and implementation of this Protocol."[35]

Finally, the Assembly of Heads of State and Governments may request the Commission to undertake *other tasks*. The Charter does not elaborate what these tasks may entail, but it is notable that the Commissioners have been requested to observe elections in various African countries.[36]

However, the Commission continues to be the chief body in what refers to protection of individual human rights. Its protective mandate is intrinsically bound to the enforcement and implementation mechanisms which are discussed in the next subsection.

2. Specific Mandate: Enforcement and Implementation

The African Charter, in articles 46 to 59, vests the Commission with the specific mandate to watch over its enforcement and implementation. Article 46 establishes that "the Commission may resort to any appropriate method of investigation; it may hear from the Secretary General of the Organization of African Unity or any other person capable of enlightening it." The main enforcement mechanisms provided by the Charter are communications and State-reporting procedures.[37] Communications may be inter-State communications and individual and/or NGO communications.

The procedure for the consideration of the communications depends on whether the complaint has been submitted by a State or by any other entity. The procedure for each is discussed below.

2.1 Inter-State Communications

The procedure for dealing with communications from States is provided for from Article 47 to Article 54 of the Charter. There are two

---

[35] See Protocol to the African Charter on Human and Peoples' Rights on the Rights of Women in Africa, adopted by the 2nd Ordinary Session of the Assembly of the Union, in Maputo, on 11th July 2003.

[36] For example, *9th Annual Activity Report of the African Commission on Human and Peoples' Rights* (1995-6), ACHPR/RPT/9th, para. 15: [t]*wo Commissioners who were part of the OAU observer teams presented reports on elections in Tanzania and the Comoros Islands.*

[37] See Evans, M.D., "State Reporting Mechanism under the African Charter", in Evans and Murray (Ed), *The African Charter on Human and Peoples' Rights: the system in practice 1986-2006*, Cambridge University Press, Cambridge, 2008, at 49.

forms under which a State may submit complaints. The first involves a State Party which believes that another State has violated the provisions of the Charter drawing up a written communication so as to bring the matter to that State's attention.[38] The communication is also copied to the Secretary General of the AU and the Chairman of the Commission.

The State to which the communication is addressed is given three months within which to respond to the enquiring State in the form of a written explanation or statement which includes, as much as possible, relevant information relating to the laws and rules of procedure applied or applicable, as well as the redress already given or any course of action that is available. If the matter is not peacefully settled within three months to the satisfaction of the two States, then either State may submit the matter to the Commission. The issue is also referred to the Commission if the State party to which the communication is addressed fails to react to the request made under Article 47 of the Charter within the three months' period of time.

The second method is provided for under Article 49 of the Charter. A State party to the Charter which considers that another State has violated the provisions of the Charter may refer the matter directly to the Commission without going through the aforementioned procedure. The State addresses the communication to the Chairman, the Secretary General of the AU, and the State concerned.

Once a communication is received by the Secretariat of the Commission in Banjul, it is registered under a file number in the Commission's Official Register of Communications. The Secretariat acknowledges receipt of the author's letter of complaint. It should be noted, however, that registration of a communication is no guarantee that it is going to be handled by the Commission.

---

[38] For example, Comm. 227/03: *Democratic Republic of Congo v. Burundi, Rwanda and Uganda*, where the Commission found the application admissible and finally found the Respondent States in violation of Articles 2, 4, 5, 12(1) and (2), 14, 16, 17, 18(1) and (3), 19, 20, 21, 22, and 23 of the African Charter on Human and Peoples' Rights. The Commission urged the Respondent States to abide by their obligations under the Charters of the United Nations, the Organisation of African Unity, the African Charter on Human and Peoples' Rights, the UN Declaration on Principles of International Law Concerning Friendly Relations and Co-operation among States and other applicable international principles of law and withdraw its troops immediately from the complainant' territory. See *http://www.achpr.org/english/_info/index_Decision_ Uganda.html*

Once a communication has been registered, the Commission has to take possession of it. The Secretariat waits for a response from at least seven of the eleven commissioners to indicate that they have received the communication and approved seizure. If the Secretariat does not receive at least seven responses, the communication is presented to all the commissioners at the Commission's next session. At this session, the Commission decides whether to be seized of the communication by determining whether it alleges any *prima facie* violation of the Charter, or whether it is properly submitted according to the provisions of article 55 of the Charter.

There has been so far one inter-State Communication since the Commission's creation. It was the Communication made by the Democratic Republic of the Congo (DRC) to the African Commission alleging violations of the African Charter on Human and Peoples' Rights and international law, including the Geneva Conventions 1949 and Additional Protocols, the UN Charter and UN Declaration on Friendly Relations by Burundi, Rwanda and Uganda.[39]

The DRC alleged that armed forces from Burundi, Uganda and Rwanda had occupied its border provinces in the eastern part of the country and committed mass human rights violations, including the mass killing of civilians and the siege of a hydroelectric dam (civilian run) resulting in the cut off of electricity to homes, schools and hospitals – which led to the deaths of patients dependent on life support systems. Particularly worrisome was the mass rape accusations and spread HIV/AIDS by Ugandan soldiers. Further allegations were the mass looting of civilian property and the natural mineral wealth in the region, as well as the forced movement of populations from the region into 'concentration camps' in Rwanda in order to establish a 'Tutsi land'.

The violation of law included acts against the African Charter on Human and Peoples' Rights Articles 2, 4, 5, 12(1) and (2), 14, 16, 17, 18(1) and (3), 19, 20, 21, 22, and 23, The Geneva Convention relative to the Protection of Civilian Persons in Time of War 1949 and Additional

---

[39] Communication 227/99, *Democratic Republic of Congo v. Burundi, Rwanda and Uganda* is well summarised by Equal Rights Trust. We have partially reproduced the most relevant section in the next paragraph. The full text is available at: *https://docs.google.com/viewer?url=http%3A%2F%2Fwww.equalrightstrust.org%2Fertdocumentbank%2FDRC%2520v%2520Burundi%2C%2520Rwanda%2520and%2520Uganda.pdf*

Protocol 1 to the Geneva Conventions, the UN Charter and the UN Declaration on Friendly Relations Between Nations.

Rwanda denied all the charges of human rights abuses and justified the presence of soldiers as a security measure designed to protect its own territory from the actions of armed rebel groups hiding in the Congolese provinces and receiving support from the DRC. Uganda made similar claims to justify the presence of soldiers on Congolese territory, it referred to an invitation it received in 1997 following the installation of the Kabila Government, to stop the activities of Ugandan rebels in the eastern provinces. The invitation was revoked in 1998 following a new rebellion in the DRC which was blamed on Rwandan and Ugandan forces. Uganda further denied that its soldiers committed human rights abuses and argues that with a lack of independent verification of the facts the case is inadmissible.

The Commission moved to consider the merits of the case. Rwanda and Uganda did not participate beyond submissions on the admissibility. Burundi did not respond to any of the submissions.

Having considered the matter, the Commission asserted that there was an effective occupation on DRC territory which constituted a violation of the Charter. The alleged human rights violations stemmed from this illegal occupation and were in direct violation of the Charter and international law. The Commission also held that there was a violation of Article 2 of the African Charter concerning non-discrimination in the enjoyment of rights, as the violations were directed at victims based on their national origin.

Further violations of specific rights in the African Charter were found including violation against the family as the fundamental unit of society, the violation against freedom and the forced displacement of the population.[40]

The Commission requested all States to abide by international law and urged Rwanda, Uganda and Burundi to withdraw from DRC territory. The Commission also recommended that reparation be made on behalf of the victims of human rights violations committed by the armed forces of the respondent States whilst in effective occupation of DRC territory.[41]

---

[40] See *Ibid.*

[41] Certainly by the time the decision was reached the countries in question had already withdrawn and the matter of reparation was never addressed.

Although the Republic of Rwanda and the Republic of Uganda did respond to the Commission in its request for information on the allegations, the Republic of Burundi refused to react.[42] Regrettably there was no sanction imposed on Burundi, and the lack of the Commission's executive legal functions coupled with the lack of political support from the AU organs, often renders the Commission's decisions obsolete or mere human rights aspirations. The challenge is both political and legal. Nonetheless, for practical purposes it is expected that henceforth States may take their complaints directly to the Court instead of the Commission, especially if they expect concrete legal redress.

2.2 Individual Communications

The Charter also provides for communications brought by parties other than States.[43] This mechanism is employed by private individuals, groups of individuals and NGOs who feel that a State party has violated rights contained in the Charter. The African Charter, however, does not explicitly speak of individual and NGO complaints but uses the term 'other communications' to distinguish these communications from those submitted by States.

The admissibility requirements are provided for by Article 56 of the Charter. There are seven requirements. The first requirement is that communication should indicate its authors. The author must be identified, even if he or she requests anonymity. If the author requests to remain anonymous, the communication is given a letter of the alphabet as is also customary in other bodies.[44] Secondly, the communication must be compatible with the African Charter. It must allege a violation by a State party of a right or duty guaranteed by the African Charter which took place after the Charter became legally binding on that State. A communication which does not establish a *prima facie* case shall not be examined.[45] Third, the complaint must not be written in disparaging or

---

[42] See Murray, R., "African Commission on Human and Peoples' Rights", *Max Planck Encyclopedia of Public International Law*, *www.mpepil.com*, Oxford University Press, (2007), para. 18.

[43] See Viljoen, F., *International Human Rights Law in Africa,* Oxford University Press, Oxford, 2007, at 319 and 320.

[44] For example Communication 283/03, where the complainant, a Kenyan suspended judge requested anonymity and was therefore identified as *B v. Kenya.*

[45] For example in *Communication* 57/91 and *Communication* 1/88, the failure to prove a *prima facie* violation rendered the communication inadmissible. Also, an allegation in a general manner is not enough, according to *Communication* 63/92.

insulting language. It should simply state the facts and indicate how they constitute a violation of a right or duty protected by the Charter, without insulting remarks. Coarse or abusive language will render a communication inadmissible, irrespective of the seriousness of the complaint.[46] Fourth, the complaint must not be based exclusively on information gathered from media reports. The author of the communication must ascertain the truth of the facts before requesting the Commission's intervention. Fifth is the requirement of the exhaustion of local remedies.[47]

The Commission may be approached only once the matter has been pursued in the highest court of the country in question, without success, or a *reasonable* prospect of success. This requirement is founded on the principle that the State should be given the opportunity to remedy the violation before it is called to an international body. This also prevents the international body from acting as a court of first instance rather than as a body of last resort. In *Jawara v The Gambia*, the Commission stated that "a remedy is considered available if the petitioner can pursue it without impediment, it is deemed effective if it offers a prospect of success, and it is found sufficient if it is capable of redressing the complaint."[48] The exception to this requirement is if it is obvious that the procedure is unduly prolonged. The complaint should indicate which national remedies have been tried and the results.

Sixth, the communications should be submitted within a reasonable period from the time local remedies are exhausted, or within a reasonable period from the time the Commission is seized with the matter. Though the Charter does not give a specific time period, it is advisable to submit a complaint as early as possible. Seventh, the communication must not deal with cases that have been settled by the States involved in accordance with the principles of the Charter of the United Nations, the Charter of the OAU or the African Charter.[49] Communications should not be about cases that have been or are being considered by another treaty monitoring body.

---

[46] For example *Communication* 65/92 was declared inadmissible for using words such as *regime of tortures* and *a government of barbarism.*

[47] ACHPR, *Communications* 43/ 90 and 45/90. The non-exhaustion of local remedies rendered the communications inadmissible.

[48] ACHPR, *Communication* 147/95 and 149/96 - *Sir Dawda K Jawara v. The Gambia,* No. 32.

[49] For example, in *Communication* 15/88, the United Nations Human Rights Committee had decided the case in favour of the victim. Subsequently, he submitted the same *Communication* to the Commission. It was declared inadmissible.

If the Commission decides that a communication is inadmissible under the Charter, it informs the complainant and if it has been transmitted to a State party, it also informs that State.[50] This, however, does not hinder the case being reopened later by the Commission, which may reconsider its decision at a later date upon a request for reconsideration.

Rule 104 of the Rules of Procedure provides that the Commission, through the Secretary, may request the author of a communication to provide clarifications on the applicability of the Charter to his or her communication. The Commission gives the author a time period within which this should be done, so as to avoid unreasonable delay in the procedure. Such a request for clarification does not prevent the inclusion of the communication on the lists of communications submitted by the Secretary to the Commission for its consideration.

All communications received by the Secretariat are transmitted to the Commission. The Commission then determines whether or not to consider a communication, based on the aforementioned criteria. Article 55(2) empowers a simple majority of the Commission to make such a decision.

Article 58 of the Charter gives the Commission authority to refer special cases which reveal the existence of a chain of serious or massive violations of human and peoples' rights to the Assembly of Heads of State and Government. The Assembly may then request the Commission to undertake an in-depth study of these cases and make a factual report which includes findings and recommendations.

In emergency cases, for example where the victim's life, personal integrity or health is in imminent danger, the Commission has the powers under Rule 111 of its Rules of Procedure, to adopt provisional measures.[51] This is to ensure that the State concerned does not take any action that would cause irreparable damage to the victim until the substantive issues have been dealt with by the Commission. The Commission may also adopt other urgent measures as it deems fit.

Communications are gradually gaining admissibility in recent years.[52] However, comparatively speaking, the admissible ones are still a small

---

[50] ACHPR, *Rules of Procedure*, Rule 118.

[51] These provisional measures may include a preventive injunction of constitutional nature that aims at protecting the alleged victim while the substantive matter is under consideration.

[52] As a matter of fact, a great number of communications presented to the Commission have been declared inadmissible. In 1988 the following

percentage of the total communications presented. For instance, only 9 communications out of hundreds introduced in 2005 have already been decided.[53] Nevertheless, all the communications presented in 2005 were examined in greater detail, which did not use to be the case fifteen years earlier, and the Commission's decision on inadmissibility has since become more laborious.

2.2.1 The supporting role of the NGOs

The Commission has had an important relationship with NGOs, not only at the level of communication but also training and reporting. NGOs sometimes submit shadow reports which provide vital information as to

---

Communications were presented: 1/88: Frederick Korvah / Liberia, 2/88: Iheanyichukwu A Ihebereme / USA, 3/88: Centre for the Independence of Judges and Lawyers / Yugoslavia, 4/88: Coordinating Secretary of the Free Citizens Convention / Ghana, 5/88: Prince J. N. Makoge / USA, 6/88: Dr. Kodji Kofi / Ghana, 7/88: Committee for the Defence of Political Prisoners / Bahrain, 8/88: Nziwa Buyingo / Uganda, 9/88: International Lawyers Committee for Family Reunification/Ethiopia, 10/88: Gatachew Abebe / Ethiopia, 11/88: Henry Kalenga/Zambia,12/88: Mohemed El-Nekheily / OAU, 13/88: Hadjali Mohamad / Algeria, 14/88: Dr. Abd Eldayem A. E. Sanussi / Ethiopia, 15/88: Mpaka-Nsusu Andre Alphonse / DRC, 16/88: Comité Culturel pour la Démocratie au Benin / Benin, 17/88: Badjogoume Hilaire / Benin, 18/88: El Hadj Boubacar Diawara / Benin, 19/88: International PEN / Malawi, Ethiopia, Cameroon and Kenya, 20/88: Austrian Committee Against Torture / Morocco 21/88: Centre Haitien des Libertés Publiques / Ethiopia, 22/88: International PEN / Burkina Faso, 24/89: Union Nationale de Liberation de Cabinda/Angola. All of them were either declared inadmissible or the substantive matter was not dealt with due to the release of prisoners or amicable settlement quickly reached as happened in 11/88, 16-18/88 and 22/88. All the others were inadmissible. It was in 1989, when the first communication was admitted (25/89) which was joined to 47/90, 56/91 and 100/93, in the case of *Free Legal Assistance Group, Lawyers' Committee for Human Rights, Union Interafricaine des Droits de l'Homme, Les Témoins de Jehovah v. DRC.*

[53] These are: 297/05: Scanlen and Holderness / Zimbabwe; 299/05: Anuak Justice Council / Ethiopia; 300/05: Socio Economic Rights and Accountability Project / Nigeria; 304/05: FIDH, National Human Rights Organisation (ONDH)and Rencontre Africaine pour la Defence des Droits de l'Homme (RADDHO) / Senegal; 307/05: Mr. Obert Chinhamo / Zimbabwe; 308/05: Michael Majuru / Zimbabwe; 21 0/05: Darfur Relief and Documentation Centre / Republic of Sudan; 312/05: Interights and the Egyptian Initiative for Personal Rights / Egypt; 313/05: Kenneth Good / Republic of Botswana. Only 2 of them (297/05 and 313/05) were declared admissible.

the actual human rights situation in the countries in which they operate. Further, NGOs sometimes lobby States and Commissioners to take action.

A large number of NGOs have been granted observer status by the Commission. In its 25th Session in Bujumbura, Burundi, the Commission adopted a Resolution on the Criteria for Granting and Enjoying Observer Status to Non-Governmental Organizations Working in the Field of Human Rights with the African Commission on Human and Peoples' Rights. The resolution requires that these accredited organizations must have objectives and activities in consonance with the fundamental principles of the African Charter. They should also be organizations working in the field of human rights, declare their financial status, and have an established structure. The organizations should furnish the Commission with their statutes, proof of legal existence, list of members, constituent organs, sources of funding, latest financial statements, as well as a statement on activities carried out. The statement of activities should cover the past and present activities of the Organization, its plan of action and any other information that may help to determine the identity of the organization, its purpose and objectives, as well as its field of activities.

NGOs with observer status are invited to be present at the opening and closing sessions of the African Commission. They are allowed to make statements and proposals in the Commission's sessions. However, they cannot make comments during the examination of State reports. They have access to the non-confidential documents of the Commission provided that the documents deal with issues that are of relevance to their interests.

NGOs have been of paramount importance in the development of human rights in Africa. Their positive advocacy has, on some occasions, triggered the annulment of domestic laws that are found in contradiction to the Charter. For example, in *Civil Liberties Organization in respect of the Nigerian Bar Association v. Nigeria,*[54] a Nigerian NGO brought the communication to protest against the Legal Practitioners' Decree, which established a new governing body of the Nigerian Bar Association, namely the Body of Benchers. The Body of Benchers was dominated by representatives of the government and had wide discretionary powers. The decree excluded recourse to the Courts and was retrospective. The communication argued that the prohibition on litigation violated Article 7 of the African Charter and further that the Body of Benchers violated Nigerian lawyers' freedom of association guaranteed by Article 10 of the African Charter. The Commission found that there had been a violation of

[54] ACHPR, *Communication* 101/93.

Articles 6, 7, and 10 of the African Charter and held that the Decree be annulled.[55]

NGOs are required to establish close relations of co-operation with the African Commission and to engage in regular consultations with it on all matters of common interest. They should present their activity reports to the Commission every two years.

2.2.2 State Reporting

According to David Kretzmer, States' reports are the basis for international monitoring of human rights conventions. He asserts that,

> "The first provision requiring such reports appeared in the International Labour Organization (ILO) Constitution, adopted at the Versailles Peace Conference in April 1919. The League of Nations Covenant required all mandatory powers to submit an annual report to the League's Council 'in reference to the territory committed to its charge.' A permanent commission was established 'to receive and examine the annual reports of the Mandatories and to advise the Council on all matters relating to the observance of the mandates.' After establishment of the United Nations, reports on State compliance with international human rights standards were requested by the UN Economic and Social Council (ECOSOC). Acting on the recommendation of the UN Commission on Human Rights, in August 1956 ECOSOC passed a resolution instituting periodic reporting on State compliance with human rights standards.[56] States were asked to submit a report every three years, in which they described human rights developments and progress. The reports were to discuss rights mentioned in the 1948 Universal Declaration of Human Rights as well as the right to self-determination. This system was amended in 1965 and States were now required to report annually in a three-year continual cycle. In the first year they were to report on civil and political rights, in the second on economic, social and cultural rights and in the third on freedom of information."[57]

---

[55] *African Charter*, Article 1 of the African Charter provides that member States *shall undertake to adopt legislative or other measures* to give effect to the Charter. The States are to take measures to ensure that their national laws comply with the provisions of the Charter. In certain instances, the Commission may require a State which has been found in violation of the Charter to annul or repeal the offending legislation.

[56] UN ECOSOC, Res 624 (XXII) of 1st August 1956,22nd session, sup.1, 12.

[57] Kretzmer, D., "Human Rights, State Reports", *Max Planck Encyclopaedia of Public International Law*, *www.mpepil.com*, Oxford University Press, (2008), para. 1-3

Outlined in Article 62 is the State reporting procedure under which States parties are required to submit reports on the legislative and other measures taken with the view of giving effect to the rights and freedoms recognized and guaranteed by the Charter. It was introduced as a means of continually monitoring State compliance with the Charter. This procedure has been described as the backbone of the mission of the Commission in its monitoring of the implementation of the Charter by States.[58] It is a critical and analytical appraisal of the human rights situation of a country, which affords the State an opportunity to review its performance in line with its obligations. In addition, the State reporting exercise facilitates the sharing of experiences, best practices and lessons learnt. Various other human rights monitoring bodies use this process to evaluate the progress made by their members in the fulfilment of their obligations.[59]

The reports should contain information on the human rights situation within the country and should indicate, where possible, the factors and difficulties impeding the implementation of the provision of the Charter.[60] The reports are considered by the Commission during its sessions. Before a report is considered, the Commission first ensures that the report provides all the necessary information. If the Commission is of the opinion that the information is inadequate, it may request the State to provide additional information within a certain time period.[61] In case of non-submission, the Commission may send a report or reminder to the State party.

The initial report is due two years after ratification of the Charter. Periodic reports are due every two years thereafter. In practice, however, State parties have failed to submit their reports. Consequently, in order to encourage compliance, the Commission has permitted Member States to combine overdue reports. By May 2010 the Status on submission of State reports indicated that only one State member had presented 4 reports (Rwanda), seven States had presented 3 reports, fifteen States had

---

[58] Badawi El-Sheikh, I., "The African Commission on Human and Peoples' Right: Prospects and Problems", *Netherlands Quarterly of Human Rights*, vol 7, (1989) at 281.

[59] For example the reporting requirements found in Article 40 of the International Covenant on Civil and Political Rights, Article 16 of the International Covenant on Social, Economic and Cultural Rights and Article 9 of the International Convention on the Elimination of all Forms of Racial Discrimination.

[60] ACHPR, *Rules of Procedure*, Rule 81(1).

[61] ACHPR, *Rules of Procedure*, Rule 85.

presented 2 reports, seventeen States had presented only 1 report and thirteen States have presented no report at all.[62]

According to the 27thActivity Report of the ACHPR this means that only 3 States had submitted all their Reports and were to present the next Report at the 47th Ordinary Session of the African Commission. Additionally, 12 States had submitted and presented all their Reports but were not going to submit at the 47th Session. 26 States had submitted one (1) or two (2) Reports but still owe more Reports, and 12 States had not submitted any Report at all. This indicates that 72% of State members of the AU have defaulted several times the State reporting procedure; and that 23% of State members have never presented any report.[63] Regrettably, no compulsory measures are available for the Commission to be able to enforce the State's obligation to report and the greatest means available still remains peer-pressure.

The Commission informs the member States as early as possible of the opening date, duration and venue at which their respective reports shall be considered. The State parties may then send representatives to participate in the sessions in which their reports are being considered.[64] The representatives may need to clarify matters arising, answer questions and provide additional information from the State as may be necessary. The aim of the procedure is to create a constructive dialogue between the Commission and the State.[65]

It is not compulsory for a State to send representatives to sessions where reports are being considered. At its 23rd Ordinary Session, the Commission decided that if a State fails to send a representative to present its report it shall be notified twice. If still there is no response, the Commission will go ahead with examination of the report and forward its comments to the State concerned.

After the examination of State reports, the Commission usually sends a follow-up dispatch to the State concerned, summing up the examination

---

[62] Data available at:
http://www.achpr.org/english/_info/statereport_considered_en.html

[63] 27th Activity Report of the ACHPR. The States which have no presented any report are: Comoros, Côte d'Ivoire, Djibouti, Equatorial Guinea, Eritrea, Gabon, Guinea-Bissau, Liberia, Malawi, Sao Tome & Principe, Sierra Leone and Somalia.

[64] ACHPR, *Rules of Procedure*, Rule 83.

[65] ACHPR, *Guidelines for National Periodic Reports, Second Annual Activity Report of the African Commission on Human and Peoples' Rights* (1988-9), ACHPR/RPT/2nd, Annex XII at para. 1.

and putting in writing the questions that were not given satisfactory answers, if any. This is in accordance with Rule 85(3). The State is then requested to submit to the Secretariat of the Commission any additional information that it may require.

Rule 86(2) provides that the Commission may also transmit to the Assembly, the observation accompanied by copies of the reports it has received from the States, as well as the comments supplied by the latter if possible.

The State's reporting system of the African Commission is still in its developing stages. Unlike the UN Human Rights Committee, the African Commission examines very few reports during each of its sessions. For example, in its May 2011 session only three (3) reports are on the agenda: The Peoples' Bureau of the Great Socialist People's Libyan Arab Jamahiriya, the Republic of Burkina Faso and the Republic of Namibia. To develop this system further, the Commission would need greater cooperation from States and stronger lobbying from NGOs and civil society.[66]

The African Court on Human and People's Rights

The second organ created under the African Charter is the African Court on Human and People's Rights, hereinafter referred to as the Court. It is a specialized judicial body created to be an impartial arbiter in African human right issues. The Court complements and reinforces the protective mandate of the Commission. The Court's judgments on cases are final and binding upon the State parties concerned. Out of the 53 States that have ratified the Charter, only twenty-six have ratified the Court's Protocol.[67]

---

[66] See *http://www.achpr.org/english/_info/state_procedure_en.html*

[67] These States are Algeria, Burkina Faso, Burundi, Côte d'Ivoire, Comoros, Congo, Gabon, Gambia, Ghana, Kenya, Libya, Lesotho, Mali, Malawi, Mozambique, Mauritania, Mauritius, Nigeria, Niger, Rwanda, South Africa, Senegal, Tanzania, Togo, Tunisia and Uganda. The AU and the Commission used all possible persuasive arguments and ways to encourage the ratification of the Court's Protocol. In 2000, the African Commission approved the following resolution: *65ACHPR/Res.60(XXXI)02: Resolution on the Ratification of the Protocol to the African Charter on the Establishment of an African Court (2002) The African Commission on Human and Peoples' Rights, meeting at its 31st Ordinary Session in Pretoria, South Africa, from 2nd to 16th May 2002 ; RECALLING that the Assembly of Heads of States and of Governments of the Organisation of African Unity (OAU) adopted the Protocol to the African Charter*

The Court's judgments are final and non-appealable. The Court may order appropriate remedies, including fair compensation and reparations.[68] The judgment is notified to the member States of the AU and the AU Commission.[69] The Executive Council is responsible for monitoring the execution of the judgment. If a State party fails to comply with the decision of the ACtHPR, the AU may impose sanctions.[70] However, only one substantive matter has been decided by the court, though the full trial is still pending.

1. Establishment and Composition

The Court consists of eleven judges appointed from among the AU States and elected in their individual capacity from among jurists of high moral character and of recognized practical, judicial or academic competence and experience in the field of human and peoples' rights. The judges are elected for a six-year or four-year term and may be re-elected only once. The Court is hosted in Arusha, Tanzania. In the election of judges, the Assembly should ensure that there is representation from the major regions of Africa and of their principal legal traditions, as well as ensuring adequate gender representation. The judges are not representatives of the States of which they are nationals. They undertake to discharge their duties impartially and faithfully. The Court elects its own president and vice-president who serve for a period of two years, and may be re-elected only once. All judges except the president perform their functions on a part-time basis.[71]

---

on Human and Peoples' Rights on the Establishment of an African Court on Human and Peoples' Rights at its 19th Ordinary Session on 9 July 1998 in Ouagadougou, Burkina Faso; NOTING with satisfaction that 36 States have signed the Protocol to the African Charter on Human and Peoples' Rights on the establishment of an African Court on Human and Peoples' Rights; CONSIDERING that only 5 States have up to now ratified the said Protocol: Burkina Faso, Gambia, Mali, Senegal and Uganda; RECALLING that 15 ratifications or accessions are necessary for the entry into force of the Protocol on the Establishment of an African Court on Human and Peoples' Rights; URGES all the OAU Member States to ratify or accede as soon as possible to the Protocol on the Establishment of an African Court on Human and Peoples' Rights. Done in Pretoria, South Africa 16th May 2000.

[68] *Protocol to the African Court on Human and Peoples' Rights* (1998), Article 27.

[69] *Protocol to the African Court on Human and Peoples' Rights* (1998), Article 29.

[70] *African Union, Constitutive Act* (2001), Article 23.

[71] See *supra* note no. 56 about the Judges' election.

Judicial independence is ensured. Judges therefore must not sit in any case concerning the State of their nationality. Further, no judge may hear any case in which he or she had previously taken part as agent, counsel or advocate for one of the parties or as a member of a national or international court or a commission of enquiry or in any other capacity. The judges of the Court enjoy the immunities extended to diplomatic agents in accordance with international law. As regards professional ethics, a judge must not carry out any activity which is incompatible with the demands of office or which might interfere with his or her independence or impartiality.

Article 19 of the Court's Protocol provides that a judge shall not be suspended or removed from office unless, by the unanimous decision of the other judges of the Court, the judge concerned has been found to be no longer fulfilling the required conditions to be a judge of the Court. Such a decision of the Court shall become final unless it is set aside by the Assembly at its next session.

The Court's official languages are the same as those of the African Union: Arabic, English, French and Portuguese.

2. Jurisdiction of the Court

By the term 'jurisdiction' we refer to the organ's authority on the judicial control of the legality of its decisions that involves the legitimacy and application of its decisions and the obligation of Parties to comply.[72]Jurisdiction is usually understood *ratione materiæ* on those substantive issues a court has power to deal with, *ratione personæ* on the subjects of law who are allowed to access the Court, and *ratione temporis* on submission brought before the Court within a reasonable period of time. There is also Advisory jurisdiction which grants the Court a general power to interpret certain instruments under its scope.

The jurisdiction *ratione materiæ* of the African Court on Human and Peoples' Rights is defined by article 3 of the Protocol as follows:

> "1. The jurisdiction of the Court shall extend to all cases and disputes submitted to it concerning the interpretation and application of the Charter,

---

[72] See Oliver, C.T., "The Jurisdiction (Competence) of States", in Bedjaoui, M., *op. cit.*, at 307.In this definition we have made partial use of a wider definition Oliver makes referring to the general jurisdiction of a State and we have modified it accordingly and applied it the international judicial body in question.

> this Protocol and any other relevant Human Rights instrument ratified by the States concerned.2. In the event of a dispute as to whether the Court has jurisdiction, the Court shall decide."

Such jurisdiction is rather broad and it could bring this Court into conflict with the sub-regional courts in Africa or even international human rights courts and tribunals.

The jurisdiction *ratione personæ* of the African Court on Human and Peoples' Rights is regulated by Article 5(1) that reads:

> "Article 5 *Access to the Court*
> 1. The following are entitled to submit cases to the Court
> a. The Commission;
> b. The State Party which has lodged a complaint to the Commission;
> c. The State Party against which the complaint has been lodged at the Commission;
> d. The State Party whose citizen is a victim of human rights violation;
> e. African Intergovernmental Organizations.
> 2. When a State Party has an interest in a case, it may submit a request to the Court to be permitted to join.
> 3. The Court may entitle relevant Non-Governmental Organizations (NGOs) with observer status before the Commission, and individuals to institute cases directly before it, in accordance with article 34 (6) of this Protocol."[73]

And the jurisdiction *ratione temporis* is determined by Article 6(2) of the protocol, which says that the "Court shall rule on the admissibility of cases taking into account the provisions of article 56 of the Charter." Article 56 of the Charter says:

> "Communications relating to Human and Peoples' rights referred to in Article 55 received by the Commission [in this case 'the Court'], shall be considered if they: 6. Are submitted within a reasonable period from the time local remedies are exhausted or from the date the Commission is seized with the matter."

Certainly, if the exhaustion of local remedies is unduly prolonged the Court may also possess the matter as stated by article 55(5).

Thus, when jurisdiction *ratione materiæ* and *ratione temporis* are so wide and all-inclusive, jurisdiction *ratione personæ* becomes the 'filter' to prevent overloading the system. From a political perspective this 'filter'

---

[73] See Protocol to the African Charter on Human and Peoples' Rights on the Establishment of an African Court on Human and Peoples' Rights, Article 5.

seems to us the most accepted one because stringent regulations *ratione materiæ* or *ratione temporis* would have been perceived as attempts to tamper with substantive human rights which would contradict today's permissive understanding of human rights.

Understandably, the Protocol had to somehow place limits on the Court's jurisdiction or else no State would have signed it. In the end the filter was placed by limiting or conditioning access to the Court, thus not denying the existence of a right, but limiting access in such a way that the Court could be rendered almost ineffective.

Article 5(3) of the Protocol opened a 'window of opportunity' when it granted the possibility of allowing the Court to consider cases of human rights complaints brought by individuals or NGOs with observer status before the African Commission. For the Court to grant access to these individual complaints and NGOs with observer status before the Commission, the State against which the complaint has been lodged must first have recognized the competence of the Court to receive such petitions pursuant to Article 34(6) of the Protocol.[74]

Therefore, the declaration of the State pursuant article 34(6) is the legal act whereby the Court is expressly granted jurisdiction to receive individual and certain NGOs complaints. However, for some this requirement seems to impose an unreasonable limitation to the access to justice and more so in a context where it is usually the State that is the greatest human rights aggressor. For as long as Governments have to sign a declaration the Court's work and effectiveness will be limited. This is, perhaps, a political problem related to the failure of the State in Africa. The *Declaration of the State* allowing individual petitions seems to make the Court accessibility depend on the will of the State, which makes little sense in a human rights context where African States are the greatest perpetrators of abuse. As of January 2014 only 7 countries had signed the declaration: Ghana, Malawi, Burkina Faso, Mali, Tanzania, Rwanda and most recently Côte d'Ivoire. This makes it all the more important to convince States to delete the clause on declaration in the future court. Logically, facilitating access to justice is of paramount importance for a human rights system.

---

[74] Article 34(6) reads: "At the time of the ratification of this Protocol or any time thereafter, the State shall make a declaration accepting the competence of the Court to receive cases under article 5(3) of this Protocol. The Court shall not receive any petition under article 5 (3) involving a State Party which has not made such a declaration."

As a matter of fact, this requirement was at the centre of the first case ever to be presented at the Court: *Michelot Yogogombaye v The Republic of Senegal*,[75] decided on 15th December 2009. In a short ruling accompanied by a separate opinion by Judge Fatsah Ouguergouz, the Court unanimously dismissed the case for lack of jurisdiction. The applicant, Michelot Yogogombaye, a Chadian living in Switzerland initiated proceedings against Senegal in August 2008, seeking an order to prevent Senegalese authorities from prosecuting former President Hissène Habré, who ruled Chad for eight years and sought asylum in Senegal, after being deposed in December 1990. Habré is allegedly responsible for ordering the torture and deaths of up to forty thousand Chadians during his eight-year rule. Yogogombaye attempted to get the Court to establish its jurisdiction over the case. He also claimed that the Country had made the required declaration by Article 34(6) of the Court's Protocol allowing individual petitions.

This judgment did not go into the merits of the case, but instead dealt with the issue of the jurisdiction of the Court. The Court held that it did not have jurisdiction to deal with the matter for Senegal had never made the required declaration under article 34 as claimed by Yogogombaye. The importance of the judgment, however, is that it provided an interpretation of Articles 5(3) and 34(6) of the Protocol, as well as looking into the issues of the *locus standi* to bring cases before the Court and the personal jurisdiction of the Court. Regrettably, a case that should have been resolved in a speedy manner by the Registrar took a year and a full pronouncement by the Court in *plenary*.

The complainant wrongly asserted that Senegal had made the voluntary declaration while it had not. Weldehaimanot explains that the Registrar of the Court gave the benefit of the doubt to the complainant without confirming from the AU Commission in Addis Ababa, Ethiopia, which is depository of AU treaties, ratifications, reservations, and declarations related to a particular treaty. This was clearly a blunder from the Registrar of the Court, whose duty includes getting from the AU Commission regular update son the voluntary declarations of States and any other relevant signature, declaration or ratification. The Registrar, without establishing if Senegal had made the voluntary declaration proceeded to serve Senegal with a copy of the application and asked the State to defend it.

---

[75] ACtHPR, Application No. 001/2008.

Ouguergouz points out in a separate opinion that "[Senegal] could have limited itself to indicating that it had not made the declaration and that, consequently, the Court had no jurisdiction."[76] However, Senegal was willing to defend the case and this aggravated the Registrar's error. It was wrong for the Registrar to serve Senegal without ascertaining deposit of its declaration and it was wrong for Senegal not to point out the matter early enough. Thus, the blunders of the Registrar and Senegal were further aggravated when he committed the case to trial after Senegal had clearly stated that it has not made the declaration. As a result, the Court went into a full-scale trial.[77]

The case of *Michelot Yogogombaye v The Republic of Senegal*, although a costly error of the Registrar and worsened by the State Party, it allowed the Court to examine in depth certain aspects of jurisdiction. The Court focused the matter on the term 'receive' as the key establishing jurisdiction. In its decision, the Court stated:

> "The Court further notes that the second sentence of Article 34(6) of the Protocol provides that 'it shall not *receive* any petition under Article 5(3) involving a State Party which has not made such a declaration' (emphasis added). The word 'receive' should not however be understood in its literal meaning as referring to 'physically receiving' nor in its technical sense as referring to 'admissibility' It should instead be interpreted in light of the letter and spirit of Rule 34(6) in its entirety and, in particular, in relation to the expression 'declaration accepting the competence of the Court to receive applications [emanating from individuals or NGOs]' contained in the first sentence of this provision. It is evident from this reading that the objective of the aforementioned Rule 34(6) is to prescribe the conditions under which the Court could hear such cases; that is to say, the requirement that a special declaration should be deposited by the concerned State Party, and to set forth the consequences of the absence of such a deposit by the State concerned."[78]

It is clear that the complainant made a mistake by instituting a cause against a State that had not signed the declaration established by Article

---

[76] Separate opinion of Judge Fatsah Ouguergouz in the case of *Michelot Yogogombaye v. the Republic of Senegal*, Application No. 001/2008.

[77] See Weldehaimanot, S. M., "Towards Speedy Trials: Reforming the Practice of Adjudicating Cases in the African Human Rights System", *The University for Peace Law Review*, vol. 14, No. 1, (2010) at 14-38. Available at *http://www.lawreview. upeace.org/pdf/vol1issue1article2.pdf]*

[78] ACtHPR, case of *Michelot Yogogombaye v. the Republic of Senegal*, Application No. 001/2008, No. 39.

34(6) of the Protocol. It is also clear that the Registrar should have confirmed if Senegal has signed the declaration before including the complaints in the Court's general list. According to Ouguergouz he should have "rejected *de plano* by simple letter"[79] the submission. It is further clear that Senegal should not have entered into the matter by raising preliminary objections in its 'statement of defence'. Therefore, the matter raises the following question: Can Senegal's statement of defence be taken as an implicit or tacit act of acceptance of jurisdiction? Judge Fatsah Ouguergouz, in his separate opinion argues that the matter should have been considered by the Court. Ouguergouz states that:

> "consideration by the Court of Senegal's preliminary objections, in a judgment, required that it addresses the question of its jurisdiction in a more comprehensive manner by developing in particular the possibility of a *forum prorogatum*. This possibility is all the more suggested in paragraph 37 of the Judgment where the Court, on the grounds of its ruling that Senegal has not made the optional declaration, concluded that the said State, on that basis, 'has not accepted the jurisdiction of the Court to hear cases instituted directly against the Country by individuals or non-governmental organizations'."[80]

Judge Ouguergouz is in fact pointing at the possibility of the Court having interpreted Senegal's disposition and argumentation during Court's proceedings as an implicit or tacit acceptance of jurisdiction through the principle of *forum prorogatum*, "because under this doctrine, effective participation in proceedings by addressing the merits of a case, for example, could be taken to imply a tacit endorsement of jurisdiction."[81] The term *forum prorogatum* or 'prorogation of jurisdiction' appears to have been coined by the judges of the PCIJ when they discussed the proposed amendments to the Rules of Court in 1934.[82]According to Yee, it finds its origins in Roman law and has been inherited by many national legal systems. Traditionally understood, *forum prorogatum* meant the

---

[79] ACtHPR, case of *Michelot Yogogombaye v. the Republic of Senegal*, Application No. 001/2008, Separate Opinion of Judge Fatsah Ouguergouz, No. 40.
[80] *Ibid.*, No. 37.
[81] See Bederman, D.J. and Jalloh, C.C., "Michelot Yogogombaye v. Republic of Senegal", *The American Journal of International Law*, Vol. 104, No. 4, (2010) pp. 620-628.
[82] See Yee, S., "Forum Prorogatum Returns to the International Court of Justice", *Leiden Journal of International Law*, vol. 16, (2003) at 703.

extension of jurisdiction of a court by agreement of the parties in a case where the court was originally without jurisdiction.[83]

However, Pouliot tells us that concerns have also been expressed in "relation to some legal consequences of resorting to *forum prorogatum* when the Court relies on tacit consent to its jurisdiction."[84] This is a delicate issue which also involves internal law and the consequences should not be overlooked. For example, it may be said that the organ of the State that has argued the merits does not have the power to confer jurisdiction, especially when it comes to pointing out which State organs have the authority to confer jurisdiction to the African Court.[85] Therefore, "ruling that to plead on the merits of the case constitutes tacit acceptance of the jurisdiction of the Court means conferring such powers to the Agents of the Parties regardless of the domestic law of that State. This is perhaps one of the reasons why *forum prorogatum* has so far been rarely used... In fact, between the *Haya de la Torre* case in 1951, and the case concerning *Certain Criminal Proceedings in France* in 2003, the ICJ not once relied on *forum prorogatum* to establish its jurisdiction."[86]

Thus, Ouguergouz is stating that the Court should have examined in depth the reasons that led the Court to give a solemn judgment when apparently the matter could have been resolved in a rather short time. Mujuzi, for example, asserts that in light of Article 34(6) of the Protocol, Judge Ouguergouz is of the view that 'consent by a State Party is the only condition for the Court to exercise jurisdiction with regard to applications brought by individuals.' This consent may be expressed by the submission of the declaration alluded to by Article 34(6) at the time of ratification or later.[87] The difficult matter would be to define whether this declaration may be done only by a formal act of declaration, or it could be done informally or implicitly through *forum prorogatum*,[88] and if it is implicitly

---

[83] *Ibid.*

[84] Pouliot, V., "Forum Prorogatum before the International Court of Justice: The Djibouti v. France case", *Hague Justice Journal*, vol 3, No. 3, (2008) at 35.

[85] Pouliot makes this parallelism referring to the ICJ. See *Ibid.*

[86] *Ibid.*

[87] See Mujuzi, J.D., "Michelot Yogogombaye v The Republic of Senegal: The African Court's First Decision", *Human Rights Law Review*, Oxford, vol. 10, No. 2, (2010) at 372-381.

[88] See Wittich, S., "Permissible Derogation from Mandatory Rules? The Problem of Party Status in the Genocide Case", *European Journal of International Law*, vol. 18, (2007) at 602.

done there must be 'an unequivocal indication' on the part of the respondent State to accept the jurisdiction of the Court.[89]

Hence, the essential question in the *Michelot Yogogombaye v The Republic of Senegal* case is whether Senegal accepted, either expressly or tacitly, through decisive acts or an unequivocal behaviour, the Court's jurisdiction to judge over complaints submitted by individuals. If this matter had been accepted, *forum prorogatum* would have given potential applicants to the African Court hope on more than one way through which a State Party to the Protocol can consent to the Court's jurisdiction over individual complaints.[90] What remains clear is that the primary and least contentious way is the formal one, whereby States make the required acceptance of jurisdiction at the time of ratification or thereafter through a formal declaration as per article 34(6) of the Protocol.

Forum prorogatum is likely to be controversial. Jurisprudence on this matter will clarify alternative means to establish jurisdiction over States which have not submitted the aforementioned declaration. Certainly, *forum prorogatum* must fulfil certain conditions that lead the Court to ascertain unequivocally the consent of the State and that this consent which implies in Mujuzi's terms the "voluntary and indisputable acceptance of the Court's jurisdiction"[91] does not contradict the State's domestic laws.

As has already been stated, the Court also enjoys advisory jurisdiction whereby it is competent to hear all matters concerning the interpretation and application of the African Charter, the Protocol to the Charter on the Establishment of the African Court on Human and Peoples' Rights, and any other relevant human rights instruments ratified by the States concerned. The Court may also give its advisory opinion on any legal matter in relation to the Charter or any other relevant human rights instrument, provided that the matter is not being examined by the Commission.

---

[89] See Hammer, "Allowing Genocide? An Analysis of Armed Activities on the Territory of the Congo, Jurisdictional Reservations, and the Legitimacy of the International Court of Justice", *Minnesota Journal of International Law*, vol. 16, (2007) at 506.Hammer discusses in this article the Rwanda-Congo conflict and the approach taken by the ICJ.

[90] See generally Mujuzi, J.D., *op. cit.*, at 372-381.

[91] *Ibid.*

3. Lodging complaints

Cases are submitted to the Registrar,[92] at the seat of the Court in Arusha, Tanzania, in accordance with Rule 25 and Rule 34. The Registrar has custody of the seal and official stamp of the Court to officially acknowledge receipt of any submission. Applications must be in writing, in one of the official languages of the Court and must be signed by the applicant or a representative.

Applications must indicate: the names and addresses of the persons designated as the applicant's representative; a summary of the facts of the case and of the evidence that will be adduced; clear particulars of the applicant and of the party (or parties) against whom the application has been brought; specification of the alleged violation; evidence of exhaustion of local remedies or of the inordinate delay of such local remedies and the orders or injunctions sought. Where an applicant on his or her own behalf or on behalf of the victim wishes to be granted reparation, the application should include the request for reparation.

In cases of extreme gravity and urgency, and when necessary to avoid irreparable harm to persons, the Court may adopt provisional measures as necessary.[93] This has recently happened in the case of the *African Commission on Human and Peoples' Rights v. Great Socialist People's Libyan Arab Jamahiriya*,[94] where the Court, in accordance with Rule 51,[95]

---

[92] See *http://www.african-court.org/en/court/registry/.* The Registrar had been Aboubakar Diakité since the Court's foundation until January 2011. He has been replaced by an acting Registrar, Dr Robert Eno. According to Mr Diakité they expected several cases to arrive within a year. *The office of the Registry is located at the Court's seat in Arusha, Tanzania. The Registry is headed by the Registrar who is responsible for the supervision and coordination of all the operations and activities of the Registry. Among other things it is the duty of the Registry to keep a list of all cases, to prepare minutes of the Court's sittings and to notify the parties to a case about the Court's decisions.*

[93] See 1998 *Protocol*, Article 27: "1. If the Court finds that there has been violation of a human or peoples' right, it shall make appropriate orders to remedy the violation, including the payment of fair compensation or reparation. 2. In cases of extreme gravity and urgency, and when necessary to avoid irreparable harm to persons, the Court shall adopt such provisional measures as it deems necessary."

[94] ACtHPR, application no. 004/2011.

[95] ACtHPR, Rule 51 (Interim Measures): "1. Pursuant to article 27(2) of the Protocol, the Court may, at the request of a party, the Commission or on its own accord, prescribe to the parties any interim measure which it deems necessary to adopt in the interest of the parties or of justice. 2. In case of extreme urgency, the

issued on 25th March 2011, an Order for Provisional Measures against Libya to prevent further and irreparable abuses against human rights.

These are the first provisional measures ever granted by the African Court. The case was submitted to the Court by the African Commission, which alleges serious violations against human and peoples' rights in Libya. Although the Commission did not request the Court to issue an order for provisional measures, the Court decided *motu proprio* to issue them. The Court explains that it is satisfied *prima facie* that it appears to have jurisdiction and it also indicated that these measures – being provisional in nature – do not prejudice its findings on jurisdiction, admissibility and merits of the case.[96] The Court unanimously ordered:

> "1) The Great Socialist People's Libyan Arab Jamahiriya must immediately refrain from any action that would result in loss of life or violation of physical integrity of persons, which could be a breach of the provisions of the Charter or of other international human rights instruments to which it is a party.
>
> 2) The Great Socialist People's Libyan Arab Jamahiriya must report to the Court within a period of fifteen (15) days from the date of receipt of the Order, on the measures taken to implement this Order."[97]

It is quite remarkable and positive that Libya has answered the Court within the fifteen days period and with a lengthy report on the matter. Libya's response is not public yet, but it is an important step in the judicial function the Court exercises in Africa. It also elevates the hope Africa and its human rights system has placed on the Court.

4. Consideration of Cases

In considering cases, the Court shall apply the provisions of the Charter and any other relevant human rights instruments ratified by the States concerned. The Charter provides that the sources of law that apply for the monitoring of the implementation of the Charter are international law on human and peoples' rights, particularly from the provisions of various African instruments on human and peoples' rights, the Charter of

---

President may convene an extraordinary session of the Court to decide on measures to be taken.(…)"

96 ACtHPR, application no. 004/2011, *In the Matter of the African Commission on Human and Peoples' rights v. Great Socialist Peoples' Libyan Arab Jamahiriya*, Order for Provisional Measures of 25th March 2011.

97 *Ibid*. No. 25, at 7.

the United Nations, the Charter of the Organization of African Unity (now the Constitutive Act of the African Union), the Universal Declaration of Human Rights, other instruments adopted by the United Nations and by African countries in the field of human and peoples' rights, as well as from the provisions of various instruments adopted within the Specialized Agencies of the United Nations of which the parties to the Charter are members. The Court also has the prerogative to consider a case or to transfer it to the Commission.

In this context, given the multicultural and multi-ethnic diversity of the African Continent, it seems reasonable to foresee that the application of the 'margin of appreciation' doctrine[98] will become a relevant tool for decisions on consideration of cases, referrals as well as the equitable consideration of substantive issues. The margin of appreciation doctrine has a two-fold area of operations: First, it opens the doors for the Court to ponder the Charter and its application taking into consideration the historic, cultural and societal divergences between African States. Second, this doctrine also allows States to have certain flexibility in the application of general norms contained in the Charter without necessarily contradicting local customs and usages. Thus, margin of appreciation may become a useful tool in the African human rights system. As stated by the ECHR in *Handyside v. The United Kingdom*,

> "Article 10(2) leaves to the Contracting States a margin of appreciation. This margin is given both to the domestic legislator ("prescribed by law") and to the bodies, judicial amongst others, that are called upon to interpret and apply the laws in force … Nevertheless, Article 10(2) does not give the Contracting States an unlimited power of appreciation. The Court, which, with the Commission, is responsible for ensuring the observance of those States' engagements … is empowered to give the final ruling on whether a "restriction" or "penalty" is reconcilable with freedom of expression as protected by Article 10. The domestic margin of appreciation thus goes hand in hand with a European supervision."[99]

Therefore the margin of appreciation allows a delicate balancing act which gives the Court and the State the necessary flexibility to respect certain principles of equity.

---

[98] This doctrine was used for the first time by the European Court of Human Rights in the case of *Handyside v. The United Kingdom*, (Application no. 5493/72), Strasbourg, 7th Dec. 1976.

[99] ECHR, (Application no. 5493/72), *Handyside v. The United Kingdom*, Strasbourg, 7th Dec. 1976.

Article 10 of the Protocol stipulates that the Court shall conduct its proceedings in public, unless it is decided in particular instances, to hold them in chambers. Any party to a case is entitled to be represented by a legal representative of choice. Free legal representation or assistance may be provided where the interests of justice so require and in accordance with international law, any person, witness or representative of the parties who appears before the Court is provided with the necessary protection and facilities.[100] Quorum for cases' examination will be constituted if at least seven judges review the matter.

The Court hears submissions by all parties and, if necessary, holds an inquiry. The States concerned have a duty to assist the Court by providing relevant facilities for the efficient handling of the case. The Court may receive all elements of proof that it considers appropriate, whether written or oral evidence. It also considers expert testimonies. The Court then makes its decision on the basis of the evidence provided by the parties. It may, however, try to reach an amicable settlement while the case is still pending before it.[101]

In considering admissibility of cases, the Court takes into consideration the provisions of article 56 of the Charter,[102] just as the Commission is required to do so. Further, the Court may request the opinion of the Commission on the issue of admissibility and the Commission is required to give this opinion as soon as practicable.

---

[100] See 1998 *Protocol*, Article 10 (3).

[101] See 1998 *Protocol*, Article 26.

[102] *Africa Charter*, Article 56 states: *Communications relating to human and peoples' rights referred to in 55 ... shall be considered if they: 1. Indicate their authors even if the latter request anonymity, 2. Are compatible with the Charter of the Organization of African Unity or with the present Charter, 3. Are not written in disparaging or insulting language directed against the State concerned and its institutions or to the Organization of African Unity, 4. Are not based exclusively on news discriminated through the mass media, 5. Are sent after exhausting local remedies, if any, unless it is obvious that this procedure is unduly prolonged, 6. Are submitted within a reasonable period from the time local remedies are exhausted or from the date the Commission is seized of the matter, and 7. Do not deal with cases which have been settled by these States involved in accordance with the principles of the Charter of the United Nations, or the Charter of the Organization of African Unity or the provisions of the present Charter.*

5. Court Judgments and their Execution

Once the Court has finished examining the case, it renders its judgment within ninety days of the completion of its deliberations. The judgment of the Court decided by majority is final and not subject to appeal.

If the Court finds that there has been a violation of rights, it issues appropriate orders to remedy the violation, including the payment of fair compensation or reparation. The Court should also foster amicable settlement in cases pending before it in accordance with the provisions of the Charter.

As regards judgments, the Court has the jurisdiction to interpret a judgment it has rendered and it can also review its own judgment in the light of new evidence. A party may apply for a judgment review within six months after the party acquires knowledge of the evidence discovered.[103]

Each judge is entitled to add his or her separate or dissenting opinion to the majority decision of the Court. The reasons for the judgment must be given. The judgment is read in open court, due notice having been given to the parties.[104]

The parties to the case are notified of the judgment of the Court and it is transmitted to the Member States of the AU and to the Commission. The Council of Ministers is also notified of the judgment so that it monitors its execution on behalf of the Assembly.[105] In accordance with Article 30, the States Parties to the Protocol undertake to comply with the judgment in any case to which they are parties and to guarantee execution within the time stipulated by the Court. If a State party does not comply with the Court's judgment, the Court notifies the Assembly through the report that it submits to each regular session of the Assembly.

The execution of the judgments of the African Court will determine its efficacy and efficiency within the African Human Rights System. Ordinarily, the enforcement of foreign judgments is associated with the reciprocal recognition and enforcement of judgments between States, which is frequently regulated by bilateral treaty or multilateral international conventions. However, judgments from the African Court should not be considered 'foreign judgments' but, rather, 'supranational judgments'. Enforcing foreign judgments involves the application of the local court's

---

[103] See 1998 *Protocol*, Article 28.

[104] *Ibid.*

[105] See 1998 *Protocol*, Article 29.

powers to give effect to the foreign court's decision without the plaintiff having to re-litigate the merits of the dispute.[106] Conversely, enforcing supranational judgments has not yet found a harmonious and consistent practice in Africa.

In the African scenario, nonetheless, the problem the African Court will face at the time of execution is double: On the one hand the African State is naturally and historically reluctant to allow any form of external interference, and the Court is no exception to this.[107] On the other hand, most African States have not developed, in practice, a tangible and genuine constitutional and administrative system of internal checks and balances.[108] These two aspects undermine the protection of human rights and the enforcement of international decision to the core.[109] First, because the decision comes from a supranational body, and second, because the internal procedures for execution of domestic judgments against the State are ineffective and often designed to frustrate its execution and evade State responsibility. Nigeria is perhaps an example of a State that is essentially dualist in regards to treaty incorporation but has no practical experience in regards to the incorporation of international judicial decisions.[110] If a

---

[106] BCLI, British Columbia Law Institute, "Report on the Enforcement of Non-Money Judgments from Outside the Province", *Report*, No 8, (1999) at 6.

[107] This obeys the historical reasons we have explained at length in the historical summary (*supra*) of the so-called *scramble for Africa*.

[108] See Chapter I and II *supra*.

[109] This issue about enforcement of judgements will be analysed in greater detail below.

[110] For example, Nigeria's recognition of foreign judgments is governed by two statutes: the Reciprocal Enforcement of Foreign Judgments Ordinance, Cap 175 and the Foreign Judgments (Reciprocal Enforcement) Act, Cap 152. However, the High Court's jurisprudence is contradictory as to which of these two statutes regulates the enforcement of foreign judgments. In principle, for a foreign judgment to be enforceable in Nigeria, it must be pronounced by a superior court of the country of the original court and the judgment must also be final and conclusive as between the parties. Regarding human rights judgments, the only experience comes from decisions by the ACHPR, which has issued several communications against Nigeria with some degree of expeditious enforcement, mostly at the will of the executive. For example in the case of *Centre for Free Speech v. Nigeria* [ACHPR, C. No. 206/97 (1999)], where the Commission found that Nigeria had violated the journalists' rights to personal liberty, a fair trial, and the guarantee of the independence of the courts (Article 26). It recommended that the government release them, and the Government complied [Viljoen, F. and Louw, L.,"State Compliance with the Recommendations of the African Commission on Human and Peoples' Rights,1993–2004", *American Journal of*

decision against Nigeria is reached by the African Court, the Nigerian Government would apply a similar procedure as with domestic decisions. Such decisions go to the attorney general who gives the go-ahead for their execution.[111] This is often difficult. Therefore, a decision from the African Court would have to be taken by the interested party to the Nigerian Attorney General and request its execution.[112]

However, Nigeria has been exemplary in handling several cases decided by the African Commission regarding human rights complaints.[113]

International Law, vol 101, No. 1, (2007), at 10]. There is also the case of *Constitutional Rights Project (in respect of Zamani Lakwot and 6 Others) v. Nigeria*. In this case, the Commission found that Nigeria had violated the African Charter's fair trial protection when it tried seven prominent leaders of the Kataf ethnic minority in a military tribunal and sentenced them to death [Okafor, O. C., "The African system on Human and Peoples' Rights, quasi-constructivism, and the possibility of peace-building within African States", *The International Journal of Human Rights*, Volume 8, Issue 4, (2004), at 424]. After the Commission announced grave violations of due process and recommended that Nigeria release the men in 1996, they were released later that year. Other cases involving Nigeria where the Commission did not provide a recommendation, include the case of *Rights International v. Nigeria.* [ACHPR, C. No. 215/98 (1999)], where the Commission found that the State of Nigeria had violated rights under the African Charter when it arrested and tortured the plaintiff. However, at the end of its report on the case, the Commission merely concluded that Nigeria had violated certain provisions of the charter without suggesting a remedy. Similarly, in *Huri-Laws v. Nigeria* the Commission found that Nigeria had violated its obligations under the Charter. Nevertheless, it failed to recommend steps Nigeria should have taken to remedy the situation.

[111] Soniyi, T., 14th April 2010. Available at:
http://www.nigerianbestforum.com/index.php?topic=71414.0
This bureaucratic step seems to make judges afraid to decide cases against the State. This is the reason why on 14th April 2010, Justice George Oguntade, who retired from the Nigerian Supreme Court on March 10, 2010 at the age of 70 *called on judges not to be afraid to give judgments against the government of the day. In an emotion-laden speech he read at a session at the Supreme Court in Abuja to mark his retirement from the Bench, Oguntade said that courts must guide both the people and the government on how to live in a society governed by the rule of law. He said, 'Nowadays, judges hesitate to give judgments against the government. This is an untenable approach. For me it is irrelevant who the parties are in a case.' The former Justice of Supreme Court also argued that laws were no longer enforced, saying that it was regrettable that impunity was everywhere.*

[112] These domestic obstacles will require a constitutional audit in the State parties to establish clear mechanisms and remove possible administrative hurdles.

[113] See

Nigeria has complied with some degree of expeditious enforcement, mostly at the will of the executive. For example, in the case of *Centre for Free Speech v. Nigeria*[114] the Commission found that Nigeria had violated the journalists' rights to personal liberty, a fair trial, and the guarantee of the independence of the courts (Article 26). The Commission recommended that the government releases them, and the Government complied.[115] There is also the case of *Constitutional Rights Project (in respect of Zamani Lakwot and 6 Others) v. Nigeria.*[116] In this case, the Commission found that Nigeria had violated the African Charter's fair trial protection when it tried seven prominent leaders of the Kataf ethnic minority in a military tribunal and sentenced them to death.[117] After the Commission announced grave violations of due process and recommended that Nigeria releases the men in 1996, they were released later that year.

Since the Court has fully pronounced itself on only one substantive matter in the case of *Mtikila v. Tanzania* on 14 June 2013, it may be prudent to peep into the possible future scenario based on the current compliance level of decisions from the Commission. In this regard, Viljoen and Louw undertook a compliance survey of decisions issued by the Commission between 1993 and 2004.[118] They focused their studied on nineteen (19) decisions[119] of which only six (6)[120] were enforced by the State involved. Although they did not manage to establish in a comprehensive

---

http://www.achpr.org/english/ _info/List_Decision_Communications.html.
It must also be noted that Nigeria has been the Country with the highest number of complaints before the Commission. As of January 2011, 31 complaints where Nigeria was party had been decided by the Commission.

[114] ACHPR, C. No. 206/97 (1999).

[115] See Viljoen, F. and Louw, L., "State Compliance with the Recommendations of the African Commission on Human and Peoples' Rights,1993–2004", *American Journal of International Law*, vol 101, No. 1, (2007), at 10.

[116] ACHPR, *Comm.* 87/93: The Constitutional Rights Project (in respect of Zamani Lakwot and six others) / Nigeria.

[117] Okafor, O.C., "The African system on Human and Peoples' Rights, quasi-constructivism, and the possibility of peace-building within African States", *The International Journal of Human Rights*, Volume 8, Issue 4, (2004), at 424.

[118] See Viljoen, F. and Louw, L., *op. cit.*, at 32 ff

[119] The cases were *Mazou v. Cameroon, Zambian Deportation, Nigerian Detention, Nigerian Journalists, Modise, Sierra Leone Coup, Zairian Torture, Zairian Mass Violations, Mekongo, Angolan Expulsion, Mauritanian Widows, Nigerian Torture, Bwampamye, Ouko, Nigerian Military Tribunals, Sudanese Military Court, Suleiman, Sudanese Picnic* and *Gambian Mental Health.*

[120] Cf. *Mazou, Zambian Deportation, Nigerian Detention, Nigerian Journalists, Modise* and *Sierra Leone Coup.*

manner the causes that helped compliance, they did assert that the domestic system of enforcement should be studied at the national level and that the Commission should have been clearer and more assertive. In certain decisions the Commission limited itself to declare the infringement of a right without proposing any specific remedies to redress the situation.[121]

The Court of Justice of the African Union

The Constitutive Act of the African Union requires the creation of several organs within the AU system. One of these organs is the Court of Justice of the African Union.[122] The drafting of the Protocol of the Court of Justice commenced in 2002 and was later approved by a Ministerial Conference in June 2003. It was then adopted at the 2nd Ordinary Assembly Session of the Assembly of Heads of State and Government of the African Union meeting in Maputo, Mozambique, on 11th July 2003.[123] It entered into force on 11th February 2009 after the 15th State deposited its ratification. However, it is not yet operational.

The Court of Justice has ample jurisdiction *ratione materiæ* to resolve disputes between the AU member States or between member States and the AU[124] and to interpret and implement the Constitutive Act of the AU, other AU treaties, and the acts and decisions of the AU.[125] The Court could also be conferred with wider jurisdiction, as may be necessary, by the AU through agreements among the member States or with the African

---

[121] This happened, for example, in the case of *Rights International v. Nigeria* [ACHPR, C. No. 215/98 (1999)], where the Commission found that the State of Nigeria had violated rights under the African Charter when it arrested and tortured the plaintiff. However, at the end of its report on the case, the Commission merely concluded that Nigeria had violated certain provisions of the Charter without suggesting a remedy. Similarly, in *Huri-Laws v. Nigeria* [Comm. 225/98] the Commission found that Nigeria had violated its obligations under the Charter, but it failed to recommend steps Nigeria should have taken to remedy the situation.

[122] The *Constitutive Act of the African Union*, Art. 5.

[123] AU. Doc. Assembly/AU/Dec.25 (II), *Decision on the Protocol of the Court of Justice of the African Union,* , based on the recommendations made by the Executive Council, AU Doc. Dec. EX/CL/58 (III), *Decision on the Draft Protocol of the Court of Justice.*

[124] Motala, A. C., *The African Court: Prospects for the Effective Protection of Human Rights on the Continent*, Open Society Initiative for Southern Africa, Open Society Foundations, New York, (2002), at 77.

[125] The *Protocol to the African Court of Justice*, Art. 28.

Union.[126] Its jurisdiction *ratione personæ* extended to all State parties acting in their capacity as *de iure* subjects of international law. Furthermore, the Court of Justice was also bestowed with advisory jurisdiction to give opinions at the request of organs of the AU or a regional economic community.[127] Thus, the African Court of Justice was designed to be the principal judicial organ of the AU.[128]

The Court of Justice's judgments would be binding on the parties to the dispute.[129] Its decisions would be final and not subject to appeal. However, a party could apply for a revision of the Court of Justice's decision if a new fact of a decisive nature that was unknown to the Court of Justice or to the party requesting revision came up.[130] Parties to a dispute were obliged to comply with the Court's judgment within the time stipulated by the Court.[131] If a party failed to comply, the Court could refer the matter to the AU Assembly through reports[132] for it to determine the measures to be taken to give effect to the judgment.[133] The Court's decisions on the interpretation and application of the Constitutive Act of the African Union were meant to be binding on all member States and organs of the AU.[134]

This Court of Justice has not been constituted, and will never be, since in July 2004 the Assembly of Heads of State and Government directed that the possible merger with the African Court on Human and Peoples' Rights be studied and an appropriate protocol be drafted.[135] The aims were to salvage the dormant idea of a Court of Justice and to avoid overlapping of jurisdictions and multiplications of regional bodies thus easing out the heavy financial implications this meant for the struggling African economies and reducing administrative costs of running the AU. The central point was to merge the judicial bodies of the African Union into one Court with different sections. Originally there were two sections: The

---

[126] Motala, A. C., *op. cit.*, at 77. See The *Protocol to the African Court of Justice*, Article 19.
[127] The *Protocol to the African Court of Justice*, Art. 44.
[128] The *Protocol to the African Court of Justice*, Art.2 (1).
[129] The *Protocol to the African Court of Justice*, Art. 37.
[130] The *Protocol to the African Court of Justice*, Art. 41.
[131] The *Protocol to the African Court of Justice*, Art. 51.
[132] The *Protocol to the African Court of Justice*, Art. 53.
[133] The *Protocol to the African Court of Justice*, Art. 52.
[134] The *Protocol to the African Court of Justice*, Art. 38.
[135] African Union, Assembly/AU/Dec.45 (III) Rev.1, *Decision on the Seats of the Organs of the Union*.

general one and the human rights section. However, recent opinions and negotiations seem more inclined towards a third section, a criminal section, to handle certain crimes against humanity committed in Africa. Each section would have its jurisdiction defined and administrative and procedural costs would be shared under one body so as to make the financial burden lighter on both the AU and the State parties.

This would encourage African States to ratify a new Merger Protocol and fulfil the pledge of justice of the African Union. Negotiations took shape and a merger protocol was approved in 2008 although it is not yet operational.

Other African Supranational Judicial Organs and their Impact on the Human Rights System

Odinkalu explains that there are across the African Continent a multiplicity of sub-regional courts and tribunals with mandates that overlap with those of the ACtHPR and the ACHPR.[136] Certainly, there are multiple judicial bodies dealing with human rights issues within defined regional structures. In a recent meeting of sub-regional courts with judges of the African Court on Human and People's Rights, its President, Justice Gérard Niyungeko suggested that the ACtHPR should act as the appeal court of all these regional bodies in order to harmonize Continental dispensation of justice and give unifying criteria to the decisions. Sub-regional courts were however reluctant to subject themselves to a higher instance and the proposal did not go far.[137] The sub-regional courts position seems justified as they were created for and with specific jurisdiction and autonomy they would not, and sometimes cannot, relinquish.

This position of sub-regional courts "reflects the fact that, in international jurisdiction, there is, in general, only one first and last instance. This is due, *inter alia*, to the fact that in international law there is no mandatory jurisdiction and, consequently, no hierarchical court system

---

[136] Odinkalu, C.A., "Complementarity, Competition or Contradiction: The Relationship between the African Court on Human and Peoples' Rights and Regional Economic Courts in East and Southern Africa", *Presentation to Conference of East and Southern African States on the Protocol Establishing the African Court on Human and Peoples' Rights*, Gaborone, Botswana, 9-10 December 2003 (Unpublished).

[137] Justice Niyungeko (President of the Court). *Records at the President's Office*, Arusha, Tanzania, 2010.

as in national law. In particular, there were not even institutionalized courts and tribunals in the early days of international jurisdiction but only *ad hoc* arbitral tribunals which are *functus officio* once the award is rendered."[138]

Among the relevant existing judicial bodies at the sub-regional level we find the Court of Justice of the Economic Community of West African States (ECOWAS).[139] ECOWAS was established on 28th May, 1975 and its Court became operational on 22nd August, 2002. Its seat is located in Lagos, Nigeria and it has jurisdiction over the States of Benin, Burkina Faso, Cape Verde, Côte d'Ivoire, Gambia, Ghana, Guinea, Guinea-Bissau, Liberia, Mali, Niger, Nigeria, Senegal, Sierra Leone, and Togo. It has received more than 30 cases. Originally, only the Authority of Heads of State and Government and the Member States acting as such were permitted to initiate a contentious case in the Court. The power to request advisory opinions on the Treaty was also limited and the Court was idle for years.

In January 2005, the Community adopted the Additional Protocol to permit persons to bring suits against Member States. The Council also revised the jurisdiction of the Court and included violations of human rights in all Member States. It was then clear that the sources of law to be applied by the Court under its original Protocol would include general principles of international law as well as those in relation to human rights. The Court is composed of seven judges appointed by the Authority of Heads of State and Government from a list of up to two persons nominated by each Member State.

It received its first case in 2004. This landmark first case[140] was filed by an individual businessman against the government of Nigeria for a violation of Community law in the closing of the border with Benin. The Court ruled that under the Protocol only Member States could institute cases. The Protocol was later amended to allow for legal and natural persons to have access to the Court. The Additional Protocol also gave

---

[138] Oellers-Frahm, K., "Judicial and Arbitral Decisions, Validity and Nullity", The Max Planck Encyclopedia of Public International Law, Oxford University Press, 2011, online edition, [*http://www.mpepil.com/ViewPdf/epil/entries/law-9780199231690-e1057.pdf? style sheet=EPIL-display-full.xsl*], last accessed on 1.05.2011

[139] The *Protocol* establishing the ECOWAS Court was adopted in 1991. The Court itself is created as an institution of ECOWAS in Article 6(1) of the Revised ECOWAS *Treaty*, 1993.

[140] ECOWAS, case of *Olajide Afolabi v. Federal Republic of Nigeria.*

national courts of Member States the right to seize the ECOWAS Court for a ruling on the interpretation of Community law.

Since the adoption of the Additional Protocol, the Court has received several cases from individuals. Between January 2006 and June 2007, the Court received 26 applications and held 63 sessions.[141]

Another Court is the Court of the *Union économique et monétaire de l'Afrique de l'ouest* (UEMOA).[142] The Court's seat is located in Ouagadougou, Burkina Faso and its jurisdiction reaches Benin, Burkina Faso, Côte d'Ivoire, Guinea-Bissau, Mali, Niger, Senegal, and Togo.

In an attempt to avoid the delay in the entry into force of the Protocol Establishing the African Court on Human and Peoples' Rights, the Treaty provided that the

> "Protocol on the Court would be an integral part of the Treaty with no need for ratifications. Addressing further the Continental problem of implementation, the Treaty required that the Court come into being within six months of the Treaty entering into force. With financial help from France and the European Union, these Treaty provisions were fulfilled and the first judges of the Court were sworn in on January 27, 1985. Not meeting the three month deadline in the Treaty, the judges fully operationalized the Court by promulgating the Rules of Procedure in July 1986. In 1997, the addition of Guinea-Bissau to Union Treaty resulted in the expansion of the bench to nine judges."[143]

The Protocol on the Union Court grants equal standing before the Court to legal and natural persons to bring such disputes regarding the legality of the legal acts of the Union and its organs to the Court. It also requires national jurisdictions from which there is no appeal to refer cases when necessary to the Court. This ensures that the Court is the final arbiter on the interpretation of the Treaty and the laws of the Union.

The Court's control over interpretation is solidified by a procedure ensuring that national courts do not stray from the Court's jurisprudence. Such interpretations are then binding on all jurisdictions and authorities

As the member States of UEMOA are also members to the ECOWAS both organs have envisioned a merger of their monetary and trade

---

[141] See *http://www.aict-ctia.org/courts_subreg/ecowas/ecowas_home.html*
[142] See *http://www.uemoa.int/Organes/CourdeJustice.aspx*
[143] African International Courts and Tribunals Website. Available at: *http://www.aict-ctia.org/courts_subreg/waemu/waemu_home.html*

functions in 2004. While this merger has been postponed indefinitely, it could compel the needed rationalization of the roles of the two courts in these overlapping economic legal harmonization schemes.[144]

The Court of Justice of the East African Community (EACJ) was established on 30th November, 1999 and became operational on 30th November, 2001.[145] The seat is located in Arusha, Tanzania and it extends its jurisdiction to the following States: Burundi, Kenya, Rwanda, Uganda and Tanzania. It replaced the defunct East African Court of Appeals that was dissolved with the East African Community in 1977. With the revival of the East African Community in 1999, the Treaty contemplated a different type of Court. While the East African Court of Appeals was a high court for criminal and civil matters incorporated within the legal system of each Member State, the new Court came to be a sub-regional supranational Court of Justice.

In principle there is no provision for the enforcement of human rights law by this Court. However, the powers to interpret treaty law are so wide that this possibility could occur. According to the *African International Courts and Tribunals*, "in June of 2005, the East African Law Society suggested to President Yoweri Museveni of Uganda that the time had come to initiate the Treaty provision for expansion of the jurisdiction of the EACJ to cover appellate jurisdiction. Call has come also for use of that provision to expand the Court's jurisdiction to human rights. In June of 2007, the Summit approved the operationalization of the Appellate Division of the Court, reconstituting the Court effective as of July 1, 2007."[146]

There is also the Court of Justice of the Common Market of East and Southern African States (COMESA - formerly the Preferential Trading Area, PTA) has been operational in Lusaka, Zambia, since 1998.[147]

The COMESA Court is based in Khartoum, Sudan. It was established on 8th December, 1994 and became operational in 1998. Its jurisdiction covers: Angola, Burundi, Comoros, Democratic Republic of Congo, Djibouti, Egypt, Eritrea, Ethiopia, Kenya, Libya, Madagascar, Malawi, Mauritius, Namibia, Rwanda, Seychelles, Sudan, Swaziland, Uganda, Zambia and Zimbabwe. The Treaty created a judicial organ to oversee the

---

[144] *Ibid.*

[145] Created under the *East African Community Treaty* of 1999 and constituted and established in 2002 with its seat in Arusha, Tanzania.

[146] See *http://www.aict-ctia.org/courts_subreg/eac/eac_home.html*

[147] See Odinkalu, C.A., *op. cit.*, at 3.

implementation and interpretation of the COMESA agreement. The Court is allowed to receive cases from member States and from natural and legal persons, directed against the Council to determine the legality of any act, directive, regulation or decision made. Persons also are permitted standing under the Treaty to sue a member State in the COMESA Court regarding the legality under the Treaty of any act, directive, regulation or decision of such Member State.[148]

However, all national remedies must be exhausted which places an important restriction on individual petitions. It should also be pointed out that the Treaty does not specify that the Court will have jurisdiction over human rights issues within the Community, although they may be received by extension if they touch upon matters relating to the Treaty itself. According to the AICT, the COMESA Court continues to receive cases. However, due to lack of funds the Court is unable to hear all cases. The Council of Ministers has decided to fund only one sitting per year.[149]

An additional Court, the Court of Justice of the Economic Community of Central African States (ECCAS) was established on 18th December, 1984. It is not yet operational and does not have a seat. Its potential jurisdiction encompasses: Angola, Burundi, Cameroon, Central African Republic, Chad, Congo Democratic Republic, Congo, Equatorial Guinea, Gabon, Rwanda, and Sao Tome and Principe. Under the Union Treaty, the Court is designed to ensure that "the law is observed" in the interpretation and application of the Treaty. To do so, the Court is given jurisdiction to rule on the legality of decisions, directives and regulations of the Community.[150]

In northern Africa, the *Instance Judiciaire* of the Arab Maghreb Union (AMUIJ) was established on 30thNovember, 1999 and became operational on 30thNovember, 2001. The seat is located in Nouakchott, Mauritania and the States subject to its jurisdiction are: Algeria, Libya, Mauritania, Morocco and Tunisia.

This Court functions under the 1989 Treaty of Marrakech's Arab Maghreb Union (AMU). The *Instance Judiciaire* is composed of two judges from each Member State with six year terms. Pursuant to the Court's statute the Court cannot sit without the presence of at least one judge from each Member State and a quorum of eight judges. The Court is

[148] See *http://www.aict-ctia.org/courts_subreg/comesa/comesa_home.html*
[149] *Ibid.*
[150] *Ibid.*

charged with resolving disputes on the interpretation and application of the Treaty of Marrakech and other documents adopted by the Union. The Court also has advisory jurisdiction regarding potential disputes between the Union and its employees. The *Instance Judiciaire* does not seem to have supranational characteristics in that its decisions are, according to the Treaty of Marrakech, final and enforceable without the need for domestication of the decisions, which is a very interesting characteristic. "In making its decisions, the AMUIJ applies first the Treaty, agreements made under the Union and decisions of the Union organs. Secondarily, the Court applies general principles of law common to the jurisprudence of the Member States' legal systems, along with general principles of international law as long as the latter are compatible with the provisions of the Treaty. Lastly, the Court can apply international jurisprudence and doctrines in making its decisions."[151] Nonetheless, the AMU is practically dormant nowadays.[152]

Finally, the Southern African Development Community Tribunal (SADC Tribunal),[153] which has been operational since 18th November, 2005 and is located in Windhoek, Namibia. The States subject to its jurisdiction are: Angola, Botswana, DRC, Lesotho, Madagascar, Malawi, Mauritius, Mozambique, Namibia, South Africa, Swaziland, Tanzania, Zambia and Zimbabwe.

SADC Tribunal's tale is perhaps one of the most relevant in the area of human rights enforcement. In fact, the forcible execution of a judgment issued by the SADC (Southern African Development Community) Tribunal[154] against Zimbabwe has resulted in this tribunal being disbanded. This happened in the case of *Mike Campbell (PVT) Ltd et al v The Republic of Zimbabwe* that examined the lawfulness of the Zimbabwean Government's policy of land reclamation based on racial discrimination. The Zimbabwean Government was determined not to obey the SADC ruling and fiercely objected to the presence of a regional tribunal and its ability to review their domestic human rights record. Mike Campbell Ltd

---

151 See *http://www.aict-ctia.org/courts_subreg/amu/amu_home.html*

152 See *http://www.dfa.gov.za/foreign/Multilateral/africa/amu.htm*

153 SADC *Treaty*, Article 9, created the SADC Tribunal, also as an institution of the SADC. (Windhoek, SADC *Summit* of 2000).

154 The SADC was established in 1992 with the Windhoek Declaration, and set out its common aims of greater economic, political and security cooperation. Like other regional bodies, the SADC has an adjudicative tribunal to resolve disputes between member States and hear individual petitions on matters of community law. See *http://www.sadc.int/*

made an application to the North Gauteng High Court (formerly the Transvaal Provincial Division) which is a division of the High Court of South Africa. A writ of execution was issued by the North Gauteng High Court for a costs order against the Zimbabwean government of R 113,000 awarded by the Southern African Development Community (SADC) Tribunal in Windhoek last year.[155] Before the attachment of Zimbabwean properties was effected, William Spies, a human rights activist stated that "this is a symbolic message to the Zimbabwean government that, contrary to President Robert Mugabe's statements that the SADC rulings are of no consequence to Zimbabwe, they are enforceable in South Africa."[156]

During the SADC summit in Windhoek in August 2010, Mugabe threatened to block any discussion of Zimbabwe. The fact was that the summit *communiqué* stated "that it was decided that a review of the role, functions and terms of reference of the SADC Tribunal should be undertaken and concluded within six months." At the end of the summit, Joao Samuel Caholo, Deputy Executive Secretary of the SADC, declared that the Tribunal would not be able to conclude any old cases or take on new ones, before the end of the review process to be carried out by SADC Justice Ministers. Thereafter the Judges' contracts were not renewed and the Tribunal remains in 'Limbo.'[157]

Perhaps the forcible expropriation of Zimbabwean property on South African soil sent the wrong signal across other Member States and eroded their political will to support such jurisprudence of what could be termed as a real practical solution to a human rights abuse hidden behind the veil of a misunderstood and misused sovereignty.

Sub-regional African judicial bodies have been constituted primarily to supervise the operation of the treaties establishing the Regional Economic Communities (RECs) and for dispute resolution between the member States thereof. It is evident that there is certain overlap, potential

---

[155] Apparently a few days before the execution took place the South African government intervened. It is not clear at this moment if the South African Sheriff actually managed to execute the writ or not.

[156] See Spies, W., AfriForum legal representative. Available at: *http://www.businessday. co.za/Articles/Content.aspx?id=104924*

[157] See generally Cowell, F., "The suspension of the Southern African Development Community Tribunal: A threat to human rights", *Consultancy Africa Intelligence*, 17 October 2010. Available at: *http://www.consultancyafrica.com/index.php?option=com_ content&view=article&id=583:the-suspension-of-the-southern-african-development-community-tribunal-a-threat-to-human-rights&catid=91: rights-in-focus&Itemid=296*

competition and possible complementarity.[158] It also presents rich possibilities for forum shopping in the enforcement of regional human rights standards in Africa. Indeed, the most active courts are the ECOWAS and the SADC tribunal until it was disbanded. From the political point of view there seems to be little commitment to a harmonious set of working judicial bodies for the protection of human rights in Africa. From the legal perspective, the system needs to be rationalised and competing or complementary jurisdictions should be harmonised. From this viewpoint, Justice Niyungeko's proposal of considering the ACJHPR as the appellate court and highest instance on human rights matters for all sub-regional judicial bodies makes sense. It is a proposal that is gorged by legal expertise and an extremely practical sense of facilitating access to justice vis-à-vis the financial concerns of the parties involved. Nonetheless, the political point of view seems to prevail and each sub-regional body is reluctant to relinquish their own little area of influence.

The consideration of the ACJHPR as being the highest appellate Court in the African Human Rights System should be given due consideration, but our concern is focused, first and foremost, on the nature and composition of the ACJHPR. If sub-regional courts are to accept this Court as an appellate body, and if parties in Africa are to have recourse to it as the primary human rights body, then the Court must be properly constituted and count on a solid institutional structure that is able to dispense justice. Certainly, the structure and the hope of a working Court will be the ultimately argument to win over the political will of the States involved.[159] Perhaps time and experience will make coordination easier and demarcate in a clearer way the diverse jurisdictional powers of these judicial bodies.

Conclusion

The African Human Rights Charter expressly captured the existence of a quasi-judicial organ: The African Commission on Human and Peoples' Rights as a supervisory mechanism for the protection and promotion of human rights.

---

[158] See Odinkalu, C.A., *op. cit.*, at 3.

[159] See generally Yuval, S., *The Competing Jurisdictions of International Courts and Tribunals*, International Courts and Tribunal Series, Oxford University Press, New York, 2005.

The Commission has not been as effective as expected in curbing human rights abuses despite the Commissioners' commitment. Perhaps the Commission's greatest weaknesses may be summarised as follows: First, it cannot issue binding opinions or grant specific remedies.[160] In fact, there is a recent case *Centre for Minority Rights Development (Kenya) and Minority Rights Group International on behalf of Endorois Welfare Council v. Kenya*,[161] where there was a complaint against the Kenyan government for the forced removal of the Endorois peoples from their ancestral lands and violation of Indigenous Rights, among others.[162] The Commission found that the Kenyan government had violated the Endorois' rights under the African Charter, Articles 8, 14, 17, 21 and 22. For these violations, the Commission recommended that the government recognizes the Endorois' rights of ownership, grants the restitution of their ancestral lands, compensates their losses, and ensures the Endorois benefit from the royalties and employment opportunities within the game reserve. The Commission's decision was formally approved by the African Union at its January 2010 meeting. The Commission's decision calls upon the State to report on the implementation of its recommendations within three months from the date of notification and further recommends collaboration with the Endorois in implementing these remedies. This was the first time the Commission had recognized indigenous peoples' rights over traditionally owned land and their right to development under the African Charter. However, to this date Kenya has not reported on this decision's enforcement. Instead it has requested the Commission for more time to

---

160 See Udombana, N.J., *Yale Human Rights and Development Law Journal*, vol. 3, (2000), at 62.Further challenges to enforcement are the *clawback* clauses in the Charter that allow member States to limit the rights that the Charter guarantees through domestic legislation.

161 ACHPR, *Communication* 276/2003.

162 See ESCR-Net - *International Network for Economic, Social and Cultural Rights. In the 1970s, the Kenyan government evicted hundreds of Endorois families from their land around the Lake Bogoria area in the Rift Valley to create a game reserve for tourism. The Endorois, an indigenous people, had been promised compensation and benefits, but these were never fully implemented, and the community's access to the land was restricted to the discretion of the Game Reserve Authority. This prevented the community from practicing their pastoralist way of life, using ceremonial and religious sites, and accessing traditional medicines. Complainants (Centre for Minority Rights Development, Kenya and Minority Rights Group International on behalf of the Endorois Welfare Council) submitted this claim before the African Commission on Human Rights after domestic legal efforts and action failed to constitute an effective remedy for the violations alleged.*

implement.[163] Actually, it has transpired that Kenya does not have any administrative procedure in place for enforcement of the Commission's recommendations.

Second, access to the Commission is dependent on exhaustion of local remedies.[164] This may be a reasonable step in stable democracies but not in many nearly failed States in Africa, where the judiciary is not independent and judicial review of the executive is often approached with caution and even with fear. Third, its proceedings are conducted in secrecy hence it is not open to scrutiny.[165] Fourth, it lacks the adequate finances to fulfil its mandate.[166] And fifth, its location does not seem to have been

---

[163] See *A Call To Re-Evaluate The Status Of Minority And Indigenous Rights In Kenya: Decision on the Endorois Communication Before The African Commission on Human and Peoples' Rights* (ACHPR) by CEMIRIDE (Undated), available at *www.cemiride.or.ke.* Yobo Rutin, director of CEMIRIDE, stated that the recommendations by the ACHPR in this case are of immense value to all minority and indigenous communities in Kenya and if adhered to will effectively address the concerns of the routinely marginalized communities of the republic and contribute to the wider goal of achieving national cohesion in Kenya. We therefore call on the organs of the National Reform Agenda namely: the Committee of Experts on Constitutional Review (CoE), the Truth Justice and Reconciliation Commission (TJRC) and the National Cohesion and Integration Commission (NCICK) to take cognizance of the recommendations in this case while fulfilling their mandates and effectively restore the dignity and rights of these communities that have largely gone unrecognized in the past.

[164] *African Charter*, Arts 50, 52 and 56(5).

[165] See Equality Now, *op. cit.*, at 12. Moreover the Commission's decision or recommendations may take years to come and the shroud of secrecy makes it all the more discouraging. For example, since 2003, Equality Now has been involved in the case of Woineshet Zebene Negash, who was abducted, raped and forced into marriage at age 13. Partly through the Adolescent Girls' Legal Defense Fund (AGLDF), Equality Now continues to seek justice for Woineshet whose case was mishandled by the Ethiopian legal authorities. In May 2007, together with the Ethiopian Women Lawyers' Association (EWLA), Equality Now (EN) took Woineshet's case to the African Commission on Human and Peoples' Rights (the African Commission) after local remedies had been exhausted. The Ethiopian government asked EN to reach a 'friendly settlement' of the case. However, despite EN efforts, a settlement had not been reached in 2009. EN may likely request the African Commission to declare the case admissible and rule on its merits. Meanwhile, 8 years have gone by.

[166] Nmehielle, V. O., *Annual Survey of International and Comparative Law*, vol. 6, 2000, at 30-31. Frans Viljoen also asserts that due to this lack of resources the Commission is unable to order publication of its reports and activities. See Viljoen, F., *Brooklyn Journal of International Law*, vol. 30, No. 1, (2004), at 21.

strategically or adequately chosen. Certainly, The Gambia has taken gigantic steps towards development in the last decade, but at the time of the signature of the hosting agreement, Banjul was a rather inaccessible, removed and costly destination and it remains so for most Africans.[167]

However, any temptation to dismiss the Commission as a worthless institution today must be regarded as premature, ill-informed or both.[168] Certainly, there are great challenges ahead but the Commission's constitution has represented a milestone in the advancement of human rights legislation and awareness within the African system. As Pityana says, the greatest challenge facing the Commission is to advance human rights doctrine as reflected in Article 45(1-b) and (3) of the Charter.[169] To do this the Commission will have to improve its consideration of communications.[170] The more this is done, the more the people of Africa will entrust to the Commission their complaints about human rights violations. The more effective the Commission is in considering communications, the more States will take serious note of the work of the Commission and the more its decisions and recommendations will take an authoritative force to be obeyed especially by the States.[171]

Certainly, the implementation and enforcement levels of the Commission's decisions and recommendations have been dramatically low. This is partly due to the fact that recommendations are not binding and do not provide the State in question specific mechanisms for implementation. Moreover, the Commission does not have an institutionalized follow-up

---

[167] See generally Mukundi, G. and Ayinla, A., "Twenty Years of Elusive Enforcement of the Recommendations of the African Commission on Human and Peoples' Rights: A possible remedy", in: *African Human Rights Law Journal*. Juta Law Ed., vol. 6, nº 2 (2006), at 465-492. Available at: *http://www.escr-net.org/usr_doc/AJHR_Twenty_years_of_elusive_enforcement_in_ACHPR.pdf*

[168] Odinkalu, C.A., "The Individual Complaints Procedures of the African Commission on Human and Peoples' Rights: A Preliminary Assessment", *Transnational L. and Contemporary Problems*, vol. 8, (1998), at 359.

[169] Pityana, B., *op. cit.*, at 126.

[170] See ACHPR, "Commission's Research and Information Visit to Libya on 11-25 August 2005" adopted at the Commission's 40th Ordinary Session, 15-29 November 2006.For example, a 48-page report on the Commission's Research and Information Visit to Libya on 11-25 August 2005 ended with a mostly vague 10-point set of recommendations on urging, calling upon and encouraging Libya to do or refrain from doing.

[171] See generally Murray, R., *The African Commission on Human and Peoples' Rights and International Law*, Hart Publishing, Portland, Oregon, 1998.

system, even though some *ad hoc* follow-up and inconsistent measures had been initiated on few occasions. An important part of the work of the Commission has consisted in the appointment of Special Rapporteurs and the creation of Working Groups on specific themes.

Furthermore, the possible merger of the still inexistent African Court of Justice with the African Court on Human and Peoples' Rights to become the African Court of Justice and Human and Peoples Rights is still under way. It aims at avoiding overlapping of jurisdictions and multiplications of regional bodies thus easing out the heavy financial implications this meant for the struggling African economies and reducing administrative costs of running the AU. The original idea was to merge the judicial bodies of the African Union into one Court with two different sections, a general one and a human rights section. However, a third section, a criminal section, has been suggested to the proposed merged body. This new section will complete a sphere of ample jurisdiction. Thus, States will not be required to carry the greater financial burden of creating a new body for criminal offences.

At the same time, there should be a properly coordinated and harmonious relation between the Commission and the Court. This will certainly grant the Commission greater chances of compliance and success and enhance the eventual enjoyment and protection of human rights in Africa.

Finally, it is necessary to study the constitutional regulation of the foreign affairs power at the domestic level, identifying possible loopholes that may jeopardize the enforcement of decisions issued by the Commission and the Court. We analyse this point in greater detail in the next chapter and we will then conclude by making concrete proposals for the rationalisation of domestication mechanisms at national levels as well as the rationalisation of judicial structures at the African level.

CHAPTER FIVE

TOWARD AN ENHANCED AFRICAN HUMAN RIGHTS JUDICIAL SYSTEM

We have already seen that Constitutional law and international law relate and influence each other through the foreign affairs power in general, and specifically through two elements of this power, namely, treaty-making and diplomacy. Diplomacy, and specifically multilateral diplomacy, plays a key role in the negotiation and drafting of international instruments that constitute international organizations. Treaty-making delineates the way and manner these instruments will be accessed, incorporated, applied and executed according to the domestic laws of each State.

Accession to a treaty is usually regulated by Constitutional law, which distributes the powers and functions within the State and puts in place the necessary checks and balances to guarantee identification between, among others, peoples and policies. Thus, from a domestic point of view, the creation of international organizations and the authority bestowed on them are primarily the result of the exercise of certain powers and functions constitutionally given to specific State offices.

The fulfilment or the aim of a treaty that has been negotiated, signed and ratified or accessed may have certain effects at the national level. These treaties need to be incorporated into the domestic forum. This incorporation process may be through a monist or dualist system and it is governed by Constitutional law and practice. Indeed, an inappropriate or poorly designed constitutional system for domestication and enforcement of international law can frustrate and has actually frustrated the enforcement of many a treaty.

The power that allows the State to create an international organization may be used for constituting organs of judicial nature as was the case of the African Court on Human and peoples' Rights. Judicial decisions from such bodies will not, in principle, follow the same domestication process as foreign judgments, for they do not come from a foreign court but from a supranational court. Instead, international decisions will follow the process as may be specified in the constitutive instruments creating them.

Frequently, constitutive instruments declare a general obligation to enforce judgments at the domestic level without specifying the legal means and ways to do so.[1] This brings legal experts face to face with a twofold challenge. On the one hand, a political challenge for such enforcement may depend on the political will of the government in question. On the other hand, a legal challenge on what specific ways and means should be used to actualize judgments' enforcement. In this case, it is essential to conduct an audit or study of each domestic jurisdiction and determine the best constitutional approach and manner to domesticate the judgment.[2] The intricacies and complexities will increase or decrease depending on whether the State follows the dualist or the monist system for the incorporation of international law. If the State follows the dualist model, then the decision will have to be incorporated following a process similar to the usual treaty ratification process, unless the constitutive treaty prescribes otherwise. If the State follows the monist system, then it will be important to determine whether international law has primacy over the constitutional or legal norm or not. If it does not have primacy and the judgment seems to contradict internal norms it may be rendered unenforceable and this may pose a legal challenge that should be foreseen prior to ratification. If international law has primacy over domestic law, then these decisions will automatically become part of the internal law and they should be executed in a similar fashion to other comparable judgments.

Thus, the key to effective domestication is found in the primacy of laws:[3] If the domestic system grants primacy to the international order over the internal one, then judgments will follow avenues for automatic domestication through administrative processes analogous to internal judgments. But if the domestic system — even monist — grants primacy to the national law, then judgments may be rejected and the process

---

[1] This is the case, for example, of the ACHPR and the Protocol on the ACtHPR.

[2] We have conducted a sample study, although not comparatively, in *supra* chapter II.

[3] See Ruiz Miguel, C., "Las Sentencias del Tribunal Europeo de Derechos Humanos: Su Ejecución desde la Perspectiva del Derecho Constitucional Comparado y Español", *V Congreso Iberoamericano de Derecho Constitucional*, Instituto de Investigaciones Jurídicas/UNAM, México, (1998), at 845.

jeopardised.[4] If the system is monist, the rank of international law within the domestic legal order should be clearly ascertained, whether it is above the Constitution as, for example, in Cameroon or below, as Equatorial Guinea or Madagascar. If it is a dualist system, then parliamentary approval is desirable before ratification so as to avoid a situation where the executive is embarrassed by ratifying a treaty which may be rejected afterwards.[5]

Hence, to guarantee the enforcement of international judgments it is of paramount importance that the domestic law foresees and guides the actual enforcement in a more detailed manner. It is not enough to make general statements of moral obligation to comply. International judicial decisions may be, ultimately, understood to be the result of the exercise of a constitutional power granted by the national constitution to a section of the

---

[4] This actually happened in Venezuela. See TSJ/SC, decision Nº 1.942 of 15-7-03. The Supreme Court contradicted itself by stating the treaties in Venezuela have constitutional rank but then went on to say that sovereignty was above all things. The court stated: "Whereas: The treaties, pacts and conventions on human rights signed and ratified by Venezuela, as provided for by Article 23 of the Constitution of the Bolivarian Republic of Venezuela, have constitutional status and therefore its legal interpretation is entrusted to the Constitutional Chamber of the Supreme Court. And Whereas: The decisions of the Supreme Court in its various Chambers, are not subject to any review by international bodies because they express the full exercise of our sovereignty and they are issued according to the Country's legal order and on behalf of the Venezuelan people as expression of a free country…" The full text is available at the official website of the Venezuelan Supreme Court: *www.tsj.gov.ve*.

[5] See *The National Assembly Official Report*, Republic of Kenya, Vol. XVI (Part I) 2 Sep. 1968 - 4 Oct. 1968, Geneva Conventions (Second Reading), column 1240. This almost happened in Kenya in several instances, for example, in 1968, while discussing the Geneva Conventions Bill, which contained the four 1949 Geneva Conventions, Mr. Argwings-Kodhek, Minister of State, President's Office stated that the Geneva Conventions Bill was a "*Bill for an Act of Parliament enabling effect to be given to certain international conventions done in Geneva on the 12th Aug. 1949... The object of this Bill ... is to make provision for the implementation of the following four Geneva Conventions set out in the schedule of this Bill to which Kenya has already acceded.*" To this statement Mr. Shikuku, MP responded, *"Mr. Speaker, Sir, whereas it is just a question of formality of the foregone conditions that this House should be used as a rubber stamp, which I admit we are going to be to be used as in this case, that we just give our approval to whatever has been agreed in Geneva."*

government with the aim, at least in theory, of attaining or securing the common good of the political society.[6]

The revision of the theoretical foundations of the foreign affairs power and its regulation across several countries is, perhaps, the first stage of a comprehensive reform and harmonization of legal systems in the African continent. However, the process extends and goes deeper. In this chapter we look into those further aspects that are necessary to promote, foster and take into consideration: First, judicial domestication, and second, the rationalization and harmonization of the judicial structures in the African judicial system.

Judicial domestication entails the incorporation of judicial decisions into the domestic system. This process of incorporation takes place ordinarily through the systems established by the constitution for the regulation of the foreign affairs power, and extraordinarily through an innovative and open-minded consideration of international law by local judges following principles of equity aimed at dispensing justice, even when domestic legislation falls short or deficient.

The rationalization and harmonization of the judicial structures in the African judicial system leads us into a deep analysis of the merger of the African Court on Human and Peoples' Rights and the African Court of Justice. In this regard, it seems necessary to make concrete amendments to the protocol that establishes the new court: The African Court of Justice and Human and Peoples Rights (ACJHPR).

The world's globalization process has increased the practical importance of the application of foreign judgments[7] and it has created the necessity of counting with certain rules for their application. This is especially so in the area of human rights.

---

[6] We may also say that the State has the *moral duty* to ascertain that there is no conflict between the constitution and the treaties ratified or accessed. But the State has *the legal duty* to apply the decisions coming from such jurisdictions as if they were its own.

[7] Garnett, R., "The Internationalisation of Australian Jurisdiction and Judgments Law",*Australian Bar Review*, vol. 25, No. 3, (2004), at 205.

Judicial Domestication: Incorporation of International Judicial Decisions into the Domestic System

Philippe Sand argues that there has been a judicial and jurisprudential transformation in the international order where there now exists an international judiciary,

> "The powers of which seem to be ever more extensive and, consequentially, intrusive upon areas previously thought to lie exclusively within national sovereignty. It is a judiciary that increasingly relates to or impinges upon proceedings in domestic courts and to which litigants can turn to in their efforts to asserts rights and enforce obligations. Indeed, in many countries international litigation – that is to say litigation before international courts – is often front-page news."[8]

Undeniably, the traditional view held by some countries is that human rights instruments would be likely to interfere with matters which fall within the domestic jurisdiction of States and thus result in the infringement of national sovereignty, which is, according to D'Sa, preposterous.[9] Such matters are no longer exclusively within the domestic jurisdiction of States, because they now constitute international legal obligations to promote and respect human rights, if not solely by virtue of the obligations contained in the UN Charter and the 1948 Universal Declaration of Human Rights (UDHR), then certainly as a result of legal obligations acquired through the regional constitutive documents,[10] in our case the African Charter and its Protocols.

Perhaps the greatest challenge for a human rights system is to seek appropriate and effective ways to enforce its decisions within the domestic field with sufficient independence from the political will of the State involved. This challenge is perhaps greater in Africa, where the executive is still perceived as the 'sovereign' who is not subject to any authority but his own will. This approach jeopardises judicial independence and compromises the enforcement of human rights decisions.

Therefore, enforcement from a domestic perspective requires a clear set of norms regarding the constitutional regulation of the foreign affairs

---

[8] Sands, P. and Others, *Manual on International Courts and Tribunals*, 2nd Edition, Oxford University Press, New York, 2010, at 9-10.

[9] D'Sa, R.M., "The African Charter on Human and Peoples' Rights: Problems and Prospects for Regional Action", *Australian Year Book of International Law*, vol 102, (1981) at 101.

[10] See *Ibid.*

power, the consideration of international law by local judges, and proper attention and reverence to the cultural inheritance of the people through the adequate use of the margin of appreciation.

1. Domestication through the Constitutional Regulation of the Foreign Affairs Power

In order to unveil the allocation of foreign affairs powers scholars and judges have had constant recourse to the constitutional practice since the exclusive reference to the constitutional text is — in some cases — deficient. In Africa most constitutions are reasonably written and they enshrine rights and systems that are inspired by a fair desire for justice, at least in theory. Nonetheless, there has been a constant tendency to copy and incorporate constitutional aspirations, rights and institutions from other continents, and particularly from Europe, and specifically from the former great colonisers, Britain and France. These two countries have had an undeniable influence on the formation of Africa's constitutional law as we know it today. African constitutions tend to have beautifully designed human rights bills and aspirations. Nonetheless, these aspirations are often compromised by poor and abstract drafting or claw-back clauses.

Thus, the African challenge should aim first and foremost at a constitutional revision of the norms that regulate the foreign affairs power and then focus its attention on stronger judicial systems that are honest, just and independent from outside pressure.[11]As Polakiewicz asserts it is essential to take into consideration that,

> "international human rights courts have been set up with the purpose of offering individuals an ultimate possibility to challenge definitive decisions by national authorities. Instead of deciding international legal disputes between States, they mostly decide disputes between an individual and a State, often the State of which the individual is a national or resident. They pronounce directly upon the compatibility of domestic law and practices with internationally recognized human rights standards. Although no international human rights court has been given the competence to annul, repeal or modify legislative provisions or individual decisions taken

[11] See *supra* note no. 16. The Commission on Human and Peoples' Rights has experienced dramatic low levels of implementation of its recommendations; with a rate which is currently around 12%

by national authorities, their decisions directly affect the application of national law in the Member States."[12]

It is, then, essential to ascertain whether the constitution makes the State dualist or monist. However, the assumption of a monistic or dualistic international law domestication model is not the only decisive issue for the enforceability of international judgments. Indeed, it is usually understood that if a country follows the monist system incorporation will be straightforward and that the contrary occurs in dualist jurisdictions. Nonetheless, it is possible to enforce judgments in dualist systems and deny them in monistic systems. The key is really found in the primacy of laws:[13] If the domestic system grants primacy to the international order over the internal one, then judgments will follow avenues for automatic domestication through administrative processes analogous to internal judgments. But if the domestic system — even monist — grants primacy to the national law, then judgments may be rejected and the process jeopardised.[14]If the system is monist, the rank of international law within the domestic legal order should be clearly ascertained, whether it is above or below the Constitution. If it is a dualist system, then parliamentary approval is desirable before ratification so as to avoid a situation where the

---

[12] Polakiewicz, J., "International Law and Domestic (Municipal) Law, Law and Decisions of International Organizations and Courts", *Max Planck Encyclopedia of Public International Law*, www.mpepil.com, Oxford University Press, (2011). Available at:
http://www.mpepil.com/ViewPdf/epil/entries/law-9780199231690-e1057.pdf?stylesheet=EPIL-display-full.xsl

[13] See Ruiz Miguel, C., "Las Sentencias del Tribunal Europeo de Derechos Humanos: Su Ejecución desde la Perspectiva del Derecho Constitucional Comparado y Español", *V Congreso Iberoamericano de Derecho Constitucional*, Instituto de Investigaciones Jurídicas/UNAM, México, (1998), at 845.

[14] See TSJ/SC, decision Nº 1.942 of 15-7-03. This actually happened in Venezuela. The Supreme Court contradicted itself by stating the treaties in Venezuela have constitutional rank but then went on to say that sovereignty was above all things. The court stated: "Whereas: The treaties, pacts and conventions on human rights signed and ratified by Venezuela, as provided for by Article 23 of the Constitution of the Bolivarian Republic of Venezuela, have constitutional status and therefore its legal interpretation is entrusted to the Constitutional Chamber of the Supreme Court. And Whereas: The decisions of the Supreme Court in its various Chambers, are not subject to any review by international bodies because they express the full exercise of our sovereignty and they are issued according to the Country's legal order and on behalf of the Venezuelan people as expression of a free country…" The full text is available at the official website of the Venezuelan Supreme Court: *www.tsj.gov.ve*

executive is embarrassed by ratifying a treaty that is rejected later on. Once the treaty is ratified, then it should be domesticated. This will allow decisions from international judicial bodies to be accepted and appropriately enforced within the domestic forum.

Indeed, it is essential that the arrangement presents an effective system of constitutional checks and balances for the exercise of the foreign affairs power and that those checks and balances do not overburden, compromise or jeopardise the efficient conduct of foreign affairs.

2. Consideration of International Law by Local Judges

There is a growing tendency to consider international law precepts in domestic courts, even when there has been no formal act of incorporation. Domestic courts may go as far as "to refuse to enforce private transactions which are contrary to international recommendations."[15] This tendency has faced risks. As Justice Enoch Dumbutshena says,

> "Judges are not the same. Countries in Africa are also not the same. Some accept independent judiciaries, others do not. Is it not surprising that after attending the Judicial Colloquium in Harare in April1989 one of the judges who contributed much to this passage: 'But fine statements in domestic laws or international regional instruments are not enough. Rather it is essential to develop a culture of respect for internationally stated human rights norms which sees these norms applied in the domestic laws of all nations and given full effect. They must not be seen as alien to domestic law in national courts,' was detained when he returned to his home country. One would have thought that his country would have been proud of him."[16]

For Dumbutshena, the judicial development of human rights requires two essentials to be met. First, the personal philosophy of the judge should have a "bias in favour of fairness and justice."[17] Second, "there must exist an activist court. Judicial activism in human rights cases is a prerequisite for the development of human rights jurisprudence."[18]

---

[15] See Polakiewicz, J., *op. cit.,* Available at: *http://www.mpepil.com/ViewPdf/epil/entries/law-9780199231690-e1057.pdf?stylesheet=EPIL-display-full.xsl*

[16] Dumbutshena, E., "The Role of the Judge in Advancing Human Rights", *Commonwealth Law Bulletin*, vol. 18, (1992), at 1298.

[17] *Ibid.*, at 1301.

[18] *Ibid.*

However, this type of activism could be understood from a positive perspective, where the judge applies the law regardless of political or financial pressure, or from a negative perspective by having a judiciary that assumes an arbitrary law-making function beyond the scope of its natural competence.

Mirna Adjami has made a detailed survey of the modes of application of international and comparative sources in certain African national courts. Adjami asserts,

> "The Supreme Court [of Zimbabwe] addressed a ... question on the constitutionality of corporal punishment sentencing provisions in *State v. Ncube*. Justice Gubbay began his opinion with a survey of Zimbabwean law, which contained six statutes that authorize the sentence of whipping as a punishment for various crimes. After his exposition of the State of the law on corporal punishment in Zimbabwe, Justice Gubbay proceeded to establish the legal status of corporal punishment in various countries, canvassing South Africa, the United Kingdom, Canada, Australia, and the United States of America. In this comparative survey, Justice Gubbay sought to establish whether there exists a universal standard on such corporal punishment. He concluded that 'modern conceptions of justice and humanity have led most European and Scandinavian countries totally to deny the utility of corporal punishment. And, I believe, the same is true of Argentina, Mexico, India, Ghana, Jamaica, and Belize'."[19]

Adjami also looked at *Ephrahim v. Pastory*, where the "Tanzanian High Court faced the issue of determining the constitutionality of a discriminatory customary law provision on inheritance in light of the provisions of the Tanzanian Bill of Rights that was incorporated into the Tanzanian Constitution in 1984."[20] The provision denied women (Holaria Pastory) the power to sell clan land. The case was instituted by Pastory's nephew and the District Court ruled in favour of Pastory. The matter was appealed to the High Court and,

> "Justice Mwalusanya recognized that not only was the customary law clear on this matter as it is codified in the Laws of Inheritance of the Declaration of Customary Law, but also that Tanzanian precedent mandated that the courts are 'bound by the Customary law' at issue. Nonetheless, he claimed that this precedent must be re-examined in light of the incorporation in 1984 of the Bill of Rights into the Tanzanian Constitution, including the

---

[19] Adjami, M., "African Courts, International Law, and Comparative Case Law: Chimera or Emerging Human Rights Jurisprudence?",*Michigan Journal of International Law*, vol 24, (2002) at 153 ff.
[20]*Ibid.*

> non-discrimination provision in section 13(4), despite the fact that the Bill of Rights had been deemed by some to be a 'dead letter.' Justice Mwalusanya proceeded to list the international human rights instruments ratified by Tanzania that also guarantee non-discrimination. Having established Tanzania's commitment to international human rights norms, he concluded: 'The principles enunciated in the above named documents are a standard below which any civilized nation will be ashamed to fall…' Having determined that the customary law provision is unconstitutionally discriminatory, Justice Mwalusanya turned to deciding the appropriate action of the court. Section 5(1) of the Tanzanian Constitution, added after the constitution was amended to include the Bill of Rights, mandates that 'the courts will construe the existing law, including customary law ... with such modification, adoptions, qualifications and exceptions as may be necessary to bring it into conformity with [the Bill of Rights].' Adopting the purposive approach to statutory interpretation, he determined that the Parliament's intention behind section 5(1) and the Bill of Rights was to 'do away with all oppressive and unjust laws in the past.'[21]

In certain dualist jurisdictions, judges are also innovative in the use of international law. The greatest challenge in these cases is posed by the judgments' execution. For example, as we already explained,[22] a decision against Nigeria would trigger a similar procedure as with domestic decisions against the government. Such decisions go to the attorney general who gives the go-ahead for their execution.

Adjami further analyses *Rattigan v. Chief Immigration Officer* of Zimbabwe, and jurisprudence from Botswana, South Africa and Zambia. Mirna Adjami concludes that "in the absence of domestic precedent, African courts have looked beyond their borders for persuasive authority to determine the scope of their constitutional rights guarantees. Indeed several of the opinions examined … reveal that African judges view their role as one of bringing their own domestic fundamental rights jurisprudence in line with prevailing international norms."[23]

Adjami's approach has actually found its way into the South African constitutional dispensation. The South African Constitution provides in Section 39, on the interpretation of the Bill of Rights, that:

> "(1) When interpreting the Bill of Rights, a court, tribunal or forum -

---

[21] *Ibid.*
[22] See *supra* note 110 in Chapter IV.
[23] Adjami, M., *op. cit.*, at 166.

(a) must promote the values that underlie an open and democratic society based on human dignity, equality and freedom;

(b) must consider international law; and

(c) may consider foreign law.

(2) When interpreting any legislation, and when developing the common law or customary law, every court, tribunal or forum must promote the spirit, purport and objects of the Bill of Rights.

(3)The Bill of Rights does not deny the existence of any other rights or freedoms that are recognised or conferred by common law, customary law or legislation, to the extent that they are consistent with the Bill."

The innovative ways African judges are seeking to incorporate international jurisprudence is a window of hope and opportunity that could be used for the enforcement of international judicial decisions emanating from the African Court. Perhaps, the margin of appreciation allowing that delicate balancing act which gives the necessary flexibility to respect certain principles of equity could be one of the most important legal tools in this regard.

If judges develop what Justice Enoch Dumbutshena calls a personal philosophy with a bias in favour of fairness and justice, as well as rationally guided activist court work, then jurisprudence will influence the development of a human rights culture; a culture where human rights must be enforced and in which no prejudiced political will can oppose.

Rationalising the Judicial Structure in the African Judicial System

The existing African Court on Human and Peoples' Rights consists of eleven judges elected for a six-year term with ample *ratione materiæ* jurisdiction that extends to all cases and disputes submitted to it concerning the interpretation and application of the Charter, the Protocol and any other relevant human rights instrument. The jurisdiction *ratione personæ* entitles the Commission, State parties and African inter-governmental organizations to submit cases to the Court. The Court may entitle relevant Non-Governmental Organizations (NGOs) with observer status before the Commission, and individuals to institute cases directly before it if the relevant State party has signed the declaration established by article 34(6) of the Protocol. This declaration seems to make the Court accessibility depend on the will of the State, which is perhaps undesirable in a human rights context.

The Court also enjoys advisory jurisdiction to hear all matters concerning the interpretation and application of the African Charter and other relevant human rights instruments as explained before.

In considering cases, the Court shall apply the provisions of the Charter and any other relevant human rights instruments ratified by the States concerned. Given the multicultural and multi-ethnic diversity of Africa, it is foreseeable that the application of the 'margin of appreciation' doctrine may become a relevant tool for the equitable consideration of substantive issues. This doctrine may allow the Court to keep the delicate balancing and flexibility to respect certain principles of equity grounded on culture and society.

If the Court finds that there has been a violation of rights, it issues appropriate orders to remedy the violation, including the payment of fair compensation or reparation. The Court should also foster amicable settlement in accordance with the provisions of the Charter. Once the Court renders its judgment it is final and not subject to appeal. In accordance with Article 30, the States Parties undertake to comply with the judgment and to guarantee execution within the time stipulated by the Court. If a State party does not comply with the Court's judgment, the Court notifies the Assembly through the report that it submits to each regular session of the Assembly.

Ordinarily, the enforcement of foreign judgments is associated with the reciprocal recognition and enforcement of judgments between States. This is frequently regulated by bilateral treaty or multilateral international conventions. Enforcing foreign judgments involves the application of the local court's powers to give effect to the foreign court's decision without the plaintiff having to re-litigate the merits of the dispute.[24]

However, judgments emanating from the African Court are not foreign judgments but supranational judgments. Nonetheless, the African State, as any other, is bound to be reluctant to any form of external interference, and the African Court is no exception to this. Moreover, as has already been pointed out, most African States have not developed a practical constitutional and administrative system of internal checks and balances. Their own internal procedures for execution of domestic judgments against the State are ineffective and often designed to frustrate its

---

[24] BCLI, British Columbia Law Institute, "Report on the Enforcement of Non-Money Judgments from Outside the Province", *Report*, No 8, (1999), at 6.

execution and evade State responsibility.[25] The African Court will not be spared of this.

Therefore, it seems desirable to rethink the new African Court of Justice and Human and Peoples Rights taking into consideration the positive experience from the existing Court and the demands of the new merged body. We will point out below the specific structural aspects of the judicial system that led to the merger proposal and the concrete recommendations for changes to the so-called Merger Protocol.

1. The Merger of Courts: The New African Court of Justice and Human and Peoples Rights

The idea of merging the Court of Justice of the African Union and the African Court on Human and Peoples' Rights was first raised during the negotiation of the draft protocol on the African Court of Justice in April and June 2003 respectively.[26] The deliberations focused on article 56 of the draft protocol of the Court of Justice, which had a special provision for creating special chambers.[27] This pointed to the possible incorporation of the African Court on Human and Peoples' Rights into the Court of Justice as a special chamber on human rights issues. Another strong argument in favour of the merger was the financial issue; the AU was already quite constrained from a budgetary point of view.[28]

However, opponents of the merger argued that the process would relegate human rights issues.[29] In fact, when the negotiations became

---

[25] For example, the case of Nigeria was mentioned in this regard. See *supra* note 110 in Chapter IV.

[26] Summary of Procedures of the First Meeting of Experts/Judges and the PRC on the Draft protocol of the Court of Justice of the African Union, 22-24 April 2003, Expt.Judg/Draft/Prot/ACJ/Rpt. (1); Ministerial Conference on the Draft Protocol of the Court of Justice of the African Union, 7-8 June 2003, Grand Baie, Mauritius, Min/Draft/Prot/ACJ/Rpt. (1).

[27] Article 56 states: *The Court may from time to time form one or more chambers, composed of three (3) or more Judges as the Court may determine, for dealing with particular categories of cases.*

[28] Nonetheless, considering that the ACtHPR operational budget is approximately USD 7.5 million and that they are heavily financed and supported by European donors, this figure would appear to be quite sufficient. See *infra* note no.55for a comparison of budgets among regional human rights courts.

[29] Summary of Proceedings of the Second Meeting of Experts/Judges and PRC on the Draft Protocol of the African Court of Justice of the African Union, 4 – 6 June 2003, Expt.Judg/Draft/Prot/ACJ/Rpt. (ll) para 20.

heated, the Executive Council of the African Union ruled that: "the African Court on Human and Peoples' Rights shall remain a separate and distinct institution from the Court of Justice of the African Union..."[30]

Surprisingly, the merger issue re-emerged during the 3rd Ordinary Session of the Assembly Heads of State and Government of the AU in July 2004. They decided on this occasion "that the African Court on Human and Peoples' Rights and the Court of Justice should be integrated into one Court"[31] and further requested "the Chairperson to work out the modalities on implementing [the merger decision] and submit a report to [its] next Ordinary Session."[32]

This move was criticized as being futile and the fruit of lack of initiative from the AU to effectively run the African Court on Human and Peoples' Rights. The most notable concern was raised by the Commission. The Commission was of the opinion that the two courts had "essentially different mandates and litigants and that the decision could have a negative impact on the establishment of an effective African Court on Human and Peoples' Rights."[33] The Commission called upon States to ratify the Protocol on the Establishment of the African Court on Human and Peoples' Rights (the Original Protocol) so that this Court could be established while the merger discussions were going on, and this is in fact what happened.

Three years later, in Sharm El-Sheikh, Egypt, on 1st July 2008, the 'Protocol on the Statute of the African Court of Justice and Human Rights' (the Merger Protocol) was adopted at the African Union Summit. At this point it was clear that the merger was irreversible.[34] This merged court,

---

[30] Decision on the Draft *Protocol of the Court of Justice*, Doc. EX/CL/59 (111) / 58 (111), para 2.

[31] African Union, Assembly/AU/Dec.45 (III), No. 3.

[32] African Union, Assembly/AU/Dec.45 (III) Rev.1, *Decision on the Seats of the Organs of the Union*, No. 5.

[33] African Commission on Human and Peoples' Rights, Res.76 (XXXVII) 05: "Resolution on the Establishment of an Effective African Court on Human and Peoples' Rights", adopted in Banjul, the Gambia on 11th May 2005.

[34] See African Union, Assembly of the AU, Decision on the Seats of the Organs of the African Union, AU Doc. Assembly/AU/Dec.45 (Ill) Rev.1 (Jan. 2004); African Union, Assembly of the AU, Decision on the Merger of the African Court on Human and Peoples' Rights and the Court of Justice of the African Union, AU Doc. Assembly/AU/Dec. 83 (V) (Jul. 2005). This is also discussed by Rainey, C., "The African Court: Building a Continental Benchmark for Justice", unpublished document, Available at:

that has already been renamed 'the African Court of Justice and Human and Peoples Rights' (ACJHPR), will become operational thirty days after the fifteenth ratification or accession is deposited.[35]

The Merger Protocol replaces the Original Protocol adopted in 1998 and the Protocol of the Court of Justice of the African Union which was adopted in 2003. The Original Protocol shall remain in force for a transitional period of a year to enable it implement the required measures for the transfer of its prerogatives, assets, rights, and obligations to the ACJHPR.

Once the Merger Protocol enters into force the cases being heard by the African Court on Human and Peoples' Rights will be transferred to the human rights section of the ACJHPR.[36] According to the Merger Protocol, the judges of the African Court on Human and Peoples' Rights will step down and new judges be elected.[37]

The ACJHPR, as per the Merger Protocol, is divided into two sections: the general section and the human rights section. The general section is for disputes over matters such as the powers of the AU and breaches of States' treaty obligations. The human rights section handles cases against States for violations of human rights. After considering cases on human rights brought before it, the ACJHPR can issue binding judgments.[38] Where violations are found, it may award compensation and other justified remedies to victims.[39]

The parties that can submit cases in the ACJHPR are State parties, the African Commission on Human and Peoples' Rights, the African Committee of Experts on the Rights and Welfare of the Child, African inter-governmental organisations and the African National Human Rights Institutions.[40] Individuals and NGOs can only submit cases against States if the State concerned has made a declaration accepting the competence of

---

http://www.raineydevine.com/wp-content/uploads/2010/09/Feb2007.pdf

[35] It has not yet entered into force. Only five countries: Mali, Libya, Burkina Faso, Tanzania and Côte d'Ivoire have ratified it as of 1st January 2014.

[36] *Ibid.*, at 6.

[37] *Ibid.*

[38] The *Statute of the African Court of Justice and Human Rights*, Article 46 2.

[39] Sceats, S., "Africa's New Human Rights Court: Whistling in the Wind?", *Chatham House International Law Briefing Paper*, (IL BP 09/01), (2009) at 6. Available at:
http://www.chathamhouse.org.uk/publications/papers/view/-/id/721/

[40] The *Statute of the African Court of Justice and Human Rights*, Article 29 1(b).

the Court to do so.[41] This seems to be a set-back to proposals on direct access to individuals and NGOs. Therefore, unless a State makes the declaration, this limitation may frustrate access to justice for human rights victims. As a matter of fact, some ACtHPR sitting judges opine that member States should be encouraged to ratify the ACJHPR Protocol while at the same time they make the declaration allowing for individual petitions.

The merger also raises several thorny legal issues. Both the Original Protocol[42] and the Court of Justice Protocol are already in force. The former is operational but the latter is not.[43] This means that the African Court on Human and People's Rights will be 'merged' with a court whose protocol is in force but which has not been constituted. It is also challenging the fact that the Merger Protocol has only been signed by four States and so far the merger decision is in limbo for it will only become a reality when fifteen States ratify the Merger Protocol.[44]

Despite these limitations, the merger should offer some benefits. It gives States and other interested parties a time to examine the experience gathered and propose ways to improve the Court's working procedures. It will also expand its jurisdiction and centralize similar functions in one

---

[41] *Merger Protocol,* Article 8(3) is similar to the current declaration States are supposed to make before the court can examine any individual complaint.

[42] The fifteenth instrument of ratification was deposited with the African Union Commission on 26th December 2003, bringing the Protocol to the African Charter on Human and Peoples' Rights (the Protocol) establishing the African Court on Human and Peoples' Rights, into force on 25 January 2004.

[43] The *Protocol of the Court of Justice of the African Union* entered into force on 11th February 2009 and it has so far been ratified by 16 States. However, the Court has never been constituted.

[44] The situation has been rather confusing from the start: On April 2004, just before the proposed merger, the AU invited States Parties to the Protocol of the ACtHPR to submit nominations for appointees of judges to the court. [BC/OLC/66.5/8/Vol.V, 5 April 2004] By July 2004, ten States Parties had already submitted their nominations for judges to serve on the African Court on Human and Peoples' Rights. The Executive Council of the African Union, at its 5th ordinary session from 25th June to 3rd July 2004, confirmed the proposal for the election of judges to the ACtHPR to take place at its next ordinary session in the first six months of 2005. [*Progress Report of the Chairperson on the Operationalization of the African Court on Human and Peoples' Rights*, Executive Council, 5th Ordinary Session, 25 June – 3 July 2004, EX.CL/98 (V) Rev.1.] This apparent confusion is puzzling. A month later, the Assembly Heads of State and Government of the AU pass a resolution for the merger of the courts.

institution instead of having a myriad of institutions performing competing functions.[45] Certainly there is always the risk of relegating the human rights section of the ACJHPR to second priority as compared to the general section, especially if the human rights section becomes too 'vigilant' on the issue of human rights at the expense of the member States of the AU.[46]

Nevertheless, the idea of an African Court of Justice and Human and Peoples Rights (ACJHPR) has been maturing over time. It did not end with the drafting of the Merger Protocol. Many of the gaps of the Merger Protocol are being filled by on-going discussions as to the final nature of the merger. For example, the Merger protocol envisioned the replacement of the old Court, i.e. the existing African Court on Human and Peoples' Rights, by the new Court, i.e. the African Court of Justice and Human and Peoples Rights. It also advocated the establishment of two sections: One of human rights and the other on all other matters pertaining to the non-existing African Court of Justice. However, there are still new emerging ideas and the judges from the African Court on Human and Peoples' Rights are actively engaged in solving organizational and jurisdictional problems in a deep yet practical approach.

It seems essential to look into four key aspects that will help the new Court succeed. First, the court should safeguard its institutional memory. Second, the jurisdiction of the Court should be enlarged and access to justice facilitated. Third, the financial implications and sustainability should be given due consideration, and fourth, the judicial hierarchy and the extent of the Courts' powers over sub-regional bodies should be appropriately addressed and clarified.

First, 'Safeguarding institutional memory' is better achieved if one court absorbs the other, instead of replacing it. The drafting of the Merger Protocol foresees replacement of one court by another. Judges must resign, and the Merger Protocol also stipulates a fresh start for Registrar and staff members. In principle the idea behind the drafting is aimed at demarcating a clear difference between the ACtHPR and the ACJHPR. However, this has placed the court in a 'practical, institutional and political' dilemma that the drafters did not foresee. 'Practical', because the expense involved in starting a new Court afresh are enormous. It also gives the impression to

---

[45] Sceats, S., *op. cit.*, at 6.

[46] An African sub-regional tribunal (the SADC Tribunal) was practically disbanded in August 2010 for taking a bold decision against Zimbabwe's land expropriation policy. See *supra* note no. 156 in Chapter IV.

State members and donors of having unproductively wasted large resources invested in the ACtHPR for the past five years. 'Institutional', because the institutional memory is lost; the ACtHPR has already been operational for five years and it has produced only one judgment, which did not enter into substantive issues. The Court is just starting to breathe and grow aware of its responsibilities. Therefore, the passing of one Court to other should have been by way of absorption instead of replacement so that institutional memory should not be lost and systems remain in place with the experience and skills already gathered.[47] Finally 'political', because States usually guard with great jealousy the political and representative influence they exercise on such bodies. The idea of asking every judge to resign would actually mean the risk of losing the sitting judge at the Court in question. Besides, some judges could possibly advise their governments not to ratify the Merger Protocol.[48] As a matter of fact,

---

[47] For example, the substitution of one court by another is perhaps desirable only when there is a need of breaking with the past, as happened with the PCIJ and the ICJ, in which a World War made humanity seek a new beginning. In that case, the ICJ actually replaced the Permanent Court of International Justice (PCIJ), which had been established under the Covenant of the League of Nations. During its existence, the PCIJ heard a total of 66 cases. It also rendered a total of 27 advisory opinions and 32 judgments. The PCIJ underwent its first major revision in 1926. This was followed by a significant overhaul of its rules followed in 1936. World War II marked the end of the PCIJ. It held its last wartime session in The Hague in February 1940. Delegates at the Dumbarton Oaks Conference in Washington, DC discussed the development of a new International Court of Justice, which would work in association with the United Nations. Another delegate's conference held in San Francisco approved the new International Court of Justice (June 1945) as one of the principal organs of the United Nations (Article VII) and as the UN's chief judicial organization (Article XCII). In October 1945, the members of the PCIJ held their last session. The judges of the PCIJ all resigned on 31 January 1946, and the election of the first Members of the International Court of Justice took place on 6 February 1946, at the First Session of the United Nations General Assembly and Security Council. In April 1946, the PCIJ was formally dissolved, and the International Court of Justice, meeting for the first time, elected as its President Judge José Gustavo Guerrero (El Salvador), the last President of the PCIJ. The Court appointed the members of its Registry (largely from among former officials of the PCIJ) and held an inaugural public sitting, on the 18th of that month. The first case was submitted in May 1947. It concerned incidents in the *Corfu Channel* and was brought by the United Kingdom against Albania.

[48] Currently, the political organs are revising certain aspects of the merger. They are talking of absorption and not replacement, and they also want to extend the Court's jurisdiction to criminal cases but it is up to the country to decide the fate of the judges.

this could have been one of the many reasons why governments are generally reluctant or slow in ratifying the merger.

Second, 'The Court's jurisdiction' needs to be re-studied as well. The original ACJHR extended the current court's jurisdiction by creating two sections: One for human rights and another for general matters.[49] However, a new concern is rising in Africa. It is related to the high levels of impunity for crimes against humanity, peoples and persons. In some cases these crimes were carefully designed or condoned by the State apparatus. Parallel to this, there is perhaps justified and generalised reluctance to accept foreign intervention on African soil. Africa should be able to resolve its own problems. When Luis Moreno-Ocampo, the Prosecutor of the International Criminal Court (ICC) accused five high level politicians and a journalist in Kenya[50] of crimes against humanity for organising, funding and/or taking part in the post-election violence, there were reproaches against the ICC for focusing on Africa.[51] This has made the African leaders more aware of the importance of a regional court that could deal with such cases. Discussions have been held and according to Justice Niyungeko, President of the Court, the AU political organs are now revising certain aspects of the merger. One of them is the possible

[49] Statute of the African Court of Justice and Human Rights, Article 16 (Sections of the Court) establishes: *The Court shall have two (2) Sections; a General Affairs Section composed of eight (8) Judges and a Human Rights Section composed of eight (8) Judges.* Article 17 says: *1. The General Affairs Section shall be competent to hear all cases submitted under Article 28 of this Statute save those concerning human and/or peoples' rights issues. 2. The Human Rights Section shall be competent to hear all cases relating to human and/or peoples' rights.* In the 2013 AU negotiations a third section has been added to deal with certain international crimes.

[50] Uhuru Kenyatta (Former Deputy Prime Minister and current President), Francis Muthaura (Secretary to the Cabinet and Head of Civil Service), William Ruto (Former Minister of Higher Education and Kalenjin political leader, now the Deputy President), Henry Kosgei (Former Minister of Trade), General Hussein Ali (Postal Corporation CEO and former Commissioner of Police) and Joshua Sang (Journalist). Eventually charges against Muthaura, Kosgei and Ali were dropped.

[51] See Daily Nation, Special Report by Alphonce Shiundu, Wednesday 22nd December 2010, at 19. On 21st December 2010, the Kenyan Parliament passed a motion proposed by the then MP for Chepangulu, Isaac Ruto, which requests *that the Government* [of Kenya] *suspends any links, cooperation and assistance to the International Criminal Court forthwith.* As a matter of fact, this motion triggered the lobbying of Kenya to gather the support of the AU in pulling out of the ICC as a block.

extension of the ACJHR's jurisdiction to criminal cases.[52] The political organs of the AU are currently studying this possibility and have consensually agreed on a merged Court with 3 sections: criminal, human rights and general matters, and that the human rights and the general section would absorb the existing ACtHPR. This merged court with an added criminal section will be called the African Court of Justice and Human and Peoples Rights (ACJHPR).

Third, 'financial implications' of the merger which need to be foreseen. In relative terms, the ACtHPR is perhaps the best funded among the Inter-American and European counterparts. The ACtHPR's budget for 2010 reached USD 7,939,375.[53] It is a small court, still with a comparatively low volume of work and composed of part-time judges.[54] European governments are among the biggest donors. Certainly, the European Court of Human Rights had a 2010 budget allocation of more than USD 70 million[55] but it issued hundreds of judgments and it seats 47 judges on a full-time basis. The Inter-American Court's budget instead reached a little more than 4 per-cent of the European Court, i.e. between USD 3.5 and 4 million. Its work volume was also far superior and not comparable to the African Court. Therefore, the finances of the African Court seem to be so far convenient and sufficient. The main constraints for the future Court will be to attain sustainable income so that it stops being heavily dependent on donor funding, which is unsustainable and could also compromise the Court's freedom and independence on human right issues. The growth of the Court will imply bigger grants because African States' commitment to the AU bodies has been below standards. Furthermore, unless the Court relaxes admission procedures thus increasing

---

[52] See *supra* note no. 137.

[53] See AU, Decision on the Budget of the African Union for the 2010 Financial Year, adopted by the Sixteenth Ordinary Session of the Executive Council in Addis Ababa, Ethiopia on 1st February 2010, Doc. EX.CL/537(XVI). The budgeted amount means a substantial improvement since its foundation in 2006 when the Court received, in its first year, 2006-2007, a budget of US$ 2,378,750 from the A.U. See "A Guide: African Court on Human and People's Rights", published by the *Coalition for an Effective African Court on Human and Peoples' Rights*, Arusha, Tanzania (*www.africancourtcoalition.org*), September 2008.

[54] With the exception of the Court's President, who resides permanently at the Court in Arusha, as mentioned before.

[55] See: *www.echr.coe.int/ECHR/EN/Header/The+Court/How+the+Court+works/Budget.* Euros 58,588,600 (2010).

access to justice and produces tangible results it will sooner or later face donor fatigue.

Fourth, the 'judicial hierarchy over sub-regional jurisdictions.' The ACtHPR's jurisdiction, provided under Article 3(1) of the Original Protocol, extends to all cases and disputes submitted to it regarding the interpretation and application of the Charter, the Court's Protocol and any other relevant human rights instrument ratified by the States concerned. The jurisdiction of the Court is advisory, adjudicatory as well as of amicable settlement. Under advisory jurisdiction, the Court gives non-binding opinions on legal matters relating to the Charter or any other relevant human rights instruments. The Court also has adjudicatory jurisdiction. This allows the Court to handle cases and disputes submitted to it concerning interpretation and application of the Charter, the Protocol and any other relevant human rights instrument ratified by the States concerned. Lastly, the Court has the power to resort to amicable settlement. This settlement that the Court provides has to be in accordance with the provisions of the Charter. Indeed, Justice Niyungeko's idea of considering the ACJHR or ACJHPR as the appellate court and highest instance over all sub-regional judicial bodies would be desirable in practical terms.[56] However, this implies a dramatic legal shift that may be incompatible with the constitutive instruments of sub-regional entities. Moreover, sub-regional judicial organs are zealous of their powers and will repel any interference or attack on the absolute jurisdiction they enjoy within their sphere of competence and their foundational mission. It should be considered that international courts are not founded on a hierarchical relationship as national courts do.[57] To change this *status quo* will require amendments to each and every constitutive treaty, which entails bringing every State party together and having them agree to subject each sub-regional court to have the ACJHPR as their appellate body. This will ultimately depend on the political will of the States involved.

2. *Proposed Amendments to the Protocol on the Statute of the African Court of Justice and Human Rights*

The Merger Protocol and its Statute are currently undergoing further amendments during negotiations being hosted by the African Union. As a

---

[56] See *supra* note no. 137 in Chapter IV.

[57] See generally Yuval, S., *The Competing Jurisdictions of International Courts and Tribunals*, International Courts and Tribunal Series, Oxford University Press, New York, 2005.

matter of fact, the latest proposals have changed the name of the merged court from African Court of Justice and Human Rights (ACJHR) to African Court of Justice and Human and Peoples Rights (ACJHPR). The Executive Council in its Twenty-Second Ordinary Session, met in Addis Ababa, on 21st to 25th January 2013, and produced a revised Draft Protocol on Amendments to the Protocol on the Statute of the African Court of Justice and Human Rights.[58]

There are two main avenues to seek approval of the proposed amendments. The first avenue is through the political organs of the AU as provided by the 1998[59] and 2003[60] Protocols. The second, and perhaps more desirable one, is by drafting a new modified Protocol and opening it up for signature and ratification. This new Protocol should consider the absorption (instead of replacement) of the ACtHPR into the new ACJHPR and include a third section (criminal) to encompass certain crimes against humanity as per the constitutive documents of the AU. It should also contemplate a slightly higher number of judges so as to cater for the new criminal section, as well as the extended jurisdiction over personal cases, provided local remedies have been exhausted or there has been an unreasonable and/or unjustified delay in dispensing justice at the domestic level. Finally, the protocol should determine in a more forceful manner the

---

[58] See Exp/Min/IV/Rev.7, Original: English. Draft Protocol on Amendments to the Protocol on the Statute of the African Court of Justice and Human Rights. Report of the Meeting of Government Experts and Ministers of Justice/Attorneys General on Legal Matters, Addis Ababa, Ethiopia. This document is reproduced in Appendix I

[59] ACtHPR, 1998 *Protocol*, Article 35 states: *1.The present Protocol may be amended if a State Party to the Protocol makes a written request to that effect to the Secretary-General of the OAU. The Assembly may adopt, by simple majority, the draft amendment after all the State Parties to the present Protocol have been duly informed of it and the Court has given its opinion on the amendment. 2. The Court shall also be entitled to propose such amendments to the present Protocol as it may deem necessary, through the Secretary-General of the OAU. 3. The amendment shall come into force for each State Party which has accepted it thirty days after the Secretary-General of the OAU has received notice of the acceptance.*

[60] ACJ, 2003 *Protocol*, Article 45 states: *1. This Protocol may be amended if a State Party makes a written request to that effect to the Chairperson of the Assembly. 2. Proposals for amendment shall be submitted to the Chairperson of the Commission who shall transmit same to Member States within thirty (30) days of receipt thereof. 3. The Assembly may adopt by a simple majority, the draft amendment after the Court has given its opinion on the amendment.*

duty of State parties to enforce judgments and pair such enforcement to an appropriate local agency.

In any case, it seems necessary to replace all existing protocols and submit to the AU a final comprehensive version of the Merger Protocol in order to harmonize the African process and prevent possible conflicts of jurisdiction between this new ACJHPR and other existing courts.

This new version of the Merger Protocol should take into consideration the theoretical aspects that have been analysed hereinbefore and the experience and opinion of judges of the existing African Court on Human and Peoples' Rights. This new version should aim at facilitating the working of the court, its output and the enforcement of its decisions at a domestic level.[61]

The current working draft proposes the creation of an International Criminal Law section. This new section has been put forward in the African context so as to deal regionally with certain crimes against humanity. A new concern is rising in Africa; it is related to the high levels of impunity for crimes against humanity, peoples and persons. In some cases these crimes were carefully designed by the State apparatus. This awareness reached its climax with the Rwanda genocide and continued with the massacres in Darfur, the orchestrated post-election violence in Kenya, massive expropriations in Zimbabwe, the election-rigging practices throughout several countries, including Côte d'Ivoire, the crisis in Tunisia, Egypt and Libya. Reluctance to Western interventionism has made African leaders more aware of the importance of a regional court that could deal with certain criminal cases.

Obiageli Oraka opines that "expanding the African Court to prosecute criminal cases would put enormous burdens on the court. African countries should also ensure that an expanded African Court would not impede the ICC's role as a crucial court of last resort."[62]

---

[61] The reader should take note that the African Court of Justice and Human Rights (ACJHR) is referred to in the latest editions of the revised draft as the African Court of Justice and Human and Peoples Rights (ACJHPR). See appendix I for the full version of the revised Draft Protocol.

[62] Oraka O., "AU: Support Justice for Gravest Crimes - 125 Groups Across Africa Call for ICC Support at Summit", *Human Rights Watch*, Johannesburg, 27th June 2011. Available at *http://www.hrw.org/fr/news/2011/06/27/au-support-justice-gravest-crimes*.

Certainly, a Criminal section will imply a great burden for the Court, but at the same time there is an imperative need to end the prevalent impunity reigning in the Continent. African human rights groups and civil society stakeholders are struggling and focused on this goal and their strength is based on the premise: 'African problems must be resolved by Africans.' Francois-Xavier Bangamwabo states that "since Africa does not have a continental criminal tribunal or court, and since domestic courts are neither well prepared nor willing to deal with individual criminal responsibility for international crimes, crimes of an international nature committed on African continent have been referred to either *ad-hoc* international criminal tribunals or the (permanent) International Criminal Court."[63] This International Criminal Court,[64] whose foundations were forged to a large extent by African Countries, has already been accused of being a neo-colonial tool for the persecution of African leaders. Indeed, on-going proceedings relate to cases in Africa.[65] Girke and Kamp say that "on the African government's part there have been repeated accusations that the ICC only concentrates on illegal actions in Africa and is blind to crimes on other continents. Many African governments believe that the ICC is a neo-colonial tool used by Western States to exert influence indirectly on Africa. To a certain extent this perception explains the reaction to the al-Bashir case, in which the court was not convened at the invitation of the signatory country involved, unlike other proceedings."[66]

---

[63] Bangamwabo, F.X., "International criminal justice and the protection of human rights in Africa", published online by the Konrad Adenauer Stiftung, KAS International. Available at:
http://www.kas.de/upload/auslandshomepages/namibia/Human_Rights_in_Africa/5_Bangamwabo.pdf

[64] The Rome Statute of the International Criminal Court was adopted on 17th July 1998. It entered into force on 1st July 2002 after 60 ratifications were reached on 11th April 2002. The first Session of the Assembly of States Parties was held from 3rd to 10th Sep 2002.

[65] The cases being investigated by the ICC involve African cases mostly: the Situation in Uganda (ICC–02/04), The Situation in the Democratic Republic of Congo (ICC–01/04), and Prosecutor v Lubanga (ICC–01/04–01), The Situation in Darfur referred to the ICC by the UN Security Council in terms of Article 13 of the Rome Statute; The Situation in the Central African Republic [see Bangamwabo, F.X, op. cit., at 113]. This is perhaps due to the fact that justice and judicial services in Africa are deficient. More recent cases are also focused on Africa: Kenya, Ivory Coast and Libya.

[66] Girke, P. and Kamp, M., "Africa and the International Criminal Court: Stocktaking in Uganda", KAS International Reports, vol. 10, Sankt Augustin, (2010) at 76-77.

Thus, the experience so far seems to indicate that States are prone to accept regional judicial structures rather than international ones, especially in Africa. Unquestionably, the International Criminal Tribunal for Rwanda, the Special Court for Sierra Leone, the International Criminal Tribunal for the former Yugoslavia, the UN *ad-hoc* hybrid criminal courts established in Cambodia, East Timor and Kosovo, have all produced tangible results that were generally accepted by the States involved.[67]This experience is particularly relevant in the African context and it should be taken into consideration.

According to Article 28A of the working Draft, the international criminal jurisdiction of the African Court will extend to the following crimes: Genocide, crimes against humanity, war crimes, the crime of unconstitutional change of government,[68] piracy, terrorism, mercenarism, corruption, money laundering, trafficking in persons, trafficking in drugs, trafficking in hazardous wastes, illicit exploitation of natural resources and the crime of aggression.

Regrettably, this draft has reintroduced the requirement of State Declaration accepting the competence of the Court to receive cases or applications submitted to it directly by parties other than States and AU organs. This may complicate and jeopardise due processes. Article 30 of the Draft asserts that:

> The following entities shall also be entitled to submit cases to the Court on any violation of a right guaranteed by the African Charter, by the Charter on the Rights and Welfare of the Child, the Protocol to the African Charter on Human and Peoples' Rights on the Rights of Women in Africa, the crimes specified under this Protocol or any other legal instrument relevant to human rights ratified by the States Parties concerned:
>
> a) State Parties to the present Protocol;
>
> b) The African Commission on Human and Peoples' Rights;
>
> c) The African Committee of Experts on the Rights and Welfare of the Child;
>
> d) African Intergovernmental Organizations accredited to the Union or its organs;
>
> e) African National Human Rights Institutions;
>
> f) African individuals or African Non-Governmental Organizations with Observer Status with the African Union or its organs or institutions, but only with regard to a State that has made a Declaration accepting the

[67] Bangamwabo, F.X., *op. cit.*, at 128.

[68] It must be noted that the definition of this specific crime has been quite contentious due to Egypt's situation after the military overthrow of

> competence of the Court to receive cases or applications submitted to it directly. The Court shall not receive any case or application involving a State Party which has not made a Declaration in accordance with Article 9(3) of this Protocol.

Rather than imposing the declaration requirement, which lends itself to the politicization of justice, it would have been advisable to open the Court's jurisdiction on matters relating to Human and Peoples' Rights to individuals and certain Non-Governmental Organizations. Certainly, considering the nature of the Court, the fact that its judges are part-time and the limited financial resources available, it would be necessary to insist on the exhaustion of local remedies before granting access to individuals and NGOs. The international rule of exhaustion of local remedies before taking on international remedies is one of the basic rules in international law. The object of the rule is to enable the respondent State the first opportunity to make redress and dispense justice, for it is fitting in a democratic system that the State makes use of its different powers to check and balance one another for the common good.

Thus, access to an international organ should be available, but only as a last resort, after the domestic remedies have been exhausted. If no domestic remedies are available or there is an unreasonable delay on the part of national courts in granting a remedy, clearly, there should be the possibility of gaining access to international remedies.[69] In this way, States are given the opportunity to redress an alleged wrong within the framework of its own domestic legal system before its international responsibility can be called into question at the level of regional or international organs.

Charles Rainey argues that currently "the Court does not possess the authority to impose sanctions upon non-compliant States, thus rendering it incapable of enforcing its decisions."[70] This is the reason why it seems advisable to borrow from article 52(1) of the African Court of Justice Protocol, which reads: "Where a party has failed to comply with a judgment, the Court may, upon application by either party, refer the matter to the Assembly, which may decide upon measures to be taken to give effect to the judgment." This article, Rainey says, "goes on to specify that such sanctions may include, 'denial of transport and communications links

---

[69] *http://www.un.org/esa/socdev/enable/comp201.htm*

[70] Rainey, C., "The African Court: Building a Continental Benchmark for Justice", at 45. Available at:
http://www.raineydevine.com/wp-content/uploads/2010/09/Feb2007

with other Member States, and other measures of a political and economic nature to be determined by the Assembly'."[71]

It will be the task of each State party to scrutinize the State's enforcement machinery so that the judgment may produce the desired effects. As we have observed, African States have not generally developed, in practice, a tangible and genuine constitutional and administrative system of internal checks and balances, upsetting to the core the protection of human rights and the enforcement of international decisions.[72] This is why it seems appropriate to mention subsidiary means for enforcement to cater for cases where domestic law has not foreseen the execution of international judgments and where constitutional law and jurisprudence have not developed a constant practice.

Additionally, if a proper understanding of sovereignty as a type of autonomy — which is subject to democratic checks and balances — is grasped it will facilitate the understanding of the State's responsibility to protect. Should the State fail to fulfil this responsibility in the area of human rights, then the international community has the subsidiary responsibility to protect through lawful means and guarantee the rights and the survival of the political society for whom the State was born and exists but can no longer protect or guarantee.

Warioba observes that international courts do not have power of enforcement because there is no world executive similar to national governments."[73] However, in our opinion, the realm of human rights is essentially — and by nature — devolved. The world does not need an executive because the national governments have the duty and task of executing human rights judgments.[74] Certainly, when a person accesses

---

[71] *Ibid.*, at 195.

[72] For example if a decision is reached by the African Court against Nigeria, where there is no practical experience in relation to such decisions from a Human Rights Court, the Nigerian Government would apply a similar procedure as to their domestic decisions. This means that such decisions have to go to the attorney general so as to be granted the go-ahead prior to execution.

[73] Warioba, J. S., *op. cit*, at 49

[74] The fact is that, as the Commission on Global Governance has stated, *the very essence of global governance is the capacity of the international community to ensure compliance with the rules of society. In a country in which the rule of international law was respected, enforcement procedures would not be needed. In a world in which it is not, universal enforcement may not be achievable*. Report of the Commission on Global Governance, Chapter Six, quoted in Warioba, J. S., *op. cit.*, at 41

international jurisdiction in order to reclaim a right that has been violated, he or she is essentially requesting a type of redress that his or her State had the duty to dispense but it has either denied and/or may not be in a position to dispense.[75] Therefore, the relationship created between the party and the judicial power entrusted with the matter is not an 'international' relationship in the traditional sense. It is rather a devolved relationship, where the State allows access to supranational organs in order to guarantee what the State itself has failed or may fail to guarantee. It also seems fitting to the universality of human rights that these courts should be addressed as universal or regional courts instead of international courts, a term that rightly applies to, for example, the International Court of Justice but should not apply to the African Court on Human and Peoples' Rights or the European Court of Human Rights and other similar human rights judicial bodies.

Therefore, we can speak of a devolved relationship between the ratification or accession of a supranational judicial body and the decisions it may reach in order to dispense justice. This is also why a proper understanding of the nature of the State and its relationship toward the person justifies the responsibility to protect as a viable legal action.

Conclusion

One of the greatest challenges human rights systems face refers to the enforcement of its decisions within the domestic field and with sufficient independence from the political will of the State involved. This challenge is perhaps greater in Africa, where judicial independence is often compromised and tends to bend toward the will of the executive.

Africa's constitutional evolution has been fast-tracked. A process that took hundreds of years to develop in Europe and America was compressed into less than fifty years in Africa. Indeed, if this pace is to be kept certain parameters must be respected. An essential parameter is the sacredness of the rule of law, which in human rights law is deeply related to enhancing the enforcement of human rights decision. This is a clear sign of maturity in a system of law. Human rights decisions are usually directed against the State and they help keep the State within constitutional checks and balances to prevent abuse of power and ensure the actual fulfilment of the bill of rights.

---

[75] This is a universally accepted fact in what regards human rights protection and enforcement.

Consequently, as has been studied in this chapter, the African system needs certain reforms to develop the enforcement of its judicial decisions. These reforms may be grouped into subjective reforms, which are the necessary constitutional and judicial changes within the domestic legislation of State parties, and objective reforms, which refer to the regional judicial structures, set up within the African human rights system.

Regarding subjective reforms, it is desirable to count on a clear set of norms concerning the constitutional regulation of the foreign affairs power. It is essential to ascertain whether the constitution makes the State dualist or monist, although the assumption of a monistic or dualistic international law domestication model is not the only decisive issue for the enforceability of international judgments. Indeed, it is usually understood that if a country follows the monist system incorporation will be straightforward and that the contrary occurs in dualist jurisdictions. Nonetheless, it is possible to enforce judgments in dualist systems and deny them in monistic systems. What really matters is the primacy of laws. If the domestic system grants primacy to the international order over the internal one, then judgments will follow avenues for automatic domestication through administrative processes analogous to internal judgments. But if the domestic system — even monist — grants primacy to the national law, then judgments may be rejected and the process jeopardised. If the system is monist, the rank of international law within the domestic legal order should be clearly ascertained, whether it is above the Constitution or below.

Apart from a constitutional audit to identify appropriate domestication channels, it is also appropriate for local judges to give due consideration to international law. Some have called this 'judicial activism', which seems a repugnant and superficial term. It should rather be seen as 'judicial innovation' which points at the use of innovative ways the judge may use, within certain boundaries, to achieve justice.[76] In this sense, there is a growing tendency to consider international law precepts in domestic courts, even when there has been no formal act of incorporation.

On the other hand, objective reforms refer to the judicial body set up within the African human rights system: The African Court on Human and People's Rights and its eventual successor, the African Court of Justice and Human and Peoples Rights, whose 'Protocol on the Statute of the African Court of Justice and Human and Rights' (the Merger Protocol)

---

[76] This requires that the personal philosophy of the judge should have a 'bias in favour of fairness and justice.'

was adopted at the African Union Summit in July 2008 and is currently undergoing modifications. This merged court, the African Court of Justice and Human and Peoples Rights (ACJHPR), is not yet operational but it is part of an irreversible process that is bound to take place.

There are four key aspects that will need to be taken into consideration for this new Court to succeed: First, the court should safeguard its institutional memory. Second, the jurisdiction of the Court should be enlarged and access to justice facilitated. Third, the financial implications and sustainability[77] should be given due consideration, and fourth, the judicial hierarchy and the extent of the Courts' powers over sub-regional bodies should be appropriately addressed and clarified. We have taken these four aspects into consideration and proposed relevant amendments to the proposed merger Protocol. We also have taken into consideration a fifth key aspect, which, however, falls outside the human rights scope, but that has been widely discussed and agreed by the political organs of the AU: a criminal section for the new Court.

---

[77] See AU, EX.CL/773(XXII), Annex 2 Rev: *Report on the financial and structural implications of extending the jurisdiction of the African Court of Justice and Human Rights to encompass international crimes*. The report called for three principles to be taken into consideration: (1) Pragmatism in institutional design, (2) gradualism in institutional growth and development, and (3) flexibility in current and future developments at the Court. The working group asserted that in summary, the extension of jurisdiction and expansion of the Court will entail: a) Election of new Judges (but retaining the overall number of sixteen already adopted in the Sharm el Sheikh Protocol); b) Establishment of the Office of the Prosecutor with investigative, prosecutorial and other staff; c) Enlargement of the Registry, furnishing it with more powers and more staff of different calibre and cadre; d) Expansion/ increase of the working premises of the Court i.e. Courtroom facilities, office, registry, library, information and communication technology (ICT) and other facilities; e) Establishment and maintenance, in conjunction with the Host State, of penitentiary (detention) facilities adjacent or proximate to the Court; f) Operational requirements for enhancing and maintaining the security of the Court; g) Procurement of furniture, equipment and working accessories commensurate with the numbers and categories of staff recruited; h) Operational requirements of investigations across (and sometimes beyond) the continent; i) Funds for the benefit of victims, and for Legal Assistance to accused persons; j) Funds to cater for contingencies and emergencies. Estimates on the possible financial requirements of the Court were based on comparative costing to that of the Special Chamber to try the former President of Chad, Hissène Habré (in Euros): Year 1: 3,802,560; Year 2: 2,106,251; Year 3:1,125,550. Total approximate cost increase: 7,034,361.

Certainly, if the aforementioned key aspects are allowed to enlighten the amendments to the merger Protocol this will help the harmonization of the judicial decision-making process and subsequent domestication and enforcement. It will also simplify the financial obligations of State parties by preventing a mushrooming of expensive organs which Africa cannot afford to pay for. Such a Court, belonging to Africa and financially sustained by Africa, will encounter a more willing political support, where the national autonomy is not perceived as abused, compromised or attacked. Sovereignty cannot be used as a sensible and credible excuse against the enforcement of judicial decisions coming from the African Court of Justice and Human and Peoples Rights.

EPILOGUE

Indeed, constitutional democracy should have the rule of law at its core. It demands a proper understanding of the purpose and function of the State, which is not an *absolute entity*, and whose existence prompts the presence of limitations that are actualized in the form of constitutional checks and balances. State functions are under constant scrutiny by the judicial function. This scrutiny is exercised through checks and balances placed inside or outside the structures of the State. They are inside if they are defined by constitutional law or practice; they may be found outside through international judicial organs with jurisdiction. This judicial function requires independence, which must be real and present at all levels, which is, perhaps, nation building's greatest challenge.

In the past, judiciary independence was jeopardized mainly through executive interference. Nowadays these factors have multiplied themselves: ideologization, cultural pressure, peer-pressure, political, economic and media manipulation, etc. We are constantly witnessing judicial decisions at national and international levels that seem to focus on ideological, cultural and developmental factors thus consigning justice to a second place.[1]

International jurisdiction may be accessed directly by the State through an administrative decision called treaty ratification. This administrative decision is founded on the State's prerogative to exercise the foreign affairs power, which we have defined as a constitutional function that regulates the capacity of a State to become an active player in the realm of international relations. International jurisdiction may also be accessed directly by the people through national referenda.[2] Both manners of ratification or accession are subject to constitutional checks and balances, which act as regulators or valves that limit the strength and method with

[1] For example, ECHR (2010) in the case of *A,B, & C v. Ireland*, which has been criticised as an ambiguous decision that avoided defining substantive issues. The same may be said of several decisions from the African Commission, where the Commission limited itself to stating human rights abuses without proposing any action to remedy the wrong. See generally *supra* Chapter V, 1.

[2] See *supra* note no. 204.

which the State may use its powers and the extent of those powers over its subjects.

Those checks and balances subject the State to rule of law, and this subjection compels the presence and intervention of the judiciary. For national matters the domestic judiciary will be expected to safeguard the rule of law. For international matters, including human rights as may be applicable, international bodies with appropriate jurisdiction will be called for in a subsidiary or complementary way.[3]

Therefore, the State's act of ratification or accession to a treaty creating a supranational judicial organ imposes the inalienable duty to enforce those decisions as if they were domestic decisions. Human Rights decisions thus should trigger the judicial enforcement apparatus of the State as if they were domestic decisions. Furthermore, it seems convenient in the African human rights international judicial system to entrust in a more detailed manner the execution of decisions to specific domestic organs, for example, to the highest domestic tribunal or court. This may set into motion the administrative apparatus and guarantee a greater level of success.

Human rights international constitutive instruments should also count on a proper understanding of the term 'sovereignty' so that it may not be used as a tool to frustrate compliance. Sovereignty should not hang over international human rights institutions like the sword of Damocles,[4] a constant threat and reminder that the real power is held by a sovereign State. Sovereignty is rightly embraced again and again and cautiously

---

[3] See Corao, C. M., *La Ejecución de Sentencias de la Corte Interamericana de Derechos Humanos*, *Estudios Constitucionales*, vol. 5, Universidad de Talca, (2007), at 128.

[4] Cícero, Tvscvlanarvm Dispvtationvm Liber Qvintvs, XXI. Cicero relates the story as follows: *Dionysius (II) was a fourth century B.C. tyrant of Syracuse, a city in Magna Graecia, the Greek area of southern Italy. To all appearances Dionysius was very rich and comfortable, with all the luxuries money could buy, tasteful clothing and jewellery, and delectable food. He even had court flatterers to inflate his ego. One of them was the court sycophant, Damocles, who used to make comments to the king about his wealth and luxurious life. Dionysius turned to Damocles and said, 'If you think I'm so lucky, how would you like to try out my life?' Damocles readily agreed ... until he noticed a sharp sword hovering over his head. It was suspended from the ceiling by a horse hair. This, the tyrant explained to Damocles, was what life as ruler was really like. Damocles, alarmed, quickly revised his idea of what made up a good life, and asked to be excused.* Available at: *http://www.thelatinlibrary.com/cicero/*

cherished in every national constitution;[5] it is widely spoken about and revered as the quintessence against foreign abuse. Regrettably, it is also used as an excuse to justify horrors and crimes against humanity. If a proper understanding of sovereignty as a type of autonomy, which is subject to democratic checks and balances, is grasped it will facilitate the understanding of the State's responsibility to protect. Should the State fail to protect human rights, then the international community has the immediate responsibility to protect through lawful means to guarantee the rights and survival of the political society for whom the State was born and exists but which it can no longer protect or guarantee.[6]

Certainly, when a person accesses an international jurisdiction in order to claim a right that has been violated, he or she is essentially requesting a type of redress that his or her State had the duty to dispense but which it has either denied, abused and/or may not be in a position to protect.

---

[5] In most national constitutions, sovereignty will be among the first articles; in some cases 2nd or 3rd. Only in one case (Ethiopia's) it comes under no. 8. Certainly, the holder of sovereignty may vary from State to People or Nation. See for example: Ukraine, Article 1. Turkey, Article 6. Estonia, Article 1. Croatia, Article 2. Afghanistan, Article 4. Jordan, Article 1. Myanmar, Section 1. Eritrea, Article 1. Laos, Article 1. Nigeria, Section 2. Switzerland, Article 3. Sudan, Section 1. Russia, Article 3. South Africa, Section 1. Albania, Article 2. Spain, Article 1. Portugal, Article 1. Finland, Section 1. Slovak, Article 1. (1) Nicaragua, Article 1. Egypt, Article 3. Kazakhstan, Article 2. Romania, Article 1. Ethiopia, Article 8. Latvia, Article 2. Uruguay, Article 4. Nepal, Section 2. Rwanda, Article 1. El Salvador, Article 1. Lithuania, Article 2. Antigua and Barbuda, Section 1. (1). Greece, Article 1. France, Article 3. Azerbaijan, Article 2. Zambia, Section 1. Uganda, Section 1. Serbia, Article 1. Haiti, Article 1. Brazil, Article 1. Kyrgyzstan, Article 1. Morocco, Article 2. Venezuela, Article 1. Zimbabwe, Section 1. Iraq, Article 1. Mali, Article 2. Benin, Article 1. Namibia, Article 1. Bosnia and Herzegovina, Section 2. New Zealand, Section 2. Cambodia, Article 1. Cuba, Article 1. Montenegro, Article 1. Czech Republic, Article 1. Moldova, Article 1. East Timor, Section 1. Armenia, Article 1. Indonesia, Article 1. Hungary, Article 2.

[6] For example, after the post-election violence that Kenya witnessed in 2007-2008, the State machinery was clearly unable to dispense justice. The country was deeply divided and perpetrators and masterminds of the crimes committed were in some cases powerful politicians. The Kenyan Parliament requested that the International Criminal Court (ICC) should take charge of the situation. In December 2010 the ICC Prosecutor, Luis Moreno-Ocampo, requested the pre-Trial Chambers to issue summons on five powerful political figures and one journalist. This shows that the *body politic* was clearly aware that the State and its machinery did not have the capacity and/or political will to dispense justice given the complicated ethnical nature of the charges, the bias of the national court system and the extent of the country-wide damage caused by the violence.

Therefore, the relationship created between the party and the judicial power entrusted with the matter is not an international relationship in the traditional sense. It is rather a devolved relationship, where the State allows the access to supranational organs in order to guarantee what the State has failed or may fail to guarantee.[7]

Therefore, human rights decisions should be automatically domesticated and enforced; the State has the duty to put in place the necessary mechanisms to guarantee that this may be so. This is the reason why it can be said that the realm of human rights is essentially — and by nature — devolved, where the national government is entrusted with the legal and moral duty of executing human rights judgments.[8]

In Human Rights we should not attempt to separate the *right* from what is *human* or else law may be turned into a weapon against the person, where justice is no longer the goal. As Martin Luther King Jr. wrote on 16th April 1963 in his Letter from a Birmingham Jail:

> "A just law is a man-made code that squares with the moral law or the law of God. An unjust law is a code that is out of harmony with the moral law. To put it in the terms of St. Thomas Aquinas: An unjust law is a human law that is not rooted in eternal law and natural law. Any law that uplifts human personality is just. Any law that degrades human personality is unjust… Thus I can urge them to disobey segregation ordinances, for they are morally wrong. (…) We should never forget that everything Adolf Hitler did in Germany was 'legal' and everything the Hungarian freedom fighters did in Hungary was 'illegal.' It was 'illegal' to aid and comfort a Jew in Hitler's Germany. Even so, I am sure that, had I lived in Germany at the time, I would have aided and comforted my Jewish brothers."[9]

---

[7] As we have also said, it seems to befit the universality of human rights that these courts should be referred to as universal or regional courts instead of international courts, a term that rightly applies to, for example, the International Court of Justice but should not apply to the African Court on Human and Peoples' Rights or the European Court of Human Rights and other similar human rights jurisdictions.

[8] The fact is that, as the Commission on Global Governance has stated, *the very essence of global governance is the capacity of the international community to ensure compliance with the rules of society. In a country in which the rule of international law was respected, enforcement procedures would not be needed. In a world in which it is not, universal enforcement may not be achievable*. Report of the Commission on Global Governance, Chapter Six, quoted in Warioba J. S., *op. cit.*, at 41

[9] Luther King, M. Jr., "Letter from a Birmingham Jail", 16th April 1963, published by the African Studies Center - University of Pennsylvania. Available at: *http://www.africa.upenn.edu/Articles_Gen/Letter_Birmingham.html*

CONCLUSIONS

Constitutional law and international law relate and influence each other through the foreign affairs power in general, and specifically through two elements of this constitutional power, namely, treaty-making and diplomacy. Treaty-making delineates the way and manner these instruments will be accessed, incorporated, applied and executed in the domestic forum of each State. Diplomacy plays a key role in the negotiation and drafting of international instruments that constitute international organizations.

The power of treaty ratification, accession or acceptance is usually regulated by Constitutional law, which distributes powers and functions within the State and puts in place the necessary checks and balances to guarantee identification between, among others, peoples and policies. Thus, from a domestic point of view, the creation of international organizations and the authority bestowed on them are primarily the result of the exercise of certain powers and functions constitutionally given to specific State offices.

Human rights treaties – regardless the instrument's name –are bound to have internal effects, because they tend to deal with rights and/or aspirations usually contained in the bills of rights of domestic constitutions or considered by constitutional practice. In this sense, human rights standards call on the State, first, to aim at the highest possible protection, which is done primarily through the constitution's bill of rights. Second, to respect international law's peremptory norms and the treaties it has ratified or accessed. Third, to realise that if the State fails to protect human rights the political society has the right to activate available and legal means to secure such protection.

Hence, human rights treaties require incorporation into the domestic forum. This incorporation process may be carried out through a monist or dualist system, which is ruled by Constitutional law and practice.

It is essential to ascertain whether the constitution makes the State dualist or monist, but the assumption of a monistic or dualistic international law domestication model is not the only decisive issue for the enforceability of international judgments. It is possible to enforce judgments in dualist systems and deny them in monistic systems. The key is really found in the primacy of laws: If the domestic system grants primacy to the international order over the internal one, then judgments will follow avenues for automatic domestication through administrative processes analogous to internal judgments. But if the domestic system — even monist — grants primacy to the national law, then judgments may be rejected and the process jeopardised.

Perhaps the greatest challenge for a human rights system is to seek appropriate and effective ways to enforce its decisions within the domestic field with sufficient independence from the political will of the State involved. This is challenge is perhaps greater in most African States, where the executive is still perceived as the 'sovereign' who is not subject to real and substantial checks and balances. This approach jeopardises judicial independence and compromises the enforcement of human rights decisions.

To guarantee the enforcement of international judgments it is of paramount importance that the domestic law foresees and guides the actual enforcement in a more detailed manner. It is not enough to make general statements of moral obligation to comply. Judicial decisions from such bodies should not, in principle, follow the same domestication process as foreign judgments, for they do not come from a foreign court but from a supranational court, whose jurisdiction has been accepted, strictly speaking, as an extension of the domestic system.

The African Human Rights Charter captured the existence of a quasi-judicial organ: The African Commission on Human and Peoples' Rights as a supervisory mechanism for the protection and promotion of human rights. This Commission was the only original body conceived for the promotion and protection of human rights in Africa. The three main functions of the Commission are promotion, ensuring protection and interpretation. The enforcement and implementation mechanisms of its decisions are State-reporting and communications. Communications may be inter-State communications and individual and/or NGO communications.

The African Human Rights Charter also implicitly paved the way for a judicial organ, a court that could become the principal human rights judicial organ of the AU, with jurisdiction over human rights matters in Africa. This court was created and it is now functional. It is known as: The African Court on Human and Peoples' Rights. The Court complements and reinforces the protective mandate of the Commission. It may allow Non-Governmental Organizations (NGOs) with observer status before the

Commission, and individuals to institute cases directly before it, provided the State involved made a declaration allowing this type of complaints. The Court's judgments on cases are final and binding upon the State parties concerned.

Besides, the Constitutive Act of the African Union had foreseen the creation of the Court of Justice of the African Union that was never constituted. In 2004 the African Union decided that this African Court of Justice and the African Court on Human and People's Rights should be merged. To this effect they approved a merger Protocol, which is still under negotiation. To help this merged Court succeed it appears essential to look into four key aspects of the merger process: First, absorption is preferable to replacement so as to safeguard its institutional memory. Second, the jurisdiction *ratione personæ* of the Court should be enlarged and access to justice facilitated. Third, the financial implications of the merger and the Court's self-sufficiency should be given due consideration, and fourth, the judicial hierarchy and the extent of the Courts' powers over sub-regional bodies should be appropriately addressed and clarified.

It seems clear that in order to enhance the enforcement of judicial decisions emanating from the ACJHPR four tasks need to be undertaken: First, there should be an audit of the constitutional norms that regulate the foreign affairs power of State parties and assess their viability. Second, foster stronger domestic judiciary systems that are honest, just, independent and innovative and train judicial officers along these lines. Third, rationalise the structure of the new ACJHPR by facilitating access to justice, establishing the appropriate number of sections and their jurisdictions, and specifying the enforcement means as far as practicable. Fourth, amend or re-draft the merger protocol and open it for ratification, this will prevent conflicting ratifications and discordant accessions into the new African Judicial Court system.

CHRONOLOGY OF AFRICAN HUMAN RIGHTS

1900:	Manchester Pan-African gathering of intellectuals, presided over by Menelik II.
1904, 1-8:	Pan-Africanist Leader, Marcus Garvey, brought together scattered African Communities worldwide.
1919:	Treaty of Versailles redistributes and shares Africa among major European powers.
1945:	End of WW II and foundation of the UN.
1948:	UDHR.
1961, Jan:	First Congress of African Lawyers in Africa, Lagos, Nigeria.
1963, 25-5-:	Birth of the OAU at a Meeting of Independent African States, in Addis Ababa.
1967:	The Dakar Declaration: a conference of jurists from Francophone Africa was convened in Dakar.
1968:	Tehran Conference.
1969:	Cairo Seminar.
1977:	UNGA appeal to create instruments for human rights promotion & protection.
1978 July:	Meeting of Jurists in Butare, Rwanda.
1978 Sep:	Dakar Colloquium on Human Rights and Economic Development.
1978 Sep:	Monrovia Proposal for an African Commission.
1979 Nov:	Dakar meeting of Experts.
1980 Jun:	Banjul Meeting.
1981 Jan:	Second Banjul Meeting.
1981 Jun:	Adoption of Banjul Charter in Nairobi.

1986, 21-10:	Banjul Charter enters into force.
1987 Jun:	Election of first Commissioners of the African. Commission on Human and Peoples' Rights (ACHPR).
1987, 2-11:	Inauguration of the ACHPR.
1990:	OAU adopts African Charter on the Rights and Welfare of the Child.
1995 Mar:	WILDAF meeting in Lomé, Togo.
1995:	Cape Town meeting of experts on a Draft Protocol to the African Charter on the Establishment of an ACtHPR.
1995 Jun:	OAU asks ACHPR to develop a protocol on women.
1997:	Nouakchott Draft & Addis Ababa Draft on an ACtHPR.
1998 Jun:	Adoption of ACtHPR Original Protocol in Ouagadougou, Burkina Faso.
1999:	African Charter on the Rights and Welfare of the Child enters into force.
2001:	AU replaces the OAU.
2002:	Commencement of the drafting of the ACJ Protocol.
2003:	Equality Now's conference of women's groups.
2003 Jul:	Maputo Protocol on the Rights of Women is adopted by the AU.
2003 Jul:	ACJ Protocol is adopted.
2004, 25-1:	ACtHPR Protocol enters into force.
2005:	Maputo Protocol enters into force.
2006 Jan:	First judges of the ACtHPR are elected and appointed.
2007 Aug:	ACtHPR moves to Arusha, its permanent seat.
2008 Jul:	Protocol on the Statute of the African Court of Justice and Human Rights is adopted in Sharm El-Sheikh, Egypt.
2009, 11-2:	Protocol on the ACJ enters into force.

2009, 15-12: The ACtHPR decides its first matter: *Michelot Yogogombaye v The Republic of Senegal.*

2010/2013: On-going discussions for the Merger of ACtHPR and the ACJ into the ACJHPR.

2011, 25-3: First Provisional Measures' order is issued by the ACtHPR, in the case of *Commission on Human and Peoples' Rights v. Great Socialist Peoples' Libyan Arab Jamahiriya.*

APPENDIX I

DRAFT PROTOCOL ON AMENDMENTS TO THE PROTOCOL ON THE STATUTE OF THE AFRICAN COURT OF JUSTICE AND HUMAN RIGHTS[1]

The Member States of the African Union parties to the Constitutive Act of the African Union;

RECALLING the objectives and principles enunciated in the Constitutive Act of the African Union, adopted on 11 July 2000 in Lome, Togo, in particular the commitment to settle their disputes through peaceful means;

FURTHER RECALLING the provisions of the Protocol on the Statute of the African Court of Justice and Human Rights and the Statute annexed to it adopted on 1 July 2008 in Sharm-El-Sheikh, Egypt;

RECOGNIZING that the Protocol on the Statute of the African Court of Justice and Human Rights had merged the African Court on Human and Peoples Rights and the Court of Justice of the African Union into a single Court;

BEARING IN MIND their commitment to promote peace, security and stability on the continent, and to protect human and peoples" rights in accordance with the African Charter on Human and Peoples Rights and other relevant instruments;

FURTHER RECOGNIZING the efforts and contribution of the African Commission on Human and Peoples Rights in the promotion and protection of human and peoples" rights since its inception in 1987;

---

[1] See (AU) Exp/Min/IV/Rev.7. See also the Protocol's original version available at: *http://www.au.int/en/sites/default/files/PROTOCOL_STATUTE_AFRICAN_COURT_JUSTICE_AND_HUMAN_RIGHTS.pdf*

NOTING the steady growth of the African Court on Human and Peoples Rights and the contribution it has made in protecting human and peoples‟ rights on the African continent as well as the progress towards the establishment of the African Court of Justice and Human and Peoples Rights;

FURTHER BEARING IN MIND the complementary relationship between the African Commission on Human and Peoples Rights and the African Court on Human and Peoples Rights, as well as its successor, the African Court of Justice and Human and Peoples Rights;

FURTHER RECALLING their commitment to the right of the Union to intervene in a Member State pursuant to a decision of the Assembly in respect of grave circumstances, namely: war crimes, genocide and crimes against humanity as well as a serious threat to legitimate order to restore peace and stability to the Member State of the Union upon the recommendation of the Peace and Security Council;

REITERATING their respect for democratic principles, human and peoples‟ rights, the rule of law and good governance;

FURTHER REITERATING their respect for the sanctity of human life, condemnation and rejection of impunity and political assassination, acts of terrorism and subversive activities, unconstitutional changes of governments and acts of aggression;

FURTHER REITERATING their commitment to fighting impunity in conformity with the provisions of Article 4(o) of the Constitutive Act of the African Union;

ACKNOWLEDGING the pivotal role that the African Court of Justice and Human and Peoples Rights can play in strengthening the commitment of the African Union to promote sustained peace, security and stability on the Continent and to promote justice and human and peoples‟ rights as an aspect of their efforts to promote the objectives of the political and socio-economic integration and development of the Continent with a view to realizing the ultimate objective of a United States of Africa;

FURTHER RECALLING Assembly Decision Assembly/AU/Dec.213 (XII) adopted by the Twelfth Ordinary Session of the Assembly in Addis Ababa, Federal Democratic Republic of Ethiopia, on 3 February 2009 on the implementation of the Assembly's Decision on the Abuse of the Principle of Universal Jurisdiction;

FURTHER RECALLING Assembly Decision Assembly/AU/Dec.263 (XIII) adopted by the Thirteenth Ordinary Session of the Assembly in Sirte, Great Socialist People's Libyan Arab Jamahiriya, on 3 July 2009 on the transformation of the African Union Commission to the African Union Authority;

FURTHER RECOGNIZING the need to take the necessary measures to amend the legal instruments of the principal organs of the African Union in the light of the aforementioned Assembly Decisions;

CONVINCED that the present Protocol will complement national, regional and continental bodies and institutions in preventing serious and massive violations of human and peoples" rights in keeping with Article 58 of the Charter and ensuring accountability for them wherever they occur;

HAVE AGREED to adopt the present amendments to the Protocol on the Statute of the African Court of Justice and Human Rights and the Statute annexed thereto as follows:

CHAPTER I

In CHAPTER I of the Protocol (MERGER OF THE AFRICAN COURT ON HUMAN AND PEOPLES RIGHTS AND THE COURT OF JUSTICE OF THE AFRICAN UNION) the deletion of the existing title, Articles and their provisions in their entirety and the insertion in their place of the following:

CHAPTER I - GENERAL PROVISIONS

Article 1

Definitions

In this Protocol:

"Assembly" means the Assembly of Heads of State and Government of the African Union;

"Chairperson" means the Chairperson of the Assembly;

"Charter" means the African Charter on Human and Peoples Rights;

"Commission" means the Commission of the African Union;

"Court" means the African Court of Justice and Human and Peoples Rights;

"Member State" means a Member State of the Union;

"President" means the President of the Court;

"Protocol" means the Protocol on the Statute of the African Court of Justice and Human Rights;

"Single Court" has the same meaning as the Court;

"Statute" means the present Statute;

"Union" means the African Union established by the Constitutive Act of the African Union;

"Vice President" means the Vice President of the Court.

Article 2

Organs of the Court

The Court shall be composed of the following organs:

1. The Presidency;
2. The Office of the Prosecutor;
3. The Registry.

Article 3

Jurisdiction of the Court

1. The Court is vested with an original and appellate jurisdiction, including international criminal jurisdiction, which it shall exercise in accordance with the provisions of the Statute annexed hereto.

2. The Court has jurisdiction to hear such other matters or appeals as may be referred to it in any other agreements that the Member States or the Regional Economic Communities or other international organizations recognized by the African Union may conclude among themselves, or with the Union.

Article 4

Relationship between the Court and the African Commission on Human and Peoples Rights

The Court shall, in accordance with the Charter and this Protocol, complement the protective mandate of the African Commission on Human and Peoples Rights.

CHAPTER II - TRANSITIONAL PROVISIONS

Article 5

Term of Office of the Judges of the African Court on Human and Peoples Rights

In Article 4 (Term of Office of the Judges of the African Court on Human and Peoples Rights), replace the existing provision including its title, with:

Article 4

Term of Office of the Judges of the African Court on Human and Peoples Rights

1. Upon the coming into force of the Protocol on the Statute of the African Court of Justice and Human Rights, the terms and appointment of the Judges of the African Court on Human and Peoples Rights shall terminate.

2. Without prejudice to paragraph 1, the Judges of the African Court on Human and Peoples Rights shall remain in office until the judges of the African Court of Justice and Human and Peoples Rights are sworn in.

Article 6

Pending Cases

At the entry into force of this Protocol, where any matter affecting any State had already been commenced before either the African Court on Human and Peoples‟ Rights or the African Court of Justice and Human Rights, if in force, such a matter shall be continued before the relevant Section of the African Court of Justice and Human and Peoples‟ Rights, pursuant to such Rules as may be made by the Court.

Article 6bis

Temporary Jurisdiction

At the entry into force of this Protocol, until a Member State ratifies it, any jurisdiction which has hitherto been accepted by such Member State with respect to either the African Court on Human and Peoples‟ Rights or the African Court of Justice and Human Rights shall be exercisable by this Court.

Article 7

Registry of the Court

1. The Registrar of the African Court on Human and Peoples Rights shall remain in office until the appointment of a new Registrar for the African Court of Justice and Human and Peoples Rights.

2. The staff of the African Court on Human and Peoples Rights shall be absorbed into the Registry of the African Court of Justice and Human and Peoples Rights, for the remainder of their subsisting contracts of employment.

CHAPTER III - FINAL PROVISIONS

Article 8

Nomenclature

In the Protocol and the Statute wherever it occurs "African Court of Justice and Human Rights" is deleted and replaced with "African Court of Justice and Human and Peoples Rights."

Article 9

Signature, Ratification and Accession

1. This Protocol and the Statute annexed to it shall be open for signature, ratification or accession by Member States, in accordance with their respective constitutional procedures.

2. The instruments of ratification or accession to this Protocol and the Statute annexed to it shall be deposited with the Chairperson of the Commission.

3. Any Member State may, at the time of signature or when depositing its instrument of ratification or accession, or at any time thereafter, make a declaration accepting the competence of the Court to receive cases under Article 30 (f).

Article 10

Depository Authority

1. This Protocol and the Statute annexed to it, drawn up in four (4) original texts in the Arabic, English, French and Portuguese languages, all four (4) texts being equally authentic, shall be deposited with the Chairperson of the Commission, who shall transmit a certified true copy to the Government of each Member State.

2. The Chairperson of the Commission, shall notify all Member States of the dates of deposit of the instruments of ratification or accession, and shall, upon the entry into force of this Protocol, register the same with the Secretariat of the United Nations.

Article 11

Entry into force

1. This Protocol and the Statute annexed to it shall enter into force thirty (30) days after the deposit of instruments of ratification by fifteen (15) Member States.

2. For each Member State which shall accede to it subsequently, this Protocol and Annexed Statute shall enter into force on the date on which the instruments of ratification or accession are deposited.

3. The Chairperson of the Commission shall notify all Member States of the entry into force of this Protocol.

Article 12

Amendments

1. This Protocol and the Statute annexed to it may be amended if a State Party to the Protocol makes a written request to that effect to the Chairperson of the Commission. The Assembly may adopt, by simple majority, the draft amendment after all the States parties to the present Protocol have been duly informed of it and the Court has given its opinion on the amendment.

2. The Court shall also be entitled to propose such amendments to the present Protocol or the Statute annexed to it as it may deem necessary, through the Chairperson of the Commission.

3. The amendments shall come into force for each State Party which has accepted it thirty (30) days after the Chairperson of the Commission has received notice of the acceptance.

Adopted by the … Session of the Assembly of the African Union held in …, …, on …, 20…

Statute of the African Court of Justice and Human and Peoples Rights

Article 1

Definitions

1. In Article 1 of the Statute (Definitions), the deletion from the chapeau of the words "except otherwise indicated, the following shall mean"

2. The insertion of the following words and the definitions ascribed to them:

"Chairperson" means the Chairperson of the Commission;

"Child" means any person under eighteen years of age;

"Court" means the African Court of Justice and Human and Peoples Rights;

"Full Court" means the three Sections of the Court sitting together in plenary;

"Person" means a natural or legal person;

"President" means the President of the Court unless otherwise specified;

"Section" means the General Affairs or Human and Peoples" Rights or International Criminal Law Section of the Court;

"Statute" means the Statute of the African Court of Justice and Human and Peoples Rights;

"Vice President" means the Vice President of the Court.

Article 2

Composition

In Article 3 of the Statute (Composition), add the following paragraph 4:

"4. The Assembly shall ensure that there is equitable gender representation in the Court."

Article 3

Qualifications of Judges

Article 4 of the Statute (Qualifications of Judges) is replaced with the following:

"The Court shall be composed of impartial and independent Judges elected from among persons of high moral character, who possess the qualifications required in their respective countries for appointment to the highest judicial offices, or are juris-consults of recognized competence and experience in international law, international human rights law, international humanitarian law or international criminal law."

Article 4

List of Candidates

Article 6 of the Statute (List of Candidates) is replaced with the following:

"1. For the purpose of election, the Chairperson of the Commission shall establish three (3) alphabetical lists of candidates presented as follows:

i. List A containing the names of candidates having recognized competence and experience in International law;

ii. List B containing the names of candidates having recognized competence and experience in international human rights law and international humanitarian law; and

iii. List C containing the names of candidates having recognized competence and experience in international criminal law.

2. States Parties that nominate candidates possessing the competences required on the three (3) lists shall choose the list on which their candidates may be placed.

3. At the first election, five (5) judges each shall be elected from amongst the candidates on lists A and B, and six (6) judges shall be elected from amongst the candidates of list C respectively.

4. The Chairperson of the Commission shall communicate the three lists to Member States, at least thirty (30) days before the Ordinary Session of the Assembly or of the Council during which the elections shall take place."

Article 5

Term of Office

Article 8 of the Statute (Term of Office) is replaced with the following:

"1.The Judges shall be elected for a single, non-renewable term of nine (9) years. The terms of office of five (5) of the judges elected at the first election shall end after three (3) years, and the terms of another five (5) of the judges shall end after six (6) years.

2. The Judges whose term of office shall end after the initial periods of three (3) and six (6) years shall be determined by lot drawn by the Chairperson of the Assembly or the Executive Council, immediately after the first election.

3. A Judge elected to replace another whose term of office has not expired shall complete the term of office of his or her predecessor.

4. All the Judges, except the President and the Vice President, shall perform their functions on a part-time basis.

5. The Assembly shall, on the recommendation of the Court, decide the time when all the Judges of the Court shall perform their functions on a full time basis."

Article 6

Structure of the Court

Article 16 of the Statute (Sections of the Court) is replaced with the following:

"Article 16

Structure of the Court

1. The Court shall have three (3) Sections: a General Affairs Section, a Human and Peoples Rights Section and an International Criminal Law Section.

2. The International Criminal Law Section of the Court shall have three (3) Chambers: a Pre-Trial Chamber, a Trial Chamber and an Appellate Chamber.

3. The allocation of Judges to the respective Sections and Chambers shall be determined by the Court in its Rules."

Article 7

Assignment of matters to Sections of the Court

Article 17 of the Statute (Assignment of matters to Sections) is replaced with the following:

"Article 17

Assignment of matters to Sections of the Court

1. The General Affairs Section shall be competent to hear all cases submitted under Article 28 of the Statute except those assigned to the Human and Peoples Rights Section and the International Criminal Law Section as specified in this Article.

2. The Human and Peoples Rights Section shall be competent to hear all cases relating to human and peoples" rights.

3. The International Criminal Law Section shall be competent to hear all cases relating to the crimes specified in this Statute."

Article 8

Revision and Appeal

Article 18 (Referral of matters to the Full Court) is replaced with the following:

"Article 18

Revision and Appeals

1. In the case of the General Affairs Section and the Human and Peoples' Rights Section, a revision of a judgement shall be made in terms of the provisions of Article 48.

2. In the case of the International Criminal Law Section, a decision of the Pre-Trial Chamber or the Trial Chamber may be appealed against by the Prosecutor or the accused, on the following grounds:

(a) A procedural error; (b) An error of law; (c) An error of fact.

3. An appeal may be made against a decision on jurisdiction or admissibility of a case, an acquittal or a conviction.

4. The Appellate Chamber may affirm, reverse or revise the decision appealed against. The decision of the Appellate Chamber shall be final."

Article 9

Chambers of the Court

Article 19 of the Statute (Chambers) is replaced with the following:

"Chambers of the Court

1. The General Affairs Section, Human and Peoples Rights Section or International Criminal Law Section may, at any time, constitute one or more Chambers in accordance with the Rules of Court.

2. A Judgment given by any Chamber shall be considered as rendered by the Court."

Article 9 Bis

Powers and Functions of the Chambers of the International Criminal Law Section

After Article 19 of the Statute (Chambers) add the following as Article 19 Bis:

"Article 19 Bis

Powers and Functions of the Chambers of the International Criminal Law Section

1. The Pre-Trial Chamber shall exercise the functions provided for in Article 46F of this Statute.

2. In addition, the Pre-Trial Chamber may also at the request of the Prosecutor issue such orders and warrants as may be required for an investigation or prosecution.

3. The Pre-Trial Chamber may issue such orders as may be required to provide for the protection and privacy of witnesses and victims, the presentation of evidence and the protection of arrested persons.

4. The Trial Chamber shall conduct trials of accused persons in accordance with this Statute and the Rules of Court.

5. The Trial Chamber shall receive and conduct appeals from the Pre-Trial Chamber in accordance with Article 18 of this Statute.

6. The Appeals Chamber shall receive and conduct appeals from the Trial Chamber in accordance with Article 18 of this Statute.

Article 10

Quorum

Article 21 of the Statute (Quorum) is replaced with the following:

1. The General Affairs Section of the Court shall be duly constituted by three (3) judges.

2. The Human and Peoples Rights Section of the Court shall be duly constituted by three (3) judges.

3. The Pre-Trial Chamber of the International Criminal Law Section of the Court shall be duly constituted by one (1) judge.

4. The Trial Chamber of the International Criminal Law Section of the Court shall be duly constituted by three (3) judges.

5. The Appellate Chamber of the International Criminal Law Section of the Court shall be duly constituted by five (5) judges.

Article 11

Presidency and Vice Presidency

Article 22 (Presidency, Vice-Presidency and Registry) is replaced with the following:

"Article 22

Presidency and Vice Presidency

1. At its first ordinary session after the election of the Judges, the Full Court shall elect a President and a Vice President of the Court.

2. The President and Vice President shall serve for a period of two (2) years, and may be re-elected once.

3. The President and Vice President shall, in consultation with the Members of the Court and as provided for in the Rules of Court, assign Judges to the Sections.

4. The President shall preside over all sessions of the Full Court. In the event of the President being unable to sit during a session, the session shall be presided over by the Vice President.

5. The President and Vice President shall reside at the seat of the Court."

Article 12

Presidency and Vice Presidency

After Article 22 (Presidency and Vice-Presidency) add the following as Articles 22A and 22B:

"Article 22A

The Office of the Prosecutor

1. The Office of the Prosecutor shall comprise a Prosecutor and two Deputy Prosecutors.

2. The Prosecutor and Deputy Prosecutors shall be elected by the Assembly from amongst candidates who shall be nationals of States Parties nominated by States Parties.

3. The Prosecutor shall serve for a single, non-renewable term of seven (7) years.

4. The Deputy Prosecutors shall serve for a term of four (4) years, renewable once.

5. The Prosecutor and the Deputy Prosecutors shall be persons of high moral character, be highly competent in and have extensive practical experience in the conduct of investigations, trial and prosecution of criminal cases.

6. The Office of the Prosecutor shall be responsible for the investigation and prosecution of the crimes specified in this Statute and shall act independently as a separate organ of the Court and shall not seek or receive instructions from any State Party or any other source.

7. The Office of the Prosecutor shall have the power to question suspects, victims and witnesses and collect evidence, including the power to conduct on-site investigations.

8. The Prosecutor shall be assisted by such other staff as may be required to perform the functions of the Office of the Prosecutor effectively and efficiently.

9. The staff of the Office of the Prosecutor shall be appointed by the Prosecutor in accordance with the Staff Rules and Regulations of the African Union.

10.The remuneration and conditions of service of the Prosecutor and Deputy Prosecutors shall be determined by the Assembly on the recommendation of the Court made through the Executive Council.

Article 22B

The Registry

1. The Registry shall comprise of a Registrar and three Assistant Registrars.

2. The Court shall appoint the Registrar and Assistant Registrars, in accordance with the Staff Rules and Regulations of the African Union.

3. The Registrar shall serve for a single, non-renewable term of seven years.

4. The Assistant Registrars shall serve for a term of four (4) years, renewable once.

5. The Registry shall be headed by a Registrar who, under the direction of the President, shall be responsible for the non-judicial aspects and servicing of the Court. The Registrar shall be the principal administrative and accounting officer of the Court, and shall ensure that proper books of accounts are kept in accordance with the financial rules and regulations of the African Union.

6. The Registrar and Assistant Registrars shall be persons of high moral character, be highly competent in and have extensive practical managerial experience.

7. The Registrar shall be assisted by such other staff as may be necessary for the effective and efficient performance of the functions of the Registry.

8. The staff of the Registry shall be appointed by the Court in accordance with the Staff Rules and Regulations of the African Union.

9. The Registrar shall set up, within the Registry:

a. A Victims and Witnesses Unit, which shall provide, in consultation with the Court and the Office of the Prosecutor, as appropriate, protective measures and security arrangements, counselling and other appropriate assistance for witnesses, victims who appear before the Court and others who are at risk on account of testimony given by such witnesses. The Unit personnel shall include experts in the management of trauma.

b. A Defence Counsel and Detention Management Unit, which shall provide services to the defence and manage the conditions of detention of suspects and accused persons.

10.The salaries and conditions of service of the Registrar, Assistant Registrars and other staff of the Registry shall be determined by the Assembly on the proposal of the Court, through the Executive Council.

Article 12Bis

Conditions of Service of the Registrar and Members of the Registry

Article 24 of the Statute (Conditions of Service of the Registrar and Members of the Registry) is deleted.

Article 13

Under Chapter III (*Competence of the Court*) In Article 28 of the Statute (*Jurisdiction of the Court*), the insertion of a new sub-paragraph (d) as follows, with consequential renumbering of the existing paragraphs (d) to (h).

"… (d) The crimes contained in this Statute, subject to a right of appeal…"

Article 14

International Criminal Jurisdiction of the Court

Immediately after Article 28 (Jurisdiction of the Court), the insertion of new Articles 28A, 28B, 28C, 28D, 28E, 28F, 28G, 28H, 28I, 28I Bis, 28J, 28K, 28L, 28L Bis, 28M and 28N as follows:

"Article 28A

International Criminal Jurisdiction of the Court

1. Subject to the right of appeal, the International Criminal Law Section of the Court shall have power to try persons for the crimes provided hereunder:

1. Genocide
2. Crimes Against Humanity
3. War Crimes
4. The Crime of Unconstitutional Change of Government;
5. Piracy
6. Terrorism
7. Mercenarism
8. Corruption

9. Money Laundering
10. Trafficking in Persons
11. Trafficking in Drugs
12. Trafficking in Hazardous Wastes
13. Illicit Exploitation of Natural Resources
14. The Crime of Aggression

2. The Assembly may extend upon the consensus of States Parties the jurisdiction of the Court to incorporate additional crimes to reflect developments in international law.

3. The crimes within the Jurisdiction of the Court shall not be subject to any statute of limitations.

Article 28 B

Genocide

For the purposes of this Statute, "genocide" means any of the following acts committed with intent to destroy, in whole or in part, a national, ethnical, racial or religious group, as such:

a. Killing members of the group;

b. Causing serious bodily or mental harm to members of the group;

c. Deliberately inflicting on the group conditions of life calculated to bring about its physical destruction in whole or in part;

d. Imposing measures intended to prevent births within the group;

e. Forcibly transferring children of the group to another group;

f. Acts of rape that are intended to change the identity of a particular group.

Article 28 C

Crimes Against Humanity

1. For the purposes of this Statute, "crime against humanity" means any of the following acts when committed as part of a widespread or systematic attack or enterprise directed against any civilian population, with knowledge of the attack or enterprise:

a. Murder;

b. Extermination;

c. Enslavement;

d. Deportation or forcible transfer of population;

e. Imprisonment or other severe deprivation of physical liberty in violation of fundamental rules of international law;

f. Torture, cruel, inhuman and degrading treatment or punishment;

g. Rape, sexual slavery, enforced prostitution, forced pregnancy, enforced sterilization, or any other form of sexual violence of comparable gravity;

h. Persecution against any identifiable group or collectivity on political, racial, national, ethnic, cultural, religious, gender or other grounds that are universally recognized as impermissible under international law;

i. Enforced disappearance of persons;

j. The crime of apartheid;

k. Other inhumane acts of a similar character intentionally causing great suffering, or serious injury to body or mental or physical health.

2. For the purpose of paragraph 1:

a. "Attack directed against any civilian population" means a course of conduct involving the multiple commission of acts referred to in paragraph 1 against any civilian population, pursuant to or in furtherance of a State or organizational policy to commit such attack;

b. "Extermination" includes the intentional infliction of conditions of life, inter alia the deprivation of access to food and medicine, calculated to bring about the destruction of part of a population;

c. "Enslavement" means the exercise of any or all of the powers attaching to the right of ownership over a person and includes the exercise of such power in the course of trafficking in persons, in particular women and children;

d. "Deportation or forcible transfer of population" means forced displacement of the persons concerned by expulsion or other coercive acts from the area in which they are lawfully present, without grounds permitted under international law;

e. "Torture" means the intentional infliction of severe pain or suffering, whether physical or mental, upon a person in the custody or under the control of the accused; except that torture shall not include pain or suffering arising only from, inherent in or incidental to, lawful sanctions;

f. "Forced pregnancy" means the unlawful confinement of a woman forcibly made pregnant, with the intent of affecting the ethnic composition of any population or carrying out other grave violations of international law. This definition shall not in any way be interpreted as affecting national laws relating to pregnancy;

g. "Persecution" means the intentional and severe deprivation of fundamental rights contrary to international law by reason of the identity of the group or collectivity;

h. "The crime of apartheid" means inhumane acts of a character similar to those referred to in paragraph 1, committed in the context of an institutionalized regime of systematic oppression and domination by one racial group over any other racial group or groups and committed with the intention of maintaining that regime;

i. "Enforced disappearance of persons" means the arrest, detention or abduction of persons by, or with the authorization, support or acquiescence of, a State or a political organization, followed by a refusal to acknowledge that deprivation of freedom or to give information on the fate or whereabouts of those persons, with the intention of removing them from the protection of the law for a prolonged period of time.

Article 28 D

War Crimes

For the purposes of this Statute, "war crimes" means any of the offences listed, in particular when committed as part of a plan or policy or as part of a large scale commission of such crimes.

a. Grave breaches of the Geneva Conventions of 12 August 1949, namely, any of the following acts against persons or property protected under the provisions of the relevant Geneva Convention:

i. Wilful killing;

ii. Torture or inhuman treatment, including biological experiments;

iii. Wilfully causing great suffering, or serious injury to body or health;

iv. Extensive destruction and appropriation of property, not justified by military necessity and carried out unlawfully and wantonly;

v. Compelling a prisoner of war or other protected person to serve in the forces of a hostile Power;

vi. Wilfully depriving a prisoner of war or other protected person of the rights of fair and regular trial;

vii. Unlawful deportation or transfer or unlawful confinement;

viii. Taking of hostages.

b. Grave breaches of the First Additional Protocol to the Geneva Conventions of 8 June 1977 and other serious violations of the laws and customs applicable in international armed conflict, within the established framework of international law, namely, any of the following acts:

i. Intentionally directing attacks against the civilian population as such or against individual civilians not taking direct part in hostilities;

ii. Intentionally directing attacks against civilian objects, that is, objects which are not military objectives;

iii. Intentionally directing attacks against personnel, installations, material, units or vehicles involved in a humanitarian assistance or peacekeeping mission in accordance with the Charter of the United Nations, as long as they are entitled to the protection given to civilians or civilian objects under the international law of armed conflict;

iv. Intentionally launching an attack in the knowledge that such attack will cause incidental loss of life or injury to civilians or damage to civilian objects or widespread, long-term and severe damage to the natural environment which would be clearly excessive in relation to the concrete and direct overall military advantage anticipated;

v. Intentionally launching an attack against works or installations containing dangerous forces in the knowledge that such attack will cause excessive loss of life, injury to civilians or damage to civilian objects which will be excessive in relation to the concrete and direct overall military advantage anticipated;

vi. Attacking or bombarding, by whatever means, towns, villages, dwellings or buildings which are undefended and which are not military objectives;

vii. Killing or wounding a combatant who, having laid down his arms or having no longer means of defence, has surrendered at discretion;

viii. Making improper use of a flag of truce, of the flag or of the military insignia and uniform of the enemy or of the United Nations, as well as of the distinctive emblems of the Geneva Conventions, resulting in death or serious personal injury;

ix. The transfer, directly or indirectly, by the Occupying Power of parts of its own civilian population into the territory it occupies, or the deportation or transfer of all or parts of the population of the occupied territory within or outside this territory;

x. Intentionally directing attacks against buildings dedicated to religion, education, art, science or charitable purposes, historic monuments, hospitals and places where the sick and wounded are collected, provided they are not military objectives;

xi. Subjecting persons who are in the power of an adverse party to physical mutilation or to medical or scientific experiments of any kind which are neither justified by the medical, dental or hospital treatment of the person concerned nor carried out in his or her interest, and which cause death to or seriously endanger the health of such person or persons;

xii. Killing or wounding treacherously individuals belonging to the hostile nation or army;

xiii. Declaring that no quarter will be given;

xiv. Destroying or seizing the enemy's property unless such destruction or seizure be imperatively demanded by the necessities of war;

xv. Declaring abolished, suspended or inadmissible in a court of law the rights and actions of the nationals of the hostile party;

xvi. Compelling the nationals of the hostile party to take part in the operations of war directed against their own State, even if they were in the belligerent's service before the commencement of the war;

xvii. Pillaging a town or place, even when taken by assault;

xviii. Employing poison or poisoned weapons;

xix. Employing asphyxiating, poisonous or other gases, and all analogous liquids, materials or devices;

xx. Employing bullets which expand or flatten easily in the human body, such as bullets with a hard envelope which does not entirely cover the core or is pierced with incisions;

xxi. Employing weapons, projectiles and material and methods of warfare which are of a nature to cause superfluous injury or unnecessary suffering or which are inherently indiscriminate in violation of the international law of armed conflict;

xxii. Committing outrages upon personal dignity, in particular humiliating and degrading treatment;

xxiii. Committing rape, sexual slavery, enforced prostitution, forced pregnancy, enforced sterilization, or any other form of sexual violence also constituting a grave breach of the Geneva Conventions;

xxiv. Utilizing the presence of a civilian or other protected person to render certain points, areas or military forces immune from military operations;

xxv. Intentionally directing attacks against buildings, material, medical units and transport, and personnel using the distinctive emblems of the Geneva Conventions in conformity with international law;

xxvi. Intentionally using starvation of civilians as a method of warfare by depriving them of objects indispensable to their survival, including wilfully impeding relief supplies as provided for under the Geneva Conventions;

xxvii. Conscripting or enlisting children under the age of eighteen years into the national armed forces or using them to participate actively in hostilities;

xxviii. Unjustifiably delaying the repatriation of prisoners of war or civilians;

xxix. Wilfully committing practices of apartheid and other inhuman and degrading practices involving outrages upon personal dignity, based on racial discrimination;

xxx. Making non-defended localities and demilitarised zones the object of attack;

xxxi. Slavery and deportation to slave labour; xxxii. Collective punishments; xxxiii. Despoliation of the wounded, sick, shipwrecked or dead;

c. In the case of an armed conflict not of an international character, serious violations of article 3 common to the four Geneva Conventions of 12 August 1949, namely, any of the following acts committed against persons taking no active part in the hostilities, including members of armed forces who have laid down their arms and those placed hors de combat by sickness, wounds, detention or any other cause:

i. Violence to life and person, in particular murder of all kinds, mutilation, cruel treatment and torture;

ii. Committing outrages upon personal dignity, in particular humiliating and degrading treatment;

iii. Taking of hostages;

iv. The passing of sentences and the carrying out of executions without previous judgment pronounced by a regularly constituted court, affording all judicial guarantees which are generally recognized as indispensable.

d. Paragraph 1 (c) applies to armed conflicts not of an international character and thus does not apply to situations of internal disturbances and tensions, such as riots, isolated and sporadic acts of violence or other acts of a similar nature.

e. Other serious violations of the laws and customs applicable in armed conflicts not of an international character, within the established framework of international law, namely, any of the following acts:

i. Intentionally directing attacks against the civilian population as such or against individual civilians not taking direct part in hostilities;

ii. Intentionally directing attacks against buildings, material, medical units and transport, and personnel using the distinctive emblems of the Geneva Conventions in conformity with international law;

iii. Intentionally directing attacks against personnel, installations, material, units or vehicles involved in a humanitarian assistance or peacekeeping mission in accordance with the Charter of the United Nations, as long as they are entitled to the protection given to civilians or civilian objects under the international law of armed conflict;

iv. Intentionally directing attacks against buildings dedicated to religion, education, art, science or charitable purposes, historic monuments, hospitals and places where the sick and wounded are collected, provided they are not military objectives;

v. Pillaging a town or place, even when taken by assault;

vi. Committing rape, sexual slavery, enforced prostitution, forced pregnancy, enforced sterilization, and any other form of sexual violence also constituting a serious violation of article 3 common to the four Geneva Conventions;

vii. Conscripting or enlisting children under the age of eighteen years into armed forces or groups or using them to participate actively in hostilities;

viii. Ordering the displacement of the civilian population for reasons related to the conflict, unless the security of the civilians involved or imperative military reasons so demand;

ix. Killing or wounding treacherously a combatant adversary;

x. Declaring that no quarter will be given;

xi. Subjecting persons who are in the power of another party to the conflict to physical mutilation or to medical or scientific experiments of any kind which are neither justified by the medical, dental or hospital treatment of the person concerned nor carried out in his or her interest, and which cause death to or seriously endanger the health of such person or persons;

xii. Destroying or seizing the property of an adversary unless such destruction or seizure be imperatively demanded by the necessities of the conflict;

xiii. Employing poison or poisoned weapons;

xiv. Employing asphyxiating, poisonous or other gases, and all analogous liquids, materials or devices;

xv. Employing bullets which expand or flatten easily in the human body, such as bullets with a hard envelope which does not entirely cover the core or is pierced with incisions;

xvi. Intentionally using starvation of civilians as a method of warfare by depriving them of objects indispensable to their survival, including wilfully impeding relief supplies;

xvii. Utilizing the presence of a civilian or other protected person to render certain points, areas or military forces immune from military operations;

xviii. Launching an indiscriminate attack resulting in death or injury to civilians, or an attack in the knowledge that it will cause excessive incidental civilian loss, injury or damage;

xix. Making non-defended localities and demilitarised zones the object of attack;

xx. Slavery;

xxi. Collective punishments;

xxii. Despoliation of the wounded, sick, shipwrecked or dead

f. Paragraph 1 (e) applies to armed conflicts not of an international character and thus does not apply to situations of internal disturbances and tensions, such as riots, isolated and sporadic acts of violence or other acts of a similar nature. It applies to armed conflicts that take place in the territory of a State when there is protracted armed conflict between governmental authorities and organized armed groups or between such groups.

g. Using nuclear weapons or other weapons of mass destruction.

"BRACKETED"

[Article 28E *

The Crime of Unconstitutional Change of Government[2]

---

[2] Due to an objection placed by Egypt, where a coup d'état had legitimised the government, the AU formed an *ad-hoc* committee to study this specific crime. This committee met in 2012 and 2013 and its following observations and comments ensued: i) The Peace and Security Council (PSC) is the Organ responsible for determining that an unconstitutional change of government has occurred in conformity with the various legal instruments of the Union (i.e. PSC Protocol and African Charter on Democracy, Elections and Governance); ii) Involving political bodies in judicial processes is not advisable; iii) Need to specify the penalties for the crime of an unconstitutional change of government as a deterrent; iv) Replace 'democratically elected government' with just 'government' so as not to legitimize the overthrow of any government irrespective of how that government came into power; v) What are the criteria for determining that an uprising is popular? vi) Sub-paragraph 3 should be deleted all together as it is more political than legal and in any case does not add or subtract from the Court its jurisdiction over this crime; vii) Sub-paragraph 2 which reads: "For purposes of this Statute, 'democratically elected government' has the same meaning as contained in AU instruments", should be deleted since the term 'democratically elected government' is not only defined under AU legal instruments but also under international law; viii) Those who act violently to overthrow a government within the context of a popular uprising should be protected under the draft Protocol as well; ix) Criminal responsibility is not collective but an individual one, hence it is difficult to criminalize an uprising that is undertaken collectively; x) The eventual

1. For the purposes of this Statute, "unconstitutional change of government" means committing or ordering to be committed the following acts, with the aim of illegally accessing or maintaining power:

a. A *putsch* or *coup d'état* against a democratically elected government;

b. An intervention by mercenaries to replace a democratically elected government;

c. Any replacement of a democratically elected government by the use of armed dissidents or rebels or through political assassination;

d. Any refusal by an incumbent government to relinquish power to the winning party or candidate after free, fair and regular elections;

e. Any amendment or revision of the Constitution or legal instruments, which is an infringement on the principles of democratic change of government or is inconsistent with the Constitution;

f. Any substantial modification to the electoral laws in the last six (6) months before the elections without the consent of the majority of the political actors.

2. For purposes of this Statute, "democratically elected government" has the same meaning as contained in AU instruments.

3. [Any act of a sovereign people peacefully exercising their inherent right which results in a change of government shall not constitute an offence under this

Article.] "]

---

wording of the definition should not reflect a right to overthrow a government through a popular uprising, but should be worded in a way that will not encourage a change of government other than the constitution provides and which may act as catalysts to destabilize most of the fledgling democracies on the continent. After extensive deliberations, the workshop decided not to propose any amendments to sub-articles 1 and 2 of Article 28E as adopted by the Assembly but agreed to amend sub-article 3 which was the only contentious provision. In this regard, the workshop adopted a reformulated sub-article 3 to read as follows: "*Where the Peace and Security Council of the African Union determines that the change of government through popular uprising is not an unconstitutional change of government, the Court shall not be seized of the matter.*"

Article 28F

Piracy

Piracy consists of any of the following acts:

a. any illegal acts of violence or detention, or any act of depredation, committed for private ends by the crew or the passengers of a private boat, ship or a private aircraft, and directed:

i. on the high seas, against another boat, ship or aircraft, or against persons or property on board such boat, ship or aircraft;

ii. against a boat, ship, aircraft, persons or property in a place outside the jurisdiction of any State

b. any act of voluntary participation in the operation of a boat, ship or of an aircraft with knowledge of facts making it a pirate boat, ship or aircraft;

c. any act of inciting or of intentionally facilitating an act described in subparagraph (a) or (b).

Article 28 G

Terrorism

For the purposes of this Statute, "terrorism" means any of the following acts:

A. Any act which is a violation of the criminal laws of a State Party, the laws of the African Union or a regional economic community recognized by the African Union, or by international law, and which may endanger the life, physical integrity or freedom of, or cause serious injury or death to, any person, any number or group of persons or causes or may cause damage to public or private property, natural resources, environmental or cultural heritage and is calculated or intended to:

1. intimidate, put in fear, force, coerce or induce any government, body, institution, the general public or any segment thereof, to do or abstain from doing any act, or to adopt or abandon a particular standpoint, or to act according to certain principles; or

2. disrupt any public service, the delivery of any essential service to the public or to create a public emergency; or

3. create general insurrection in a State.

B. Any promotion, sponsoring, contribution to, command, aid, incitement, encouragement, attempt, threat, conspiracy, organizing, or procurement of any person, with the intent to commit any act referred to in sub-paragraph (a) (1) to(3).

C. Notwithstanding the provisions of paragraphs A and B, the struggle waged by peoples in accordance with the principles of international law for their liberation or self-determination, including armed struggle against colonialism, occupation, aggression and domination by foreign forces shall not be considered as terrorist acts.

D. The acts covered by international Humanitarian Law, committed in the course of an international or non-international armed conflict by government forces or members of organized armed groups, shall not be considered as terrorist acts.

E. Political, philosophical, ideological, racial, ethnic, religious or other motives shall not be a justifiable defence against a terrorist act.

Article 28H

Mercenarism

1. For the purposes of this Statute:

a. A mercenary is any person who:

i. Is specially recruited locally or abroad in order to fight in an armed conflict;

ii. Is motivated to take part in the hostilities essentially by the desire for private gain and, in fact, is promised, by or on behalf of a party to the conflict, material compensation;

iii. Is neither a national of a party to the conflict nor a resident of territory controlled by a party to the conflict;

iv. Is not a member of the armed forces of a party to the conflict; and

v. Has not been sent by a State which is not a party to the conflict on official duty as a member of its armed forces.

b. A mercenary is also any person who, in any other situation:

i. Is specially recruited locally or abroad for the purpose of participating in a concerted act of violence aimed at:

1. Overthrowing a legitimate Government or otherwise undermining the constitutional order of a State;

2. Assisting a government to maintain power;

3. Assisting a group of persons to obtain power; or

4. Undermining the territorial integrity of a State;

ii. Is motivated to take part therein essentially by the desire for private gain and is prompted by the promise or payment of material compensation;

iii. Is neither a national nor a resident of the State against which such an act is directed;

iv. Has not been sent by a State on official duty; and

v. Is not a member of the armed forces of the State on whose territory the act is undertaken.

2. Any person who recruits, uses, finances or trains mercenaries, as defined in paragraph (1) (a) or (b) above commits an offence.

3. A mercenary, as defined in paragraph (1) (a) or (b) above, who participates directly in hostilities or in a concerted act of violence, as the case may be, commits an offence.

Article 28I

Corruption

1. For the purposes of this Statute, the following shall be deemed to be acts of corruption if they are of a serious nature affecting the stability of a state, region or the Union:

a. The solicitation or acceptance, directly or indirectly, by a public official, his/her family member or any other person, of any goods of monetary value, or other benefit, such as a gift, favour, promise or advantage for himself or herself or for another person or entity, in exchange for any act or omission in the performance of his or her public functions;

b. The offering or granting, directly or indirectly, to a public official, his/family member or any other person, of any goods of monetary value, or other benefit, such as a gift, favour, promise or advantage for himself or herself or for another person or entity, in exchange for any act or omission in the performance of his or her public functions;

c. Any act or omission in the discharge of his or her duties by a public official, his/her family member or any other person for the purpose of illicitly obtaining benefits for himself or herself or for a third party;

d. The diversion by a public official, his/her family member or any other person, for purposes unrelated to those for which they were intended, for his or her own benefit or that of a third party, of any property belonging to the State or its agencies, to an independent agency, or to an individual, that such official has received by virtue of his or her position;

e. The offering or giving, promising, solicitation or acceptance, directly or indirectly, of any undue advantage to or by any person who directs or works for, in any capacity, a private sector entity, for himself or herself or for anyone else, for him or her to act, or refrain from acting, in breach of his or her duties;

f. The offering, giving, solicitation or acceptance directly or indirectly, or promising of any undue advantage to or by any person who asserts or confirms that he or she is able to exert any improper influence over the decision making of any person performing functions in the public or private sector in consideration thereof, whether the undue advantage is for himself or herself or for anyone else, as well as the request, receipt or the acceptance of the offer or the promise of such an advantage, in consideration of that influence, whether or not the influence is exerted or whether or not the supposed influence leads to the intended result;

g. Illicit enrichment;

h. The use or concealment of proceeds derived from any of the acts referred to in this Article.

2. For the purposes of this Statute "Illicit enrichment" means the significant increase in the assets of a public official or any other person which he or she cannot reasonably explain in relation to his or her income.

Article 28I Bis

Money Laundering

1. For the purposes of this Statute, “Money Laundering” means: any act of

i. Conversion, transfer or disposal of property, knowing that such property is the proceeds of corruption or related offences for the purpose of concealing or disguising the illicit origin of the property or of helping any person who is involved in the commission of the offence to evade the legal consequences of his or her action.

ii. Concealment or disguise of the true nature, source, location, disposition, movement or ownership of or rights with respect to property which is the proceeds of corruption or related offences;

iii. Acquisition, possession or use of property with the knowledge at the time of receipt, that such property is the proceeds of corruption or related offences

iv. Participation in, association with or conspiracy to commit, attempts to commit and aiding, abetting, facilitating and counselling the commission of any of the offences established in accordance with this article.

2. Nothing in this article shall be interpreted as prejudicing the power of the Court to make a determination as to the seriousness of any act or offence.

Article 28J

Trafficking in persons

For the purposes of this Statute:

1. "Trafficking in persons" means the recruitment, transportation, transfer, harbouring or receipt of persons, by means of the threat or use of force or other forms of coercion, of abduction, of fraud, of deception, of the abuse of power or of a position of vulnerability or of the giving or receiving of payments or benefits to achieve the consent of a person having control over another person, for the purpose of exploitation.

2. Exploitation shall include the exploitation of the prostitution of others or other forms of sexual exploitation, forced labour or services, slavery or practices similar to slavery, servitude or the removal of organs;

3. The consent of a victim of trafficking in persons to the intended exploitation set forth in subparagraph (1) of this article shall be irrelevant where any of the means set forth in subparagraph (1) have been used;

4. The recruitment, transportation, transfer, harbouring or receipt of a child for the purpose of exploitation shall be considered "trafficking in persons" even if this does not involve any of the means set forth in subparagraph (1) of this article;

Article 28K

Trafficking in drugs

1. For the purposes of this Statute, “trafficking in drugs” means:

a. The production, manufacture, extraction, preparation, offering, offering for sale, distribution, sale, delivery on any terms whatsoever, brokerage, dispatch, dispatch in transit, transport, importation or exportation of drugs;

b. The cultivation of opium poppy, coca bush or cannabis plant;

c. The possession or purchase of drugs with a view to conducting one of the activities listed in (a);

d. The manufacture, transport or distribution of precursors knowing that they are to be used in or for the illicit production or manufacture of drugs.

2. The conduct described in paragraph 1 shall not be included in the scope of this Statute when it is committed by perpetrators for their own personal consumption as defined by national law.

3. For the purposes of this Article:

a. “Drugs” shall mean any of the substances covered by the following United Nations Conventions:

> a. the 1961 Single Convention on Narcotic Drugs, as amended by the 1972 Protocol Amending the Single Convention on Narcotic Drugs of 1961;
>
> b. The 1971 Vienna Convention on Psychotropic Substances.

b. “Precursors” shall mean any substance scheduled pursuant to Article 12 of the United Nations Convention against Illicit Traffic in Narcotic Drugs and Psychotropic Substances of 20 December 1988.

Article 28L

Trafficking in Hazardous Wastes

1. For the purposes of this Statute, any import or failure to re-import, trans-boundary movement, or export of hazardous wastes proscribed by the Bamako Convention on the Ban of the Import into Africa and the Control of Trans-boundary Movement and Management of Hazardous Wastes within Africa, adopted in Bamako, Mali, in January 1991 shall constitute the offence of trafficking in hazardous waste.

2. The following substances shall be "hazardous wastes" for the purpose of this statute:

a. Wastes that belong to any category contained in Annex I of the Bamako Convention;

b. Wastes that are not covered under paragraph (a) above but are defined as, or are considered to be, hazardous wastes by the domestic legislation of the State of export, import or transit;

c. Wastes which possess any of the characteristics contained in Annex II of the Bamako Convention;

d. Hazardous substances which have been banned, cancelled or refused registration by government regulatory action, or voluntarily withdrawn from registration in the State of manufacture, for human health or environmental reasons.

3. Wastes which, as a result of being radioactive, are subject to any international control systems, including international instruments, applying specifically to radioactive materials are included in the scope of this Convention.

4. Wastes which derive from the normal operations of a ship, the discharge of which is covered by another international instrument, shall not fall within the scope of this Convention.

5. For the purposes of this Article, "failure to re-import" shall have the same meaning assigned to it in the Bamako Convention.

6. The export of hazardous waste into a Member State for the purpose of rendering it safe shall not constitute an offence under this Article.

Article 28L Bis

Illicit Exploitation of Natural Resources

For the purpose of this Statute, "Illicit exploitation of natural resources" means any of the following acts if they are of a serious nature affecting the stability of a state, region or the Union:

a. Concluding an agreement to exploit resources, in violation of the principle of peoples" sovereignty over their natural resources;

b. Concluding with state authorities an agreement to exploit natural resources, in violation of the legal and regulatory procedures of the State concerned;

c. Concluding an agreement to exploit natural resources through corrupt practices;

d. Concluding an agreement to exploit natural resources that is clearly onesided; (sic)

e. Exploiting natural resources without any agreement with the State concerned;

f. Exploiting natural resources without complying with norms relating to the protection of the environment and the security of the people and the staff; and

g. Violating the norms and standards established by the relevant natural resource certification mechanism.

Article 28M

Crime of Aggression

A. For the purpose of this Statute "Aggression " means the use, intentionally and knowingly, of armed force or any other hostile act by a state, a group of States, an organization of States or non-State actor(s) or by any foreign or external entity, against the sovereignty, political independence, territorial integrity and human security of the population of a State Party, which, by its character, gravity and scale, constitutes a manifest violation of the Charter of the United Nations or the Constitutive Act of the African Union.

B. The following shall constitute acts of aggression, regardless of a declaration of war by a State, group of States, organizations of States, or non-State actor(s) or by any foreign entity:

1. The use of armed forces against the sovereignty, territorial integrity and political independence of any state, or any other act inconsistent with the provisions of the Constitutive Act of the African Union and the Charter of the United Nations.

2. The invasion or attack by armed forces against the territory of a State, or military occupation however temporary, resulting from such an invasion or attack, or any annexation by the use of force of the territory of a State or part thereof.

3. The bombardment by the armed forces of a State against the territory of another State or the use of any weapons by a State against the territory of another State.

4. The blockade of the ports, coasts or airspace of a State by the armed forces of another State.

5. The attack by the armed forces of a State on the land, sea or air forces, or marine and fleets of another State.

6. The use of the armed forces of one State which are within the territory of another State with the agreement of the receiving State, in contravention of the conditions provided for in the African Union Non-Aggression and Common Defence Pact or any extension of their presence in such territory beyond the termination of the agreement.

7. The action of a State in allowing its territory, which it has placed at the disposal of another State to be used by another State for perpetrating an act of aggression against a third State.

8. The sending by ,or on behalf of a State or the provision of any support to armed bands, groups , irregulars , mercenaries and other organized transnational criminal groups which may carry out hostile acts against a State ,of such gravity as to amount to the acts listed above ,or its substantial involvement therein.

9. Technological assistance of any kind, intelligence and training to another state for use in committing acts of aggression against another State.

Article 28N

Modes of Responsibility

An offence is committed by any person who, in relation to any of the crimes or offences provided for in this Statute:

i. Incites, instigates, organizes, directs, facilitates, finances, counsels or participates as a principal, co-principal, agent or accomplice in any of the offences set forth in the present Statute;

ii. Aids or abets the commission of any of the offences set forth in the present Statute;

iii. Is an accessory before or after the fact or in any other manner participates in a collaboration or conspiracy to commit any of the offences set forth in the present Statute;

iv. Attempts to commit any of the offences set forth in the present Statute.

Article 15

Entities Eligible to Submit Cases to the Court

In paragraph 1(b) of Article 29 of the Statute (Entities Eligible to Submit Cases to the Court), immediately after the words "The Assembly" insert:

"the Peace and Security Council"

Add a new paragraph (d)

(d) "The Office of the Prosecutor"

Article 16

Other Entities Eligible to Submit Cases to the Court

The deletion of paragraph (f) of Article 30 of the Statute (Other Entities Eligible to Submit Cases to the Court), and the insertion of the following new paragraph:

"(f) African individuals or African Non-Governmental Organizations with Observer Status with the African Union or its organs or institutions, but only with regard to a State that has made a Declaration accepting the competence of the Court to receive cases or applications submitted to it directly. The Court shall not receive any case or application involving a State Party which has not made a Declaration in accordance with Article 9(3) of this Protocol."

Article 17

Institution of Proceedings before the International Criminal Law Section

UNDER CHAPTER FOUR (PROCEDURE), immediately after Article 34 of the Statute (Institution of Proceedings before the Human Rights Section, the insertion of new Articles 34A and 34B as follows:

"Article 34A

Institution of Proceedings before the International Criminal Law Section

1. Subject to the provisions of Articles 22A and 29, cases brought before the International Criminal Law Section of the Court shall be brought by or in the name of the Prosecutor.

2. The Registrar shall forthwith give notice of the case to all parties concerned, as well as the Chairperson of the Commission.

Article 34B

Institution of Proceedings before the Appellate Chamber

The Court shall define the procedures for appeals in its Rules."

Article 18

Representation of Parties

In Article 36 of the Statute (Representation of the Parties), the insertion of a new paragraph (6) as follows, with consequential renumbering of the existing paragraph 6:

"… 6. A person accused under the international criminal jurisdiction of this Court shall have the right to represent himself or herself in person or through an agent…"

Article 19

Sentences and Penalties

Immediately after Article 43 of the Statute (Judgments and Decisions) the insertion of a new Article 43A as follows:

"Article 43A

Sentences and Penalties under the International Criminal Jurisdiction of the Court

1. Without prejudice to the provisions of Article 43, the Court shall pronounce judgment and impose sentences and/ or penalties, other than the death penalty, for persons convicted of international crimes under this Statute.

2. For the avoidance of doubt, the penalties imposed by the Court shall be limited to prison sentences and/ or pecuniary fines.

3. The sentences and/ or penalties shall be pronounced in public and, wherever possible, in the presence of the accused.

4. In imposing the sentences and/ or penalties, the Court should take into account such factors as the gravity of the offence and the individual circumstances of the convicted person.

5. In addition to the sentences and/ or penalties, the Court may order the forfeiture of any property, proceeds or any asset acquired unlawfully or

by criminal conduct, and their return to their rightful owner or to an appropriate Member State."

Article 20

Compensation and Reparations to Victims

Article 45 of the Statute (Compensation), including its title, is deleted in its entirety and substituted with the following:

"Article 45

Compensation and Reparations to Victims

1. Without prejudice to the provisions of paragraph (i) of Article 28, the Court shall establish in the Rules of Court principles relating to reparations to, or in respect of, victims, including restitution, compensation and rehabilitation. On this basis, in its decision the Court may, either upon request or on its own motion in exceptional circumstances, determine the scope and extent of any damage, loss or injury to, or in respect of, victims and will state the principles on which it is acting.

2. With respect to its international criminal jurisdiction, the Court may make an order directly against a convicted person specifying appropriate reparations to, or in respect of, victims, including restitution, compensation and rehabilitation.

3. Before making an order the Court may invite and take account of representations from or on behalf of the convicted person, victims, other interested persons or interested States.

4. Nothing in this article shall be interpreted as prejudicing the rights of victims under national or international law."

Article 21

Binding Force and Execution of Judgments

Paragraph 2 of Article 46 of the Statute (Binding Force and Execution of Judgments) is deleted and substituted with the following: -

"… 2. Subject to the provisions of Article 18 (as amended) and paragraph 3 of Article 41 of the Statute, the judgment of the Court is final…"

Article 22

Provisions Specific to the International Criminal Jurisdiction of the Court

Under Chapter IV (PROCEDURE), immediately at the end of Article 46 (Binding Force and Execution of Judgments), the insertion of a new CHAPTER IVA and new Articles 46A to 46L as follows:

"CHAPTER IVA: PROVISIONS SPECIFIC TO THE INTERNATIONAL CRIMINAL JURISDICTION OF THE COURT

Article 46A

Rights of Accused

1. All accused shall be equal before the Court.

2. The accused shall be entitled to a fair and public hearing, subject to measures ordered by the Court for the protection of victims and witnesses.

3. The accused shall be presumed innocent until proven guilty according to the provisions of this Statute.

4. In the determination of any charge against the accused pursuant to this Statute, he or she shall be entitled to the following minimum guarantees, in full equality:

a. To be informed promptly and in detail in a language that he or she understands of the nature and cause of the charge against him or her;

b. To have adequate time and facilities for the preparation of his or her defence and to communicate freely with counsel of his or her own choosing;

c. To be tried without undue delay;

d. To be tried in his or her presence, and to defend himself or herself in person or through legal assistance of his or her own choosing; to be informed, if he or she does not have legal assistance, of this right; and to have legal assistance assigned to him or her, in any case where the interests of justice so require, and without payment by him or her in any such case if he or she does not have sufficient means to pay for it;

e. To examine, or have examined, the witnesses against him or her and to obtain the attendance and examination of witnesses on his or her behalf under the same conditions as witnesses against him or her;

f. To have the free assistance of an interpreter if he or she cannot understand or speak the language used in the Court;

g. Not to be compelled to testify against himself or herself or to confess guilt.

h. To have the judgment pronounced publicly

i. To be informed of his /her right to appeal.

Article 46B

Individual Criminal Responsibility

1. A person who commits an offence under this Statute shall be held individually responsible for the crime.

2. Without prejudice to the immunities provided for under international law, the official position of any accused person, whether as Head of State or Government, Minister or as a responsible government official, shall not relieve such person of criminal responsibility nor mitigate punishment.

3. The fact that any of the acts referred to in article 28A of the present Statute was committed by a subordinate does not relieve his or her superior of criminal responsibility if he or she knew or had reason to know that the subordinate was about to commit such acts or had done so and the superior failed to take the necessary and reasonable measures to prevent such acts or to punish the perpetrators thereof.

4. The fact that an accused person acted pursuant to the order of a Government or of a superior shall not relieve him or her of criminal responsibility, but may be considered in mitigation of punishment if the Court determines that justice so requires.

Article 46C

Corporate Criminal Liability

1. For the purpose of this Statute, the Court shall have jurisdiction over legal persons, with the exception of States.

2. Corporate intention to commit an offence may be established by proof that it was the policy of the corporation to do the act which constituted the offence.

3. A policy may be attributed to a corporation where it provides the most reasonable explanation of the conduct of that corporation.

4. Corporate knowledge of the commission of an offence may be established by proof that the relevant knowledge was possessed within the corporation and that the culture of the corporation caused or encouraged the commission of the offence.

5. Knowledge may be possessed within a corporation even though the relevant information is divided between corporate personnel.

6. The criminal responsibility of legal persons shall not exclude the criminal responsibility of natural persons who are perpetrators or accomplices in the same crimes.

7. For the purpose of this section:

"Corporate culture" means an attitude, policy, rule, course of conduct or practice existing within the body corporate generally or within the area of the body corporate in which the relevant activities take place.

Article 46D

Exclusion of Jurisdiction over Persons under the age of eighteen

The Court shall have no jurisdiction over any person who was under the age of eighteen (18) years at the time of the alleged commission of a crime.

Article 46E

Temporal Jurisdiction

1. The Court has jurisdiction only with respect to crimes committed after the entry into force of this Protocol and Statute.

2. If a State becomes a Party to this Protocol and Statute after its entry into force, the Court may exercise its jurisdiction only with respect to crimes committed after the entry into force of this Protocol and Statute for that State.

Article 46E bis

Preconditions to the exercise of Jurisdiction

1. A State which becomes a Party to this Protocol and Statute thereby accepts the jurisdiction of the Court with respect to the crimes referred to in Article 28A.

2. The Court may exercise its jurisdiction if one or more of the following conditions apply:

(a) The State on the territory of which the conduct in question occurred or, if the crime was committed on board a vessel or aircraft ,the State of registration of that vessel or aircraft.

(b) The State of which the person accused of the crime is a national.

(c) When the victim of the crime is a national of that State.

(d) Extraterritorial acts by non-nationals which threaten a vital interest of that State.

3. If the acceptance of a State which is not a Party to this Statute is required under paragraph 2, that State may, by declaration lodged with the Registrar, accept the exercise

Article 46F

Exercise of Jurisdiction

The Court may exercise its jurisdiction with respect to a crime referred to in article 28A in accordance with the provisions of this Statute if:

1. A situation in which one or more of such crimes appears to have been committed is referred to the Prosecutor by a State Party;

2. A situation in which one or more of such crimes appears to have been committed is referred to the Prosecutor by the Assembly of Heads of State and Government of the African Union or the Peace and Security Council of the African Union.

3. The Prosecutor has initiated an investigation in respect of such a crime in accordance with article 46G.

Article 46G

The Prosecutor

1. The Office of the Prosecutor may initiate investigations proprio motu on the basis of information on crimes within the jurisdiction of the Court.

2. The Office of the Prosecutor shall analyse the seriousness of information received. For this purpose, he or she may seek additional information from States, organs of the African Union or United Nations, intergovernmental or non-governmental organizations, or other reliable sources that he or she deems appropriate, and may receive written or oral testimony.

3. If the Office of the Prosecutor concludes that there is a reasonable basis to proceed with an investigation, it shall submit to a Pre-Trial Chamber a request for authorization of an investigation, together with any supporting material collected. Victims may make representations to the Pre-Trial Chamber, in accordance with the Rules of the Court.

4. If the Pre-Trial Chamber, upon examination of the request and supporting material, considers that there is a reasonable basis to proceed with an investigation, and that the case appears to fall within the jurisdiction of the Court, it shall authorize the commencement of the investigation, without prejudice to subsequent determinations by the Court with regard to the jurisdiction and admissibility of a case.

5. The refusal of the Pre-Trial Chamber to authorize the investigation shall not preclude the presentation of a subsequent request by the Office of the Prosecutor based on new facts or evidence regarding the same situation.

6. If, after the preliminary examination referred to in paragraphs 1 and 2, the Office of the Prosecutor concludes that the information provided does not constitute a reasonable basis for an investigation, it shall inform those who provided the information. This shall not preclude the Office of the Prosecutor from considering further information submitted to him or her regarding the same situation in the light of new facts or evidence.

Article 46H

Complementary Jurisdiction

1. The jurisdiction of the Court shall be complementary to that of the National Courts, and to the Courts of the Regional Economic Communities where specifically provided for by the Communities.

2. The Court shall determine that a case is inadmissible where:

a. The case is being investigated or prosecuted by a State which has jurisdiction over it, unless the State is unwilling or unable to carry out the investigation or prosecution;

b. The case has been investigated by a State which has jurisdiction over it and the State has decided not to prosecute the person concerned, unless the decision resulted from the unwillingness or inability of the State to prosecute;

c. The person concerned has already been tried for conduct which is the subject of the complaint;

d. The case is not of sufficient gravity to justify further action by the Court.

3. In order to determine that a State is unwilling to investigate or prosecute in a particular case, the Court shall consider, having regard to the principles of due process recognized by international law, whether one or more of the following exist, as applicable:

a. The proceedings were or are being undertaken or the national decision was made for the purpose of shielding the person concerned from criminal responsibility for crimes within the jurisdiction of the Court;

b. There has been an unjustified delay in the proceedings which in the circumstances is inconsistent with an intent to bring the person concerned to justice;

c. The proceedings were not or are not being conducted independently or impartially, and they were or are being conducted in a manner which, in the circumstances, is inconsistent with an intent to bring the person concerned to justice.

4. In order to determine that a State is unable to investigate or prosecute in a particular case, the Court shall consider whether, due to a total or substantial collapse or unavailability of its national judicial system, the State is unable to obtain the accused or the necessary evidence and testimony or otherwise unable to carry out its proceedings.

Article 46I

Non bis in idem

1. Except as provided in this Statute, no person shall be tried before the Court with respect to conduct which formed the basis of crimes for which the person has been convicted or acquitted by the Court.

2. Except in exceptional circumstances, no person who has been tried by another court for conduct proscribed under Article 28A of this Statute shall be tried by the Court with respect to the same conduct unless the proceedings in the other Court:

a. Were for the purpose of shielding the person concerned from criminal responsibility for crimes within the jurisdiction of the Court;

b. Otherwise were not conducted independently or impartially in accordance with the norms of due process recognized by international law and were conducted in a manner which, in the circumstances, was inconsistent with an intent to bring the person concerned to justice.

3. In considering the penalty to be imposed on a person convicted of a crime under the present Statute, the Court shall take into account the extent to which any penalty imposed by another Court on the same person for the same act has already been served.

Article 46J

Enforcement of Sentences

1. A sentence of imprisonment shall be served in a State designated by the Court from a list of States which have indicated to the Court their willingness to accept sentenced persons.

2. Such imprisonment shall be as provided for in a prior agreement between the Court and a receiving State and in accordance with the criteria as set out in the Rules of Court.

Article 46Jbis

Enforcement of fines and forfeiture measures

1. States Parties shall give effect to fines or forfeitures ordered by the Court without prejudice to the rights of bona fide third parties, and in accordance with the procedure provided for in their national law.

2. If a State Party is unable to give effect to an order for forfeiture, it shall take measures to recover the value of the proceeds, property or assets ordered by the Court to be forfeited, without prejudice to the rights of bona fide third parties.

3. The Court shall determine in its Rules how real or movable property obtained by a State as a result of its enforcement of a judgment or order may be dealt with.

Article 46K

Pardon or Commutation of Sentences

If, pursuant to the applicable law of the State in which the convicted person is imprisoned, he or she is eligible for pardon or commutation of sentence, the State concerned shall notify the Court accordingly. There shall only be pardon or commutation of sentence if the Court so decides on the basis of the interests of justice and the general principles of law.

Article 46L

Co-operation and Judicial Assistance

1. States Parties shall co-operate with the Court in the investigation and prosecution of persons accused of committing the crimes defined by this Statute.

2. States Parties shall comply without undue delay with any request for assistance or an order issued by the Court, including but not limited to:

a. The identification and location of persons;

b. The taking of testimony and the production of evidence;

c. The service of documents;

d. The arrest, detention or extradition of persons;

e. The surrender or the transfer of the accused to the Court."

f. The identification, tracing and freezing or seizure of proceeds, property and assets and instrumentalities of crimes for the purpose of eventual forfeiture, without prejudice to the rights of bona fide third parties.

g. Any other type of assistance which is not prohibited by the law of the requested State, with a view to facilitating the investigation and prosecution of crimes within the jurisdiction of the court.

3. The Court shall be entitled to seek the co-operation or assistance of regional or international courts, non-States Parties or co-operating partners of the African Union and may conclude Agreements for that purpose.

Article 46M

Trust Fund

1. The Assembly shall, by a Decision, establish, within the jurisdiction of the Court, a Trust Fund for legal aid and assistance and for the benefit of victims of crimes or human rights violations and their families.

2. The Court may order money and other property collected through fines or forfeiture to be transferred, by order of the Court, to the Trust Fund.

3. The Trust Fund shall be managed according to criteria to be determined by the Assembly.

Article 23

Annual Activity Report

Article 57 of the Statute (Annual Activity Report) is deleted and substituted with the following:

"The Court shall submit to the Assembly an annual report on its work during the previous year. The report shall specify, in particular, the pending and concluded investigations, prosecutions and decisions and the cases in which a party has not complied with the judgment, sentence, order or penalty of the Court."

APPENDIX II

DRAFT PROTOCOL ON AMENDMENTS TO THE PROTOCOL ON THE STATUTE OF AFRICAN UNION (DRAFT) MODEL NATIONAL LAW ON UNIVERSAL JURISDICTION OVER INTERNATIONAL CRIMES[1]

PREAMBLE

Recognizing that certain crimes are of most serious concern to the Member States of the African Union and the international community as a whole that they must not go unpunished;

Recalling the Constitutive Act of the African Union, and in particular Article 4(h) which provides for the right of the Union to intervene in respect of grave circumstances namely genocide, war crimes and crimes against humanity;

Further recalling the African Charter on Human and Peoples' Rights;

Mindful of the need for effective prosecution to be ensured by taking appropriate measures at the national level in order to enhance international co-operation;

Recognizing also that the primary responsibility for the prosecution of international crimes rests with States;

Now be it enacted by (Parliament, etc. of the country) as follows:

---

[1] See (AU) EXP/MIN/Legal/VI Rev.1. This model national law has been prepared pursuant to concerns expressed in successive Decisions of the Assembly of Heads of State and Government of the Union, in Decisions Assembly/AU/Dec. 199(XI), Assembly/AU/Dec. 213(XII), Assembly/AU/Dec. 233(XIII), Assembly/AU/Dec. 292(XV) and Assembly/AU/Dec. 335(XVI). The intention and expectation is that Member States will adopt this Model Law and will legislate accordingly, in accordance with their national constitutional arrangements.

1. Purpose

A law to provide for the exercise by (name of the country) of universal jurisdiction over international crimes and for connected matters and to give effect to its obligations under international law.

2. Definitions

Except where otherwise expressly indicated or where the context otherwise requires, the following definitions shall apply throughout the law:

"Court" means the highest Court with original jurisdiction;

"1961 Convention" means Single Convention on Narcotic Drugs adopted in 1961 and entered into force on 13 December 1964;

"1961 Convention as amended" means Singe Convention on Narcotic Drugs, 1961, as amended by the 1972 Protocol amending the Single Convention on Narcotic Drugs;

"1972 Protocol" means the Protocol amending the Single Convention on Narcotic Drugs, 1961.

3. Objectives

The objectives of this law are to:

a) Combat impunity for crimes under this law, and prevent and punish such crimes;

b) Confer jurisdiction on the courts to try crimes under this law;

c) Define the jurisdiction of the courts over such crimes;

d) Define the crimes that are punishable under this law, and provide for the power to prosecute those responsible for such crimes;

e) Ensure fair trial of persons accused of such crimes;

f) Give effect to immunities enjoyed by foreign State officials under international law;

g) Provide for the extradition of persons accused of committing the crimes in this law;

h) Provide for mutual legal assistance and co-operation amongst States;

i) Provide for the punishment of the persons convicted of the crimes under this law; and

j) Provide for rehabilitation and reparation for victims.

4. Jurisdiction

4(1). The Court shall have jurisdiction to try any person alleged to have committed any crime under this law, regardless of whether such a crime is alleged to have been committed in the territory of the State or abroad and irrespective of the nationality of the victim, provided that such a person shall be within the territory of the State.

4(2). In exercising jurisdiction under this law, a Court shall accord priority to the court of the State in whose territory the crime is alleged to have been committed, provided that the State is willing and able to prosecute.

5. Power to Prosecute

The Prosecuting Authority shall have the power to prosecute before the Court any person in the territory of the State who is alleged to have committed an offense under this law where the information available to the Prosecuting Authority provides a reasonable basis to believe that a crime under this law has been or is being committed.

6. Rights of an Accused Person

A person alleged to have committed a crime under this law shall have the highest standard of rights guaranteed to any accused person in the State.

7. Witness Protection

The Prosecuting Authority and the Court shall ensure that any witness is accorded the necessary protection.

8. Crimes

The following crimes shall be punishable under this law: Genocide, Crimes against humanity, War Crimes, Piracy, Trafficking in drugs and Terrorism.

9. Genocide

1. For the purposes of this Law, "genocide" means any of the following acts committed with intent to destroy, in whole or in part, a national, ethnical, racial or religious group, as such:

a. Killing members of the group;

b. Causing serious bodily or mental harm to members of the group;

c. Deliberately inflicting on the group conditions of life calculated to bring about its physical destruction in whole or in part;

d. Imposing measures intended to prevent births within the group;

e. Forcibly transferring children of the group to another group;

f. Acts of rape that are intended to change the identity of a particular group.

10. Crimes against Humanity

1. For the purposes of this Law, "crime against humanity" means any of the following acts when committed as part of a widespread or systematic attack or enterprise directed against any civilian population, with knowledge of the attack or enterprise:

a. Murder;

b. Extermination;

c. Enslavement;

d. Deportation or forcible transfer of population;

i. Imprisonment or other severe deprivation of physical liberty in violation of fundamental rules of international law;

j. Torture, cruel, inhuman and degrading treatment or punishment;

k. Rape, sexual slavery, enforced prostitution, forced pregnancy, enforced sterilization, or any other form of sexual violence of comparable gravity;

l. Persecution against any identifiable group or collectivity on political, racial, national, ethnic, cultural, religious, gender or other grounds that are universally recognized as impermissible under international law;

m. Enforced disappearance of persons;

n. The crime of apartheid;

o. Other inhumane acts of a similar character intentionally causing great suffering, or serious injury to body or mental or physical health.

2. For the purpose of paragraph 1:

a. "Attack directed against any civilian population" means a course of conduct involving the multiple commission of acts referred to in paragraph 1 against any civilian population, pursuant to or in furtherance of a State or organizational policy to commit such attack;

b. "Extermination" includes the intentional infliction of conditions of life, inter alia the deprivation of access to food and medicine, calculated to bring about the destruction of part of a population;

c. "Enslavement" means the exercise of any or all of the powers attaching to the right of ownership over a person and includes the exercise of such power in the course of trafficking in persons, in particular women and children;

d. "Deportation or forcible transfer of population" means forced displacement of the persons concerned by expulsion or other coercive acts from the area in which they are lawfully present, without grounds permitted under international law;

e. "Torture" means the intentional infliction of severe pain or suffering, whether physical or mental, upon a person in the custody or under the control of the accused; except that torture shall not include pain or suffering arising only from, inherent in or incidental to, lawful sanctions;

f. "Forced pregnancy" means the unlawful confinement of a woman forcibly made pregnant, with the intent of affecting the ethnic composition of any population or carrying out other grave violations of international law. This definition shall not in any way be interpreted as affecting national laws relating to pregnancy;

g. "Persecution" means the intentional and severe deprivation of fundamental rights contrary to international law by reason of the identity of the group or collectivity;

h. "The crime of apartheid" means inhumane acts of a character similar to those referred to in paragraph 1, committed in the context of an institutionalized regime of systematic oppression and domination by one racial group over any other racial group or groups and committed with the intention of maintaining that regime;

i. "Enforced disappearance of persons" means the arrest, detention or abduction of persons by, or with the authorization, support or acquiescence of, a State or a political organization, followed by a refusal to acknowledge that deprivation of freedom or to give information on the fate or whereabouts of those persons, with the intention of removing them from the protection of the law for a prolonged period of time.

11. War Crimes

For the purposes of this Law, "war crimes" means any of the offences listed , in particular when committed as part of a plan or policy or as part of a large scale commission of such crimes.

a. Grave breaches of the Geneva Conventions of 12 August 1949, namely, any of the following acts against persons or property protected under the provisions of the relevant Geneva Convention:

ix. Wilful killing;[2]

x. Torture or inhuman treatment, including biological experiments;

xi. Wilfully causing great suffering, or serious injury to body or health;

xii. Extensive destruction and appropriation of property, not justified by military necessity and carried out unlawfully and wantonly;

xiii. Compelling a prisoner of war or other protected person to serve in the forces of a hostile Power;

xiv. Wilfully depriving a prisoner of war or other protected person of the rights of fair and regular trial;

xv. Unlawful deportation or transfer or unlawful confinement;

xvi. Taking of hostages.

b. Grave breaches of the First Additional Protocol to the Geneva Conventions of 8 June 1977 and other serious violations of the laws and customs applicable in international armed conflict, within the established framework of international law, namely, any of the following acts:

xxxiv. Intentionally directing attacks against the civilian population as such or against individual civilians not taking direct part in hostilities;

xxxv. Intentionally directing attacks against civilian objects, that is, objects which are not military objectives;

xxxvi. Intentionally directing attacks against personnel, installations, material, units or vehicles involved in a humanitarian assistance or peacekeeping mission in accordance with the Charter of the United

[2] We have reproduced here the same numbering as the original report.

Nations, as long as they are entitled to the protection given to civilians or civilian objects under the international law of armed conflict;

xxxvii.Intentionally launching an attack in the knowledge that such attack will cause incidental loss of life or injury to civilians or damage to civilian objects or widespread, long-term and severe damage to the natural environment which would be clearly excessive in relation to the concrete and direct overall military advantage anticipated;

xxxviii. Intentionally launching an attack against works or installations containing dangerous forces in the knowledge that such attack will cause excessive loss of life, injury to civilians or damage to civilian objects which will be excessive in relation to the concrete and direct overall military advantage anticipated;

xxxix. Attacking or bombarding, by whatever means, towns, villages, dwellings or buildings which are undefended and which are not military objectives;

xl. Killing or wounding a combatant who, having laid down his arms or having no longer means of defence, has surrendered at discretion;

xli. Making improper use of a flag of truce, of the flag or of the military insignia and uniform of the enemy or of the United Nations, as well as of the distinctive emblems of the Geneva Conventions, resulting in death or serious personal injury;

xlii. The transfer, directly or indirectly, by the Occupying Power of parts of its own civilian population into the territory it occupies, or the deportation or transfer of all or parts of the population of the occupied territory within or outside this territory;

xliii. Intentionally directing attacks against buildings dedicated to religion, education, art, science or charitable purposes, historic monuments, hospitals and places where the sick and wounded are collected, provided they are not military objectives;

xliv. Subjecting persons who are in the power of an adverse party to physical mutilation or to medical or scientific experiments of any kind which are neither justified by the medical, dental or hospital treatment of the person concerned nor carried out in his or her interest, and which cause death to or seriously endanger the health of such person or persons;

xlv. Killing or wounding treacherously individuals belonging to the hostile nation or army;

xlvi. Declaring that no quarter will be given;

xlvii. Destroying or seizing the enemy's property unless such destruction or seizure be imperatively demanded by the necessities of war;

xlviii. Declaring abolished, suspended or inadmissible in a court of law the rights and actions of the nationals of the hostile party;

xlix. Compelling the nationals of the hostile party to take part in the operations of war directed against their own country, even if they were in the belligerent's service before the commencement of the war;

l. Pillaging a town or place, even when taken by assault;

li. Employing poison or poisoned weapons;

lii. Employing asphyxiating, poisonous or other gases, and all analogous liquids, materials or devices;

liii. Employing bullets which expand or flatten easily in the human body, such as bullets with a hard envelope which does not entirely cover the core or is pierced with incisions;

liv. Employing weapons, projectiles and material and methods of warfare which are of a nature to cause superfluous injury or unnecessary suffering or which are inherently indiscriminate in violation of the international law of armed conflict

lv. Committing outrages upon personal dignity, in particular humiliating and degrading treatment;

lvi. Committing rape, sexual slavery, enforced prostitution, forced pregnancy, enforced sterilization, or any other form of sexual violence also constituting a grave breach of the Geneva Conventions;

lvii. Utilizing the presence of a civilian or other protected person to render certain points, areas or military forces immune from military operations;

lviii. Intentionally directing attacks against buildings, material, medical units and transport, and personnel using the distinctive emblems of the Geneva Conventions in conformity with international law;

lix. Intentionally using starvation of civilians as a method of warfare by depriving them of objects indispensable to their survival, including wilfully impeding relief supplies as provided for under the Geneva Conventions;

lx. Conscripting or enlisting children under the age of eighteen years into the national armed forces or using them to participate actively in hostilities;

lxi. Unjustifiably delaying the repatriation of prisoners of war or civilians;

lxii. Wilfully committing practices of apartheid and other inhuman and degrading practices involving outrages upon personal dignity, based on racial discrimination.

lxiii. Making non-defended localities and demilitarised zones the object of attack;

lxiv. Slavery and deportation to slave labour;

lxv. Collective punishments;

lxvi. Despoliation of the wounded, sick, shipwrecked or dead;

c. In the case of an armed conflict not of an international character, serious violations of article 3 common to the four Geneva Conventions of 12 August 1949, namely, any of the following acts committed against persons taking no active part in the hostilities, including members of armed forces who have laid down their arms and those placed hors de combat by sickness, wounds, detention or any other cause:

v. Violence to life and person, in particular murder of all kinds, mutilation, cruel treatment and torture;

vi. Committing outrages upon personal dignity, in particular humiliating and degrading treatment;

vii. Taking of hostages;

viii. The passing of sentences and the carrying out of executions without previous judgment pronounced by a regularly constituted court, affording all judicial guarantees which are generally recognized as indispensable.

d. Paragraph c) applies to armed conflicts not of an international character and thus does not apply to situations of internal disturbances and tensions, such as riots, isolated and sporadic acts of violence or other acts of a similar nature.

e. Other serious violations of the laws and customs applicable in armed conflicts not of an international character, within the established framework of international law, namely, any of the following acts:

xxiii. Intentionally directing attacks against the civilian population as such or against individual civilians not taking direct part in hostilities;

xxiv. Intentionally directing attacks against buildings, material, medical units and transport, and personnel using the distinctive emblems of the Geneva Conventions in conformity with international law; xxv. Intentionally directing attacks against personnel, installations, material, units or vehicles involved in a humanitarian assistance or peacekeeping mission in accordance with the Charter of the United Nations, as long as they are entitled to the protection given to civilians or civilian objects under the international law of armed conflict;

xxvi. Intentionally directing attacks against buildings dedicated to religion, education, art, science or charitable purposes, historic monuments, hospitals and places where the sick and wounded are collected, provided they are not military objectives;

xxvii. Pillaging a town or place, even when taken by assault;

xxviii. Committing rape, sexual slavery, enforced prostitution, forced pregnancy, enforced sterilization, and any other form of sexual violence also constituting a serious violation of article 3 common to the four Geneva Conventions;

xxix. Conscripting or enlisting children under the age of eighteen years into armed forces or groups or using them to participate actively in hostilities;

xxx. Ordering the displacement of the civilian population for reasons related to the conflict, unless the security of the civilians involved or imperative military reasons so demand;

xxxi. Killing or wounding treacherously a combatant adversary;

xxxii. Declaring that no quarter will be given;

xxxiii. Subjecting persons who are in the power of another party to the conflict to physical mutilation or to medical or scientific experiments of any kind which are neither justified by the medical, dental or hospital treatment of the person concerned nor carried out in his or her interest, and which cause death to or seriously endanger the health of such person or persons;

xxxiv. Destroying or seizing the property of an adversary unless such destruction or seizure be imperatively demanded by the necessities of the conflict;

xxxv. Employing poison or poisoned weapons;

xxxvi. Employing asphyxiating, poisonous or other gases, and all analogous liquids, materials or devices;

xxxvii.Employing bullets which expand or flatten easily in the human body, such as bullets with a hard envelope which does not entirely cover the core or is pierced with incisions

xxxviii. Intentionally using starvation of civilians as a method of warfare by depriving them of objects indispensable to their survival, including wilfully impeding relief supplies;

xxxix. Utilizing the presence of a civilian or other protected person to render certain points, areas or military forces immune from military operations;

xl. Launching an indiscriminate attack resulting in death or injury to civilians, or an attack in the knowledge that it will cause excessive incidental civilian loss, injury or damage;

xli. Making non-defended localities and demilitarised zones the object of attack;

xlii. Slavery;

xliii. Collective punishments;

xliv. Despoliation of the wounded, sick, shipwrecked or dead

f. Paragraph e) applies to armed conflicts not of an international character and thus does not apply to situations of internal disturbances and tensions, such as riots, isolated and sporadic acts of violence or other acts of a similar nature. It applies to armed conflicts that take place in the territory of a State when there is protracted armed conflict between governmental authorities and organized armed groups or between such groups.

g. Using nuclear weapons or other weapons of mass destruction.

12. Piracy

For the purpose of this law, Piracy consists of any of the following acts:

a. any illegal acts of violence or detention, or any act of depredation, committed for private ends by the crew or the passengers of a private boat, ship or a private aircraft, and directed:

i. on the high seas, against another boat, ship or aircraft, or against persons or property on board such boat, ship or aircraft;

ii. against a boat, ship, aircraft, persons or property in a place outside the jurisdiction of any State

d. any act of voluntary participation in the operation of a boat, ship or of an aircraft with knowledge of facts making it a pirate boat, ship or aircraft;

e. any act of inciting or of intentionally facilitating an act described in subparagraph (a) or (b).

13. Trafficking in drugs

1. For the purposes of this Law, trafficking in drugs means:

e. The production, manufacture, extraction, preparation, offering, offering for sale, distribution, sale, delivery on any terms whatsoever, brokerage, dispatch, dispatch in transit, transport, importation or exportation of drugs;

f. The cultivation of opium poppy, coca bush or cannabis plant;

g. The possession or purchase of drugs with a view to conducting one of the activities listed in (a);

h. The manufacture, transport or distribution of precursors knowing that they are to be used in or for the illicit production or manufacture of drugs.

2. The conduct described in paragraph 1 shall not be included in the scope of this Statute when it is committed by perpetrators for their own personal consumption as defined by national law.

3. For the purposes of this Article:

c. "Drugs" shall mean any of the substances covered by the following United Nations Conventions:

i. the 1961 Single Convention on Narcotic Drugs, as amended by the 1972 Protocol Amending the Single Convention on Narcotic Drugs of 1961;

ii. the 1971 Vienna Convention on Psychotropic Substances.

d. "Precursors" shall mean any substance scheduled pursuant to Article 12 of the United Nations Convention against Illicit Traffic in Narcotic Drugs and Psychotropic Substances of 20 December 1988.

14. Terrorism

For the purposes of this Law, "terrorism" means any of the following acts:

A. Any act which is a violation of the criminal laws of a State Party, the laws of the African Union or a regional economic community recognized by the African Union, or by international law, and which may endanger the life, physical integrity or freedom of, or cause serious injury or death to, any person, any number or group of persons or causes or may cause damage to public or private property, natural resources, environmental or cultural heritage and is calculated or intended to:

4. intimidate, put in fear, force, coerce or induce any government, body, institution, the general public or any segment thereof, to do or abstain from doing any act, or to adopt or abandon a particular standpoint, or to act according to certain principles; or

5. disrupt any public service, the delivery of any essential service to the public or to create a public emergency; or

6. create general insurrection in a State.

B. Any promotion, sponsoring, contribution to, command, aid, incitement, encouragement, attempt, threat, conspiracy, organizing, or procurement of any person, with the intent to commit any act referred to in sub-paragraph (a) (1) to(3).

C. Notwithstanding the provisions of paragraphs A and B, the struggle waged by peoples in accordance with the principles of international law for their liberation or self-determination, including armed struggle against colonialism, occupation, aggression and domination by foreign forces shall not be considered as terrorist acts.

D. The acts covered by international Humanitarian Law, committed in the course of an international or non-international armed conflict by government forces or members of organized armed groups, shall not be considered as terrorist acts.

E. Political, philosophical, ideological, racial, ethnic, religious or other motives shall not be a justifiable defence against a terrorist act.

15. Individual Criminal Responsibility

An offence is committed by any person who, in relation to any of the crimes or offences under this law:

I. Incites, instigates, organizes, directs, facilitates, finances, counsels or participates as a principal, co-principal, agent or accomplice in any of the offences set forth in the present law;

II. Aids or abets the commission of any of the offences set forth in the present law;

III.Is an accessory before or after the fact or in any other manner participates in a collaboration or conspiracy to commit any of the offences set forth in the present law;

IV.Attempts to commit any of the offences set forth in the present law.

16. Jurisdictional Immunities

The jurisdiction provided under Article 4 of this law shall apply subject to any national or international law on immunities.

17. Extradition

17 (1). The crimes under this law shall be extraditable offences.

17(2). The State shall endeavour to expedite extradition requests, provided that fair trial standards and other procedural guarantees are assured.

17(3). Where the State does not extradite a person alleged to have committed a crime prohibited under this law, the Prosecuting Authority shall prosecute such a person, subject to jurisdictional immunities as provided for in this law.

18. Mutual Legal Assistance

18(1). The Prosecuting Authority shall request and afford other States, to the extent possible, the widest measure of mutual legal assistance in investigations, prosecutions and judicial proceedings in relation to the prosecution of the crimes in this law.

18 (2). Mutual legal assistance to be afforded in accordance with this clause may be requested for any of the following purposes:

a) Taking evidence or statements from persons;

b) Effecting service of judicial documents;

c) Executing searches and seizures;

d) Examining objects and sites;

e) Providing information and evidentiary items;

f) Providing originals or certified copies of relevant documents and records, including bank, financial, corporate or business records;

g) Identifying, tracing or confiscating proceeds, property, instrumentalities or other things for evidential and preservation purposes.

18(3).The Prosecuting Authority may afford other States any other forms of mutual legal assistance under this law.

18(4). The provisions of this clause shall not affect the obligations under any other treaty, bilateral or multilateral, which governs or will govern, in whole or in part, mutual legal assistance in criminal matters.

19. Punishment

1. Any person convicted under this law shall be liable to a sentence commensurate with the gravity of the offence and the individual circumstances of the convicted person.

2. In imposing a sentence, the Court may deduct the time, if any, previously spent in detention in accordance with an order of the Court. The Court may deduct any time otherwise spent in detention in connection with conduct underlying the crime.

3. In addition to imprisonment, the Court may order:

a) A fine

b) A forfeiture of proceeds, property and assets derived directly or indirectly from that crime, without prejudice to the rights of bona fide third parties.

4. The Court may make an order directly against a convicted person specifying appropriate reparations to, or in respect of, victims, including restitution, compensation and rehabilitation.

5. Before making an Order the Court may invite and take account of representations from or on behalf of the convicted person, victims, other interested persons or interested States.

20. Entry into force

This law shall enter into force at such time as the State or Minister responsible shall determine.

BIBLIOGRAPHY

ADACHI, S., "The Asian Concept", in *International Dimensions of Humanitarian Law*, Edited by Henry Dunant Institute and UNESCO, Martinus Nijhoff, Dordrecht, (1988). Pp. 13-20.

ADJAMI, M., "African Courts, International Law, and Comparative Case Law: Chimera or Emerging Human Rights Jurisprudence?", *Michigan Journal of International Law*, vol. 24, (2002). Pp. 103-167.

AFRICAN (BANJUL) CHARTER ON HUMAN AND PEOPLES' RIGHTS. Adopted 27th June 1981.

AFRICAN COMMISSION ON HUMAN AND PEOPLES' RIGHTS, *Annual Activity Reports* 1987-2010.

—. *Commission's Research and Information Visit to Libya on 11-25 August 2005*, adopted at the Commission's 40th Ordinary Session, 15-29 November 2006.

—. *Guidelines for National Periodic Reports*, 1988-9.

—. *The Robben Island Guidelines or RIG*, 32nd Ordinary Session in October 2002. Approved by the Conference of Heads of State and Government of the African Union, Maputo, Jul 2003.

—. *Rules of Procedure* of the ACHPR.

AFRICAN COURT ON HUMAN AND PEOPLES' RIGHTS, *Rules of Procedure of the ACtHPR.*

—. Case of *Michelot Yogogombaye v. the Republic of Senegal*, Application No. 001/2008, No. 39

—. Case of *Michelot Yogogombaye v. the Republic of Senegal*, Application No. 001/2008, Separate Opinion of Judge Fatsah Ouguergouz, No. 40

—. Application no. 004/2011, In the Matter of *African Commission on Human and Peoples' rights v. Great Socialist Peoples' Libyan Arab Jamahiriya*, Order for Provisional Measures, 25th March 2011.

AFRICAN UNION, *African Charter on the Rights and Welfare of the Child*, 1999.

—. *Constitutive Act* (2001).

—. *Decision on the Budget of the African Union for the 2010 Financial Year*, adopted by the Sixteenth Ordinary Session of the Executive Council in Addis Ababa, Ethiopia on 1st February 2010, Doc. EX.CL/537(XVI).

—. *Protocol to the African Charter on Human and Peoples' Rights on the Establishment of an African Court on Human and Peoples' Rights*, 1998.

—. *Protocol of the Court of Justice of the African Union*, adopted by the 2nd Ordinary Session of the Assembly of the Union, Maputo, 11th July 2003.

—. *Protocol on the Statute of the African Court of Justice and Human Rights*, adopted by the Assembly of the Union, Sharm El-Sheikh, Egypt, July 2008.

—. *Protocol to the African Charter on Human and Peoples' Rights on The Rights of Women in Africa*, adopted by the 2nd Ordinary Session of the Assembly of the Union, in Maputo, on 11th July 2003.

—. *Draft Protocol on Amendments to The Protocol on The Statute of The African Court of Justice and Human Rights, Revisions up to September 2013, Exp/Min/Iv/Rev.7.*

—. *African Union (Draft) Model National Law on Universal Jurisdiction over International Crimes, EXP/MIN/Legal/VI Rev.1*

—. *Report on Workshop on the Definition of Crimes of Unconstitutional Change of Government and Financial and Structural Implications of an international crimes section within the African Court of Justice and Human Rights, 19-20 December 2012, Arusha, Tanzania, AfCHPR/ LEGAL/DOC.3.*

AGUILAR CAVALLO, G., "La Internacionalización del Derecho Constitucional", *Estudios Constitucionales*, vol. 5, No. 001, Centro de Estudios Constitucionales, Santiago de Chile, (2007).Pp. 223-281.

AHMED and APPIAGYEI-ATUA, "Human Rights in Africa – A New Perspective on Linking the Past to the Present", *McGill Law Journal*, vol 41, (1995-1996). Pp. 819-854.

AKEHURST, M., *A Modern Introduction to International Law*, George Allen and Unwin Ltd, London, 1970.

ALSTON, P., "A Third Generation of Solidarity Rights: Progressive Development or Obfuscation of International Human Rights Law?",*Netherlands International Law Review*, vol. 29, No. 3, (1982). Pp. 307-322.

AMOAKO BAAH, R., *Human Rights in Africa: The Conflict of Implementation*, University Press of America, Lanham, Maryland, 2000.

ANZILOTTI, D., "Volonta e responsabilita nella stipulazione dei trattati intemazionali", *Rivista di diritto internazionale*, (1910). Pp. 3-46.

AQUINAS, T., *The Summa Theologica*, Treatise on Law, Benziger Bros. Ed, New York, 1947, questions 90-108.

—. *Summa Theologica*, Secunda Secundae, Christian Classics, Westminster, Maryland, 1920, question 40.

ARISTOTLE, *The Politics*, Book 7(1). Translated by Carnes Lord, The University of Chicago Press, Chicago, 1984.

AUSTIN, J., *Lectures on Jurisprudence or the Philosophy of Positive Law*, vol. 1, 5th Ed, R. Campbell (ed), London, 1885.

—. "The Province of Jurisprudence Determined", (1832), Available at *HeinOnline* (*http://heinonline.org*), Sat Apr 16 11:47:43 2011.

AYALA CORAO, C.M. "La Ejecución de Sentencias de la Corte Interamericana de Derechos Humanos", *Estudios Constitucionales*, vol. 5, Universidad de Talca, (2007). Pp. 127-201.

AYUGI, T., *Political Order, Complementarity and Human Equality: A Thomistic Defence of their Compatibility*, Doctoral thesis, Pontifical University of the Holy Cross, Rome, 2002.

BADAWI EL-SHEIKH, I., "The African Commission on Human and Peoples' Right: Prospects and Problems", *Netherlands Quarterly of Human Rights* - NQHR, vol 7, (1989). Pp. 272-283.

BAEHR, P.R., *The Role of Human Rights in Foreign Policy*, 2nd Edition, Macmillan, Hampshire, 1996.

BALUARTE, D. C. and De VOS, C. M., *Judgment to Justice: Implementing International and Regional Human Rights Decisions*, Open Society Justice Initiative, Open Society Foundations, New York, 2010.

BANGAMWABO, F.X., "International criminal justice and the protection of human rights in Africa", published online by the Konrad Adenauer Stiftung, KAS International. Available at: *http://www.kas.de/upload/auslandshomepages/namibia/Human_Rights _in_Africa/5_Bangamwabo.pdf*

BARICAKO, G., "Introductory Preface: The African Charter and the African Commission on Human and People's Rights", published in Malcolm, E. and Murray, R. (Eds), *The African Charter on Human and Peoples' Rights: the system in practice 1986-2006*, 2nd Edition, Cambridge University Press, Cambridge, (2008).

BEDERMAN, D.J. and JALLOH, C.C., "Michelot Yogogombaye v. Republic of Senegal", *The American Journal of International Law*, Vol. 104, No. 4, (2010). Pp. 620-628.

BEDJAOUI, M. (ed), *International Law: Achievements and Prospects*, UNESCO & Martinus Nijhoff Publishers, Paris, 1991.

BELLO, E., "The African Charter on Human and Peoples' Rights", *Recueil des Cours*, vol. 194, Académie de Droit International, The Hague, (1985). Pp. 9-268.

BENEDEK, W. "Human Rights in a Multi-Cultural Perspective: The African Charter and the Human Right to Development", in Ginther K. and W. Benedek (Ed), *New Perspectives and Conceptions of International Law. An Afro-European Dialogue*, Supplement 6, Springer Verlag, Vienna, (1983).

BENN, S.I. and STANKIEWICZ, J.W. (ed), *In Defense of Sovereignty*, Oxford University Press, New York, 1969.

—. "The Uses of Sovereignty", *Political Studies*, vol 3 (1955). Pp. 109-122.

BENTHAM, J., *Works*, vol.I, Stevenson and Co., Edinburgh, 1838.

BERGER, R., "The Presidential Monopoly of Foreign Treaties", *Michigan Law Review*, vol. 71, (1972-73). Pp. 1-58.

BHALLA, R.S., *Concepts of Jurisprudence*, Nairobi University Press, Nairobi, 1990.

BLACKSTONE, Sir W., *Commentaries on the Laws of England*, Clarendon Press, Oxford, 1765. Reprinted by Dawsons of Pall Mall, London, 1966.

BLAY, S., "Territorial Integrity and Political Independence", *Max Planck Encyclopedia of Public International Law*, *www.mpepil.com*, Oxford University Press, (2011).

BLIX, H., "The Requirement of Ratification", *British Year Book of International Law*, vol. 30, (1953).Pp.352-380.

BLOOM, W., *Personal Identity, National Identity and International Relations*, Cambridge University Press, Cambridge, 1990.

BOCZEK, B.A., *International Law: A dictionary*, Scarecrow Press, Lanham, 2005.

BONFIELD, A. E., "Military and foreign affairs function rule-making under the APA", *Michigan Law Review*, vol. 71 (1972). Pp. 221-358.

BOYE, A., "The Application of the Rules of International Public Law in Municipal Legal Systems", in Bedjaoui, M. (ed), *International Law: Achievements and Prospects*, UNESCO & Martinus Nijhoff Publishers, Paris, (1991).

BREWER-CARÍAS, A., *Constitutional Protection of Human Rights in Latin America: a comparative study of 'amparo' proceedings*, Cambridge University Press, New York, 2009.

BRYCE, J., *Studies in History and Jurisprudence*, vol. 1, Clarendon Press, New York, 1901.

BURKE, C.P., "Law and Ethics", paper presented at the Strathmore Ethics Conference (2004), published in Franceschi, L. and Ritho, A. (Eds), *Legal Ethics and Jurisprudence in Nation Building*, LawAfrica, Nairobi, 2005.

CARTY, A., "International Legal Personality and the End of the Subject: Natural Law and Phenomenological Responses to New Approaches to International Law", *Melbourne Journal of International Law*, vol. 6, (2005) pp. 534-552.

CASSESE, A., *International Law in a Divided World*, Clarendon Press, Oxford, 1994.

CAVALLI-SFORZA, MENOZZI and PIAZZA, *The History and Geography of Human Genes*, Princeton University Press, Princeton, 1994.

CICERO, *Tvscvlanarvm Dispvtationvm*, Liber Qvintvs, XXI. Available at: *http://www.thelatinlibrary.com/cicero/*

COMMITTEE OF EXPERTS ON CONSTITUTIONAL REVIEW *Harmonized Draft of the Proposed Constitution of Kenya*, Government Printers, Nairobi, 17th November, 2009.

COWELL, F., "The suspension of the Southern African Development Community Tribunal: A threat to human rights", *Consultancy Africa Intelligence*, 17th October 2010. Available at: *http://www.consultancyafrica.com*

CROFTS, R.A., "The Common Good in the Political Theory of Thomas Aquinas", *The Thomist*, vol. 37, (1973). Pp. 155-173.

DAHL, R.A., *A Preface to Democratic Theory*, Charles R. Walgreen Foundation Lecturers, University of Chicago Press, Chicago, 1956.

D'ASCOLI, S. and SCHERR, K., "The Rule of Prior Exhaustion of Local Remedies in the International Law Doctrine and its Application in the Specific Context of Human Rights Protection", *European University Institute*, vol. 02, (2007). Pp. 7-31. Available at: *https://docs.google.com/viewer?url= http://cadmus.eui.eu/bitstream/handle/1814/6701/LAW_2007_02.pdf%3Fsequence%3D1*

DELBRÜCK, J., "Prospects for a Word (Internal) Law?: Legal Developments in a Changing International System", *Indiana Journal of Global Legal Studies*, vol. 9, (2001-2002), Pp. 401–431.

—. "Structural Changes in the International System and its Legal Order: International Law in the Era of Globalization", *Swiss Review of International and European Law*, vol. 1, (2001). Pp. 1-36.

—. "Transnational Federalism: Problems and Prospects of Allocating Public Authority Beyond the State", *Indiana Journal of Global Legal Studies*, vol. 11, (2004). Pp. 31-56.

DEMBINSKI, L., *The Modern Law of Diplomacy*, Martinus Nijhoff, The Hague, 1988.

DETTER De LUPIS, I., *The Concept of International Law*, Norstedts Förlag, Stockholm, 1987.

DO NASCIMENTO, D.S., "Diplomacy", in Bernhardt (Ed) *Encyclopaedia of Public International Law*, Installment 9 Amsterdam, (1986).

DONNELY, J. and HOWARD, R., in Orlu, V., *The African Human Rights System: Its Law, Practice and Institutions*, Martinus Nijhoff, The Hague, 2001.

D'SA, R.M., "The African Charter on Human and Peoples' Rights: Problems and Prospects for Regional Action", *Australian Year Book of International Law*, vol 102, (1981). Pp. 101-130.

DRAPER, G.I.A.D., "The Development of International Humanitarian Law", in *International Dimensions of Humanitarian Law*, Edited by Henry Dunant Institute and UNESCO, Martinus Nijhoff, Dordrecht, (1988). Pp. 67-90.

DUMBUTSHENA, E., "The Role of the Judge in Advancing Human Rights", *Commonwealth Law Bulletin*, vol. 18, Issue 4, Oct (1992). Pp. 1298-1305.

EISSEN, M.-A., "La Convention et les devoirs de l'individu", in *La protection internationale des droits de l'homme dans le cadre européen*, Travaux du colloque de Strasbourg, Nov. 1960, éd. Dalloz, Paris, (1961).

ESTANISLAO, J., "A View on Development as a Calling to Continuing Improvement", Paper presented at the 7th Annual Conference, Strathmore University, Nairobi, 28th and 29th October 2010. (Currently in Press).

EUROPEAN SOCIAL CHARTER, 18th October 1961, 529 *UNTS* 89.

EVANS, M.D., "State Reporting Mechanism under the African Charter", in Evans and Murray (Ed), *The African Charter on Human and Peoples' Rights: the system in practice 1986-2006*, Cambridge University Press, Cambridge, (2008).

FINNEMORE, M., *National Interests in International Society*, Cornell University Press, New York, 1996.

FLASSAN, G., *Histoire Genérale et Raisonnée de la Diplomatie Francaise; Depuis la Fondation de la Monarchie*, Giguet et Michaud, Paris, 1809.

FOLEY, M., *The Silence of the Constitutions*, Routledge, London, 1989.

FRIEDRICH, C., "Constitutions of Modern States, Constitutions and Constitutionalism", in Sils, P. L. (ed) *The International Encyclopaedia of the Social Sciences*, Vol. 3, New York, (1968).

GARDEN, W., *Traité Complet de Diplomatie, au Theorie Generale des Relations Exterieures des Puissances de l' Europe, Librairie de Treuthel et Wurtz*, vol. I, Paris, 1833.

GARNETT, R., "The Internationalisation of Australian Jurisdiction and Judgments Law, *Australian Bar Review*, vol. 25, No. 3, (2004). Pp. 205-226.

GARRIDO FALLA, F., *Comentarios a la Constitución*, 3rd Edición, Civitas, Madrid, 2001.

GIERKE, O., *Political Theories of the Middle Ages*, Translated by Maitland, Cambridge University Press, Cambridge, 1930.

GIRKE, P. and KAMP, M., "Africa and the International Criminal Court: Stocktaking in Uganda", KAS International Reports, vol. 10, Sankt Augustin, (2010),pp. 76-77.

GOSE, M., *The African Charter on the Rights and Welfare of the Child*, Published by the Community Law Centre, University of Western Cape, Bellville, 2002.

GRAHAM, M., in Murison, K. (Ed), *Africa South of the Sahara*, 34th Edition, Europa Publications Limited, Volume 33, London, 2004.

GREEN, L.C., *Law and Society*, Oceana Publications Inc. Dobbs Terry, New York, 1975.

HAGAN, J. D., *Political Opposition and Foreign Policy in Comparative Perspective*, Lynne Rienner Publisher, London, 1993.

HARDY, M., *Modern Diplomatic Law*, Manchester University Press, Manchester, 1968.

HAMED, S., "The Islamic Concept of Humanitarian Law", in *International Dimensions of Humanitarian Law*, Edited by Henry Dunant Institute and UNESCO, Martinus Nijhoff, Dordrecht, (1988). Pp. 29-40.

HAMILTON, A., "Pacifus", no. 1, in Syrett, H. C. (ed.), *Federalist*, Columbia University Press, New York, XV, vol. 70, (1973).

HAMMER, "Allowing Genocide? An Analysis of Armed Activities on the Territory of the Congo, Jurisdictional Reservations, and the Legitimacy of the International Court of Justice", *Minnesota Journal of International Law*, vol. 16, (2007). Pp. 495-524.

HEATLEY, P. D., *Diplomacy and the Study of International Relations*, Clarendon Press, Oxford, 1919.

HENKIN, L., *Foreign Affairs and the Constitution*, W.W. Norton & Company, New York, 1972.

—. *International Law: Cases and Materials*, 2nd Edition, West Publishing Co., St. Paul, Minnesota, 1987.

—. “The Role of Law and its Limitations”, in Williams, M. (ed.), *International Law in the Twentieth Century: A Reader*, Macmillan Education, London, (1989).

HERSHEY A.S., *The Essentials of International Public Law and Organisation*, Revised Edition, The Macmillan Company, New York, 1927.

HEYNS, C., *Human Rights Law in Africa*, Kluwer, The Hague, 2002.

HIGGINS, R., "Derogation Under Human Rights Treaties", *British Yearbook of International Law*, vol. 48, (1976-77). Pp. 281-320.

HOBBES, T., *Leviathan*, Michael Oakeshott Ed., Collier Books, New York, 1962.

HOLDSWORTH, Sir W. S., *A History of English Law*, Vol. V, Sweet & Maxwell, London, 1966.

HOOF G., van, *Rethinking the Sources of International Law*, Kluwer, The Netherlands, 1983.

HOWARD, R., “Evaluating Human Rights in Africa: Some Problems of Implicit Comparisons”, *Human Rights Quarterly*, vol. 6, (1984).

ILES, A., “Recent Developments”, *Harvard International Law Journal*, vol. 36, (1995), pp. 207-219.

JACKSON, J. H., “Editorial Comment: International Law Status of WTO DS Reports: Obligation to Comply or Option to ‘Buy-Out’?” *American Journal of International Law*, vol. 98, (2004). Pp. 109-125.

JEAL, T., *Stanley: The Impossible Life of Africa’s Greatest Explorer*, Yale University Press, New Haven, 2007.

JENNINGS, I., *The Law and the Constitution*, 5th Edition, University of London Press, London, 1959.

JHERING, R., *Geist des Römischen Rechts Auf den Verschiedenen Stufen Seiner Entwicklung*, vol. III, Leipzig, 1924.

JORDE, L.B. and WOODING, S.P., “Genetic Variation, Classification and Race”, in *Nature Genetics*, Vol. 36, (2004), (Published online), S28 S33.

KANT, E., *The Critique of Pure Reason*, (In commemoration of the century of its first publication), vol. 1, Translated by F. Müller, The Macmillan Co., London, 1881.

KATETE ORWA, *Foreign Relations and International Co-operation*, Official Handbook of the Ministry of Information and Broadcasting, The Government of Kenya, Kenya, 1988.

KELLER, H. and STONE SWEET, A., “Assessing the Impact of the ECHR on National Legal Systems”, *Faculty Scholarship Series*, Paper 88, (2008). Available at *http://digitalcommons.law.yale.edu/fss_papers/88*

KELSEN, H., *Principles of International Law*, The Lawbook Exchange Ltd, New Jersey, 2003.

KELSEN, H., *General Theory of Law and State*, Translated by A. Wedberg, Russel & Russel, New York, 1961.

KINDIKI, K., "A Review of the Efficacy of Select African Union Monitoring and Reporting Mechanisms", *State of the Union Continental Report*, published by the State of the Union Coalition, (2010).Available at *www.stateoftheunionafrica.net.*

KOSKENNIEMI, M., "The Place of Law in Collective Security", *Michigan Journal of International Law*, vol. 17, Issue 2 (1996). Pp. 455-492.

—. "Lauterpacht: The Victorian Tradition in International Law", *European Journal of International Law*, vol. 8, (1997).

KROMAREK, P., "Environment and Human Rights", *Human Rights Teaching*, vol. 3, UNESCO, (1982). Pp. 26-31.

LAMB, D., *The Africans*, Vintage Books, New York, 1987.

LAMM, C.B. and OTHERS, "Enforcement of Foreign Arbitral Awards in Russia", *American College of Trial Lawyers,*(2007).Pp. 1-16. Available at: *http://www.actl.com/AM/Template.cfm?Section=Home&Template=/CM/ContentDisplay.cfm&ContentID=5001*

LANE, P.H., *A Manual of Australian Constitutional Law*, 4th Ed, LawBook Co, Sydney, 1997.

LAUTERPACHT, H.,*International Law*, vol. IV, Cambridge University Press, Cambridge, 1978.

—. "The Subjects of International Law", in Lauterpacht (ed), *International Law. Being the Collected papers of Hersch Lauterpacht*, vol. I – The General Works, Cambridge University Press, London, (1970).

LOCKE, J., *Two Treatises on Government*, 7th Ed, J. Wiston Editor, London, 1689.

LUCK, E.C., "The United Nations and the Responsibility to Protect", *Policy Analysis Brief*, The Stanley Foundation, August 2008. Available at: *www.humansecuritygateway.com/documents/TSF_theUNandR2P.pdf&pli*

MAGNARELLA, P.J., "Assessing the Concept of Human Rights in Africa" (2001). Available at *http://www.du.edu/korbel/hrhw/volumes/2001/1-2/baah-magnarella.pdf*

MALANCZUK, P., *Akehurst's Modern Introduction to International Law*, Seventh Edition, Routledge ed., London, 1997.

MANSFIELD, H.C., "The Modern Doctrine of Executive Power", *Presidential Studies Quarterly*, Spring (1987). Pp. 237-252.

MARITAIN, J., *Man and The State*, Charles R. Walgreen Foundation Lectures, University of Chicago Press, Chicago, 1951.

—. "The Concept of Sovereignty", published by Stankiewicz, J.W. (ed), *In Defense of Sovereignty*, Oxford University Press, New York, (1969).

McNAIR, A.D., *The Law of Treaties*, Clarendon Press, Oxford, 1961.

McWHINNEY E., *Supreme Law and Judicial Law-Making: Constitutional Tribunals and Constitutional Review,* Martinus Nijhoff Publishers, Dordrecht, 1966.

MIRKINE-GUETZEVITCH, B., "Droit international et droit constitutionnel", *Recueil des Cours*, vol. 38, Académie de Droit International, The Hague, (1931). Pp. 307-466.

MONTESQUIEU, *Esprit des Lois*, Book XI, chapter VI. Available at: *https://docs.google.com/viewer?url=http%3A%2F%2Fwww.forgotten books.org%2Febooks%2FThe_Spirit_of_Laws_Vol_2_-_9781440067457.pdf*

PAKENHAM, T., *The Scramble for Africa: White Man's Conquest of the Dark Continent from 1876 to 1912*, Random House Publishing Group, New York, 1991.

MOTALA, A.C., *The African Court: Prospects for the Effective Protection of Human Rights on the Continent*, Open Society Initiative for Southern Africa, Open Society Foundations, New York, 2002.

MUJUZI, J.D., "Michelot Yogogombaye v The Republic of Senegal: The African Court's First Decision", *Human Rights Law Review, Oxford*, vol. 10, No. 2, (2010). Pp. 372-381.

MUKUNDI, G. and AYINLA, A., "Twenty Years of Elusive Enforcement of the Recommendations of the African Commission on Human and Peoples' Rights: A possible remedy", in: *African Human Rights Law Journal*, Juta Law Ed., vol. 6, nº 2, (2006). Pp. 465-492.

MURRAY, R., African Commission on Human and Peoples' Rights, *Max Planck Encyclopedia of Public International Law*, www.mpepil.com, Oxford University Press, (2007).

—. *The African Commission on Human and Peoples' Rights and International Law*, Hart Publishing, Portland, Oregon, 1998.

MUTUA, M., "The African Human Rights System, a Critical Evaluation", (2000). Available at: *http://hdr.undp.org/en/reports/global/hdr2000/papers/mutua.pdf*

MWAGIRU and HUNJA, "Aspects of Treaty Practice in Kenya", *Lesotho Law Journal*, vol. 6, No. 2, (1990). Pp. 7-22.

MWAGIRU, M., "Diplomacy: From Theory to Practice", Research paper, *Seminar on Diplomacy, Culture and Media of the Institute of Diplomacy and International Studies*, University of Nairobi, 1-3 August, (1991).

NDAM NJOYA, A., "The African Concept of Humanitarian Law", in *International Dimensions of Humanitarian Law*, Edited by Henry Dunant Institute and UNESCO, Martinus Nijhoff, Dordrecht, (1988). Pp. 5-12.

NEWMAN, E. and OTHERS (Editors), *Multilateralism Under Challenge*, United Nations University Press, Tokyo, 2006.

NMEHIELLE, V.O., *The African Human Rights System: Its Law, Practice and Institutions*, Martinus Nijhoff Publishers, The Hague, 2001.

—. "Towards an African Court of Human Rights: Structuring and Empowering the Court", *Annual Survey of International and Comparative Law*, vol. 6, (2000). Pp. 30-31.

ODINKALU, C.A., "The Individual Complaints Procedures of the African Commission on Human and Peoples' Rights: A Preliminary Assessment", *Transnational Law and Contemporary Problems*, vol. 8, Issue 2, (1998). Pp. 359-406.

—. "Complementarity, Competition or Contradiction: The Relationship between the African Court on Human and Peoples' Rights and Regional Economic Courts in East and Southern Africa", Presentation at the *Conference of East and Southern African States on the Protocol Establishing the African Court on Human and Peoples' Rights*, Gaborone, Botswana, 9-10 December 2003 (Unpublished).

OELLERS-FRAHM, K., "Judicial and Arbitral Decisions, Validity and Nullity", *The Max Planck Encyclopedia of Public International Law*, Oxford University Press, 2011, online edition. Available at: *http://www.mpepil.com/ViewPdf/epil/entries/law-9780199231690-e1057.pdf?stylesheet=EPIL-display-full.xsl*

OJWANG, J.B., *Constitutional Development in Kenya*, Act Press, Nairobi, 1990.

—. *Legislative Control of Executive Powers: A Comparative Study of the British and French-derived Constitutions of Kenya and Cote d'Ivoire*, University of Cambridge, Ph.D. dissertation, Cambridge, 1981.

—. *Application of Treaties, Legislative Control of Executive Powers*, Downing College, Cambridge, 1981.

OKAFOR, O.C., "The African system on Human and Peoples' Rights, quasi-constructivism, and the possibility of peace-building within

African States", *International Law Journal of Human Rights*, vol. 8, (2004). Pp. 413–450.

OKOTH-OGENDO, H.W.O., "Human and Peoples' Rights: What Point is Africa Trying to Make?" in Cohen, Hydén and Nagan (eds.), *Human Rights and Governance in Africa*, University Press of Florida, Gainesville, (1993).

OLIVER, C.T., "Historical Development of International Law: Contemporary Problems of Treaty Law", *Recueil Des Cours*, vol. 88, Académie de Droit International, The Hague, (1955). Pp. 417-508.

—. "The Jurisdiction (Competence) of States", in Bedjaoui, M. (ed), *International Law: Achievements and Prospects*, UNESCO & Martinus Nijhoff Publishers, Paris, (1991).

OPPENHEIM, L., *International Law*, 8th Edition, Longmans, London, 1955.

—. *International Law*, vol.1, (Reprint) Longmans, Green and Co. Ltd., London, 1967.

—. *Oppenheim's International Law*, Edited by Jennings, R and Watts, A., 9th Edition, Longmans, New Jersey, 1996.

ORAKA O., "AU: Support Justice for Gravest Crimes - 125 Groups Across Africa Call for ICC Support at Summit", *Human Rights Watch*, Johannesburg, 27th June 2011. Available at: *http://www.hrw.org/fr/news/2011/06/27/au-support-justice-gravest-crimes.*

ORGANIZATION OF AMERICAN STATES, *The American Declaration of the Rights and Duties of Man*, 9th International Conference of American States, Bogotá, 1948.

—. *American Convention on Human Rights*, Inter-American Specialized Conference on Human Rights, San José, Costa Rica, 22nd November 1969.

OUGUERGOUZ, F., *The African Charter on Human and Peoples' Rights: A Comprehensive Agenda for Human Dignity and Sustainable Democracy in Africa*, Martinus Nijhoff Publishers, The Hague, 2003.

OUGUERGOUZ, F., "African Charter on Human and Peoples' Rights", *Max Planck Encyclopaedia of Public International Law*, Max Planck Institute for Comparative Public Law and International Law, Heidelberg and Oxford University Press, (2010). Available at *http://www.mpepil.com*

PACKER, A.A.C., *Using human rights to change tradition: traditional practices harmful to Women's Reproductive Health in Sub-Saharan Africa*, Intersentia, Utrecht, 2002.

PASTOR RIDRUEJO, J.A., *Curso de Derecho Internacional Público y Organizaciones Internacionales*, 3rd Edición, Tecnos, Madrid, 1989.

PEREZ, A. F., "Who Killed Sovereignty - or: Changing Norms Concerning Sovereignty in International Law", *Wisconsin International Law Journal*, vol. 14, (1995-1996). Pp. 463-490.

PETERS, A., "Treaty Making Power", *Max Planck Encyclopedia of Public International Law*, www.mpepil.com, Oxford University Press, (2011).

PITYANA, N. B., "Reflections on the African Court on Human and Peoples' Rights", *African Human Rights Law Journal*, vol. 4, (2004).Pp.121-129.

POLAKIEWICZ, J., *Treaty-making in the Council of Europe*, Council of Europe Publishing, Strasbourg, 1999.

POLAKIEWICZ, J., "International Law and Domestic (Municipal) Law, Law and Decisions of International Organizations and Courts", Max Planck Encyclopedia of Public International Law, www.mpepil.com, Oxford University Press, (2011). Available at: *http://www.mpepil.com/ViewPdf/epil/entries/law-9780199231690-e1057.pdf?stylesheet=EPIL-display-full.xsl*

POULIOT, V., "Forum Prorogatum before the International Court of Justice: The Djibouti v. France case", *The Hague Justice Portal*, Jan (2009). Available at: *http://www. haguejusticeportal.net/eCache/DEF/10/170.TD1OTA.html*

PRAKASH, S. B. and RAMSEY, M. D., "The Executive Power over Foreign Affairs", *Yale Law Journal*, vol. 111, (2001). Pp. 231-356.

PRZETACZNIK, F., *Protection of Officials of Foreign States According to International Law*, Martinus Nijhoff Publishers, Boston, 1983.

RAINEY, C., "The African Court: Building a Continental Benchmark for Justice", (2010). Available at: *http://www.raineydevine.com/wpcontent/uploads/2010/09/Feb2007.pdf*

RAMSEY, M. D., *The Constitution's Text in Foreign Affairs*, Harvard University Press, Cambridge, 2007.

REUTER, P., *Introduction to the Law of Treaties*, Printers Publishers, London, 1989.

REYNOLDS P.A., *An Introduction to International Relations*, Longman, London, 1992.

RIVIER, *Principes du Droit des Gens*, vol. 2, Bibliothèque Nationale de France, Paris, 1896.

RHONHEIMER M., "Fundamental Rights, Moral Law, and the Legal Defence of Life in a Constitutional Democracy", *The American Journal of Jurisprudence*, vol. 43, (1998). Pp. 135-183.

RONCATI, E., "Diplomacy", *Max Planck Encyclopedia of Public International Law*, www.mpepil.com, Oxford University Press, (2008).
ROUSSEAU, C., *Principes Généraux du Droit International Public*, vol. I., Pedone, Paris, 1944.
RUILOBA SANTANA, E., "Una Nueva Categoría en el Panorama de la Subjetividad International; El Concepto de Pueblo", in *Estudios de Derecho Internacional. Homenaje al Profesor Miaja de la Muela*, vol. 1, Tecnos Ed, Madrid, (1979).
RUIZ MIGUEL, C., "Las Sentencias del Tribunal Europeo de Derechos Humanos: Su Ejecución desde la Perspectiva del Derecho Constitucional Comparado y Español", *V Congreso Iberoamericano de Derecho Constitucional*, Instituto de Investigaciones Jurídicas/UNAM, México, (1998). Pp. 811-846.
SALMOND, J.W., *Jurisprudence*, London, Sweet & Maxwell, 1966.
SANDS, P. and OTHERS, *Manual on International Courts and Tribunals*, 2nd Edition, Oxford University Press, New York, 2010.
SATOW, *Satow's Guide to Diplomatic Practice*, Longman, London, 1983.
SCEATS, S., "Africa's New Human Rights Court: Whistling in the Wind?", Chatham House International Law Briefing Paper, (IL BP 09/01), (March 2009). Available at:
http://www.chathamhouse.org.uk/publications/papers/view/-/id/721/
SCHMELZING, J., *Systematischer Grundriss des Völkerrechts*, vol. 3, Rudolstadt, 1818.
SCHWARZENBERGER, G., *International Law*, vol. III, Stevens & Sons, London, 1976.
SEATON and MAUTI, *Tanzania Treaty Practice*, Oxford University Press, London, 1973.
SELLÉS DAUDER, J. F., *Antropología para Inconformes*, Ediciones Rialp, Madrid, 2006.
SILVA BASCUÑÁN, A., *Tratado de Derecho Constitucional*, Editorial Jurídica de Chile, vol. XI, Santiago, 2006.
SHAW, M., *International Law*, 3rd Edition, Grotius Publications, Cambridge, 1991. (The 2nd Edition of 1986 was also consulted.)
SHIVJI, I.G., *The Concept of Human Rights in Africa*, Codesria, London, 1989.
SHORE, A.M., "A Look at Law in Judaism and Christianity: The Torah of God: Road Back or Road Block?", *Issues*, vol. 6, No. 2. (1988). Available at:
http://jewsforjesus.org/publications/issues/ 6_2/torahofgod
SOUTHERN AFRICAN DEVELOPMENT COMMUNITY TREATY, *SADC Summit*, Windhoek, 2000.

SPIRO, P.J., "Treaties, International Law, and Constitutional Rights", *Stanford Law Review*, vol. 55, (1999). Available at: *http://www.lexisnexis.com/hottopics/lnacademic/?sfi=AC00NBGenSrch&csi=7353&shr=t*

STARKE, J.G., *Introduction to International Law*, 10th Edition, Butterworths, London, 1989. (The 9th Edition of 1984 was also consulted.)

SULLIVAN, M.P., "Transnationalism, Power Politics, and the Realities of the Present System", in Williams, M. (ed.), *International Law in the Twentieth Century: A Reader*, Macmillan Education, London, (1989).

SWINARSKI, C. (ed.), *Studies and Essays on International Humanitarian Law and Red Cross Principles in honour of Jean Pictet*, Martinus Nijhoff Publishers, Geneva, The Hague, ICRC, 1984.

THOMPSON, A. and SNIDAL, D., *International Organizations*, University of Chicago, Chicago, 1999. Available at *http://encyclo.findlaw.com/9800book.pdf*

TOCQUEVILLE, A., *Democracy in America*, Regnery Publishing, Washington DC, 2002.

TUNKIN, G. I., *Teoriia Mezhdunarodnogo Prava*, (Translated by Butler, W. E. as *Theory of International Law*) Harvard University Press, Cambridge, Massachusetts, 1974.

TRIEPEL, M., "Les Rapports entre le Droit Interne et le Droit International", *Recueil des Cours*, vol. 1, Académie de Droit International, The Hague, (1923). Pp. 73-122.

UDOMBANA, N.J., "Towards the African Court on Human and Peoples' Rights: Better Late than Never", *Yale Human Rights and Development Law Journal*, vol. 3, No. 45, (2000). Pp. 75-110.

UMOZURIKE, U.O., *The African Commission on Human and Peoples' Rights*, Martinus Nijhoff Publishers, The Hague, 1997.

UNITED NATIONS CONFERENCE ON THE HUMAN ENVIRONMENT-STOCKHOLM (Declaration), Doc.A/CONF.48/14/ Rev.1., June 1972, New York, 1973.

UNITED NATIONS GENERAL ASSEMBLY, *In larger freedom: Towards development, security and human rights for all,* Report by the Secretary General, A/59/2005.

VARIOUS AUTHORS, *Final Report*, Approved for Issue at the 95th Plenary Meeting of the Constitution of Kenya Commission, held on 10th February 2005, Published by the CKRC, Nairobi, 2005.

VARIOUS AUTHORS, *Report on the Enforcement of Non-Money Judgments from Outside the Province* BCLI - *British Columbia Law Institute*, No 8, 1999.

VARIOUS AUTHORS, "Committee Of Governmental Experts for the Preparation of a Draft Convention on Harmonized Substantive Rules Regarding Intermediated Securities", *Report of the Ad hoc Working Group on Legislative Techniques for the Implementation of the Preliminary Draft Convention on Harmonized Substantive Rules Regarding Intermediated Securities*, UNIDROIT (2006), Study LXXVIII – Doc. 26, Rome, 6/14 March 2006.

VARIOUS AUTHORS, "Harvard Draft Convention on the Law of Treaties", Report on the Law of Treaties by J.L. Brierly, Special Rapporteur. Extract from the *Yearbook of the International Law Commission* (1950), vol. II A/CN.4/23. Pp. 223-248.

VARIOUS AUTHORS, "Report on the Enforcement of Non-Money Judgments from Outside the Province", *British Columbia Law Institute* ('BCLI'), Report No 8, (1999). Available at: *http://www.bcli.org/bclrg/publications*

VARIOUS AUTHORS, *The Responsibility to Protect*, International Commission on Intervention and State Sovereignty, Published by the International Development Research Center, Ottawa, Canada, Dec. 2001.

VARIOUS AUTHORS, *Bol'shaia Sovetskaia Entsiklopediia*, 2nd Edition, vol. XIV, 1958.

VARIOUS AUTHORS, "A Guide: African Court on Human and People's Rights", published by the *Coalition for an Effective African Court on Human and Peoples' Rights*, Arusha, Tanzania (*www.africancourtcoalition.org*), (September 2008).

VASAK, K. "Pour une troisième génération des droits de l'homme", in C. Swinarski (ed.), *Studies and Essays on International Humanitarian Law and Red Cross Principles in honour of Jean Pictet*, Martinus Nijhoff Publishers, ICRC, Geneva, The Hague, (1984).

VERDROSS, A., "Le Fondement Du Droit International", *Recueil des Cours*, Académie de Droit International, vol. 16, The Hague, (1927), Pp. 247-324.

VILJOEN, F., *International Human Rights Law in Africa*, Oxford University Press, Oxford, 2007.

—. "African Court on Human and Peoples' Rights (ACtHPR)", *Max Planck Institute for Comparative Public Law and International Law*, Heidelberg and Oxford University Press, (2010). Available at: *http://www.mpepil.com/ViewPdf/epil/entries/law-9780199231690-e6.pdf?stylesheet=EPIL-display-full.xsl*

—. "A Human Rights Court for Africa, and for Africans", *Brooklyn Journal of International Law*, vol. 30, No. 1, (2004). Pp. 1-66.

VILJOEN, F. and LOUW, L., "State Compliance with the Recommendations of the African Commission on Human and Peoples' Rights,1993–2004", *American Journal of International Law*, vol. 101, No. 1, (2007). Pp. 1-34.

VON GLAHN, G., *Law Among Nations, An Introduction to Public International Law*, 2nd Edition, The Macmillan Co., London, 1970.

WADE, E.C.S., and PHILIPS G., *Constitutional Law*, 6th Edition, Longmans, London, 1960.

WALKER, D., *The Scottish Legal System*, 6th Ed., W. Green/Sweet & Maxwell, Edinburgh, 1992.

WALKER, R. J. and WARD R., *English Legal System*, 7th Ed. Butterworths, London, 1994.

WATERS, M.A., "Creeping Monism: The Judicial Trend Toward Interpretive Incorporation of Human Rights Treaties", *Columbia Law Review*, vol. 107, (2007). Pp. 628-705.

WARIOBA, J. S., FROWEIN J.A., WOLFRUM R. (eds.) "Monitoring Compliance with and Enforcement of Binding Decisions of International Courts" in the *Max Planck Yearbook of United Nations Law*, vol. 5, Kluwer International, The Netherlands, (2001).

WATSON, A., *Diplomacy: The Dialogue Between States*, Routledge, London, 1991.

WELCH, C.E., *Human Rights in Africa: Roles and Strategies of Non-governmental Organizations*, University of Pennsylvania Press, Philadelphia, 1995.

WELDEHAIMANOT, S. M., "Towards Speedy Trials: Reforming the Practice of Adjudicating Cases in the African Human Rights System", *The University for Peace Law Review*, vol. 14, No. 1, (2010). Pp. 14-38. Available at: *http://www. lawreview.upeace.org/pdf/vol1issue1article2.pdf]*

WENDT, A., *Social theory of International Politics*, Cambridge University Press, Cambridge, 6th Edition, 2003

WERNER, L., *Contemporary International Law*, Westview Press, Colorado, 1979.

WICQUEFORT, *L'Ambassadeur et ses Fonctions*, Daniel Steucker Edition, Cologne, 1690. Available at: *http://books.google.co.ke/books?id=Vls_AAAAcAAJ&printsec=frontcover&dq=Wicquefort+L'Ambassadeur+et+ses+Fonctions&hl=en&ei=y0FYTfKfKMTXrQfQy7WMBw&sa=X&oi=book_result&ct=result&resnum=1&ved=0CCgQ6AEwAA#v=onepage&q=h*

WILSON, G., *Cases and Materials in Constitutional and Administrative Law*, Cambridge University Press, Cambridge, 1966.

WITZCH, G., "Foreign Relations and International Integration According to the Basic Law of the Federal Republic of Germany", *Indian Journal of International Law*, vol 7, (1967). Pp. 45-158.

WITTICH, S., "Permissible Derogation from Mandatory Rules? The Problem of Party Status in the Genocide Case", *European Journal of International Law*, vol. 18, (2007).Pp.591-618.

WOLF-PHILLIPS, L., *Constitutions of Modern States: Selected texts*, Pall Mall Press, London, 1968.

YEE, S., "Forum Prorogatum Returns to the International Court of Justice", *Leiden Journal of International Law*, vol. 16, (2003). Pp. 701-713.

YUVAL, S., *The Competing Jurisdictions of International Courts and Tribunals*, International Courts and Tribunal Series, Oxford University Press, New York, 2005.

Selected Web Resources

AFRICAN COMMISSION ON HUMAN AND PEOPLES' RIGHTS
www.achpr.org/english/info/List_Decision_Communications.html
www.achpr.org/english/_info/state_procedure_en.html

AFRICAN COURT ON HUMAN AND PEOPLES' RIGHTS
www.african-court.org

AFRICAN INTERNATIONAL COURTS AND TRIBUNALS
www.aict-ctia.org/courts_subreg/amu/amu_home.html
www.aict-ctia.org/courts_subreg/comesa/comesa_home.html
www.aict-ctia.org/courts_subreg/eac/eac_home.html
www.aict-ctia.org/courts_subreg/ecowas/ecowas_home.html
www.aict-ctia.org/courts_subreg/waemu/waemu_home.html

CENTRE FOR MINORITY RIGHTS DEVELOPMENT
www.cemiride.or.ke

CENTRAL INTELLIGENCE AGENCY LIBRARY
www.cia.gov/library/publications/the-world-factbook.

DEPARTMENT OF INTERNATIONAL RELATIONS AND COOPERATION - SOUTH AFRICA
www.dfa.gov.za/foreign/Multilateral/africa/amu.htm

HEINONLINE, *http://www.heinonline.org*

INSTITUTE FOR HUMAN RIGHTS AND DEVELOPMENT IN AFRICA (IHRDA) *http://www.ihrda.org*

LEXISNEXIS ACADEMIC, *http://www.lexisnexis.com*

MAX PLANCK ENCYCLOPEDIA OF PUBLIC INTERNATIONAL LAW, *http://www.mpepil.com*

SABINET, *http://www.sabinet.co.za*

Selected Speeches

ANNAN, K. in Luck, E.C., "The United Nations and the Responsibility to Protect", *Policy Analysis Brief*, The Stanley Foundation, August 2008. Available at: *www.humansecuritygateway.com/documents/TSF_theUNandR2P.pdf&pli*

—. Speech before the 4087th Meeting of the Security Council, 10th January 2000.

ATKIN, J.L., Judgment on behalf of the Privy Council in the case: *Attorney-General for Canada v. Attorney-General for Ontario*(1937) A.C. 326.

HOFFMANN, J., "The Universality of Human Rights", Judicial Studies Board Annual Lecture given on 19th March 2009.

LUTHER KING, M. Jr, "Letter from a Birmingham Jail", dated 16th April 1963, published by the *African Studies Center* - University of Pennsylvania. Available at: *http://www.africa.upenn.edu/Articles_Gen/Letter_Birmingham.html*

ORJIAKO, D.T., "The African Union – Our Common Home". *Keynote Address*, Delivered at North-eastern University, Boston, Massachusetts, 24th March, 2005.

SENGHOR, L.S., "Inaugural Speech", OAU Doc. CAB/LEG/67/5.

SHIUNDU, A., "Special Report", *Daily Nation*, Wednesday 22nd December 2010, p. 19.

INDEX